CIVIL PROCEDURE

CIVIL
PROCEDURE

CIVIL PROCEDURE

KEYED TO YEAZELL
NINTH EDITION

John T. Cross

Grosscurth Professor of Law

University of Louisville School of Law

The *Emanuel® Law Outlines* Series

 Wolters Kluwer

Copyright © 2016 CCH Incorporated.

Published by Wolters Kluwer in New York.

Wolters Kluwer Legal & Regulatory US serves customers worldwide with CCH, Aspen Publishers, and Kluwer Law International products. (www.WKLegaledu.com)

To contact Customer Service, e-mail customer.service@wolterskluwer.com, call 1-800-234-1660, fax 1-800-901-9075, or mail correspondence to:

Wolters Kluwer
Attn: Order Department
PO Box 990

Frederick, MD 21705

Printed in the United States of America.

3 4 5 6 7 8 9 0

ISBN 978-1-4548-6854-5

Library of Congress Cataloging-in-Publication Data

Names: Cross, John T., author. | Yeazell, Stephen C. Civil procedure. 9th ed.
Title: Civil procedure : Keyed to Yeazell / John T. Cross, Grosscurth
  Professor of Law, University of Louisville School of Law.
Description: Ninth edition. | New York : Wolters Kluwer, [2016] | Series: The
  Emanuel law outlines series
Identifiers: LCCN 2016016297 | ISBN 9781454868545
Subjects: LCSH: Civil procedure—United States—Outlines, syllabi, etc.
Classification: LCC KF8841 .C76 2016 | DDC 347.73/5—dc23
LC record available at https://lccn.loc.gov/2016016297

This book is intended as a general review of a legal subject. It is not intended as a source of advice for the solution of legal matters or problems. For advice on legal matters, the reader should consult an attorney.

About Wolters Kluwer Legal & Regulatory US

Wolters Kluwer Legal & Regulatory US delivers expert content and solutions in the areas of law, corporate compliance, health compliance, reimbursement, and legal education. Its practical solutions help customers successfully navigate the demands of a changing environment to drive their daily activities, enhance decision quality and inspire confident outcomes.

Serving customers worldwide, its legal and regulatory portfolio includes products under the Aspen Publishers, CCH Incorporated, Kluwer Law International, ftwilliam.com and MediRegs names. They are regarded as exceptional and trusted resources for general legal and practice-specific knowledge, compliance and risk management, dynamic workflow solutions, and expert commentary.

Note

This book includes analyses of nearly all of the cases treated as principal cases in Yeazell, *Civil Procedure,* Ninth Edition, 2016, as well as some cases discussed in the text. The analysis of each case discussed in Yeazell is preceded by ★ symbol.

Summary of Contents

Table of Contents

CHAPTER 1

INTRODUCTION

CHAPTER 2

PERSONAL JURISDICTION

CHAPTER 3

VENUE

CHAPTER 4

SUBJECT MATTER JURISDICTION

CHAPTER 5

THE *ERIE* DOCTRINE

CHAPTER 6

AN OVERVIEW OF LITIGATION

CHAPTER **7**

PLEADING

CHAPTER 8

DISCOVERY

CHAPTER 9

RESOLUTION WITHOUT TRIAL

CHAPTER 10

DETERMINING THE TRIER

CHAPTER 11

THE TRIAL

Chapter 12

APPEALS

CHAPTER **13**

RESPECT FOR JUDGMENTS

CHAPTER **14**

JOINDER OF CLAIMS AND PARTIES

CHAPTER **15**

CLASS ACTIONS

Preface

Welcome to Civil Procedure! Although the subject may seem strange at first, with patience and diligence you will gradually grow comfortable with it. This book is intended to help you reach that point of comfort.

Civil Procedure deals with the conduct of civil cases (which, roughly speaking, is any case other than a criminal prosecution or administrative proceeding). However, most Civil Procedure courses do not spend much time on certain specialized types of civil cases, such as divorce and child custody actions or suits against the government. Although many of the general principles of Procedure also govern these cases, you will have to wait until other courses to learn the idiosyncratic rules that apply in these areas.

Most schools offer Civil Procedure in the first-year curriculum. However, the course is different from other traditional first-year courses. First, because Procedure deals primarily with *process* rather than the substantive law, you will deal with cases involving a number of different areas of substantive law. The same procedural issue can arise in a contracts, constitutional law, or corporate law case. You will soon realize that the merits of the underlying dispute are usually not the crucial issue for purposes of Civil Procedure.

Second, the study of Procedure does not focus as heavily on case law as other courses. Most systems have codified their rules of procedure. In many situations, your primary source for a legal principle will be a statute or written rule rather than a judicial opinion. During your study of Civil Procedure, you will become very familiar with the Federal Rules of Civil Procedure as well as certain statutes dealing with the authority of the federal courts. *Bring a copy of these rules with you to every class.* Although cases are important, many cases in Civil Procedure books merely illustrate how the statute or rule applies in practice.

Because Procedure differs from state to state, Procedure professors typically focus mainly on *federal* procedure. Although many of you will never set foot in federal court, it is nevertheless useful to study how the federal courts conduct cases. The federal procedural system has had a tremendous influence on many states. In fact, a number of states have copied the Federal Rules of Civil Procedure for use in their own courts. Others, while not copying the federal rules, have borrowed many of the underlying concepts. Although every state has its own particular rules and interpretations, a study of federal Civil Procedure nevertheless provides a solid grounding for learning the particular rules in force in any U.S. jurisdiction.

Many students claim Civil Procedure is one of the most difficult courses in law school. With the benefit of hindsight, and many years teaching the course, I can assure you this is not true. The rules of Procedure are no more numerous or complex than the rules in many of your other courses. And although Procedure has its share of difficult concepts—the *Erie* doctrine, claim and issue preclusion, and the right to a jury spring to mind—other courses deal with concepts that are equally tough to grasp.

Nevertheless, although an experienced attorney or judge might not list Civil Procedure among the more difficult subjects in law school, there is no doubt that the subject *seems* difficult to the first-year student. This perception stems from the nature of the course. The problem with Procedure is that the subject is almost entirely foreign to the new law student. Other mainstream courses, such as Contracts, Torts, Constitutional Law, and Criminal Law, present real-life issues to which students can immediately relate. Because they understand the issue, students more often than not have a "gut reaction" as to what the rule of law ought to be. Civil Procedure seems cold and mechanical in comparison. The outcome of a dispute concerning whether a motion for a new trial was filed in timely fashion has no immediately obvious effect on the greater social good. Students therefore have no "hunch" as to how the dispute ought be resolved.

But do not assume that Civil Procedure comprises a set of arbitrary rules that you need only commit to memory. As in all your other courses, there is a philosophy at the core of Civil Procedure. Once you accept that there are underlying norms, and make the effort to understand the "big picture," half of the battle of understanding the subject will be won.

This book will, if properly used, help you understand Civil Procedure. Given the nature of the work, the primary focus is the individual rules. Of course, you will need to know the content of those rules in preparing for your examinations. Nevertheless, the book also attempts to offer some insight into *why* certain rules are the way they are. Understanding the policy underlying the rules will help you understand the overall policy underlying Civil Procedure.

When using this book, approach the different elements in different ways. First, when preparing for class, check the correlation chart to find the section of the book that corresponds to what you are reading. Read this material *before* reading the casebook to give yourself a basic overview of what you are covering. You may also find it helpful to reread the same section of this book after each class to reinforce what you have learned. When you finish a topic or chapter, work through the Quiz Yourself questions to check what you know and where you need work. Make sure you can apply the rules you have learned. Equally important, however, make sure you can spot the issue being addressed in the problem. Issue spotting can be especially tricky in Civil Procedure.

Second, when preparing your outline, refer again to this work for a summary of the rules. Here, however, you should also consider the general structure of this work. Great care has been taken to organize the material into a useful outline form. Although this outline generally follows the Yeazell *Civil Procedure* casebook, in places it diverges to help the reader look at the relation between concepts in a different way.

Third, review the Exam Tips when preparing for the final examination. These Tips focus on areas that students frequently find confusing. Work again through the Quiz Yourself sections, both to make sure you know the material and to help you practice your writing. Finally, take a stab at the longer essays in the essay section, which mirror the exam format used by many professors.

It should go without saying that this work is meant to complement, *not substitute for,* your casebook. You should always read the assigned material in the casebook and any supplementary materials. *Never* go into class having read only the material in this work. In addition, this work is not intended to be a "canned outline." You should always prepare your own outline for the course, at the very least because your professor will have his or her own slant and possibly bring in additional materials.

Good luck with Civil Procedure!

John Cross
June 2016

Casebook Correlation Chart

Material in Yeazell, Civil Procedure, Ninth Edition (by chapter and section heading)	Pages in Yeazell	Pages in Emanuel Law Outline
I. AN OVERVIEW OF PROCEDURE		
A. The Idea and the Practice of Procedure	1-5	1-6
B. Where Can the Suit Be Brought	5-14	6-7
C. Stating the Case	14-28	7
D. Parties to the Lawsuit	28-32	8
E. Factual Development—Discovery	32-38	8
F. Pretrial Disposition—Summary Judgment	38-44	8-9
G. Trial	44-49	9
H. Former Adjudication	49-52	9-10
I. Appeals	52-57	10
II. PERSONAL JURISDICTION		
A. The Origins	69-79	13-14
B. The Modern Constitutional Formulation of Power	80-154	14-22, 30-31
C. Consent as a Substitute for Power	154-159	22
D. The Constitutional Requirement of Notice	160-175	25-29
E. Self-Imposed Restraints on Jurisdictional Power: Long-Arm Statutes, Venue, and Discretionary Refusal of Jurisdiction	175-199	35-43
III. SUBJECT MATTER JURISDICTION OF THE FEDERAL COURTS		
A. The Idea and the Structure of Subject Matter Jurisdiction	205-208	49-50
B. Federal Question Jurisdiction	209-220	51-55
C. Diversity Jurisdiction	220-234	55-65
D. Supplemental Jurisdiction	234-242	65-69
E. Removal	242-251	70-73
IV. STATE LAW IN FEDERAL COURTS: ERIE AND ITS ENTAILMENTS		
A. State Courts as Lawmakers in a Federal System	256-267	81-84
B. The Limits of State Power in Federal Courts	267-291	84-94
V. INCENTIVES TO LITIGATE		
A. Litigation in the United States at the Start of the Twenty-First Century	299-305	not covered
B. Reasons to Litigate: Dollars, Orders, and Declarations	305-338	99-106
C. Financing Litigation	338-364	106-107
VI. PLEADING		
A. The Story of Pleading	367-415	112-118
B. Ethical Limitations in Pleading—and in Litigation Generally	416-429	132-135
C. Responding to the Complaint	429-457	118-132
VII. DISCOVERY		
A. Modern Discovery	463-464	141-142
B. The Stages of Discovery	464-481	150-161
C. The Scope of Discovery	481-502	142-150
D. Experts	502-508	147-148
E. Ensuring Compliance and Controlling Abuse of Discovery	508-522	161-164

Capsule Summary

This Capsule Summary provides a "road map" for the main body of this book. It should be used as a general overview, *not* as a substitute for the more in-depth material in the main body. The bracketed numbers provide cross-references to the page numbers in the main body.

CHAPTER 1

INTRODUCTION

I. CIVIL PROCEDURE GENERALLY

Civil Procedure is the study of how civil cases are conducted. Although it focuses primarily on litigation in courts, it also covers alternative means of resolving disputes.

A. Different from other courses: Civil Procedure differs in certain significant ways from the other first-year courses in that there is less focus on the substantive law. Nevertheless, the substantive law you learn in your other courses often affects how the rules of Procedure apply. [1-3]

B. Sources of Civil Procedure: Another difference between Civil Procedure and other courses is that the rules of Procedure are far more likely to come from a statute or written rule than from case law. [3-4]

  1. Federal Rules of Civil Procedure: The Federal Rules of Civil Procedure are especially important in the study of Procedure. [3]

  2. Cases: Although most rules come from statutes and other written rules, cases are also important insofar as they explain, fine-tune, and sometimes ignore the rules. [3-4]

II. GENERAL THEMES

A. Multiple court systems: One recurring theme in Civil Procedure is the system of parallel state and federal courts. Unlike in some other federal nations, in the United States it is often possible for either state or federal court to hear a particular dispute. [4-6]

B. Stages in a civil lawsuit: A typical lawsuit involves several stages.

  1. Determining where to sue: Plaintiff first determines where to bring the action. This decision requires consideration of *subject matter jurisdiction, personal jurisdiction,* and *venue*. [6-7]

  2. Pleading the case: Next, the party determines how to plead the case. The *complaint* is the document in which plaintiff sets out her claims. Defendant responds with a pre-answer motion and/or an answer. [7]

C. **Joinder:** It is possible for a case to involve more than one plaintiff and one defendant. If so, the parties may file various claims against each other. It is also possible for parties other than plaintiffs and defendants to be joined to a case, or, in some cases, for non-parties to join of their own volition. [8]

D. **Discovery:** Although the parties will engage in significant information gathering before the case begins, they may also *compel* the other parties, as well as non-party witnesses, to provide information during the case. [8]

E. **Resolution before trial:** Many cases are *settled* before ever going to trial. A party may also *dismiss* her case voluntarily or have her case dismissed for failure to cooperate in the litigation process. Finally, if it becomes clear that one side should prevail, the court may grant a *summary judgment* in that party's favor, which operates like a judgment after a full trial. [8-9]

F. **Trial:** If a case reaches trial, additional issues arise, primarily involving immediate appeals of rulings and use of the *jury*. [9]

G. **Post-trial:** An unfavorable judgment usually may be *appealed*, although strict rules govern the timing of the appeal. In addition, a final judgment may prevent the litigants or other parties from relitigating the claims and issues in later cases. [9-10]

Chapter 2

PERSONAL JURISDICTION

I. OVERVIEW

A. **Definition:** Personal jurisdiction is a court's power to enter a judgment that binds the parties to the case. [12]

B. **Constitutional considerations:** The U.S. Constitution limits a court's power to exercise personal jurisdiction. Numerous Supreme Court cases define when the Constitution allows jurisdiction. [12]

C. **Two categories:** Courts distinguish between two broad categories of personal jurisdiction: *in personam* (jurisdiction over the person) and *in rem* (jurisdiction over property). There are important distinctions between the two. [12-13]

II. THE CONSTITUTIONAL TEST

The Supreme Court, through a long line of cases spanning well over a century, has set out an analysis for when a court may exercise jurisdiction over a *defendant*. This test is commonly referred to as the minimum contacts test. [13-22]

A. **Pennoyer v. Neff (1877):** *Pennoyer* was the first case to hold that the Constitution limited jurisdiction. The decision set out a territorial approach to the issue, under which a state's authority usually was confined to people and property within its borders. More recent decisions have modified many (but by no means all) of *Pennoyer*'s territorial rules. [13-14]

B. International Shoe v. Washington (1945): *International Shoe* established the basic ***minimum contacts test***, which is still used today to measure jurisdiction. The Court indicated that the minimum level of contacts necessary to sustain jurisdiction would depend on whether the suit arose out of the contacts ("specific" jurisdiction) or whether it was unrelated to the contacts ("general" jurisdiction). [14-15]

C. Shaffer v. Heitner (1977): *Shaffer* held that the minimum contacts test also applied to *in rem* jurisdiction. In addition, the Court held that if property was the only contact between defendant and the state, and the cause of action did not arise directly out of the property, a state ordinarily could not exercise jurisdiction over the property or the owner. [16]

D. World-Wide Volkswagen v. Woodson (1980): *World-Wide* fleshed out the minimum contacts test, indicating it comprised two distinct elements.

1. First, there must be purposeful contacts between defendant and the forum. [17]

2. Second, the exercise of jurisdiction must be fair, as measured by five factors. [17]

E. Contract cases: In McGee v. International Life, Hanson v. Denckla, and Burger King v. Rudzewicz, the Court discussed how the minimum contacts analysis would apply to contract-based claims. These decisions make it clear that a contract can constitute purposeful availment with a state if the contract is negotiated and/or is to be performed in that state. Merely contracting with a citizen of another state, however, is not enough to qualify as a contact. [19]

F. *Nicastro*: J. McIntyre Machinery, Ltd. v. Nicastro deals with the ***stream of commerce*** problem, where a defendant injects a good into commerce through a third party. The Court indicated that mere awareness that some of your product would end up in the forum state was not enough to qualify as a contact. Instead, contacts would exist only if the party also engaged in other activities specifically directed at the forum, such as advertising. [19-20]

G. Internet cases: Because Internet users do not necessarily know the location of the people with whom they interact, the Internet poses special difficulties for the minimum contacts test. Although the Supreme Court has not dealt with the issue, the lower courts have often analyzed the nature of the website involved. While passive sites usually do not create jurisdiction, active sites, especially those where the owner takes orders, can be a sufficient contact. [20]

H. General jurisdiction. Most personal jurisdiction cases involve ***specific*** jurisdiction, where the claim arises out of defendant's contacts. However, if defendant is "essentially at home" in the state, ***general*** jurisdiction may be available even if defendant is not currently in the state. In general jurisdiction, the claim need not arise out of the contacts. [20-21]

I. Summary: These cases and others set out a basic analysis to use in determining whether most assertions of personal jurisdiction satisfy the Constitution.

1. **Two distinct steps:** The contacts and fairness portions of the test are separate steps.

   a. Contacts are always required. Unless there is at least one purposeful contact between defendant and the forum, there will not be jurisdiction.

   b. Once at least one contact is identified, a court will evaluate fairness, applying five different factors. Usually, the fairness analysis will prevent a court from exercising jurisdiction only in cases of extreme unfairness. [18]

2. **Contacts and purposefulness:** The Court has indicated that a contact does not count unless it is the result of ***purposeful availment*** by defendant of the benefits and protections of the forum. [18]

3. **Fairness:** When evaluating fairness, one must consider not only the burden on defendant but also the interests of plaintiff, the forum state, other states, and the judicial system. However, fairness is not considered unless there is at least one purposeful contact. [17-18]

III. CASES OUTSIDE THE MINIMUM CONTACTS TEST

Although the minimum contacts test of *International Shoe* replaces the territorial approach of *Pennoyer* in most circumstances, there are still situations in which the *Pennoyer* rules apply. These include:

A. the ***domicile*** of an individual [21],

B. the ***state of incorporation*** of a corporate defendant [21],

C. the ***physical presence*** of defendant in the forum state at the time of service (illustrated by Burnham v. Superior Court) [21], and

D. when defendant ***consents*** to jurisdiction. [22]

IV. NOTICE

Notice—usually a summons and copy of the complaint—is the other key prerequisite for exercising personal jurisdiction.

A. **Constitutional considerations:** The Constitution also places certain restrictions on notice. The Supreme Court held in *Mullane* that notice must be reasonably calculated to give actual notice to the parties being served. [25]

B. **How notice is provided:** State and federal courts differ on the methods of service.

1. **Long-arm statute:** Service on an out-of-state defendant in a state court action is usually effected by means of a special statute called the long-arm statute. [26]

2. **Federal courts:** Service in a federal action is governed by ***Fed. R. Civ. P. 4***.

   a. **Methods:** A federal court can serve either using the various methods listed in ***Fed. R. Civ. P. 4*** or by borrowing the law of the state in which the federal court sits or in which service occurs. Special service rules apply to certain types of defendants, such as infants, foreign defendants, and the United States. [27]

   b. **Territorial limits:** Service alone does not create jurisdiction. Instead, Fed. R. Civ. P. 4(k) provides that, in most cases, a federal court can exercise jurisdiction only if the courts of the state in which the federal court sits could exercise jurisdiction over that defendant. [27]

      i. Thus, the minimum contacts analysis discussed above applies to the federal courts, albeit indirectly. [27]

      ii. However, there are a few exceptions to this. [28]

   c. **Waiver of service:** A party suing in federal court may also ask defendant to waive service. The rule provides incentives to encourage defendants to waive. [28-29]

V. CHALLENGES TO PERSONAL JURISDICTION

Personal jurisdiction is a personal defense that can be waived by inaction or by taking inconsistent action.

A. Traditional approach: The traditional approach was very strict. If defendant participated in the case in any way, she waived the personal jurisdiction defense. [30]

B. Modern approach: The modern approach is exemplified by the Federal Rules of Civil Procedure. Under this approach, a defendant may challenge personal jurisdiction and, if he loses, go ahead and litigate the merits. [31]

CHAPTER 3

VENUE

I. BASIC PRINCIPLES

Legislatures often prescribe a particular location for litigation, which is called the venue. [35]

II. STATE VENUE

Venue in the state systems varies significantly.

III. FEDERAL VENUE

In the federal courts, venue is specifically defined by 28 U.S.C. §1391 and other statutes. [35]

A. Districts: Federal venue is defined in terms of judicial districts rather than states. Many states have more than one federal district. [36]

B. Where proper: Under §1391(b), a plaintiff may bring her action in any district in which a defendant resides (provided that all defendants reside in the same state) or in any district in which a substantial portion of the events or omissions giving rise to the cause of action occurred. If venue is not possible under either of those options, plaintiff may bring the action in any district in which any defendant is subject to personal jurisdiction. [36-37]

   1. Corporations and non-resident defendants: Section 1391(c) also contains special rules governing corporate and non-resident defendants.

      a. A corporation is deemed to reside wherever it is subject to personal jurisdiction. [37]

      b. Defendants who do not reside in the United States may be sued in any district in the United States. [37-38]

   2. Special venue: Special venue statutes apply to certain cases, such as statutory interpleader actions and cases removed from state court. [38, 274]

IV. CHALLENGES TO VENUE

The rules governing challenges to venue are the same as those that apply to challenges to personal jurisdiction. [39]

V. *FORUM NON CONVENIENS*

Forum non conveniens is a court-created doctrine, applicable in both state and federal court, that gives a court *discretion* to dismiss an action even though venue is proper. A court will dismiss a case based on *forum non conveniens* only if:

A. an alternate forum is available to hear the case [40], and

B. the court determines that the *private* and *public factors* warrant dismissal. The private factors relate generally to matters of convenience of the parties and witnesses, while the public factors consider choice of law questions and the interests of the judicial system. [40-41]

VI. TRANSFER OF VENUE

A case filed in one federal district may be transferred to another federal district.

A. If venue proper: If the original court has venue over the action, any party may ask the court to transfer the case to another federal district where venue would also be proper. 28 U.S.C. §1404. The court will grant the request if the new forum is a more convenient place for litigation. [41]

   1. As in *forum non conveniens*, the court considers both public and private factors. [42]

   2. The governing law in the new court is the same as that which would apply in the original court. [42]

B. If venue improper: If venue is improper in the original court, 28 U.S.C. §1406 allows the court to transfer the case to a district where venue would be proper, but only if transfer is more just than simply dismissing for lack of venue. [42-43]

CHAPTER 4

SUBJECT MATTER JURISDICTION

I. BASIC PRINCIPLES

A. Definition: Subject matter jurisdiction (SMJ) is a court's power to hear a particular dispute. [49]

B. All courts: SMJ is an issue in both state and federal courts.

   1. State courts: State courts have residual jurisdiction; that is, there is at least one court in every state with SMJ over every claim other than those specifically delegated to another court. [49-50]

2. **Federal courts:** Federal courts are courts of limited jurisdiction. The SMJ of federal courts is limited by the Constitution and federal statutes. There are two basic categories of federal SMJ: *federal question* and *diversity*. [49]

3. **Exceptions:** There are several exceptions to federal jurisdiction, including domestic relations and probate cases. [50]

C. **Challenges:** Unlike other defenses, any party may challenge SMJ at any time. A court may also raise the issue *sua sponte*. [50]

II. FEDERAL QUESTION JURISDICTION

28 U.S.C. §1331 gives federal courts SMJ over statutory and constitutional claims, regardless of the amount in controversy. [51]

A. **Basics**

1. **Exclusive jurisdiction:** SMJ under §1331 is usually not exclusive but is instead shared with the state courts. However, other statutes give the federal courts exclusive jurisdiction over certain claims arising under federal law. [51]

2. **Claims "arising under":** Section 1331 gives federal courts jurisdiction over claims "arising under" not only federal statutes but also under the U.S. Constitution and treaties. [52]

3. **When claim "arises under":** A claim can arise under one of these bodies of law either if the law itself creates the right, or, in some cases, when federal law is a necessary element of a state-law claim. [52-53]

B. **Well-pleaded complaint rule:** Whether a case involves a federal question is determined using the well-pleaded complaint rule. Under this rule, federal question jurisdiction exists only if the federal issue is necessary to plaintiff's case. [53-54]

III. DIVERSITY JURISDICTION

28 U.S.C. §1332 gives a federal court SMJ based on the citizenship of the parties.

A. **Basics**

1. **Actions included:** The statute grants SMJ over actions that (a) are between citizens of different states and/or foreign citizens, and (b) involve an amount in controversy greater than $75,000. [55]

2. **Not exclusive:** Diversity jurisdiction is not exclusive. The same action may be filed in state courts. [55]

3. **Exceptions:** There are certain exceptions to diversity jurisdiction, including abstention and situations of collusive joinder. [56]

4. **Complete diversity required:** Section 1332 requires complete diversity; that is, no plaintiff can be a citizen of the same state as any defendant. [56-57]

B. **Determining citizenship:** A "citizen of a state" within the meaning of §1332 is a citizen of the United States who is domiciled within a particular state.

1. **Domicile:** A person's domicile is determined by residence plus intent to remain. An individual always has only one domicile. [57-58]

2. **Corporations:** Section 1332(c) provides that a corporation is a citizen of both its state of incorporation and its principal place of business. Thus, a corporation can have two citizenships. If a corporation does business in more than one state, its principal place of business is its "nerve center," usually the corporate headquarters. [58-59]

3. **Special parties:** Special rules apply to insurance companies and representatives. [59]

4. **Foreign citizens:** Although §1332 allows suits between citizens of a state and foreign citizens, suits involving only foreigners are not covered. [60]

C. **Amount in controversy:** Section 1332 requires an amount in controversy greater than $75,000.

   1. In a case involving damages, the requirement is satisfied as long as plaintiff's complaint states a colorable claim for damages of greater than $75,000. [60]

   2. In cases involving nonmonetary relief, courts must ascertain the money value of the relief sought. [61]

   3. Plaintiff may be able to *aggregate* claims to meet the amount in controversy. [61]

D. **Skirting §1332:** Section 1359 deals with attempts to create diversity by collusive means. [61-62]

IV. SUPPLEMENTAL JURISDICTION

For a federal court to hear a case, SMJ must exist over every claim. However, §1367 allows a federal court to hear claims it could not otherwise hear when those claims are brought along with related claims over which the court has SMJ. [65]

A. **Basics:** Applying §1367 involves a *two-step process*.

   1. **§1367(a):** First, you determine if the claim in question is sufficiently related to another claim in the case over which the court has diversity or federal question jurisdiction. [65-66] A sufficient relationship exists if the two claims arise from a *common nucleus of operative fact*. [66]

   2. **§1367(b) & (c):** The second step is to determine if any of the exceptions in subsections (b) and (c) apply.

      a. Section 1367(b) prevents a federal court from exercising jurisdiction over certain claims *by plaintiffs* against parties *joined under certain rules*, when jurisdiction over the original federal claim is based *solely on diversity*. [66-67]

      b. Section 1367(c) gives a court *discretion* to refuse to hear the nonfederal claim based upon certain criteria set out in the subsection. [67-68]

V. REMOVAL OF CASES FROM STATE COURT TO FEDERAL COURT

In some situations, 28 U.S.C. §1441 allows defendant to remove a case filed in state court to federal court.

A. **When case is removable:** Generally, a case in state court may be removed when it could have been filed originally in federal court. [70]

    1. The federal court to which the case is removed must have diversity, federal question, and/or supplemental jurisdiction over all claims in the case. [70]

    2. When removal is based on diversity, special rules apply.

        a. Section 1441(b) prevents a defendant sued in her home state from removing. [71]

        b. Diversity must exist both when the case is filed and at the time of removal. [71]

        c. A case ordinarily cannot be removed based on diversity more than one year after it was first filed. [73]

    3. Section 1441(c) allows removal of federal claims brought along with certain "separate and independent" claims that are not removable. [72]

B. **Process**

    1. Only defendants may remove. [70]

    2. Defendants remove by filing a notice of removal with the federal and state court. Court permission is unnecessary. [72]

    3. Removal must occur within 30 days after defendant receives notice that she is party to a removable state court case. [72]

CHAPTER 5

THE *ERIE* DOCTRINE

I. OVERVIEW

The *Erie* doctrine requires a federal court to apply state law on certain issues.

A. **Three categories of cases:** Conceptually, there are three basic categories of *Erie* cases:

    1. those in which there is no federal statute or rule on point, and the federal court is considering applying a federal judge-made rule;

    2. those in which the federal rule is a ***Federal Rule of Civil Procedure*** or similar court rule; and

    3. those in which the federal law is a federal statute. [81-82]

B. **Federal statutes underlying *Erie*:** Two federal statutes undergird the *Erie* doctrine:

    1. The ***Rules of Decision Act*** (RODA) mirrors the basic command of *Erie*. [81-82]

    2. The ***Rules Enabling Act*** (REA) requires a different analysis for Federal Rules of Civil Procedure. [82]

II. MAIN CASES IN THE DEVELOPMENT OF THE DOCTRINE

The *Erie* doctrine developed in a line of Supreme Court cases.

A. *Erie*: Erie R.R. v. Tompkins (1938) is the source of doctrine. *Erie* held a federal court must apply state rules of tort liability instead of determining for itself what the "best" rule would be. The Court indicated that the result was mandated by federalism concerns. [83-84]

B. *Guaranty Trust*: Guaranty Trust v. York (1945) created a major exception to *Erie*, holding the doctrine does not apply to *matters of procedure*. However, the Court's test for determining whether a rule was procedural—the so-called outcome determinative test—was to prove problematic. [84]

C. *Byrd*: Byrd v. Blue Ridge Electric (1958) indicated that courts should consider the policies underlying the federal and state laws when determining whether state law applies. [85]

D. *Hanna*: Hanna v. Plumer (1965) devised a more workable test for distinguishing substance and procedure, and provided a separate analysis to be used in case of Federal Rules of Civil Procedure and similar rules. Most *Erie* issues will be analyzed under one of the two arms of the *Hanna* analysis. [85-86]

III. DEALING WITH FEDERAL JUDGE-MADE LAW

In the case of an ordinary federal judge-made rule, the issue is whether the rule is procedural. If so, federal law applies instead of state law.

A. Test: In most cases, a court applies the *Hanna* test to determine if the federal rule is procedural. A rule is procedural under this test if the difference between state and federal law would ***not be likely to cause forum-shopping*** between state and federal court. [86]

B. Exceptions: There are several exceptions to this analysis, including:

1. Judge-jury determinations are still analyzed under the test used in *Byrd*. [87]

2. Courts have recognized a limited body of purely substantive federal common law, which applies even though it clearly would lead to forum-shopping. [94]

C. Choice of law: The Supreme Court has held that state choice of law rules are substantive and must therefore be applied by a federal court. [86]

IV. DEALING WITH FEDERAL RULES OF CIVIL PROCEDURE AND SIMILAR RULES

Hanna held that a different test applied to the Federal Rules of Civil Procedure and similar rules, reflecting the different origins of these rules.

A. Rules Enabling Act: In the REA, Congress gave the Supreme Court the power to enact rules of "procedure and evidence." [89]

1. However, those rules cannot abridge, enlarge, or modify substantive rights. [90]

2. The REA is the source of the Federal Rules of Civil Procedure and other rules. [89]

B. Analysis for Federal Rules of Civil Procedure: The *Erie* doctrine binds the courts, not Congress. Therefore, because the REA delegates Congress's power, a rule made under it is valid as long as it is truly a rule of procedure, and does not abridge, enlarge, or modify substantive rights. Whether the rule would cause forum-shopping is not relevant. [90-91]

C. **Limited reading:** However, the courts will sometimes read a rule narrowly to avoid a clash with state law. [90]

V. DEALING WITH FEDERAL STATUTES

Congress is not bound by *Erie*. Therefore, if a federal statute is valid and truly applies to the issue at hand, it applies in lieu of state law. [91-92]

CHAPTER 6

LITIGATION AND ITS ALTERNATIVES

I. REMEDIES

The goal of most civil suits is obtaining an appropriate remedy.

A. **Substitutionary remedies:** Substitutionary remedies attempt to replace what the claimant has lost. [99-100]

   1. **Compensatory damages:** Damages are a frequently sought remedy. Generally speaking, the victorious plaintiff will recover a sum equal to the value of what she has lost. [100]

   2. **Other forms of damages:** In some circumstances, the law allows for the recovery of *liquidated* (amount is agreed upon ahead of time) or *statutory* (amount fixed by statute) damages. [100]

   3. **Punitive damages:** Punitive damages are not compensatory but instead are designed to punish defendant and thereby deter such behavior in the future. [100-101]

      a. Punitive damages are available only in certain narrow categories of cases, primarily in tort. [100]

      b. The Supreme Court has recognized constitutional limits on punitive damages. [101]

B. **Specific remedies:** A specific remedy orders a defendant to act, or to refrain from acting, in a certain way.

   1. **Equitable remedies:** Many (but not all) specific remedies are equitable. Equitable remedies are subject to certain limitations that do not apply to other sorts of remedies. [101]

   2. **Injunction:** The injunction is the most common specific remedy. When determining whether to grant an injunction, a court will balance the hardships as well as consider the public interest. [102]

C. **Provisional remedies:** In some cases, a party may be entitled to specific relief, such as a preliminary injunction or temporary restraining order, before the case is resolved.

   1. However, the party must make a very strong showing to obtain such relief. [102-103]

   2. *Pretrial attachment* of a defendant's assets presents special constitutional concerns. [104-105]

II. ATTORNEYS' FEES

A. Default rule: Under the so-called *American rule*, each side pays its own attorney, regardless of the outcome of the case. [106]

B. Exceptions: However, private agreements, statutes, and rules increasingly shift attorneys' fees. Litigation finance is also used with increased frequency. [106]

CHAPTER 7

PLEADING

I. OVERVIEW

Pleading is the process by which the parties inform each other and the court of their claims and defenses.

A. Historical development: Pleading has gone through centuries of evolution. At common law, pleading was highly legalistic and formalistic. The trend has been to cut back on formalism and to require more factual assertions. [112]

B. Code pleading: The system of code pleading, which remains in force in several states, requires a party to plead the facts in ordinary and concise language. [112]

C. Federal pleading: The system of notice pleading encapsulated in the Federal Rules of Civil Procedure is also used in many state systems. [112]

II. FEDERAL PLEADING—OVERVIEW

A. Pleadings allowed: The Federal Rules of Civil Procedure require a complaint, one or more answers, and, if ordered by the court, a reply.

    1. All other requests to the court are made by *motion* rather than by a pleading. [112, 113-114]

    2. Additional pleadings occur in cases where additional parties are joined to the suit. [113]

B. Format of pleadings: The Federal Rules of Civil Procedure contain certain requirements involving case information, separation of allegations, and the use of exhibits. [113]

III. FEDERAL PLEADING—CLAIMS FOR RELIEF

The term *notice pleading* describes the flexible standard for stating a claim.

A. Basic standard: Fed. R. Civ. P. 8(a) requires the claimant to make a *"short and plain statement"* of the claim. [114]

    1. In theory, as long as the claimant affords the other side notice of what legal claims she is bringing, this standard is satisfied. [114-115]

2. Recent Supreme Court decisions, however, require a pleader to include enough facts to make its legal conclusions *plausible*. [115]

3. The Federal Rules of Civil Procedure also contain special rules dealing with pleading formal matters such as capacity. [116]

B. **Prayer for relief:** The claimant must also ask for relief. [116]

C. **Jurisdiction:** A plaintiff must include a statement describing the basis for the federal court's subject matter jurisdiction. [114]

D. **Elevated pleading standards:** For some claims and issues, the Federal Rules of Civil Procedure require more detail than the basic standard set in Rule 8(a).

1. A party must provide more detail for allegations of *fraud* and *mistake*. [115]

2. Claims for *special damages* must also be set out with particularity. [115-116]

IV. FEDERAL PLEADING—DEFENDANT'S RESPONSE

A defendant's general response is her *answer*, while she can make specific responses by *motion*. [118]

A. **Pre-answer motions:** Defendants can use motions to raise both procedural and substantive challenges to the complaint. [118]

1. *Rule 12(b)* contains a special set of objections that may be made by motion, including challenges to jurisdiction, venue, and the form of the complaint. [118-119]

2. The *Rule 12(b)(6) motion* allows defendant to assert that plaintiff's complaint does not state a claim upon which relief can be granted. [119]

3. *Rule 12* also allows for a motion for a *more definite statement* and a motion to *strike* redundant, immaterial, impertinent, or scandalous material. [120]

4. *Rules 12(g) and (h)* set out certain restrictions on the timing of pre-answer motions.

    a. Defenses relating to *personal jurisdiction*, *service*, and *venue* can easily be waived by omission from the answer or failure to include them in a pre-answer motion. [120-121]

    b. The remaining Rule 12 defenses may be asserted at a later time. [121]

B. **Answer:** The answer is defendant's general response to the complaint.

1. The answer must be filed within 21 days, subject to certain exceptions. However, this time period is often extended at defendant's request. [122]

2. A defendant must *admit or deny* all allegations in the complaint.

    a. Failure to deny is deemed an admission. [122-123]

    b. An *ineffective denial*—one where defendant does not address the substance of the claims— is treated as a failure to deny, and accordingly operates as an admission. [123]

    c. If a defendant does not have sufficient information to allow him to admit or deny an allegation, he can plead insufficient information, which is treated as a denial. [123]

d. A defendant need not address each individual allegation, but can admit certain allegations and, in a single statement, deny the remainder of the entire complaint. [124]

3. Defenses: A defendant may also respond by asserting defenses: reasons why plaintiff is not entitled to the relief it has requested.

   a. There are two basic types of defenses: *ordinary* and *affirmative*. [124-125]

   i. The *ordinary defense* considers only the complaint and argues that there is a procedural, legal, or pleading defect. [124]

   ii. The *affirmative defense* introduces additional facts that prevent plaintiff from recovering. Fed. R. Civ. P. 8(c) contains a non-exclusive list of possible affirmative defenses. [125]

   b. The issue of who has the *burden of pleading* a particular issue depends on several factors. However, Fed. R. Civ. P. 8(c) and 12(b) make it clear that the burden of pleading certain issues falls on defendant. [125-126]

V. AMENDMENTS TO THE PLEADINGS

Most pleadings can be amended. However, issues can arise as to whether court permission is required and whether the amendments relate back.

A. When permission is required: Fed. R. Civ. P. 15 provides a fairly short period in which a party may amend its pleading without permission. After that, permission is necessary. [128-129]

B. Relation back: The rules also allow certain amendments to relate back to the date of the original pleading, which is important when the amendment adds a claim, but was filed or served after the statute of limitations on that claim expired.

   1. An amendment relates back if it arises from the same conduct, transaction, or occurrence as the original pleading. [129]

   2. Additional requirements must be satisfied if the amendment changes the party against whom a claim is asserted. [129-130]

C. Other changes: Fed. R. Civ. P. 15 also allows *amendments to conform to the evidence* and *supplemental pleadings*. [130]

VI. MOTION FOR JUDGMENT ON THE PLEADINGS

If the pleadings, taken as a whole, show that one party should prevail as a matter of law, the court may grant a motion for judgment on the pleadings. [132]

VII. ETHICAL LIMITATIONS ON PLEADINGS AND MOTIONS

Fed. R. Civ. P. 11 sets out detailed standards designed to ensure honesty and candor in pleadings and motions.

A. Signing requirement: The rule requires that all documents submitted to the court be signed by an attorney or the party. [132-133]

B. Representations: Signing constitutes a certification that the signer has conducted background research, that the assertions in the document are supported by law and fact, and that the document has not been filed for an improper purpose. [133-134]

C. Sanctions: Violation of Fed. R. Civ. P. 11 may result in sanctions.

    1. However, the 21-day *safe harbor provision* will afford the signer a chance to correct the problem. [134]

    2. Sanctions may be imposed not only on the signer but also on the entire law firm. [135]

    3. Monetary sanctions are usually paid to the court. [135]

CHAPTER **8**

DISCOVERY

I. OVERVIEW

A. Definition: Discovery is the formalized process by which the parties may compel other parties, as well as non-parties, to provide relevant information. A great deal of informal fact-finding not covered by the Federal Rules of Civil Procedure also occurs in most cases. [142]

B. Types: Discovery falls into two main categories.

    1. Mandatory disclosures: In the federal courts, parties are required to turn over certain information to other parties at various stages of the case. [142]

    2. Requests for information: Each party may also seek information from other parties to the case and sometimes from non- parties. [142, 150]

II. SCOPE AND SEQUENCE OF DISCOVERY

A. A party may discover most information that is *relevant* to the claim or defense of any party and *not privileged*. [142]

    1. Information is relevant as long as it helps a party prepare its case in any way. [142-143]

    2. The information can be relevant to the claim or defense of any party. [142]

    3. The law provides *privileges* for certain types of information, such as attorney-client communications. Privileged information cannot be discovered. [144-145]

    4. Work product: Fed. R. Civ. P. 26(b)(3) also places limits on the discovery of "work product": things prepared by a party or its representative in anticipation of litigation. Work product may be discovered only if the requesting party can show need. [145-146]

    5. Expert information: Facts known by and opinions of *nontestifying experts* may, like work product, be discovered only by showing need. [147]

6. The rules also place *proportionality* and *privacy* limitations to prevent abuses in the discovery process. [143-144]

B. Sequence of discovery: Discovery may occur from a very early stage in the case to a few weeks prior to trial. In federal courts, a *discovery conference* will occur early in the case. Following that conference, the parties engage in the *initial mandatory disclosures* and then may seek information from other parties and third parties. [150]

III. DISCOVERY METHODS

The Federal Rules of Civil Procedure provide for a number of different discovery methods.

A. Mandatory disclosures: The rules require the parties automatically to turn over certain information to other parties at two stages in the lawsuit. [150]

1. Soon after the discovery conference, a party must disclose various forms of evidence that he may use to support his claims or defenses. [151]

2. Prior to trial, the party must disclose all testifying experts and lay witnesses. [151-152]

B. Depositions: A deposition resembles the questioning of a witness at trial. The witness is placed under oath, and the testimony is transcribed. [152]

1. Depositions are one of the few discovery devices that can be used to force a nonparty to provide information. [152]

2. The Federal Rules of Civil Procedure limit the number of depositions that may occur in a case and the length of each deposition. [152, 154]

3. A party may notice the deposition of a corporation, in which case the corporation must produce someone with the information sought. [153-154]

4. The Federal Rules of Civil Procedure also allow for alternative forms of depositions, including a deposition prior to the commencement of the action and a deposition on written questions. [155]

C. Interrogatories: Interrogatories are written questions to another party that must be answered under oath.

1. A party may ask another party no more than 25 questions. [155]

2. The recipient has a duty to investigate before answering an interrogatory. [155-156]

D. Documents and things: Fed. R. Civ. P. 34 allows one party to inspect documents and property in the possession of another person. [156]

E. Requests for admission: A party may ask another party to admit certain facts. In effect, requests for admission operate like a second round of pleading. [157]

F. Physical and mental examinations: Fed. R. Civ. P. 35 allows a party to force another party to submit to a medical examination.

1. Unlike all other discovery devices, a party must obtain a ***court order*** in order to force the other party to submit to an examination. [158]

2. A court will grant the request for an order only if the condition is ***in controversy*** and ***good cause*** exists for an examination. Good cause exists when the information is not reasonably available from other sources. [158]

G. **Protective orders:** A court may issue a protective order to protect a person or party from overly burdensome, embarrassing, or otherwise objectionable discovery. [154]

1. Before going to court, parties must attempt to resolve the disagreement themselves. [162]

2. Two common reasons for protective orders are to protect a person's privacy and a business enterprise's trade secrets. [144]

IV. SUPPLEMENTATION OF DISCOVERY

In some situations, a party must supplement her response to an earlier discovery request. [160-161]

V. PREVENTING DISCOVERY ABUSE

The Federal Rules of Civil Procedure contain tools to help prevent discovery abuse.

A. **Signing of discovery:** Fed. R. Civ. P. 26(g) requires that all discovery documents be signed. Signing constitutes a certification that the discovery is consistent with the rules and conducted in good faith. [161]

B. **Compelling discovery:** If a person refuses to respond to a discovery request, the requesting party may ask the court to intervene.

1. Sanctions are available against a person who refuses to respond to a proper discovery request. [162-163]

2. In addition, the party may obtain an order compelling a response. [162]

3. Violation of the order may result in additional sanctions, including contempt. [163]

4. Other rules contain specific sanctions that apply to particular discovery issues, such as failure to attend one's own deposition or to supplement discovery. [164]

CHAPTER 9

RESOLUTION WITHOUT TRIAL

I. SETTLEMENT

Most pending cases are resolved by settlement, which presents few significant *legal* issues.

  A. Judicial approval: In the vast majority of cases, the court need not approve a settlement. [169]

  B. Later actions: Whether a settlement prevents plaintiff from suing again depends in large part on the terms of the settlement agreement. [170]

II. ALTERNATIVE DISPUTE RESOLUTION

The judicial system increasingly encourages alternative forms of dispute resolution to relieve the strain on court resources and parties.

  A. Mediation: Mediation, although like settlement, uses a third party to facilitate negotiation. The mediator makes no decisions. [170]

  B. Arbitration: Arbitration, by contrast, typically results in the arbitrator deciding the merits of the dispute. However, the procedure differs in many respects from court litigation. [170-172]

III. JUDICIAL MANAGEMENT OF LITIGATION

In many systems, courts play a significant role in speeding up the litigation process. In addition to dismissals and defaults (discussed below), the *discovery conference* and *pretrial conference* are two of the main tools for controlling the process. [150, 172-173]

IV. DEFAULT

A defendant who fails to respond to a complaint may be held in default.

  A. Two stages in process

    1. Entry: If a party fails to plead or otherwise defend, the clerk enters default against that party. [174]

    2. Judgment: After default is entered, the other party may obtain a default judgment. [174]

      a. Depending on the circumstances, either the court or clerk enters the judgment. [174-175]

      b. If judgment is to be entered by the court, the court may hold a hearing. The defaulting party may be entitled to notice prior to the hearing, allowing it to show up and contest damages. [175]

  B. Sanction defaults: A default judgment is sometimes imposed as a sanction against a party who violates the Federal Rules of Civil Procedure. Special rules apply to such defaults. [174]

  C. Challenges: A default judgment can be overturned by showing good cause. Default judgments are generally disfavored by the courts. [176]

V. INVOLUNTARY DISMISSAL

  A. When available: Involuntary dismissals are granted when plaintiff fails to prosecute its case or as a sanction against an uncooperative plaintiff. [176-177]

B. Effect of dismissal: In many cases, an involuntary dismissal prevents plaintiff from filing the case again. [177]

   1. However, dismissals for lack of jurisdiction or venue do not prevent refiling in a different court. [177]

   2. The effect of an involuntary dismissal in federal court is somewhat complicated because of the *Semtek* case. [177-178]

VI. VOLUNTARY DISMISSAL

A plaintiff may also dismiss his case voluntarily.

A. How accomplished: Depending on the timing, a plaintiff may be required to obtain the consent of defendants or the court in order to dismiss. [178]

B. Effect of dismissal: A voluntary dismissal may prevent plaintiff from refiling, depending on the wording of the dismissal and whether plaintiff has previously dismissed the same action. [178-179]

VII. SUMMARY JUDGMENT

If there is no genuine factual dispute in the case, a court may grant summary judgment to the party who is entitled to prevail under governing law. [181]

A. Procedure: The party seeking summary judgment files a motion, which may be supported by affidavits. [181]

B. Standard: Summary judgment is proper when there is no genuine issue of material fact and the movant is entitled to judgment as a matter of law. [181]

   1. Burdens: The burden of production directly affects how this standard is applied.

   a. It is easier for a party without the burden of production to obtain summary judgment. In this case, the movant need only show that the other side is missing evidence on at least one element of its claim or defense. [184]

   b. When the party with the burden moves, by contrast, it must show that it has uncontradicted evidence on every element of its claim or defense. [185]

   2. Evaluating evidence: The court does not weigh the evidence. If there are questions of credibility, summary judgment should be denied. [182]

   3. Inferences: Determining whether an inference may be drawn from indirect testimony is a crucial question in summary judgment.

   a. Although drawing inferences is usually a question for the jury, a court can consider the likelihood of a given inference in the summary judgment process. [182]

   b. At times, multiple inferences may be drawn from given testimony. Whether summary judgment is appropriate in such a case turns on the burden of production and on whether the inferences all favor one party. [182-183]

CHAPTER **10**

DETERMINING THE TRIER

I. RIGHT TO A JURY TRIAL

In some situations, the Seventh Amendment to the U.S. Constitution gives the parties a right to demand a jury trial.

A. Overview of Seventh Amendment

1. The amendment applies only in federal courts, not in state courts. [192]

2. The amendment also places certain restrictions on the size of the jury and on whether a unanimous verdict is required. [192]

3. A party must file a *timely demand* for a jury. [192]

B. Basic analysis: The amendment "preserves" a right to a jury in "*suits at common law.*"

1. Because the amendment preserves rather than creates a right, courts use a historical analysis in applying it. If an action would have been deemed a suit at common law in 1791, the amendment gives a right to a jury. [192-193]

2. A suit at common law is an action that traditionally would have been heard in the English courts of common law rather than in the courts of equity or admiralty. [192]

3. Distinguishing common law from equity requires a consideration not only of the *remedy* being sought but also of the underlying cause of action and procedures. [193]

C. Applying analysis to new claims: Legislatures have added to the common law by creating new statutory rights. Courts analyze these situations using a *two-part test*.

1. The first step is to find the *closest historic analogue* to the new claim and to determine whether that analogous claim would have been heard in common law or equity in 1791. [194]

2. The second step is to determine the *nature of the remedy*. [194]

3. The second step prevails over the first in cases where the two point to different conclusions. [194]

D. Applying analysis to new procedures

1. **Traditional equitable procedures:** Procedural devices that were historically available only in equity (such as the class action) do not deprive a party of the right to a jury if the underlying substantive claim would qualify as an action at common law. [195]

2. **Merger of law and equity:** Unlike in 1791, both legal and equitable claims may be joined in a single action. A party is entitled to a jury for all issues relevant to all legal claims, even if those same issues arise in the equitable claims. [195-196]

3. **Agency adjudication:** Congress may skirt the Seventh Amendment by assigning cases involving *statutory public rights* to an *agency* rather than to a court. [196]

II. SELECTING JURORS

Selecting jurors involves two main stages.

A. Selecting the pool: First, a jury pool is selected at random from the world of qualified jurors. [198]

   1. Systems differ in what groups they exclude from jury duty. The federal courts exclude relatively few groups. [199-200]

   2. The Constitution prevents systematic exclusion of jurors based on certain attributes. [200]

B. Forming the panel: The pool of jurors is narrowed through the actual panel through *voir dire.*

   1. Jurors are asked a wide range of questions to determine bias or other reasons for disqualification. [200]

   2. Jurors can be excluded for cause or by use of peremptory challenges.

     a. *Challenges for cause* are based on actual or potential bias, or for other reasons making the juror unfit to serve. [201]

     b. *Peremptory challenges* are limited in number and require no stated reason. However, if a party's use of peremptory challenges exhibits a pattern of excluding jurors of the same race, gender, or other protected attribute, the Constitution requires the party to justify the exclusion based on a reason other than the attribute. [201]

III. DISQUALIFYING JUDGES

A judge can be disqualified for personal bias, a financial or other interest in the amount in controversy, family interests, or in any other situation in which her impartiality might reasonably be questioned. [203-204]

CHAPTER 11

THE TRIAL

I. PREVENTING IMPROPER INFLUENCE ON THE JURY

Courts have several tools at their disposal to ensure the jury considers only the information it is supposed to consider.

A. Evidence: The Rules of Evidence attempt to prevent the use of unreliable evidence. [209-210]

B. Juror experimentation: It is grounds for a new trial if a juror conducts her own inspection outside the courtroom. [210]

C. Attorney misconduct: Attorneys may not provide their own personal opinions concerning the facts or make an improper appeal to the jurors' sympathy. [210]

D. Instructions: The court informs the jury about the law to be applied in a set of instructions. [210]

II. JUDGMENT AS A MATTER OF LAW

In certain cases, the evidence is so one-sided that the court can take the case away from the jury and enter judgment as a matter of law (JML).

A. **When available:** A JML is available at two points in the case: before the case is submitted to the jury or after the jury returns with a verdict. However, there are strict timing rules that apply to the postverdict JML. [211-212]

B. **Standard:** The standard for JML is that no reasonable jury could find for the party opposing the motion. [212]

  1. The standard is similar to the standard for summary judgment, although the judge has slightly more leeway to weigh the evidence. [212]

  2. As with summary judgment, both *inferences* and the *burden of production* are important factors in applying the standard for JML. [212-213]

III. NEW TRIALS

A judge can grant a new trial because the jury verdict is clearly incorrect or to remedy a procedural error.

A. Strict timing rules apply to requests for new trials. [213]

B. **New trial to cure erroneous verdict:** If a verdict is *against the great weight of the evidence*, the court may grant a new trial. [213]

  1. This standard is significantly easier to satisfy than the standard for a JML. [213-214]

  2. The party may combine a motion for new trial with a JML motion. In that case, the court must decide both even if the court grants the JML. [214]

C. **New trial to cure procedural defects**

  1. To obtain a new trial based on procedural errors, the requesting party must demonstrate he was *prejudiced* by the error. [214]

  2. The party must also *object* in timely fashion, and possibly *renew* the objection. [214]

  3. Special rules limit the *use of juror testimony* to prove procedural error. [215]

D. **Partial and conditional new trials:** A court will sometimes grant a new trial only for certain issues. In addition, the court may be able to deny a new trial if the winning party agrees to a modification of the verdict. [215-216]

CHAPTER 12

APPEALS

I. WHAT ISSUES MAY BE APPEALED

Not every issue may be appealed.

A. Adversity: The party must show that the ruling is against her interests. This showing is relatively easy to make. [221]

B. Need to raise below: The party must usually give the trial judge a chance to consider and rule on the issue. [221-222]

II. TIMING OF THE APPEAL

In the federal courts and many states, a party may appeal only a final decision of the trial court.

A. Definition: A final decision is one that completely wraps up the dispute, except for acts to collect on any judgment. All other decisions are deemed interlocutory. [223]

B. Exceptions to rule: There are several exceptions to the final decision rule.

    1. Rule 54(b): Fed. R. Civ. P. 54(b) allows a party to appeal the final resolution of a discrete "claim for relief," provided the judge makes an express determination that there is no reason to delay entry of judgment. [223-224]

    2. Injunctions: 28 U.S.C. §1292(a) allows immediate appeal of a decision granting, denying, or modifying an injunction or receivership. [224-225]

    3. §1292(b) certification: If the trial judge certifies a ruling on a controlling question of law and the court of appeals agrees to hear the case, a party may appeal the ruling immediately. [225]

    4. Class actions: A decision granting or denying class certification may be immediately appealable under Fed. R. Civ. P. 23(f). [225]

    5. Mandamus/prohibition: Technically original actions rather than appeals, writs of mandamus and prohibition provide an alternate means of challenging certain decisions of the trial court. However, such writs are rarely granted. [225]

    6. Practical finality: The court-created ***collateral order*** doctrine allows immediate appeal of a decision that:

        a. involves an important issue of law that is separate from the merits of the case,

        b. has been conclusively settled, and

        c. would be effectively unreviewable if appeal does not occur until after a final decision. This last requirement is very difficult to meet because a new trial will solve most problems. [225-226]

III. SCOPE OF APPELLATE REVIEW

An appellate court is limited in its review of lower court decisions.

A. Law: The appellate court need give no deference whatsoever to a lower court's ruling on the law. [228]

B. Fact: By contrast, the appellate court can overturn a factual finding only if the finding is ***clearly erroneous***: The same standard applies to mixed questions of law and fact. [229]

C. Discretion: If an issue lies within the discretion of the trial judge, the appellate court may overturn the finding only if there has been an ***abuse of discretion***. [229-230]

CHAPTER **13**

RESPECT FOR JUDGMENTS

I. CLAIM PRECLUSION

Claim preclusion, or *res judicata*, prevents a party from relitigating claims that he litigated, or should have litigated, in a prior case.

- **A. Standard:** A claim is barred if it, or another claim arising from the same basic event, was litigated in a prior suit that ended in a final judgment. [234]

  1. A claim is the same as one brought in a prior case if it uses the same legal theory to recover against the same defendant based on the same underlying facts. [234]

  2. Determining whether two claims arise from the same basic event is more difficult. Courts differ significantly on the test used to determine whether a claim is sufficiently related to be barred by claim preclusion. [235-236]

     a. Most look to see if the claims share a significant amount of the same core evidence. [235]

     b. Others use the narrower "same cause of action" or "same primary right" approaches. [235]

  3. Installment contracts are governed by special rules. [236]

- **B. Defense preclusion:** Claim preclusion may bar a claim even though the party asserting it was a defendant in the prior action.

  1. A **compulsory counterclaim rule** like Fed. R. Civ. P. 13(a) may bar factually related counterclaims omitted from the prior action. [236]

  2. In addition, there is a narrow common law compulsory counterclaim rule that applies when Rule 13(a) does not. This rule applies if the claim would nullify the judgment in the first suit. [236-237]

- **C. Other issues:** Other issues arise in claim preclusion.

  1. **Same parties:** Claim preclusion usually applies only when the parties are the same in the two cases. However, parties who are in *privity* with someone who was a party to the first action are also bound by the judgment. [237-238]

  2. **Final judgment on the merits:** Claim preclusion only applies if the first case resulted in a final judgment on the merits. Courts differ concerning whether certain dismissals, such as those based on failure to state a claim, are on the merits. [238-239]

  3. **Lack of jurisdiction in first court:** In most cases, claim preclusion does not apply when the first court would not have had subject matter jurisdiction over the claim in question. [239]

II. ISSUE PRECLUSION

Issue preclusion, or collateral estoppel, prevents relitigation of certain issues resolved in prior litigation. [241]

A. **Basic standard:** Issue preclusion applies if the two cases involve the *same issue*, that issue was *actually litigated* and *decided* in the first case, and the first court's ruling was *necessary* to the judgment. [241]

B. **Same issue:** Determining whether two cases involve the same issue can be difficult in situations involving differences in the burden of proof or when there is a series of related obligations or events. [241-242]

C. **Actually decided:** Whether an issue was actually decided is an important issue in cases involving multiple claims and/or defenses.

   1. An issue was actually decided a particular way only if the court logically had to decide the issue that way to reach the ultimate conclusion. [242-243]

   2. The above analysis applies when the case is decided by *general verdict*. In bench trials, the judge sets out her ruling on each claim and/or defense, making the task simpler. [243]

D. **Necessary:** The issue of whether a ruling was necessary arises both with respect to *dictum* and when the court explicitly relies on alternate bases for its holding. In the latter situation, courts are split fairly evenly as to whether each of the alternate bases has issue preclusion effect. [243]

E. **Parties affected:** Unlike claim preclusion, people who were not parties to the first case may sometimes take advantage of issue preclusion.

   1. Most courts have abandoned the old requirement of *full mutuality*, especially in cases involving defensive use of issue preclusion. [244]

   2. *Offensive use* is more problematic. Most courts place certain restrictions on offensive use of preclusion. [244-245]

   3. Issue preclusion may never be used *against* someone who was *neither a party nor in privity* with a party to the first action. [245]

III. LIMITS ON PRECLUSION

There are limits to the use of both claim and issue preclusion.

A. **Claim preclusion:** Exceptions to claim preclusion include suits to enforce a judgment and situations where the first court lacked jurisdiction. [247-248]

B. **Issue preclusion:** Exceptions to issue preclusion include situations where there has been an intervening change in the law, where there were procedural disadvantages in the first case, and where use of preclusion would defy the public interest. [248]

IV. FULL FAITH AND CREDIT

The constitutional requirement of full faith and credit (FFC) requires U.S. courts to honor the judgments of both sister state and federal courts.

A. **Basic command:** FFC extends claim and issue preclusion across state lines. If a court in the rendering state would afford either claim or issue preclusion to the judgment, all other courts in the country must ordinarily extend the same preclusive effect. [249]

B. Exceptions: Judgments rendered without jurisdiction or decreeing rights to property in another state usually are not entitled to FFC. [249-250]

C. Divorce: A state has jurisdiction to grant a divorce if at least one of the spouses is domiciled there. [250]

V. OTHER ISSUES IN PRECLUSION

A. Reopening judgments: Fed. R. Civ. P. 60(b) allows a party to reopen a judgment well after the usual 28-day period for obtaining a new trial has expired. [250-251]

    1. In some cases, the party must seek relief within a year of the judgment. [251]

    2. Relief under Fed. R. Civ. P. 60(b) is rarely granted. [251]

B. Law of the case: The doctrine of "law of the case" makes certain rulings on issues of law binding for the remainder of a given lawsuit. [251]

C. Judicial estoppel: A party may be barred from taking a position contrary to a position taken in a previous case. [251]

CHAPTER **14**

JOINDER OF CLAIMS AND PARTIES

I. JOINDER INVOLVING CURRENT PARTIES

Fed. R. Civ. P. 13 and 18 allow the existing plaintiffs and defendants to file additional claims against each other.

A. Adding claim to existing claim: Fed. R. Civ. P. 18 allows a party who already has filed an original claim, counterclaim, cross-claim, or third-party claim to add any additional claims he may have against that party. [257-258]

    1. The additional claims need not be related to the first. [257]

    2. Fed. R. Civ. P. 18 does not give the federal courts subject matter jurisdiction over the additional claims. Jurisdiction must be acquired under the jurisdictional statutes. [258]

B. Counterclaims: Rule 13 allows, and in some cases requires, defendant to file a counterclaim against plaintiff. [258]

    1. Subject only to jurisdictional considerations, a defendant may file any counterclaim it has against plaintiff, regardless of whether it is related. [258]

    2. A counterclaim is *compulsory* if it arises from the *same transaction or occurrence* as plaintiff's claim. [258]

        a. Failure to plead a compulsory counterclaim results in the claim being barred by claim preclusion. [259]

        b. Rule 13(a) lists several exceptions to the compulsory counterclaim rule. [259]

3. **Same transaction or occurrence:** Courts use two main tests to determine if two claims arise from the same transaction or occurrence. [258]

    a. The *logical relationship test* asks if the facts of the claims are logically related. [258]

    b. The *same evidence test* looks for a significant overlap in the evidence that will be used to prove both claims. [258]

4. Parties other than defendants may also be required to file counterclaims. [259]

C. **Cross-claims:** Coplaintiffs and codefendants may cross-claim against each other. A cross-claim must arise from the same transaction or occurrence as the original claim or a counterclaim. [259-260]

II. JOINDER OF PARTIES

A. **Multiple plaintiffs and defendants:** Fed. R. Civ. P. 20 allows a plaintiff to sue multiple defendants, and/or for multiple plaintiffs to join, if three requirements are met.

1. Plaintiffs are suing, or defendants are being sued, jointly, severally, or in the alternative. [260]

2. The claims arise from the same transaction or occurrence. [260]

3. The claims involve a common question of law or fact. [260-261]

B. **Adding parties to cross-claims and counterclaims:** A party may add a new party to the case in connection with a cross-claim or counterclaim if the requirements of Fed. R. Civ. P. 20 are satisfied. [261]

C. **Impleader:** If defendant may demand contribution or indemnity from a third party for all or part of plaintiff's claim, defendant may be able to join that third party to the suit under Fed. R. Civ. P. 14. [261-262]

1. Impleader is commonly used by one joint tortfeasor against another or where there is a contractual right to indemnity. [262]

2. Defendant must allege that the third party is liable to defendant, not solely to plaintiff. [262]

3. Special rules deal with service of process on the joined third party. [263]

4. The joined third party and plaintiff may file additional claims in the case. [263]

D. **Compulsory joinder:** While joinder of parties is usually optional, on occasion it is required. Fed. R. Civ. P. 19 covers compulsory joinder.

1. Compulsory joinder is primarily a *defense* raised by defendant. [265]

2. The rule sets out a three-part test for dealing with compulsory joinder.

    a. Rule 19(a) prescribes when a party should be joined if feasible. If the absence of the party may pose a significant risk to the rights of either that party or the existing parties, the person should be joined. [266-268]

    b. If the party should be joined, plaintiff must try to join her. Subject matter and personal jurisdiction may prevent joinder. [268]

    c. If the party cannot be joined, the court considers the factors listed in Rule 19(b) to determine whether to dismiss the case or to proceed without the missing party. [268-269]

E. Intervention: A nonparty may also be able to intervene as a party in the action.

　　1. Fed. R. Civ. P. 24(a) gives a party a *right to intervene* in certain situations. The grounds for intervention by right parallel the necessary party rule, Rule 19. [271-272]

　　2. Even if a party does not have a right to intervene, she may be able to intervene with the court's permission under Fed. R. Civ. P. 24(b). [270]

F. Interpleader

　　1. **When available:** Interpleader is available when a party is exposed to logically inconsistent claims to the same thing. [273]

　　2. **Two types:** Interpleader is available under both Fed. R. Civ. P. 22 (rule interpleader) and 28 U.S.C. §1335 (statutory interpleader). The two differ significantly with respect to subject matter jurisdiction, personal jurisdiction, and venue. [273-274]

　　　　a. *Rule interpleader* is subject to the usual rules governing jurisdiction and venue. [273]

　　　　b. The statutes governing *statutory interpleader* make it much easier for the court to acquire jurisdiction and venue. [273-274]

III. SEVERANCE AND CONSOLIDATION

A. Severance: If joinder of claims and parties makes the lawsuit too unwieldy or confusing, the federal rules allow the court to split the case up into several smaller suits. [276]

B. Consolidation: If two separate cases pending in a single district share a common question of law or fact, the court can consolidate them into a single action. [276]

IV. JURISDICTION AND JOINDER

Joinder of claims and parties often raises questions of subject matter and personal jurisdiction.

A. Personal jurisdiction: A court must have personal jurisdiction over all parties other than voluntary plaintiffs and intervenors. [276]

B. Subject matter jurisdiction: Courts must have subject matter jurisdiction over every claim in the case. Supplemental jurisdiction often proves very useful in establishing subject matter jurisdiction over claims brought in federal court. [276-277]

　　1. The same transaction or occurrence test used in many of the joinder rules is for all intents and purposes the same as the common nucleus of operative fact test used under 28 U.S.C. §1367(a). Therefore, if joinder is proper under these rules, the requirements of §1367(a) are usually satisfied also. [277-278]

　　2. However, even if joinder satisfies §1367(a), one must still consider subsections (b) and (c). When jurisdiction over the original claim is based on diversity, subsection (b) bars many claims by plaintiffs against nondiverse parties. [278-279]

CHAPTER 15

CLASS ACTIONS

I. OVERVIEW

A class action is a case in which one or more people represent the rights of others similarly situated. [287]

A. Plaintiff or defendant class: Although class actions usually involve groups of plaintiffs, defendant class actions are also possible. [288]

B. Control: To ensure adequate representation, the court exercises a significant degree of control over the class action. [287-288]

II. CONSTITUTIONAL CONCERNS

There are constitutional concerns in cases where one private individual represents the rights of others.

A. Representation: In *Hansberry*, the Supreme Court held that the Due Process Clause prevented the class members from being bound by a judgment when the representative did not adequately represent their interests. [289-290]

B. Personal jurisdiction: However, in *Phillips Petroleum*, the Supreme Court held that the Due Process Clause does not prevent a court from adjudicating the rights of members of a plaintiff class who have no minimum contacts with that state. [290]

III. RULE 23

The Federal Rule of Civil Procedure dealing with class actions attempts to meet the constitutional requirements set out in *Hansberry* and *Phillips Petroleum*.

A. Overview: Rule 23 requires the court to certify the case as a class action. There are two general steps in the certification process. [292]

B. Step one: Rule 23(a): Rule 23(a) requires the court to determine if the case is appropriate for a class action. In making this determination, the court considers:

1. numerosity—whether the class is so numerous that ordinary joinder is impracticable [292],

2. commonality—whether there are questions of law or fact common to the class [292-293],

3. typicality—whether the claim of the representative is typical of those of the class [293], and

4. adequacy—whether the representative will adequately represent the interests of the class. [293]

C. Step two: Rule 23(b): The court then determines whether the case falls into one of three types of class action.

1. **Rule 23(b)(1):** Cases where the members of the class would be necessary parties under Fed. R. Civ. P. 19. [293-294]

2. **Rule 23(b)(2):** Cases where the class seeks injunctive or declaratory relief pertaining to action that affects them all. [294]

3. **Rule 23(b)(3):** Cases where the common questions of law or fact predominate over the individual questions and a class action is superior to other methods for resolving the disputes. [294]

    a. In determining predominance, courts consider factors such as any individual defenses defendant may have toward some members and choice of law considerations. [295]

    b. In determining superiority, the court considers factors such as the size of the individual claims. [294-295]

D. **Procedure after certification:** Once the case is certified, additional materials may be provided to the class members.

    1. *Notice* is ordinarily provided to all members of the class. Although notice is required only in Rule 23(b)(3) class actions, courts frequently demand it in other types. The representative bears the cost of the notice. [295-296]

    2. In Rule 23(b)(3) class actions, the members must be afforded an opportunity to ***opt out*** of the class. [296]

E. **Settlement:** A class action cannot be settled without notice to the class members and court approval. [296-297]

IV. OTHER ISSUES PERTAINING TO CLASS ACTIONS

A. **Subject matter jurisdiction:** Special rules apply when determining whether a class action may be brought in federal court using diversity jurisdiction. Supplemental jurisdiction, however, may also be option. [299-300]

B. **Attorneys' fees:** Courts have considerable control over attorneys' fees in class actions. [300]

V. OTHER REPRESENTATIONAL LITIGATION

Class actions are not the only form of representational litigation. Shareholder derivative actions and actions involving unincorporated associations present many of the same sorts of issues. [300-301]

CHAPTER 1

INTRODUCTION

ChapterScope

This chapter takes a "big picture" look at the Civil Procedure course. It demonstrates how the many issues discussed in the remaining chapters are all parts of a cohesive system.

- Although Civil Procedure seems different from other first-year law school courses, it cannot be understood in isolation from those courses. The underlying substantive rules of Tort, Contract, Property, and other areas of law are always important, as they form the basis for the court's ultimate decision on the dispute.

- The rules of Civil Procedure serve two main goals: *fairness* and *efficiency*. In many situations, however, these ends conflict.

- The rules that comprise Civil Procedure come from several sources, including statutes, court-drafted rules, case law, and, in some cases, the U.S. Constitution.

- The distinction between the *federal* and *state court* systems is crucial in Civil Procedure. In many cases, a case may be litigated in either federal or state court. Nevertheless, there can be significant differences between the two systems.

- A civil case may go through several different stages before it is complete. Each stage presents its own issues.

I. CIVIL PROCEDURE GENERALLY

The Civil Procedure course focuses on the process by which civil disputes are litigated in the courts. As such, it is a vital counterpart to other courses you may be taking, such as Torts, Contracts, and Property. Civil Procedure deals with how the various claims and defenses you study in these other courses are resolved in actual practice. Understanding the procedural aspects will allow you to better understand the cases—and in some cases even the legal rules—in your other courses.

Note: Most law schools offer Civil Procedure as a first-year course. This book is accordingly written mainly for a first-year audience with a limited grasp of the substantive law. If you are taking the course as an upper-level student, you may find that the explanations typically involve basic issues of Tort, Contract, and Property law. Nevertheless, the discussion of Civil Procedure concepts is equally suited to an upper-level course.

A. How Civil Procedure differs from other courses: Because of the focus on *how* cases are litigated, discussion of cases in a Civil Procedure class often proceeds along different lines than the discussion in other substantive courses.

  1. Procedural issues: The discussion concentrates more heavily on the procedural issues in the case, such as where the parties reside, which party brought the suit, and who is claiming what against whom.

2. **Jurisdiction:** In addition, at many points in the course it is very important to remember *which court* is hearing the case.

3. **Procedural history:** When reading a Civil Procedure case, it is also important to keep the *procedural history* of the case in mind. Most cases you will read are appellate court opinions. An appellate court's power to overturn a trial court's decision varies significantly depending on the issue.

4. **Policy:** Finally, and perhaps most important, the ***underlying policy concerns*** in Civil Procedure are often quite different from those in your other courses.

   a. **Other substantive courses:** Most other courses focus on whether public policy supports making *X* pay *Y* for some injury that *X* has caused.

   b. **Civil Procedure:** Procedure, by contrast, takes that basic question for granted. The policy concerns deal more with questions of ***how a court system should operate***.

      i. **Fairness:** An often-cited policy concern in Procedure is ***fairness***. A fair system should not only reach the "right" result most of the time, but it should also *appear* fair to the litigants. Even if a party's claim or defense is weak, fairness dictates that she have a chance to be heard before a court (although not necessarily by way of a *trial*).

      ii. **Efficiency:** On the other hand, Procedure is also concerned with ***efficiency***. A system that minimizes the time that courts, parties, and (especially) attorneys must spend in preparing for and participating in a trial helps reduce the costs of litigation.

      iii. **Fairness vs. efficiency:** These concerns with fairness and efficiency often clash. Procedural rules that rush the litigation process can result in mistakes, which undermine the goal of fairness. Similarly, there are limits to the notion that a party is always entitled to a court. If a claim or defense is completely groundless, it wastes the court's and the opponent's time to conduct a full trial on the matter. Thus, the procedure system allows for summary resolution of groundless claims and defenses at several stages of the case.

B. **Common misperceptions in Civil Procedure:** Because Civil Procedure seems so "different" from the other substantive courses in the first year of law school, students often come into the course with certain basic misperceptions.

   1. **Procedure is not completely separate from the other courses:** As discussed above, there are significant differences between Procedure and the substantive courses. However, this does not mean Procedure is unrelated to those courses. Whenever you apply a case, statute, or rule, it is crucial to keep the underlying substantive law in mind.

   2. **Procedure is not more straightforward than the other courses:** Many students begin Procedure assuming—incorrectly—that learning Procedure involves simply memorizing a set of technical rules.

      a. **Underlying policy concerns:** Just as in your other substantive courses, ***policy concerns*** underlie the rules of Civil Procedure. Most rules will make more sense if you take the time to consider these policy concerns.

      b. **Procedure as a system:** On a broader level, Procedure is more than a collection of arcane rules. It is a system designed to strike a fine balance between the goals of efficiency and fairness. However, at first you probably will not appreciate how the various areas of Civil Procedure fit together into a unified whole.

3. **Procedure is not harder than the other courses:** A few weeks into Procedure, many students conclude that Procedure is more difficult than the other courses. Again, that is not necessarily true. The problem with Procedure is that the policies and rules that underlie the system are not as immediately obvious to the layman. Unlike their other classes, students often find themselves with no "gut reaction" as to how an issue should be resolved. The rules seem arbitrary at first glance.

4. **Procedure does not deal only with trials:** Certainly, the course in Procedure focuses heavily on the process of litigation. However, the litigation process involves far more than the trial. In fact, only a small portion of the Civil Procedure course deals with trials.

   a. **Pretrial:** The vast majority of an attorney's time in a typical civil case is spent with pretrial matters such as pleading and discovery.

   b. **Out-of-court resolution:** In addition, disputes are increasingly resolved without going to court at all. There is a growing trend to use *settlement, arbitration, and mediation* to resolve civil cases.

C. **Sources of Civil Procedure:** One final way in which Procedure differs from other first-year courses is in the source of the legal rules. Although cases are important, they are less important than in many other courses. Procedure instead relies much more heavily on positive law such as statutes and rules.

1. **Statutes:** Most of the statutes used in Civil Procedure are codified in title 28 of the U.S. Code (often called the "Judicial Code").

2. **Federal rules:** Another important source of positive law is the *Federal Rules of Civil Procedure*, which are promulgated by the U.S. Supreme Court (actually by an Advisory Committee to the Court) pursuant to a delegation of authority from the U.S. Congress.

   a. **Application in state court:** Although the *Federal Rules of Civil Procedure apply only in federal court*, many states have adopted similar rules for use in their courts. On the other hand, some states—including California, Illinois, and New York, which are the source of many reported decisions—do not follow the Federal Rules of Civil Procedure. The Civil Procedure systems in these states exhibit some important differences from the federal approach, although there are also core similarities.

   b. **Other federal rules:** There are other bodies of federal rules, including the Federal Rules of Appellate Procedure, the Supreme Court Rules, local rules in the various federal districts, and the Federal Rules of Evidence. These rules arise only occasionally in a basic Civil Procedure course.

3. **Importance of case law:** Although Procedure involves a much larger proportion of positive law than other first-year courses, cases are also important.

   a. **Application:** A case can illustrate how a given statute or rule applies, which can help in understanding the technical wording of statutes and rules.

   b. **Interpretation:** In addition, courts occasionally interpret a statute or rule in a way that is not obvious from the face of the statute or rule. In these cases, the judicial interpretation represents the "law" on that topic.

    c. Doctrinal sources: Finally, some Civil Procedure doctrines—such as personal jurisdiction (Chapter 2), the *Erie* doctrine (Chapter 5), and the effect of a decided case on later cases (Chapter 13)—developed primarily through case law.

II. GENERAL THEMES IN U.S. CIVIL PROCEDURE

Certain basic themes underlie Civil Procedure.

  A. Civil vs. Criminal Procedure: The course in Civil Procedure deals exclusively with the litigation process in *civil cases*. It does not deal with the procedure in *criminal cases*, a subject taught in a separate course.

    1. *Civil* defined: The easiest way to define a *civil* action is to compare it to criminal proceedings. A *criminal case* is brought by the state against a person committing a crime. The state seeks a conviction, pursuant to which defendant will be *punished*. By comparison, a civil suit usually seeks compensation or other relief, not punishment.

    2. Civil or criminal? However, it is not always immediately clear whether a case is civil or criminal.

      a. Punishment: First, civil cases may also involve punishment. In an intentional tort case, for example, plaintiff may be entitled to *punitive damages*. Although the purpose of such damages is to punish, a suit involving punitive damages is a civil case.

      b. Compensation: On the other hand, some criminal cases seek reimbursement for the victim. In many states, the prosecutor can ask for an order of *restitution*.

      c. State as party: Nor can one use the fact that a state is a party to the case as a rule of thumb. While states bring criminal prosecutions, they can also sue and be sued in civil actions.

    3. Terminology: Criminal and civil cases each have their own terminology. Avoid using criminal law terms in Procedure (as well as in courses such as Torts). For example, a defendant in a civil case is found *liable,* not guilty. Similarly, when discussing the concept of claim preclusion, do not speak of "*double jeopardy.*" Double jeopardy applies only in criminal cases.

  B. Multiple court systems: Another complicating feature of U.S. Civil Procedure is the existence of *multiple court systems*. This feature is one aspect of the United States' own unique brand of *federalism*. Strong federalism overtones exist in some Civil Procedure issues.

    1. State courts: Every state has its own court system, with at least two levels.

      a. Trial courts: Every state has multiple *trial courts*, where litigants first bring their disputes.

      b. Courts of appeals: Most states follow the federal model and have one or more *courts of appeals*, including a single *high court*. (Note that the high court is not always called the "supreme" court. For example, in New York, the "supreme court" is a trial court.) Appellate courts review cases heard in the trial courts. In a three-tier system, the high court reviews decisions from the courts of appeals.

      c. Specialized courts: Most states also have *specialized* courts to hear certain types of cases, such as a *probate court* to deal with wills, a *family court* for family matters, a *court of claims* to hear claims against the state itself, and a *small claims court* that deals with claims involving less than a certain dollar amount.

2. **Federal courts:** In addition to the state courts, the United States operates a separate, nationwide system of federal courts.

   a. **Federal courts are main focus of Procedure:** A typical Civil Procedure course focuses on the federal courts. If the procedure in your state differs significantly, your school may offer a separate course in state procedure.

      i. **State procedural rules:** However, many states have procedural rules that *mirror the federal rules*.

      ii. **Issues for federal courts only:** There are also certain issues that are *unique to the federal court system*. Examples include:

         (a) most of *subject matter jurisdiction*, discussed in Chapter 4,

         (b) the *Erie doctrine*, discussed in Chapter 5, and

         (c) the Seventh Amendment right to a *jury trial*, which applies in federal courts only and is discussed in Chapter 10.

   b. **Limited jurisdiction:** The federal courts are courts of *limited jurisdiction*, which means they may hear only certain categories of cases. Determining what cases a federal court may adjudicate involves a question of *subject matter jurisdiction*, which is discussed in Chapter 4.

   c. **Three levels:** Excluding specialized tribunals such as the Bankruptcy Court, the federal court system has three levels:

      i. **District courts:** The *district courts* serve as the trial court for most cases.

         (a) **Organization:** Every state has at least one federal district. Many have two or more districts. There are also federal district courts for the *District of Columbia*, *Puerto Rico*, and the federal territories. With one minor exception, see 28 U.S.C. §131, no federal district includes land in more than one state.

         (b) **District of Columbia:** The District of Columbia also has a separate local court system. Although this court is technically federal, it acts in many respects more like a state court.

      ii. **Courts of appeals:** The *courts of appeals* review decisions of the district courts. The appellate courts are divided into *thirteen circuits*.

         (a) **First through Eleventh and D.C. Circuits:** The First through Eleventh Circuits, and the District of Columbia Circuit, review cases from district courts located within their geographic boundaries. The D.C. Circuit also reviews many agency decisions.

         (b) **Federal Circuit:** The Thirteenth Circuit is called the *Federal Circuit*. Unlike the others, its jurisdiction is defined in terms of subject matter, not geography.

      iii. **Supreme Court:** The *U.S. Supreme Court* is the highest federal court. The Supreme Court reviews decisions of the federal courts of appeal and, in certain rare cases, hears direct appeals from the district courts.

         (a) **State court decisions:** Unlike all other federal courts, the Supreme Court may also review certain decisions of the *state high courts*. However, the U.S. Supreme

Court reviews state court decisions only when—and to the extent that—they involve questions of federal or constitutional law.

(b) Trial court: In certain rare cases, such as suits between states, the Supreme Court can sit as a trial court. This is called *original jurisdiction.*

3. **Jurisdiction often shared:** Although the United States has a wide array of different courts, it is generally true that **more than one court** is available in a given case. For example:

a. In most cases, *both state and federal courts can hear claims arising under the U.S. Constitution and federal law.*

b. Similarly, a federal court may hear **claims arising under state law** if the parties are from different states and the amount in controversy is sufficiently high.

★   **Example:** In Hawkins v. Masters Farms, Inc., 2003 WL 21555767 (D. Kan. 2003), the court found that a person who had moved to another state had established a sufficient connection to become a citizen of the new state and therefore could not sue someone from that same state in federal court.

c. A state court is *not limited* to hearing cases arising *under the law of that state.* A state court can hear cases arising under the law of any other state or foreign nation.

C. **Law vs. equity:** Historically, the legal system also operated separate courts of *law* and courts of *equity.* Today, almost all jurisdictions have merged the systems. Although this historical distinction is no longer significant for most purposes, it remains important in determining *remedies,* see Chapter 6, and in determining whether a party has a right to a *jury trial,* see Chapter 10.

III. STAGES IN A CIVIL LAWSUIT

A typical lawsuit has several stages. Different issues can arise at each stage. To understand the many issues you study in Procedure, always attempt to determine the stage at which a question arises. As the case progresses, each side usually learns more about both the underlying facts and their opponent's claims.

A. **Determining what claims to bring:** The first step is for the potential plaintiff and her attorneys to decide what claim or claims to bring in the action. This issue is largely determined by the substantive law, not the law of Civil Procedure.

B. **Determining where to sue:** The next stage is to determine *where* to sue. A plaintiff often prefers to sue in her home state. But if defendant resides elsewhere, plaintiff's home state courts might not be able to hear the case because they lack *personal jurisdiction.* Similarly, plaintiff must make sure the chosen court is a proper *venue.* Finally, regardless of which state the case ends up in, plaintiff must make a choice between the state and federal courts in that state, a choice that turns on the issue of *subject matter jurisdiction.*

1. **Personal jurisdiction (Chapter 2):** The chosen court must have authority over *every defendant.* This authority is called *personal jurisdiction.* A court's personal jurisdiction is constrained both by the *U.S. Constitution* and the *service statutes or rules* of the jurisdiction in question.

a. **Purposeful connections:** In general, the Constitution allows a court in a given state to exercise jurisdiction only over defendants who reside in a state or have established other *purposeful connections* with that state. However, defendants may consent to personal jurisdiction or waive a personal jurisdiction problem.

    b. Notice: In addition, every defendant must be given *notice* of the lawsuit.

2. Venue (Chapter 3): Like personal jurisdiction, *venue* narrows the universe of courts that are available to hear a case. Venue, however, is not a constitutional consideration. Instead, it results from statutes that attempt to place the litigation in a *convenient* forum.

3. Subject matter jurisdiction (Chapter 4): Although every state has both state and federal trial courts, a given court is an option only if it has *subject matter jurisdiction* to hear the case.

    a. Federal courts: Most discussion of subject matter jurisdiction in Civil Procedure concerns the federal courts. Federal courts may hear only certain categories of cases.

        i. Three main categories: Federal courts may hear cases in three main categories: *cases arising under federal law, state law cases between citizens of different states where the amount in controversy exceeds $75,000,* and "supplemental" jurisdiction over *state law claims that arise out of the same basic facts* as either of the prior two types of claims.

        ii. Exceptions: However, this is merely a rough guideline. There are cases in all three categories that fall outside federal jurisdiction.

    b. State courts: Subject matter jurisdiction is also an issue in state court. In some cases, a claim may be heard only in federal court.

C. Pleading the case (Chapter 7): Plaintiff commences the case by filing a *complaint* with the court and serving it on defendant. Defendant can respond in several different ways.

1. The complaint: The complaint contains the statement of plaintiff's claims. The form and contents of the complaint vary from court to court. In federal court, plaintiff must provide *notice* of the claims it is bringing, and present enough facts to convince the court the factual conclusions are *plausible*. On certain issues, however, plaintiff must go into greater detail.

2. Responding to the complaint: Defendant may respond to the complaint by filing one or more motions or by filing an answer.

    a. Motion: A motion is a request for a ruling on a specific subject. If defendant feels plaintiff's action is deficient in one or more respects, she may file a motion to *dismiss* the case. A defendant may move to dismiss if, for example, she feels the claims are not recognized at law or if the court lacks jurisdiction over the case or over defendant. Other motions are also available, such as a motion to change venue or to recuse the judge.

    b. Answer: Unlike a motion, which focuses on one or a few narrow issues, the answer is defendant's response to *all assertions in the complaint*.

        i. Types of responses: Defendant may *admit* some matters, *deny* others, and offer *affirmative defenses* that shield defendant from liability. However, a defendant who filed a pre-answer motion may be precluded from raising certain defenses in the answer.

        ii. Counterclaim: If defendant has any claims against plaintiff, she may file a *counterclaim*.

3. Amending the pleadings: The parties may be able to amend their pleadings to add new claims and defenses or cure any defects. Depending on the timing of the proposed amendment, court permission or the consent of the other party may be required to amend a pleading.

D. Determining who will sue and be sued (Chapters 14 and 15): Once the claims and court are established, the parties determine who will be litigants in the case. This stage requires consideration both of the substantive law (which determines who can be liable on a given claim) and Procedure.

    1. Plaintiffs and defendants: It is fairly common for *two or more plaintiffs* to join. Similarly, it is possible to sue *multiple defendants*.

★   **Example**: In Fisher v. Ciba Specialty Chemicals Corp., 245 F.R.D. 539 (S.D. Ala. 2007), the court denied defendants' motion to sever the claims of five plaintiffs who had joined to sue defendants. The court held the similarities in plaintiffs' claims made litigation in a single case far more efficient.

        a. Compulsory joinder: Although joinder of parties is usually optional, in certain rare situations a party must join another party to the case or risk dismissal of the action.

        b. Intervention: If a person who is not a party to the case has a significant interest in the outcome of the case, that person may be able to intervene in the case.

    2. Additional parties: Plaintiff and defendant may also bring additional parties into the case. The most common situation is *impleader*, where a defendant adds a third person to the suit by claiming that the person must reimburse defendant for all or part of any judgment rendered against defendant.

    3. Additional claims between parties: The rules of Procedure typically give a party considerable leeway to bring additional claims against the other parties. For example, one defendant may *cross-claim* against another defendant.

    4. Class actions (Chapter 15): If a significant number of people are injured in roughly the same way, those people may be joined into a class. In a class action, a representative adjudicates the rights of the class members.

E. Discovery (Chapter 8): Once the claims and parties are joined, the case is under way. The parties then prepare for trial by amassing information concerning the claims and defenses. In complex cases, discovery may take several years.

    1. Mandatory disclosures: In the federal courts, parties are required to turn over certain information to the other parties immediately after commencement of the case, and other information shortly before trial begins.

    2. Party-initiated discovery: Parties may also seek information that might be helpful to the case. Information may be obtained both from parties and from nonparty witnesses and others with information. Several discovery devices are available; the most common of these are *depositions* and *interrogatories*.

    3. Limits on discovery: Not all information a party seeks can be discovered. The *relevancy*, *privilege*, *work product*, and *expert information* rules limit discovery of certain types of information. There are also rules dealing with abuse of discovery.

★   **Example:** In Butler v. Rigsby, 1998 U.S. Dist. LEXIS 4618 (E.D. La. 1998), the court held that because a health provider's list of patients was protected by the doctor-patient privilege, it could not be discovered by another party, even though it was relevant to the party's case.

F. Resolving the case before trial (Chapter 9): Most civil actions never reach trial. Parties may negotiate a mutually acceptable settlement. In other cases, one side's position proves untenable, allowing the other side to obtain a judgment in its favor before trial ever begins.

1. **Voluntary dismissal:** If the parties settle the case, plaintiff typically dismisses the action voluntarily.

2. **Involuntary dismissal:** The court may dismiss a case if a party does not comply with the rules, if the court lacks jurisdiction, or if plaintiff's complaint does not state a legally recognized claim.

3. **Summary judgment:** After the parties have had a chance to engage in discovery, it may turn out that the facts are not really in dispute. If there is no genuine issue of fact, the court may enter a summary judgment, which resolves the case as a matter of law.

★   **Example:** Houchens v. American Home Assurance Co., 927 F.2d 163 (4th Cir. 1991), is a good example of how the summary judgment standard is applied. In that case, neither party had any direct evidence on the crucial issue of whether a person's death was accidental. Because plaintiff had the burden of proving the death was accidental, the court held summary judgment for defendant was appropriate.

G. **The trial (Chapters 10 and 11):** For those few cases that reach trial, the parties must deal with a host of issues.

1. **Jury trial issues (Chapter 10):** Many of these issues relate to the jury, the body of laypeople who decide the case. Whether a party is entitled to a jury depends on the jurisdiction and the claims in the case.

   a. **Jury selection:** Cases involving a jury may present issues concerning how the jury is selected.

   b. **Not allowed to decide:** In addition, if the evidence presented at trial overwhelmingly favors one side, the jury may not be allowed to decide the case. Instead, the court will issue a *judgment as a matter of law*.

2. **Other trial issues (Chapter 11):** The main issue at trial concerns what *evidence* is admissible. The vast majority of evidence issues are covered not in Procedure, but instead in a separate Evidence course. Issues covered in Procedure include improper influences on the jury, the form of jury instructions, and whether immediate appeals of rulings are available.

H. **Effect of a judgment (Chapter 13):** A judgment has effects beyond the actual case.

1. *Stare decisis:* One of the defining features of the common law is that courts defer to the decisions of other courts on the same issue of law. The course in Procedure usually does not focus much on this general principle.

2. **Preclusion:** Instead, the main issues in Procedure are *claim and issue preclusion*. These are a form of "super *stare decisis*," for unlike *stare decisis*, a court does not have the option to ignore a prior ruling.

   a. **Claim preclusion:** This form of preclusion prevents a party from asserting claims that were or should have been asserted in a prior case involving the *same parties*. For example, in Ison v. Thomas, 2007 WL 1194374 (Ky. App. 2007), the court held that claim preclusion prevented a plaintiff from suing to recover for personal injury after plaintiff had already sued for property damage stemming from the same accident.

★   b. **Issue preclusion:** This doctrine bars individual issues of fact. Unlike claim preclusion, issue preclusion applies only if the issue was *actually litigated* and if it is possible to determine what the prior court *actually decided*. In many jurisdictions, people who were not parties to the first action may be able to use issue preclusion against someone who was a party.

3. **Full faith and credit:** Claim and issue preclusion may apply across state lines. State and federal courts must give *full faith and credit* to each other's judgments.

I. **Appeals (Chapter 12):** Finally, an unfavorable judgment may be appealed to a higher court. There are issues concerning the timing of an appeal, as well as an appellate tribunal's authority to overturn certain findings of the trial court. Generally speaking, an appellate court has only a very limited ability to overturn a trial court's findings of fact.

1. **Interlocutory appeals.** In federal court, as well as in many states, appeals before a final judgment ("interlocutory appeals") are extremely limited.

2. **Exceptions.** However, various statutes, rules, and court-created doctrines allow for appeal of certain interlocutory orders.

CHAPTER 2

PERSONAL JURISDICTION

ChapterScope _____

This chapter deals with the rules that determine whether a court has jurisdiction over the parties to an action. A court must have personal jurisdiction over a party to enter a judgment that binds that party.

■ In most cases, the only issue is personal jurisdiction over *defendants*. A plaintiff consents to the court's jurisdiction by filing suit in that court.

■ There are two types of personal jurisdiction: *in personam* and *in rem*.

■ *Nexus* and *notice* are both required for personal jurisdiction. The Due Process Clause of the U.S. Constitution prevents a court from hearing a case unless a sufficient connection exists between the forum and defendant. In addition, defendant must receive adequate notice of the action.

■ The *minimum contacts test* determines if an adequate nexus exists. This test measures the number of contacts between defendant and the forum. In many cases, it also considers the fairness of forcing defendant to litigate in the forum.

   ■ A contact counts only if it is *purposeful*, that is, if defendant intentionally engaged in some act by which she knowingly sought the benefits or protections of the forum.

   ■ The number of contacts required to meet the constitutional test depends on whether the claim in the case *arises out of* those contacts. If the claim arises out of the contacts, even a single contact may suffice.

   ■ *Fairness* is a second and separate part of the minimum contacts test. It considers the burden on defendant in litigating in the forum as well as other factors.

■ Notice is ordinarily accomplished by *service of process*. How a party serves process is ordinarily set out in a statute or rule.

   ■ A state statute that allows service on an out-of-state defendant is often referred to as a *long-arm statute*.

■ In most cases, a *federal court* may exercise personal jurisdiction over a defendant only if the courts of the state in which that federal court sits could exercise jurisdiction.

■ *Challenges* to personal jurisdiction must be raised early in the case, or they are deemed waived. A party can waive jurisdiction explicitly or by taking action in the case inconsistent with the defense of lack of jurisdiction. Defendants may also consent to jurisdiction, either before the case or during the case.

I. OVERVIEW

A. Definition of personal jurisdiction: Personal jurisdiction is a court's power over the parties to the case. If a court does not have personal jurisdiction over a party, any order or judgment the court may render does not bind that party.

B. Subject matter jurisdiction distinguished: Personal jurisdiction is separate and distinct from subject matter jurisdiction, the focus of Chapter 4. A court must have both personal and subject matter jurisdiction in order to hear a case.

C. Constitutional requirement: Personal jurisdiction is a constitutional requirement. A judgment rendered against a person over whom the court has no personal jurisdiction violates that person's right to *due process.*

D. Two categories of personal jurisdiction: Courts have traditionally distinguished between two distinct categories of jurisdiction, *in personam* and *in rem.*

1. *In personam:* Jurisdiction *in personam* is jurisdiction over defendant herself.

2. *In rem:* Technically, jurisdiction *in rem* is not jurisdiction over a person but over a particular item of property owned by a person. Practically speaking, however, it allows the court to adjudicate claims that one or more people have to the property, and bind those people to the judgment.

    a. **True *in rem*:** A "true" *in rem* action is one in which the main purpose is to adjudicate competing legal interests in the property in question. The *quiet title* action and *mortgage foreclosure* are forms of true *in rem* actions.

    b. *Quasi in rem:* Actions brought for purposes other than determining competing rights to property are deemed *quasi in rem. Quasi in rem* actions are sometimes divided into two subcategories.

        i.   **Type 1:** If the claim before the court arises out of or is otherwise related to the property, the action is sometimes referred to as *quasi in rem type 1.* For example, if a person is injured by a hazardous condition on another person's land, and seizes the land as the basis for jurisdiction, the case involves *quasi in rem type 1 jurisdiction.*

        ii. **Type 2:** If the claim before the court is unrelated to the property, the action is sometimes referred to as *quasi in rem type 2.* In these cases, the property mainly serves as an asset to satisfy any judgment the court may enter against the owner. This type of jurisdiction was severely limited by *Shaffer,* discussed in Part II.C of this chapter.

3. **Differences:** There are several significant differences between *in personam* and *in rem* jurisdiction.

    a. **How jurisdiction obtained:** *In personam* jurisdiction is obtained by serving defendant personally with process. Jurisdiction *in rem* is obtained by seizing the property. Although notice to defendant was not historically required in *in rem* actions, more recent decisions require plaintiff to notify defendant directly if defendant can be found.

    b. **Effect of judgment**

        i.   *In personam:* If *in personam* jurisdiction exists, the judgment binds defendant personally. The judgment winner can garnish defendant's wages and bank accounts, and have certain assets owned by defendant seized and sold, to satisfy the judgment.

ii. *In rem*: A judgment in an *in rem* case binds only the property and, accordingly, is *limited to the value of the property*. Plaintiff **cannot** use the judgment to seize other property owned by defendant. However, the judgment victor can sue defendant personally to recover any deficiency between the debt owed and the value of the property.

E. **Service of process:** Proper service of process is also necessary before a court may exercise personal jurisdiction over a defendant. Any judgment rendered without reasonable notice violates defendant's *due process* rights and therefore is invalid. Statutes and rules provide various means of serving process.

II. DEVELOPMENT OF THE MODERN CONSTITUTIONAL TEST

The modern personal jurisdiction analysis is the product of numerous Supreme Court decisions spanning almost 140 years. These decisions developed the current *minimum contacts test*.

★ A. **Pennoyer v. Neff (1877):** Pennoyer v. Neff, 95 U.S. 714 (1877), was the first decision to treat personal jurisdiction as a *constitutional issue*. It set out a clear, albeit somewhat restricted, test for when a court might constitutionally exercise jurisdiction over a person or her property. Although this restrictive approach has been significantly relaxed in many respects, some aspects of *Pennoyer* remain valid.

1. **Synopsis:** *Pennoyer* involved a dispute over title to certain land. Neff originally owned the land. After Mitchell obtained a judgment against Neff, the land was sold at a sheriff's sale to Pennoyer. Neff then sued Pennoyer in a separate action to recover possession of the land. This second action eventually made it to the Supreme Court.

   a. **Judgment valid?** If the judgment in *Mitchell v. Neff* was valid, it (and the sale of the land) would be binding on Neff, and Pennoyer would prevail.

   b. **No:** However, the Supreme Court held that the earlier *judgment was invalid* because the court *lacked jurisdiction* over either Neff or the land.

2. **Analysis:** Although recognizing that the U.S. Constitution created a cooperative system among the states, the Court reasoned that the states retained many attributes of independent nations. The Court turned to basic principles of public international law to determine when a state could govern a particular situation.

   a. **Two territorial principles:** The Court held that two basic principles of international law applied to the case at hand. The first was that "every State possesses exclusive jurisdiction and sovereignty over persons and property within its territory." The second — the converse of the first — was that "no State can exercise direct jurisdiction and authority over persons and property without its territory."

   b. **Limits on jurisdiction:** From these two principles, the Court distilled the limits on personal jurisdiction.

      i. **Person or property in state:** A court could exercise *in personam* jurisdiction over any *person*, and *in rem* jurisdiction over any *property*, found within its borders at the time the suit was commenced.

         (a) **Presence sufficient:** Provided the person was served (or property seized) while in the state, jurisdiction existed regardless of how long the person or property had been in the state. In addition, a court could hear any claim, regardless of whether it related to the reason the person or her property was present in that state.

    (b) Notice: Jurisdiction also required adequate notice.

        1. *In personam*: In the case of *in personam* jurisdiction, the person herself had to be served *while in the state*.

        2. *In rem*: In the case of *in rem* jurisdiction, the court had to seize or otherwise exercise dominion over the property *at the outset of the action*.

  ii. Person or property without state: Because a state's authority ended at its borders, a person who was not in the state ordinarily could not be served *in personam*. Similarly, if that person had no property within the state, *in rem* jurisdiction was impossible.

  iii. Exceptions: However, the Court identified several exceptions to the basic rule that a court could not exercise *in personam* jurisdiction over a person who was not in the state.

    (a) Status: A court had the authority to determine the *status* of one of its citizens in relation to a nonresident. Jurisdiction over the citizen gave the court jurisdiction over the status. For example, a court could grant a *divorce* if one spouse was a citizen, even if the other spouse was not in the state.

    (b) Consent: A defendant could consent to jurisdiction. Similarly, if a person appointed an in-state agent for service of process, service on the agent was effective to create jurisdiction over the person.

c. Constitutional concerns: The Court held that these basic principles of international law were incorporated into the U.S. Constitution. The opinion discusses two separate constitutional provisions, which have different ramifications.

  i. Full faith and credit: Article IV of the Constitution requires states to enforce the judgments of sister states. *Pennoyer* held that this provision was not meant to apply to judgments that were not valid under international law. Therefore, a court *need not* enforce a judgment entered without personal jurisdiction.

  ii. Due process: *Pennoyer* also stated that the Fourteenth Amendment requirement of due process guarantees an individual that his rights can be adjudicated only by a court that has personal jurisdiction over him. Therefore, a court *cannot* enforce a judgment rendered without personal jurisdiction even if it wants to.

  Note: The discussion of due process in *Pennoyer* is technically dictum. The Due Process Clause was not yet effective when the judgment in the first case was rendered, so that judgment could not violate Neff's due process rights. Nevertheless, the courts have treated the due process discussion as good law.

★ **B.** *International Shoe* **(1945):** International Shoe Co. v. Washington, 326 U.S. 310 (1945), greatly extended the reach of jurisdiction by allowing a state to exercise jurisdiction over defendants who are not present in the state. The court replaced *Pennoyer*'s strictly territorial analysis with one that focused on a person's connections with a state. *International Shoe*'s **minimum contacts test** remains the test used to this day.

1. **Synopsis:** The state of Washington levied an unemployment tax on defendant, a corporation. When defendant did not pay, the state sued in a Washington state court.

   a. **Connection sufficient?** The corporation's only connection with Washington was that it employed salesmen in the state. These salesmen did not enter into contracts with buyers, but merely sent orders to the corporation's Missouri headquarters for acceptance.

   b. **Yes:** The Court held that Washington *had personal jurisdiction*. Although the corporation was not physically present in the state, jurisdiction was constitutional because the corporation had sufficient contacts with the state (employment of the salesmen), and the claim arose out of those contacts.

2. **Analysis:** *International Shoe* adopted an approach that considers the *connections between the defendant and the forum*.

   a. **Minimum contacts test:** The Court indicated that jurisdiction was proper over a defendant who had "certain *minimum contacts* with [the state] such that the maintenance of the suit does not offend 'traditional notions of *fair play and substantial justice.*' "

   b. **Specific and general jurisdiction:** The Court then noted that the number of contacts necessary for jurisdiction turned on whether the claim arose out of those contacts.

      i. **Arose out of:** If the claim arose from the contacts, even single or occasional acts might suffice. Today, cases where the claim arises from the contacts are referred to as cases of *specific jurisdiction*.

      ii. **Did not arise out of:** Conversely, if the claim was unrelated to the contacts, jurisdiction would be not be allowed even if there were a significant number of contacts.

      iii. **Overwhelming contacts:** However, the Court also suggested that there might be cases where the contacts were so "continuous and systematic" that jurisdiction over the corporation might be allowed even if the claim was completely unrelated to those contacts. Today, jurisdiction arising out of numerous, but unrelated, contacts is referred to as *general jurisdiction*.

      Example: *D*, a Florida corporation, produces parts in its Florida factory. It sells all of its parts to a buyer in Tennessee. Once a month, *D* sends a truck filled with parts to the buyer. On the way, the truck passes through Alabama. *P*, a citizen of Florida, works at *D*'s plant. When *P* is injured on the job, she sues in an Alabama state court. The court cannot exercise personal jurisdiction over *D* in Alabama based on these facts. Although *D* has significant contacts with Alabama, they do not rise to the level necessary to meet the minimum contacts test because *P*'s claim does not arise from the contacts. Nor are the contacts sufficiently numerous to sustain general jurisdiction.

   c. **Fairness:** The opinion provides little guidance into what constitutes "fair play and substantial justice," other than to indicate that the "inconvenience" of litigating in a distant forum is relevant.

3. **Analysis still used:** Although the Court in *International Shoe* provided few details, the Court's basic two-part minimum contacts/fairness test remains in use. Later Supreme Court opinions have filled in many of the details.

★ **C.** *Shaffer* **(1977):** *International Shoe* dealt only with *in personam* jurisdiction. Shaffer v. Heitner, 433 U.S. 186 (1977), held that the **minimum contacts test** also applies to *in rem* jurisdiction. *Shaffer*, for all intents and purposes, eviscerated the use of *in rem* jurisdiction in cases where the claim does not arise out of the property.

   1. *In rem* **as a fiction:** The Court held that the notion of an *in rem* suit as one solely against property was a legal fiction. The suit really affected a person's *interest* in that property. Because due process protects a person's interest in property, *in rem* cases should be analyzed according to the same due process standard used in *in personam* cases. Thus, courts need to consider whether the *owner* has minimum contacts with the forum.

   2. **Application of minimum contacts test to *in rem*:** The Court then applied the minimum contacts test to the situation at hand.

      a. The property involved in *Shaffer* was stock owned by defendants.

      b. The case did not arise out of the stock. Defendants were being sued because of acts they committed as corporate officers, not because of their status as shareholders.

      c. Based on these facts, the Court found that although the stock was a contact, it was not by itself enough to satisfy the minimum contacts test.

      d. The only other connection between defendants and the forum was defendants' status as officers or directors in a corporation that had been incorporated in Delaware. The claims did arise from defendants' officer status. However, because the Delaware jurisdiction statutes did not base jurisdiction on this particular connection, the Court held that the status did not count as a contact for purposes of the minimum contacts analysis.

   3. **Limits of holding in *Shaffer*:** Notwithstanding some careless assertions to the contrary, there are a number of important limits to the holding in *Shaffer*.

      a. *Shaffer* **does not destroy *in rem* jurisdiction:** *Shaffer* merely prevents the use of *in rem* jurisdiction when the **property is the only contact** and the **action has nothing to do with the property**. The practical effect of *Shaffer* is to make *quasi in rem* jurisdiction much less appealing to a plaintiff. If minimum contacts exist, the party ordinarily will forgo *in rem* jurisdiction and use *in personam*.

      b. **Property is a contact:** Property should be considered along with any other contacts in determining whether there are minimum contacts.

      c. **Property alone may be enough:** If the case directly involves ownership of the property—that is, if the case is a true *in rem* action—the property is enough of a contact to satisfy the minimum contacts test. Although the case is not clear on this point, property alone may also be a sufficient contact in a *quasi in rem type 1* action, where the claim arises out of the property.

      d. **Other limits on *in rem* remain:** Although *Shaffer* extends the test used in *in personam* cases to *in rem*, the historic limitations on *in rem* continue to exist. For example, any judgment in an *in rem* action is limited to the value of the property.

★ **D.** *World-Wide Volkswagen* **(1980):** World-Wide Volkswagen Corp. v. Woodson, 444 U.S. 286 (1980), separates the contacts and fairness portions of the minimum contacts test, and fleshes out each portion.

1. **Synopsis:** A New York resident purchased an automobile in New York. The purchaser then decided to move to Arizona, but was involved in an automobile accident in Oklahoma while in route. The purchaser sued the New York dealer, the regional distributor, and other parties in an Oklahoma state court, alleging a design defect.

2. **Holding:** The Court held that Oklahoma ***could not exercise jurisdiction*** over the dealer or distributor because the minimum contacts test was not satisfied.

3. **Analysis:** The Court found there were ***no contacts*** between the dealer and distributor and Oklahoma.

   a. **Purposeful availment test:** Although the automobile was a connection between defendants and the state, it did not count as a contact. The Court held that a connection counts as a contact only if it results from an act that defendant ***purposefully directed*** at the forum state. Because defendants did not know the automobile was going to Oklahoma, the automobile did not qualify as a purposeful contact.

   b. **Fairness:** The Court also discussed the fairness portion of the minimum contacts analysis. Fairness, the Court indicated, comprises five factors:

      i. the ***burden on the defendant***, which the Court indicated was the *"**primary concern**"*;

      ii. the interest of the ***forum*** in adjudicating the case;

      iii. ***plaintiff's interest*** in obtaining "convenient and effective relief";

      iv. the interest of the interstate judicial system in ***efficient resolution*** of controversies; and

      v. the "shared interest of the several States in ***furthering fundamental substantive social policies***."

   c. **Fairness irrelevant absent contacts:** However, the Court held that these fairness factors were not to be considered unless there is at least one purposeful contact between defendant and the forum. Because there were no contacts in the case itself, the Court listed, but did not apply, the fairness factors.

III. APPLICATION OF THE MODERN CONSTITUTIONAL TEST

The cases discussed above, together with several more recent Supreme Court rulings, provide a template for analyzing personal jurisdiction cases. However, on certain issues the Court has not been able to reach a consensus.

A. **Basic approach:** The ***minimum contacts test*** is used to analyze most questions of jurisdiction.

1. **Two-step test:** The minimum contacts test involves two discrete steps.

   a. **Contacts:** First, the court determines if there are ***any "contacts"*** between defendant and the forum. If there are no contacts, ***the analysis stops***, and there is no personal jurisdiction. If there is at least one contact, the court determines whether the claim arises out of the contact(s).

   b. **Fairness:** If there are contacts, the court then considers fairness, incorporating the five factors set out in *World-Wide Volkswagen*.

2. **Contacts:** As discussed in *World-Wide Volkswagen*, a contact is considered only if it is the result of *purposeful activity*. In more recent decisions, the Court has restated this notion as *purposeful availment of the benefits and protections of forum law*.

3. **Fairness:** The factors each deal with unique concerns.

   a. **Burden on defendant:** This factor considers not only the distance defendant must travel but also any other circumstances that make defending in the forum burdensome on defendant, such as core differences in legal systems.

   b. **Interest of the state:** A state is interested in hearing a case if any of the parties are from that state or if the dispute directly affects that state.

   c. **Interest of plaintiff:** This factor is satisfied if plaintiff is from the forum or if the forum is a convenient place to try the case because of the availability of witnesses or other evidence.

   d. **Efficient resolution:** It is inefficient when a case involving multiple parties must be split up and litigated in several different places. If the chosen forum is the only place that all claims can be heard, this factor supports jurisdiction.

   e. **Furthering social policies:** If the alternate forum does not recognize plaintiff's claim, refusing to exercise jurisdiction frustrates the policy underlying the substantive law. This is most likely to be an issue when plaintiff is forced to refile in a foreign court.

4. **Lack of fairness rarely defeats jurisdiction:** If there are purposeful contacts, it requires a *very strong showing* of unfairness to defeat jurisdiction.

   a. **Asahi:** Asahi Metal Industry Co. v. Superior Court, 480 U.S. 102 (1987), is the only case in which the Supreme Court has refused to allow jurisdiction even when there were contacts. *Asahi* involved a somewhat unique situation. A plaintiff had brought a California state-court action against a Taiwanese tube manufacturer, who in turn impleaded a Japanese valve manufacturer. All claims other than the claim by the Taiwanese defendant against the Japanese third-party defendant were settled. These facts directly affected the fairness analysis:

      i.   The burden on the valve manufacturer was large, not only in terms of distance but also because of differences in language and legal systems.

      ii. The forum had no great interest. Although the underlying accident had occurred in California, that state had no real interest in whether a Japanese party had to indemnify a Taiwanese party.

      iii. The "plaintiff" (in this case, the Taiwanese tube manufacturer) was brought into California by the original defendants and had no real interest in having the claim litigated there.

      iv. Because the remaining dispute could be litigated just as easily in Taiwan or Japan, there were no real efficiency concerns.

      v.   The underlying "substantive policies" were those of Taiwan and Japan. Therefore, the Court held that forcing the claim to be brought in one of those nations would better protect those policies.

B. **Application to particular circumstances:** Certain situations have proved troublesome to courts charged with applying the minimum contacts test.

1. **Contract cases:** Three Supreme Court cases demonstrate how the courts apply the test to contract cases.

    ★   a. *McGee*: McGee v. International Life Insurance Co., 355 U.S. 220 (1957), dealt with an *insurance policy*. A California resident purchased a life insurance policy. The insurance company then assigned the policy to a Texas insurance company. The California resident paid premiums from California to Texas until his death. When the company refused to pay, the beneficiaries sued the Texas company in California. The Court held that maintaining an insurance policy on a Californian was sufficient to establish minimum contacts between the Texas insurance company and California. Therefore, the California courts had personal jurisdiction.

    ★   b. *Hanson*: In Hanson v. Denckla, 357 U.S. 235 (1958), Donner established a trust with a Delaware trustee. Donner later moved to Florida. After Donner died, an action was brought in the Florida courts to gain the assets in the trust, which required personal jurisdiction over the Delaware trustee.

        i.   The Court held that Donner's unilateral move to Florida did not establish contacts between the Delaware trustee and Florida. The trustee did not play a role in Donner's move.

        ii. Although the trustee continued to perform under the trust agreement, the trustee had no choice in the matter. The trustee could not cancel the trust based on Donner's move.

    ★   c. *Burger King*: Burger King Corp. v. Rudzewicz, 471 U.S. 462 (1985), is the Court's most detailed discussion of how the minimum contacts test applies to contracts. That case dealt with a *commercial contract*. A Michigan person obtained a Burger King franchise from Burger King, a Florida corporation. When the agreement soured, Burger King sued the Michigan franchisee in Florida. Although defendant had never been to Florida, the Court allowed the Florida courts to exercise jurisdiction.

        i.   Merely entering into a contract with a resident of the forum is not sufficient.

        ii. However, if the contract is *negotiated* and/or to be *performed* in the forum, that is evidence that the parties have *purposefully availed* themselves of the forum. In *Burger King*, the franchisee knew he was negotiating with a Florida corporation. In addition, the contract called for the franchisee to make payments for a number of years to the Florida office, meaning that performance would take place in Florida. The Court held these activities were "purposefully directed" at Florida.

2. **Stream of commerce cases:** The stream of commerce problem has plagued the courts since shortly after *International Shoe*. The Supreme Court only recently provided a relatively clear answer to the question.

    a. **"Stream of commerce" defined:** The stream of commerce problem arises when a defendant distributes its goods in multiple states through a third party. Although defendant knows that some of its goods go to a particular state, it does not direct where the third party sends the goods. Defendant may not know exactly which products go where. Moreover, it may not particularly care if any of its product is sold in a certain state.

    b. **Stream of commerce as a contact:** The jurisdictional issue is whether *purposefully injecting goods into the stream of commerce, coupled with knowledge that some goods* *end up in the state,* constitutes purposeful availment with a state in which one of those goods causes injury.

   c. *Asahi*: The Supreme Court first dealt with the stream of commerce problem in Asahi Metal Industry Co. v. Superior Court, 480 U.S. 102 (1987). Unfortunately, the Court issued a ***plurality opinion*** with no clear guidance as to whether injecting goods into the stream of commerce counts as a contact. As discussed above, the case was decided based on fairness.

★ **d.** *Nicastro*: The Supreme Court eventually specified how to analyze stream of commerce cases in J. McIntyre Machinery, Ltd. v. Nicastro, 131 S. Ct. 2780 (2011). Although another plurality opinion, a majority of the Justices agreed that merely placing a product into the stream of commerce is *not* enough to subject a defendant to personal jurisdiction, even if defendant knows the product will end up in the forum. Instead, jurisdiction exists only if the defendant engages in activities specifically directed at the forum, such as advertising or providing service to the product in the forum. Defendant in *Nicastro* did none of these additional activities, causing the Court to find no personal jurisdiction.

3. Internet cases: The Internet presents issues that are conceptually similar to the stream of commerce problem. The Internet allows parties to interact even though neither may know where the other is located. Although the Supreme Court has not faced the question, the lower courts have developed general rules for these sorts of cases.

   a. Basic issue: The typical Internet case involves the issue of whether a plaintiff who views or is mentioned on a Web site may sue the person who operates the site in plaintiff's home state.

   b. Classification of Web site: One of the leading tests used in the Internet context — the *Zippo* test — considers the type of Web site involved.

   i. Sliding scale: *Zippo* establishes a sliding scale. In cases where defendant operates a highly interactive site, where buyers regularly place orders online, a court may ordinarily exercise jurisdiction over defendant for claims arising from the Internet activity. On the other extreme are "purely passive" Web sites, where the viewer may read the information but neither enter information nor place orders.

   ii. Intentional Torts: This analysis may be modified in cases involving intentional torts, where the victim is from the forum but the harmful act takes place elsewhere. In Walden v. Fiore, 134 S. Ct. 1115 (2014) (a non-Internet case), the Supreme Court held that jurisdiction would not exist merely because defendant harmed a victim whom defendant knows resides in the forum. Instead, jurisdiction exists only if defendant acts in the forum or somehow obtains benefits and protections of the forum.

★ **Example:** In Abdouch v. Lopez, 285 Neb. 718, 829 N.W.2d 662 (2013), the state court dealt with a case where defendant's Web site allegedly invaded plaintiff's privacy. Although the court acknowledged that defendant made significant sales from its "highly interactive" site, it noted that few of these sales were made to Nebraskans. Perhaps anticipating the Supreme Court's decision in *Walden* (discussed just above), the court found no personal jurisdiction.

4. General jurisdiction: *International Shoe* indicated in *dictum* that if a party had a substantial and continuing relationship with a state, the courts of that state could hear any claim arising against defendant, even those **unrelated to the contacts**. This form of jurisdiction is called *general jurisdiction*. More recent Supreme Court cases have made it clear general jurisdiction is limited.

★   **Example:** In Goodyear Dunlop Tires Operations, S.A. v. Brown, 131 S. Ct. 2846 (2011), the Supreme Court acknowledged that general jurisdiction could exist in a case where defendant's contacts are so significant that it is "essentially at home" in the state, but found that test was not satisfied on the facts presented.

★   **Example:** The Court further tightened the test for general jurisdiction in Daimler AG v. Bauman, 134 S. Ct. 746 (2014). The Court made it clear that a defendant corporation will ordinarily be "essentially at home" only in its state (or nation) of incorporation and its principal place of business, even if it engages in major business activities elsewhere. The Court also held that the "fairness factors" that apply in specific jurisdiction do not apply in cases of general jurisdiction. If defendant is essentially at home in a state, that state has jurisdiction without regard to fairness.

   C. Cases outside the minimum contacts test: Although *Shaffer* declared that the minimum contacts test applied to all attempts to assert jurisdiction, in some situations courts eschew the test and automatically find jurisdiction based on principles established in *Pennoyer*.

   1. Domicile: In Milliken v. Meyer, 311 U.S. 457 (1940), the Supreme Court upheld jurisdiction over a domiciliary of the state even though the person was not in the state at the time. Although this case predates the *International Shoe* minimum contacts test, its continued validity remains unquestioned. Many courts would treat the situation as one of general jurisdiction.

   2. State of incorporation: *After Daimler AG, a* state may exercise jurisdiction over a corporation in its state of incorporation, even though defendant has no assets, employees, or operations in that state.

   3. Presence: The most important part of *Pennoyer* was its rule allowing a state to exercise jurisdiction over anyone who was ***served while present*** in the state. Although the validity of jurisdiction on this basis was questionable after *Shaffer*, the Supreme Court specifically approved it in 1990.

★   **a. *Burnham*:** In Burnham v. Superior Court, 495 U.S. 604 (1990), the Supreme Court upheld California's exercise of *in personam* jurisdiction over a defendant who was served while present in the state. Defendant, a nonresident, was visiting California for three days on a matter unrelated to plaintiff's claim. However, the Court was divided, with no majority opinion.

         i. Scalia's view: Justice Scalia, joined by three others, held that the long tradition of exercising jurisdiction over people who were present was enough to show that the practice complied with traditional notions of due process. Therefore, it was ***unnecessary to apply the minimum contacts test***. That test, Justice Scalia reasoned, developed as a way to allow courts to exercise jurisdiction over people who were *not present*.

         ii. Brennan's view: Justice Brennan, joined by three others, argued that the minimum contacts test applied. However, defendant's voluntary presence, coupled with service while he was there, gave California ***general jurisdiction*** over defendant.

         iii. Stevens's view: Justice Stevens refused to join either camp, simply indicating that the dispute was "a very easy case" and that jurisdiction was present.

b. Presence as a basis for jurisdiction after *Burnham*: In most cases it does not matter if the court applies Justice Scalia's or Justice Brennan's view: Jurisdiction based on in-state service is acceptable. The only situation where the different approaches might affect the outcome is when defendant's *presence is not voluntary*. Although jurisdiction would still be acceptable under Scalia's view, under Brennan's view the presence would no longer count as a contact (because it is not "purposeful"), and therefore general jurisdiction might not be available.

4. Consent and waiver: Because personal jurisdiction is a personal defense, a party may waive it either by expressly consenting or by taking actions inconsistent with the defense.

a. Minimum contacts irrelevant: If a party consents to a court's jurisdiction, it is *unnecessary to evaluate minimum contacts*. Consent alone is sufficient to establish jurisdiction.

b. Express consent: A party may expressly consent to the jurisdiction of a particular court. The most common example of this form of consent is a *contract* specifying that disputes arising under the contract may be heard in a specific court.

    i. Enforceability: As long as the agreement is enforceable under the rules of contract law, it creates personal jurisdiction over the parties. That the consent to jurisdiction was nonnegotiable rarely renders the consent ineffective.

    ii. Forum selection clause: A twist on the contractual consent is the forum selection clause, where the parties specify that disputes can be heard *only* in a particular court. If a party sues elsewhere, the other side may move for dismissal. In most jurisdictions, forum selection clauses are enforceable provided they are *fundamentally fair*. Fairness is measured at the time the agreement is made, not when the case is filed.

★   **Note:** The Supreme Court held in Carnival Cruise Lines, Inc. v. Shute, 499 U.S. 585 (1991), that a nonnegotiable forum selection clause on a cruise ship ticket was enforceable. However, this Supreme Court decision applies only to contracts involving ships. As a general matter, the enforceability of forum selection clauses is *governed by state law*, not federal. Not all states enforce such clauses.

c. Corporate agents: Service on a corporate agent is an acceptable way to establish jurisdiction. Most courts allow such service even if the corporation has no contacts with the state, and has merely appointed an agent for service.

d. Implied consent: A party may also waive the personal jurisdiction defense by taking actions inconsistent with his argument that he does not want the court to hear the case.

    i. Plaintiffs: A plaintiff who files suit in a forum consents to personal jurisdiction for all matters arising in that lawsuit, including related counterclaims and cross-claims filed against plaintiff.

    ii. Failure to assert defense: A defendant may waive any objection to personal jurisdiction by filing other claims or defenses in the proceeding. Therefore, if a defendant files a counterclaim against plaintiff before taking any other action, she will be deemed to have consented to the court's jurisdiction. The Federal Rules of Civil Procedure have special rules governing the timing of the personal jurisdiction defense. These rules are discussed in Part V of this chapter.

Quiz Yourself on
APPLICATION OF THE MODERN CONSTITUTIONAL TEST

1. While driving through Georgia en route to Florida, Ashley, a citizen of New York, is involved in a wreck with John, a citizen of Georgia. After Ashley returns to New York, John sues Ashley in a Georgia state court. May the Georgia courts constitutionally exercise personal jurisdiction over Ashley? _____

2. Ivan invents a high-powered heater to warm his Alaska home. Ed Entrepreneur signs an agreement with Ivan under which Ed will distribute the heater nationally. Ed arranges to have an infomercial broadcast in Canada and the northernmost states in the United States. Although Ivan is aware of Ed's activities, he has no control over where Ed advertises and ships the product.

   Frieda sees Ed's infomercial while visiting a friend in North Dakota. When she returns home to Tennessee, Frieda calls the toll-free number and orders a heater from Ed. Frieda uses the heater to heat her lake cabin in Tennessee. The heater is too powerful for the temperate climate and vaporizes the varnish on Frieda's furniture, causing Frieda to become very ill. Frieda wants to sue Ivan in a Tennessee state court. Can she satisfy the minimum contacts test? _____

3. Rachel is a student attending university in Oregon. Every summer, she returns home to Virginia to live with her parents. While at home one summer, Rachel gets into a fight with Steve, who lives in Oregon but is visiting Rachel in Virginia. During this fight Rachel pours a container of caustic fluid all over the brand-new paint job on Steve's car.

   Although Rachel is still in Virginia on summer break, Steve wants to sue her in Oregon. Can he? _____

4. Tasty Taters, Inc. (TT) is a corporation chartered under the law of Delaware, but with its sole place of business located in Idaho. TT manufactures a variety of frozen potato products. TT packages its products in plastic bags. For two years now, TT has obtained its plastic bags from Herman's Hermetics, a Vermont company. The parties have a ten-year contract, which was negotiated over the phone between representatives of TT in Idaho and Herman's in Vermont. The contract requires Herman's to deliver the bags to TT in Idaho. After delivery, TT wires payment to Herman's in Vermont.

   TT has now found a cheaper source for its bags. Therefore, although eight years remain on the contract, TT refuses to accept delivery of any more bags from Herman's. Herman's sues TT for breach of contract in a Delaware state court. May the Delaware court constitutionally exercise jurisdiction over TT? _____

5. Same facts as Problem 4, except that Herman's sues in a Vermont state court. May the Vermont state court constitutionally exercise jurisdiction over TT? _____

6. Roger, a citizen of Indiana, books an Alaskan cruise with Sea Tours, which is located in Alaska. The tickets contain a forum selection clause that states that all disputes arising from the cruise can be heard only in an Alaska court. Roger slips on a wet spot in the ship's hallway, tumbles down a flight of stairs, and breaks both his legs. Roger files a negligence claim against Sea Tours in a federal court in his home state of Indiana. Will the case be dismissed? _____

Answers

1. A two-step minimum contacts test is used to establish personal jurisdiction — contacts and fairness.

To establish contacts, defendant must have taken actions that were purposefully directed toward the forum state and from which defendant derived the benefits and protections of the state's laws. Ashley's contact was driving through the state of Georgia. This is purposeful activity. While driving in Georgia, Ashley was protected by Georgia police and traffic laws.

However, even if there are minimum contacts with the forum state, the state may not exercise jurisdiction if considerations of "fair play and substantial justice" make defending the action in the forum state highly unreasonable. The burden on defendant is minimal. The distance from New York to Georgia is not that great, and Ashley has already demonstrated that she is able to travel to that state. The interest of the state of Georgia is high because John, the plaintiff, is from Georgia, and the accident occurred there. The interest of plaintiff is also high both because he would like to sue in his own state and because the witnesses and other evidence are likely to be in Georgia. The interest in efficient resolution of controversies does not apply in this case, because litigation would be roughly equally efficient regardless of whether the case is heard in Georgia or New York. Nor does the interest in furthering fundamental policies apply, as the tort laws of New York and Georgia are likely to be generally the same.

Because this is a case of specific jurisdiction, even a single contact can be enough to sustain jurisdiction. Therefore, the Georgia state courts may constitutionally exercise personal jurisdiction over Ashley in this matter.

2. At first glance, this appears to be a stream of commerce case. However, there is one potential difference. We do not know whether Ivan realizes any of his product ends up in Tennessee. If Ivan does not know that any of his product ends up in Tennessee, he cannot be subject to jurisdiction in that state.

If Ivan is aware, he is not subject to jurisdiction based on the "awareness plus" test established in the Supreme Court's *Nicastro* decision. This test requires not only awareness that the product will end up in the forum state, but also activities aimed at the forum state such as advertising, soliciting, marketing, and designing the product especially for the forum state. None of the plus factors are present in this problem.

3. Steve can sue Rachel in Oregon, although he might have to wait until Rachel returns to school in the fall.

There are three potential ways a suit in Oregon could comply with the minimum contacts test. First, it could be argued that by intentionally causing an injury to an Oregonian, Rachel established minimum contacts with that state. This theory is not likely to succeed. Although Rachel did injure someone she knew was an Oregonian, the harm happened in Virginia. As in the case of *Walden v. Fiore*, Rachel did nothing in connection with this suit to obtain the benefits and protections of Oregon law. Even though Oregon and plaintiff have an interest, the fairness factors cannot override a complete lack of contacts.

Second, if Rachel is domiciled in Oregon, Oregon could exercise *general* jurisdiction over her in this or any other suit. However, it is unlikely Rachel is an Oregon domiciliary. She attends school in Oregon, but nothing in the problem suggests she intends to remain. To the contrary, the problem indicates Virginia is still her home.

Third, Steve could wait until Rachel returns to school in Oregon and serve her personally while she is present in the state. Under *Burnham*, personal service on someone in the state gives the state jurisdiction over that person, even for claims that have nothing to do with the person's presence in the state. This is Steve's best option.

4. Delaware may exercise personal jurisdiction over TT because the corporation was incorporated in that state. *Daimler AG* indicates a corporation is essentially at home in its state of incorporation, making general jurisdiction available.

5. Vermont probably can exercise personal jurisdiction over TT. This case is closest to *Burger King*. Like in that case, TT entered into a long-term contract with someone from another state (in this case, Vermont). That contract requires TT to submit payments to the Vermont seller. It is easily foreseeable that failure to make payments—which is the breach here—will have an immediate impact on Herman's in Vermont. In this respect the case is similar to *Burger King*, where personal jurisdiction was upheld.

The fairness factors are also relevant here. There is no great burden on TT to defend in Vermont. Vermont has a strong interest in the dispute, and plaintiff Herman's has a strong interest in Vermont. The fourth and fifth fairness factors are indeterminate because efficiency and underlying policy will be furthered regardless of whether suit takes place in Vermont, Idaho, or Delaware.

6. Forum selection clauses on ships are enforced provided that they are "fundamentally fair." Fairness is measured at the time the agreement is made. A cruise is a luxury good, not a necessity, so Roger easily could have rejected the term had he found it unacceptable. The clause was on his ticket, which he should have read to find out when to board the ship. Although Roger does not live in Alaska, Sea Tours does all its business in Alaska. It is inefficient for Sea Tours to have to defend in every passenger's home state court. Because the clause is fair, the Indiana court will dismiss the case.

IV. NOTICE

Notice is the ***other primary requirement*** for exercising personal jurisdiction.

A. Constitutional requirement: The ***Due Process Clause*** of the Fourteenth Amendment to the U.S. Constitution requires that defendant receive adequate notice of the litigation. A judgment without notice is constitutionally deficient and therefore does not bind defendant.

B. Both contacts and notice required: Contacts and notice are not substitutes. Due process requires both.

C. Definition of notice: A plaintiff gives notice of a pending action when she ***serves*** the ***summons*** and a ***copy of the complaint*** on defendant. The summons commands defendant to answer the complaint within a fixed period of time.

★ **D. Adequacy of notice:** Due process requires that service of process be "***reasonably calculated***, under all the circumstances, to apprise interested parties of the pendency of the action and afford them an opportunity to present their objections." Mullane v. Central Hanover Bank & Trust Co., 339 U.S. 306 (1950).

1. Receipt of notice unnecessary: As long as the method of service meets this reasonableness standard, defendant is subject to jurisdiction even if defendant never actually receives the summons. However, if defendant never receives notice, almost every court system has a procedure whereby defendant may have the judgment set aside. See Chapter 13, Part V.A.

2. Acceptable means: In addition to the traditional means of serving defendant in hand, various forms of "substituted service" meet the reasonableness standard. Examples of substituted service include service by first-class or certified mail, service on the secretary of state with instructions to deliver it to defendant, or service to an adult who resides at defendant's usual place of residence. Courts have begun to experiment with service by email or other electronic means.

3. **Service by publication:** In some cases, notice of the pendency of a lawsuit is published in the newspaper, typically in fine print.

   a. *In rem* **cases:** Several early cases, including *Pennoyer*, held that service by publication alone was sufficient in *in rem* actions. Later **Supreme Court cases reject this old rule**, holding that when the address of the property owner can be ascertained, some other method of service that is more likely to reach defendant is required.

   b. **When publication alone is sufficient:** However, if defendant cannot be found, service by publication is the only viable option. In these cases, service by publication is acceptable in both *in rem* and *in personam* actions.

E. **How notice provided:** State and federal courts allow for various methods of service.

   1. **Who serves:** The court does not serve process. Court rules typically allow service by a private process server or the party's attorney. However, the party itself usually cannot serve. *See* Fed. R. Civ. P. 4(c)(2).

   2. **Methods of service—state court:** States typically have two sets of service rules: those pertaining to defendants who can be found within the borders of the state, and a long-arm statute allowing service on an out-of-state defendant.

      a. **Defendant in state:** States allow for a variety of service methods. Most allow for service in hand or on an agent of the defendant designated to receive service.

      b. **Defendant out of state:** Service on an out-of-state defendant is effected under the state's **long-arm statute**. These statutes are a response to the Supreme Court's decisions in *International Shoe* and later cases, which made it clear that a defendant can be sued in a state as long as contacts exist. Generally speaking, these statutes fall into two classes.

         i. **Specific cases:** Most statutes allow for service on an out-of-state defendant only in situations specifically enumerated in the statute itself. The listed situations usually represent an attempt to codify those situations where the Supreme Court has held that an out-of-state defendant can be sued.

         ★ **Example:** In Gibbons v. Brown, 716 So. 2d 868 (Fla. Dist. Ct. App. 1998), the court analyzed the Florida long-arm statute, which enumerates situations where service on an out-of-state defendant is allowed. The court held defendant was not "engaged" in activity in the state within the meaning of that statute.

         ii. **To limits of Constitution:** Some state legislatures have avoided the difficulty of codifying the precedent in a list, and simply allow service **whenever the state can exercise personal jurisdiction** over defendant consistent with the Due Process Clause. Other states interpret the list in their laws to extend to the full limits of the Constitution.

   3. **Service in federal court:** The Federal Rules of Civil Procedure specify how to serve process. In addition, the rules limit a federal court's personal jurisdiction in most cases to those situations in which the state in which the court sits could exercise jurisdiction.

a. **Methods:** *Fed. R. Civ. P. 4(e)-(j)* specify the acceptable means of service in federal court.

   i. **Defendants within United States:** For *defendants within the United States*, service can be made by serving *in hand*, leaving process at defendant's *usual place of abode* with someone of *suitable age and discretion* who also resides there, serving an *agent* authorized by contractual arrangement or law to receive service of process, or serving according to any method authorized by either the *state in which the district court sits* or the *state where service takes place*. Fed. R. Civ. P. 4(e).

   ii. **Corporations within the United States:** For *corporations and associations within the United States*, service can also be made by delivering process to an *officer or a managing or general agent*. Fed. R. Civ. P. 4(h)(1)(B).

   iii. **Special defendants:** Fed. R. Civ. P. 4 contains special service rules for *infants and incompetents*, *defendants in foreign nations*, and suits against the *federal government or government agencies or officials*.

   iv. *In rem* **actions:** A federal court may exercise *in rem* jurisdiction only when a federal statute provides for such jurisdiction or when plaintiff cannot obtain *in personam* jurisdiction over defendant by reasonable means in that district. Fed. R. Civ. P. 4(n). Because *Shaffer* (discussed above) allows *in rem* only when there are enough contacts to exercise *in personam*, Fed. R. Civ. P. 4(n) greatly limits the use of *in rem* jurisdiction in federal courts. Notwithstanding Fed. R. Civ. P. 4(n), federal courts can use *in rem* in cases where such jurisdiction is necessary, such as mortgage foreclosure actions.

b. **Territorial limits:** The Supreme Court's minimum contacts analysis was developed for *state courts*, not federal. Arguably, a federal court could exercise personal jurisdiction over a defendant whenever there are minimum contacts with the United States as a whole. A few statutes do allow federal courts to exercise nationwide jurisdiction. However, in most cases, the Federal Rules of Civil Procedure significantly limit this potential jurisdiction and require a federal court to act like a court of the state in which the federal court sits.

   i. **General rule:** *Fed. R. Civ. P. 4(k)(1)(A)* provides that service of process using any of the methods described in a.i to a.iii above is effective to establish jurisdiction over a defendant only if defendant "is subject to the jurisdiction of a court of general jurisdiction in the state where the district court is located."

      (a) To apply this test, it is necessary to consider both whether there are *minimum contacts* with the state and whether state law provides a means of *serving defendant*.

      Note: While the rule mentions a court of "general jurisdiction," it is not referring to general personal jurisdiction. Instead, the reference is to a court that can hear most tort, contract, property, and other claims, as opposed to a specialized court like family court.

      (b) However, although it is necessary to consider state service laws in determining whether a federal court may exercise personal jurisdiction, the plaintiff in federal court does not necessarily use the state law methods to effect service. Plaintiff instead *may use the methods set out in the Federal Rules of Civil Procedure*. Rule 4 also allows plaintiff to "borrow" state law service rules. See section 3.a.i above.

Example: *P* sues *D* in a federal district court in Kentucky. *P*'s attorney serves *D* at *D*'s home in South Dakota by leaving process at *D*'s home with *D*'s spouse. Because there are minimum contacts between *D* and Kentucky, a Kentucky state court could exercise personal jurisdiction over defendant. To obtain such jurisdiction, however, a plaintiff would have to use the Kentucky long-arm statute, which requires plaintiff to ask the Secretary of State to send process to defendant by certified mail. The federal court has personal jurisdiction over defendant. Even though a Kentucky state court could use only the state service methods, a federal court can use the "abode" service provided for in Rule 4(e).

ii. **Exceptions:** In some cases, a federal court is not confined by the territorial limits on jurisdiction that apply to the states.

  (a) **Impleader and involuntary plaintiffs:** Service on *third-party defendants* joined under Rule 14 and *involuntary plaintiffs* joined under Rule 19 is proper either if it meets the rule set out above or if the party is served anywhere in the United States within 100 miles of the *court issuing the summons*. Fed. R. Civ. P. 4(k)(1)(B).

  (b) **Federal statute:** Service is effective to create jurisdiction whenever authorized by a specific federal statute. Fed. R. Civ. P. 4(k)(1)(D). One example of such a case is statutory interpleader under 28 U.S.C. §1335, which allows for service anywhere in the United States.

  (c) **No state court has personal jurisdiction:** If no state court could exercise jurisdiction over defendant, service is effective if the claim *arises under federal law* and if the exercise of jurisdiction would comply with any limits imposed by the U.S. Constitution. Fed. R. Civ. P. 4(k)(2). In this case, a federal court may exercise jurisdiction as long as the minimum contacts/fairness test is met with regard to the United States as a whole, not merely with respect to the state where the federal court sits. This might exist, for example, in a case where a foreign defendant intentionally advertised in national media, but not in any particular state.

c. **Waiver of service:** *Fed. R. Civ. P. 4(d)* also allows a plaintiff to ask defendant to waive service. Waiver is an *alternative* to actual service.

  i. **Request for waiver:** A plaintiff may ask a defendant to waive by *mailing a request to waive, two copies of a waiver form*, a copy of the *complaint* and a *prepaid means of return*.

   (a) **Invalid request:** A request for waiver may not be used when defendant is an *infant, incompetent, or governmental unit or officer*.

   (b) **Date requirement:** The request must specify a date by which it must be returned, which cannot be less than 30 days from the date it was sent for defendants within the United States or less than 60 days for defendants outside the United States.

  ii. **How waiver effected:** Defendant waives service by returning the request by the specified deadline. Failure to return the request does not constitute a waiver.

  iii. **Effect of waiver:** A party who returns the request waives only the requirement of formal service. The party does *not waive* any defenses based on lack of *personal jurisdiction* or *venue*. Therefore, a defendant may argue lack of minimum contacts even if it waives service.

    iv. Failure to waive: A defendant is *not required* to waive. However, the rule provides both a carrot and a stick to encourage waiver.

      (a) Carrot: A defendant who waives service receives an automatic extension of the time to answer. Rather than the usual 21 days, defendant has 60 days following the day the request was *sent* in order to answer. If the request was sent to an address outside the United States, the time for answering is extended to 90 days following the date it was sent. Fed. R. Civ. P. 4(d)(3) and 12(a)(1)(A).

      (b) Stick: The Rule also provides that a defendant is under a "duty" to avoid unnecessary service costs. If defendant is located within the United States, failure to return the request results in an order requiring defendant to *reimburse plaintiff for the costs of actual service, together with collection fees,* unless there was good cause for the failure. Fed. R. Civ. P. 4(d)(2). Lack of personal jurisdiction does not constitute good cause.

Quiz Yourself on NOTICE

7. Pamela sues Don in a Dakota state court. Dakota law explicitly provides for service of process by first-class mail. Pamela mails the summons and complaint to Don in full compliance with this Dakota law. However, unbeknownst to Pamela, the Postal Service loses the letter, and Don does not receive it. When Don fails to answer, Pamela obtains a default judgment against Don. Is the default judgment valid? _____

8. Same facts as Problem 7, except that Pamela brings her case in a federal court situated in the state of Dakota. _____

9. Nine-year-old Jeremy is a latchkey kid who goes home after school and stays by himself until his parents get home from work. One afternoon, the doorbell rings. When Jeremy answers, a man gives Jeremy a package and tells him to give it to his dad because his dad needs to come to court. Jeremy is scared and hides the package; he does not want his dad to go to court because that is where they put people in jail. A judgment is entered against Jeremy's dad because he never showed. Is Jeremy's dad bound by the judgment? _____

10. Robert receives a request for waiver and a copy of the complaint with a prepaid envelope for return service. Robert is unsure whether to waive service. He has 30 days to decide. What are Robert's options? If Robert waives, is he consenting to the court's jurisdiction over him? _____

Answers

7. Don is bound by the judgment because the notice was reasonably calculated to reach him. First-class mail generally makes it to the recipient. That he did not actually receive notice, through no fault of Pamela, does not mean that the service was not designed to reach him. Don will almost certainly be able to reopen the judgment based on the lack of notice. But until he reopens, the judgment is valid and enforceable.

8. The judgment is valid. Unlike Dakota state rules, the Federal Rules of Civil Procedure do not explicitly authorize service by first-class mail (the Rules allow a request for waiver of service to be sent by first-class mail, but that is different from actual service of the summons and complaint). However, Fed. R. Civ. P. 4(e)(1) also allows a federal court to serve an individual using any method authorized by the law of the state in which the federal court sits. Because Dakota law allows for service by first-class mail, the federal court may also use that method.

9. Again, service need not actually reach a defendant to be valid. However, in this case the method of service does not comply with the Federal Rules of Civil Procedure. Fed. R. Civ. P. 4(e)(2)(B) specifies that service is proper when the process is left at defendant's home with someone of suitable age and discretion who also resides there. Jeremy is not of suitable age. Therefore, service is improper, and Jeremy's dad is not bound by the judgment.

10. It is definitely to Robert's advantage to waive, even though technically he is not required to do so. If Robert waives service of process, he gains an extra 39 days to answer the complaint (60 days versus 21 days — see Fed. R. Civ. P. 4(d)(3)). Unless there is a good cause for failure to waive, Robert would be ordered to reimburse plaintiff for the costs of actual service.

If Robert returns the waiver request, he waives only the formal service requirement, not jurisdiction.

V. CHALLENGES TO PERSONAL JURISDICTION

Personal jurisdiction is a *personal defense* that can be waived by inaction or by taking acts inconsistent with the defense. Courts traditionally were very strict concerning how the defense could be raised. The approach set out in the Federal Rules of Civil Procedure relaxes the rules somewhat.

A. Traditional approach: Under the traditional approach, defending yourself in any fashion waived the personal jurisdiction defense.

    1. Default and collateral attack: Therefore, defendant's only option was simply to *do nothing* in the action. If defendant never appears in an action, the court will enter a *default judgment* against defendant. Defendant could challenge jurisdiction if plaintiff attempted to enforce that default judgment elsewhere, arguing that the default judgment was invalid because the court that issued it lacked personal jurisdiction. This method is called a *collateral attack*. In Pennoyer v. Neff, Neff used a variation of this method.

    2. Dangers of collateral attack: This method of challenge was risky. First, if defendant appeared in any way in the initial action, she was deemed to have waived personal jurisdiction, thereby making collateral attack impossible. Second, the only issue that defendant could raise in the second action was *the first court's lack of personal jurisdiction*. If defendant lost on the jurisdictional question, she could not litigate the merits of the case or any other defense, but would instead be bound by the default judgment.

    3. Collateral attack still an option: Although most states allow a defendant to challenge personal jurisdiction in the first action, default and collateral attack remains an option even today. If it is clear the first court lacks jurisdiction, defendant may do nothing and collaterally attack when plaintiff attempts to enforce the judgment.

B. Special appearance: Many states ameliorated the harshness of the collateral attack approach by allowing defendant to make a *special appearance*. A special appearance is one where defendant is allowed to appear and *argue only lack of personal jurisdiction*. Some states still use this method.

1. **Limit:** Defendant making a special appearance is limited to challenging jurisdiction. A defendant who raises any other defenses or issues is deemed to have made a *general appearance* and thereby waives the jurisdictional defense.

2. **Options after jurisdiction challenge fails:** A defendant who *loses* on the jurisdictional question has two options. He can proceed to defend the case on the merits, which means he has conceded the jurisdictional question. Or, he can take no further action in the case, allow the court to enter judgment against him, and *appeal* the ruling on the jurisdictional question. Under this second avenue, however, defendant runs the same risk as under the strict traditional rule. If defendant loses on the jurisdictional question on appeal, he cannot reopen the merits of the case.

C. **Federal approach:** Most jurisdictions today follow the approach of *Fed. R. Civ. P. 12(g) and (h)*, or something close to it, when dealing with jurisdictional challenges. Because Fed. R. Civ. P. 12 is not limited to personal jurisdiction, the details of the rule—including the strict timing limits—are discussed in Chapter 7, Part IV.A.5.

   1. **Special appearance compared:** Although the pre-answer motion authorized by Rule 12 bears some facial resemblance to the special appearance rule, there are some important differences.

      a. **Not limited to jurisdiction:** A defendant may include in his pre-answer motion any and all defenses listed in Rule 12. Thus, defendant may argue both that the court lacks jurisdiction and that plaintiff's claim is not supported by any legal theory.

      b. **Ability to litigate merits:** If defendant loses her challenge to jurisdiction, she may proceed to litigate the case on the merits and still raise the jurisdictional issue (along with any other objections) on appeal.

Quiz Yourself on
PERSONAL JURISDICTION

11. Batman, a citizen of New York, has grown tired of all the dastardly deeds that his enemies have committed over the years. Batman therefore sues Joker, a citizen of Ohio, in a federal district court in Cincinnati, Ohio. Joker joins Penguin to the case under Fed. R. Civ. P. 14. Joker obtains a summons from the federal courthouse in Cincinnati and hires a private process server to serve process. The process server serves the summons and a copy of the third-party complaint on Penguin at his home in Covington, Kentucky. Even though his house is considerably closer to Cincinnati (less than ten miles) than it is to the closest federal courthouse in Kentucky, Penguin files a timely motion to dismiss the case for lack of personal jurisdiction and for improper service of process. Will the court grant the motion? _____

12. Rick, a citizen of California, is a billionaire real estate developer. Rick does most of his business on the West Coast. However, Rick also owns a rustic hunting cabin in Wyoming and decides to look into developing land in that state. Rick signs a contract to purchase a large plot of land in Wyoming. Jennifer, a citizen of Wyoming, is the real estate agent on this contract. Rick later refuses to close on the purchase.

   Jennifer sues Rick for the lost real estate commission. Because a Wyoming jury would be more sympathetic to the plight of a local citizen, she brings the action in a Wyoming state court. Jennifer does not serve Rick personally but instead uses *in rem* jurisdiction by seizing Rick's hunting cabin. Rick files a timely motion to dismiss for lack of personal jurisdiction. May Wyoming exercise *in rem* jurisdiction in this case? What are the limitations on suing Rick *in rem* as compared to *in personam*? _____

13. Sarah is a graduate student at the University of Minnesota. Sarah decides to travel by bus to her home in Atlanta, Georgia, for the holiday break. The bus travels to Nashville, Tennessee, and then takes Interstate 24 to Atlanta.

    Although Tennessee borders Georgia, Interstate 24 does not travel in a straight line. Instead, it actually dips down into Alabama for a mile or two. Sarah has not looked at a map and has no idea the bus enters Alabama. Moreover, although there are signs along the road advising people of this fact, Sarah's bus passes through this area at night, when the signs are not obvious to passengers on a bus.

    Just after the bus enters Alabama, another passenger on the bus gets up and serves Sarah with process in an Alabama state court action. The claim arises out of an automobile accident that Sarah had with a North Dakota resident in Minnesota. Because Sarah has no other contacts with Alabama, she files a timely challenge to personal jurisdiction. Will she prevail? _____

    _____

Answers

11. The facts specify the motion to dismiss is timely, so there is no need to discuss Fed. R. Civ. P. 12. Nevertheless, Penguin will lose the motion to dismiss.

    First, service is proper. Fed. R. Civ. P. 4(c)(2) allows a party to hire a process server to serve process. There is no indication that the process server is under 18 years of age. In addition, Fed. R. Civ. P. 4(e)(2)(A) explicitly allows service on a defendant personally. (Although Rule 4(e)(2)(B) mentions leaving process with *someone else* at the person's usual place of abode, that is merely another option. Nothing prevents service on defendant personally, even if it is at the place of abode.)

    Also, no constitutional problems are evident. Admittedly, in most cases, service from a federal court is effective to create personal jurisdiction over a party only if a state court of that state could exercise jurisdiction. And as discussed in Problem 1, an Ohio state court could not exercise jurisdiction. However, Fed. R. Civ. P. 4(k)(1)(B) provides that for a claim against a party joined under Fed. R. Civ. P. 14, service is also effective to establish jurisdiction if the service occurs anywhere in the United States within 100 miles of the federal courthouse—even if the location of service is in another state. The facts specify Penguin was served within ten miles of the courthouse in Cincinnati.

    Is it constitutional for a federal court in Ohio to exercise personal jurisdiction over a defendant who has no minimum contacts with Ohio? The answer is probably yes. When federal courts are involved, due process requires only that there be minimum contacts between defendant and the United States as a whole. There are clearly contacts between Penguin and the United States. And it is fair to make Penguin litigate in Ohio.

12. Jennifer can use *in rem* jurisdiction here. Admittedly, *Shaffer* places significant restrictions on the use of *in rem* jurisdiction. If the property is the only contact, *in rem* is proper only if the claim arises out of the property. The claim here clearly does not arise out of the property because it involves unrelated land.

    In this situation, however, the **land is not the only contact** between Rick and Wyoming. Rick entered into a contract to buy land in Wyoming. A Wyoming citizen was the real estate agent. Therefore, the contract, which involved Wyoming land and would affect the Wyoming agent, is a purposeful contact. And the claim clearly arises out of this contact. Because the contract alone establishes minimum contacts with Wyoming, a plaintiff suing in Wyoming may use either *in personam* or *in rem* jurisdiction.

The fairness factors do not change this result. The burden on defendant is not great, especially given that he owns a home in the forum state. Wyoming has an interest in this case because the subject matter and plaintiff are in Wyoming. Plaintiff has an interest in suing in her home state. In terms of efficiency, it might be more efficient to try this case in Wyoming. And because there is no indication that California and Wyoming law differ to any appreciable extent, the last fairness factor does not really apply in this case.

A judgment *in rem* is limited to the value of the property. Because the rustic hunting cabin may be worth far less than the real estate commission owed, Jennifer will not recover all she is owed (assuming she prevails). In addition, even if she should sue Rick in a later *in personam* action, the factual findings in the first case would not bind Rick in the later case. A judgment *in personam*, by contrast, binds defendant personally, allowing plaintiff to seize and have sold nonexempt assets owned by defendant in the forum in order to satisfy the judgment.

13. It is impossible to state for certain whether Sarah will win or lose this case. The problem involves service on a defendant while physically present in a state. *Burnham* is therefore the closest precedent. Although all of the justices in *Burnham* agreed that the in-state service was sufficient in that case, there were two competing theories, neither of which commanded a majority. Under Justice Scalia's theory, presence automatically complies with due process. If this theory represents the rule, Sarah is subject to jurisdiction. Under Justice Brennan's theory, presence qualifies as a contact for purposes of the minimum contacts test. Unlike in *Burnham*, however, it is difficult to call Sarah's presence in Alabama purposeful. Even though she is deriving protection from Alabama law, she did not realize she was in the state and did not arrange her bus ride with the knowledge she would be there. If the contact was not purposeful, it does not count.

With respect to fairness, the fairness factors are not relevant to Scalia's approach. His view is that jurisdiction over a defendant served in the state always satisfies due process and is not subject to the minimum contacts test. Under Brennan's view, the fairness factors are relevant. Application of the factors here further reinforces the conclusion that jurisdiction is not proper under Brennan's view. Because neither the plaintiff nor the accident was in Alabama, that state has no real interest in being the forum. Nor does plaintiff have any real interest in Alabama. Although the burden on defendant is not great, Alabama is not an efficient place to hear the dispute.

Exam Tips *on* PERSONAL JURISDICTION

☛ Remember that the personal jurisdiction question has two parts. Not only must the exercise of jurisdiction meet the requirements of due process, but a rule or statute must also authorize ***service***. Because the classroom discussion tends to emphasize the constitutional issues, students often overlook the question of service.

☛ Your casebook traces the development of the personal jurisdiction test over time. On the exam, however, most professors only want you to apply the test as it exists today.

☛ In every question, be sure to consider whether the challenge to personal jurisdiction is timely. The rules governing timeliness in federal court are set out in Chapter 7 Part IV.

☞ When evaluating whether minimum contacts exist, keep certain basic notions in mind.

    ☞ First, be sure to determine whether defendant's connections with the forum are ***purposeful***. If not, the connection does not count as a contact.

    ☞ In addition, carefully analyze whether the claim being brought ***arises out of*** the contact. If so, jurisdiction is quite likely. If not, jurisdiction exists only if there are enough contacts for ***general jurisdiction, which exists only if defendant is "essentially at home" in the forum***.

☞ Notwithstanding some careless statements to the contrary, *Shaffer* does not get rid of ***in rem*** jurisdiction. It merely limits the use of *in rem* when the property is the only, or the primary, contact with the forum. If the suit arises out of the property (e.g., a quiet title action), the property alone is probably a sufficient contact.

☞ In cases where jurisdiction is based on ***in-state service***, the Supreme Court offers no clear majority view as to the proper analysis. However, because the different approaches rarely make a difference in the ultimate outcome, you need not spend a great deal of time focusing on the differences.

☞ In cases involving specific jurisdiction and out-of-state defendants, do not forget to discuss the five ***fairness factors*** in the constitutional analysis. Although those factors make a difference only in a very few cases (such as *Asahi*), you nevertheless must mention them in your analysis.

☞ Remember that certain situations, including consent and possibly service on an in-state defendant, are not governed by the minimum contacts test.

☞ Have a solid grasp of the somewhat detailed service provisions, including the waiver of service option. Because service is relatively straightforward, knowing the rules well can earn you significant credit on the examination.

☞ Remember that service in a ***federal proceeding*** usually requires reference to state law. A federal court either can use the methods listed in Rule 4 or can borrow state law methods. In addition, in most cases, service in a federal proceeding creates personal jurisdiction only if the state courts could exercise personal jurisdiction over that defendant.

☞ If the exam question includes a novel method of service, consider whether that method meets the constitutional requirements set out in *Mullane*.

CHAPTER 3

VENUE

ChapterScope ─────────────────────────────────

This chapter deals with venue, the second of three main issues that control which court may hear a case.

▨ Like personal jurisdiction, venue considers convenience to the parties. However, venue restrictions come from statutes, not from the U.S. Constitution.

▨ While venue is also a factor in state courts, this chapter focuses on *federal* venue. The rules governing state venue often differ significantly from those that apply in federal court.

▨ The chapter also covers the doctrine of *forum non conveniens*, pursuant to which considerations of convenience will lead a court to refuse to hear a case even though the court has venue.

▨ A case filed in a proper venue may be *transferred* to another court of the same sovereign. Transfer may also be possible from an improper venue to a proper one.

I. BASIC PRINCIPLES OF VENUE

Venue is the place the legislature requires a particular action to be brought.

A. Both state and federal: Venue is a consideration in both state and federal courts.

B. Statutes control: Venue is primarily a creature of statute. Although state and federal venue statutes differ significantly, generally speaking all attempt to ascertain the ***most convenient place*** for litigating the case.

C. Not constitutional: The concept of venue is ***not required by the Constitution***. Therefore, a judgment issued by a court lacking venue is valid and enforceable.

II. STATE VENUE

State venue rules require an action to be filed in one or more county, district, or parish courts. The statutes look to a variety of factors, such as where the ***cause of action arose***, where ***defendant resides***, where ***defendant conducts business***, where ***plaintiff resides***, and, in a suit involving real property, where the ***property is located***.

III. FEDERAL VENUE

The primary federal venue statute is ***28 U.S.C. §1391***. Section 1391 was completely revamped in late 2011. This chapter discusses the new version. Other statutes specify venue in specific cases, but these are not covered in this chapter.

A. Overview of §1391

1. **Venue defined by district:** Unlike personal jurisdiction, venue in the federal courts is defined by *district*, not by state. While some states have only a single federal district, most have two or more. There are also districts for the District of Columbia, Puerto Rico, and federal territories.

2. **Plaintiff may choose:** In many cases, §1391 makes more than one district a proper venue. In these cases, plaintiff may freely choose the district in which she will file suit. However, a given district may hear a case only if it also has *personal jurisdiction* over all defendants.

3. **Venue in general:** Prior to the 2011 revision, §1391 distinguished between diversity cases and all other cases. The revised statute makes no such distinction. Today, venue in most federal cases is proper in *any* of the following districts:

   a. a district in which any *defendant resides, if all defendants reside in the state in which the district is located* (§1391(b)(1));

   b. any district in which a *"substantial part* of the events or omissions giving rise to the claim occurred, or a substantial part of the property that is the subject of the action is located" (§1391(b)(2)); and

   c. *if no venue is available under either (b)(1) or (b)(2),* any district in which *any defendant is subject to personal jurisdiction* (§1391(b)(3)). Note that unlike §1391(b)(1), under this "safety valve" provision only a *single defendant* needs to be subject to personal jurisdiction. Remember, though, that if one or more defendants is not subject to personal jurisdiction, that defendant can have the action dismissed for lack of personal jurisdiction, as discussed in Chapter 2.

4. **Interpreting §1391(b):** The technical language of §1391 can be difficult to apply in some situations.

   a. **Multiple defendants:** Section 1391(b)(1) allows for venue where *any defendant resides, if all defendants reside in the same state.*

      i. **Domicile vs. residence:** Although §1391(b)(1) uses the term "residence," §1391(c) specifies that a person is deemed to reside in the district where she has her domicile. Thus, where a person resides in one state but is domiciled in another, the state of domicile controls.

      ii. **Defendants in more than one state:** Note that §1391 (b)(1) applies only if *every defendant lives in the same state*. If even one defendant lives in a different state, venue cannot be determined by defendants' residence.

      iii. **All defendants in same multidistrict state:** However, if all defendants do reside in the same state, any district where at least one defendant resides is proper.

      Example: *P* sues four *D*s. Two of the *D*s reside in the Southern District of California. The third *D* resides in the Northern District of California, while the final *D* resides in the Eastern District of that state. The Northern, Eastern, and Southern Districts of California would be proper venues, but not the Central District.

   b. **Substantial part of events or omissions:** Section 1391(b)(2) allows venue where a substantial part of the events or omissions occurred. Events or omissions are "substantial" only if they are relevant to plaintiff's claim.

★ **Example:** The court in Thompson v. Greyhound Lines, Inc., 2012 WL 6213792 (S.D. Ala. 2012), applied this standard to an unusual fact situation. Plaintiff in Thompson was traveling by bus from Florida to Mississippi, changing buses in the Southern District of Alabama. After boarding the bus in Alabama, plaintiff fell asleep, and missed his connection in Mississippi. Plaintiff sued the bus driver in the Southern District of Alabama. The court dismissed for lack of venue. The driver was not a resident of that district, so §1391(b)(1) did not apply. Nor did a "substantial part" of the events and omissions occur in the Southern District of Alabama. Instead, the court held that the relevant facts were the driver's failure to wake plaintiff in Mississippi to make the connection.

5. **Corporations and other organizations as defendants:** *Section 1391(c)(2)* provides that a corporation and any other organization sued under a common name "shall be deemed to reside in any judicial district in which it is subject to *personal jurisdiction* at the time the action is commenced." Section 1391(c)(2) is not a separate venue provision for corporations, but rather a provision that defines where a corporation resides for purposes of §1391(b)(1).

    a. **Application in single-district states:** In a single-defendant case filed in a state with only one federal judicial district, §1391(c) causes the personal jurisdiction and venue analyses to dovetail. If a corporate defendant is subject to personal jurisdiction in a state, venue is also proper in the federal district for that state under §1391(b)(1).

    b. **Application in multidistrict states:** Personal jurisdiction does not necessarily equate to venue in a state with two or more districts. In these situations, §1391(d) modifies §1391(c). It *treats each district as a separate state* and provides that a corporation is deemed to reside in that district only if it has *minimum contacts with that district*.

        i. **No single district with contacts:** If no single district has sufficient contacts, but there are sufficient contacts with the state as a whole to support personal jurisdiction, the district with the *most significant contacts* is deemed to be the district where the corporation resides.

        ii. **State of incorporation:** A corporation can always be sued in *any district* in its state of incorporation. If the state of incorporation has more than one district, the corporation has sufficient contacts with *all* of those districts, regardless of whether the corporation does any business anywhere in the state.

        Example: *P* plans to sue XYZ Corporation for wrongful discharge under state law. XYZ was incorporated under the laws of Georgia, and the office where *P* worked was in Nashville, Tennessee (Middle District of Tennessee). Venue is proper under §1391(b)(1) in the Middle District of Tennessee and in any of the three districts in Georgia.

6. **Defendants who do not reside in the U.S.:** Special rules apply to parties who do not reside in the United States. Section 1391(c)(3) provides that an individual defendant who does not reside in the United States may be sued *in any district*.

    a. **Need personal jurisdiction:** As a practical matter, these parties cannot be sued in any district. The court must also have *personal jurisdiction* over the alien defendant.

    b. **Multidistrict states:** If a multidistrict state has personal jurisdiction over the non-resident defendant, venue is proper *in every district* in that state.

    c. **Case involving resident and non-resident defendants:** If a plaintiff sues both resident and non-resident defendants, courts interpret §1391(d) to mean that the *non-resident is*

deemed to reside in every district in the United States. Thus, venue would be proper under §1391(a)(1) or (b)(1) where the resident resides.

Example: *P* sues *D1*, a U.S. citizen who resides in the District of Connecticut, and *D2*, a U.S. citizen who resides in Canada. Venue is proper in the District of Connecticut because all *D*s are deemed to reside there. Of course, venue would also be proper where a substantial portion of the events or omissions giving rise to the cause of action occurred.

B. Local action exception abolished: Prior to the 2011 revisions, federal courts recognized a "local action" exception to the venue rules, under which certain actions arising in connection with land could only be brought in the district where the land was located. The 2011 revisions abolished this judge-made exception in §1391(a)(2). Now, actions involving land are subject to the same rules as apply to other actions.

C. Removal exception: If a case is properly removed from state court to federal court, ***venue*** is ***automatically satisfied*** in the district to which the case was removed, even if that district would not otherwise satisfy §1391. See §1390(c).

Quiz Yourself on APPLYING THE FEDERAL VENUE STATUTES

14. Lon Moher recently bought a new riding mower, the Megamower 2100, from Yolanda's Yard Supply in Rockford, Illinois. However, the first time Lon used the mower, it flipped and caused him serious injury.

Lon is planning to file a lawsuit in federal court against Cal Culater, the engineer who designed the mower, and Yolanda, the owner of Yolanda's Yard Supply. Lon will claim that Cal's defective design led to the accident and that Yolanda is liable for selling him a defective product. However, Lon is unsure *which* federal districts can hear the case. Yolanda lives and runs her business in the Northern District of Illinois. Cal lives in the Southern District of Illinois, and designed the Megamower 2100 in his home office.

Lon obviously prefers to bring suit in his hometown of La Crosse, Wisconsin, which is located in the Western District of Wisconsin. In the alternative, because he knows an excellent attorney in Peoria, Illinois, a city in the Central District of Illinois, Lon is not averse to suing in the Central District. List all the proper venues for Lon's case. _____

15. Same facts as Problem 14. However, instead of suing Cal, Lon decides to sue Yolanda and Megamower, Inc., the company that manufactured the mower. Megamower is a corporation incorporated under the laws of Illinois. Its headquarters and all of its operations are located in the Southern District of Illinois. However, its products are sold (typically by stores like Yolanda's) in all 50 states.

Lon still prefers to bring suit in either the Western District of Wisconsin or the Central District of Illinois. On the other hand, because Megamower is subject to personal jurisdiction everywhere in the state of Florida, and because Yolanda takes a trip to Panama City Beach, Florida, every winter, Lon is considering bringing his case in the Northern District of Florida, which encompasses Panama City. List all proper venues for Lon's suit. _____

Answers

14. The proper venues are the Western District of Wisconsin and the Northern and Southern Districts of Illinois.

The problem is governed by §1391(b). Under §1391(b)(1), jurisdiction is proper in any district in Illinois in which a defendant resides because all defendants reside in the same state. Therefore, *either* the Northern or Southern District of Illinois is proper. However, the Central District is not proper because no defendant lives there.

Under §1391(b)(2), venue is also proper where a substantial portion of the events or omissions that gave rise to the claim occurred. This again includes the Northern and Southern Districts of Illinois, as well as the Western District of Wisconsin where the injury occurred.

Section 1391(b)(3) is inapplicable because there is another district where the action can be heard.

15. In addition to the three districts listed in the prior problem, Lon could sue in the Central District of Illinois. Section 1391 again governs. However, it is necessary to determine where Megamower resides. Under §1391(c)(2), Megamower is deemed to reside in any district in which it is subject to personal jurisdiction. Because it is incorporated in Illinois, it is therefore subject to personal jurisdiction in all three districts in that state. According to §1391(c)(2), Megamower accordingly resides in all three districts. Under §1391(b)(1), *any* of those three districts would be a proper venue.

The Northern District of Florida is not a proper venue. Megamower is admittedly deemed to reside there by virtue of the fact of personal jurisdiction. However, §1391(c)(2) applies only to corporations and other organizations, not to individuals. Yolanda resides only in Illinois.

Under §1391(b)(2), venue is, as in the prior problem, proper in the Northern and Southern Districts of Illinois, as well as the Western District of Wisconsin where the injury occurred.

Section 1391(b)(3) does not apply.

IV. CHALLENGES TO VENUE

Venue, like personal jurisdiction, is a ***personal defense*** that can be waived by inaction or by taking acts inconsistent with the defense.

A. Time limits: **Fed. R. Civ. P. 12** sets strict time limits on objecting to improper venue. The rule is the same as the rule that applies to personal jurisdiction (see Chapter 7, Part IV): In federal court a party must object to venue no later than the answer, and even earlier in some cases.

B. Waiver by inconsistent action: A party may waive venue even without filing a Rule 12 motion. If the party takes actions in the case inconsistent with the venue defense, she loses her right to object to venue. For example, several courts have held that a motion to transfer the case under *28 U.S.C. §1404* (see Part VI of this chapter) waives venue because it presupposes the court is a proper venue.

V. FORUM NON CONVENIENS

Forum non conveniens is a ***court-created doctrine*** that allows a court to ***dismiss*** an action even though ***venue is proper***. Plaintiff may then refile the action in the more convenient forum.

A. Federal courts: *Forum non conveniens* does not apply that often in federal court. If plaintiff has chosen an inconvenient federal forum, the court can usually *transfer* the case under 28 U.S.C. §1404 (discussed below), a result that is far superior to dismissal and refiling. However, if the more convenient forum is a *foreign* court, federal courts will use *forum non conveniens*.

B. Considerations in the analysis: In order to dismiss based on *forum non conveniens*, the court must ascertain that there is an **alternate forum available to hear the case**. If such a forum is available, the court will then consider certain ***private*** and ***public*** factors in determining whether the chosen forum is **grossly inconvenient**.

    1. Alternate forum: The more convenient forum must have *subject matter and personal jurisdiction*.

★   **a. Differences in remedy:** Sometimes plaintiff will not be able to obtain the same relief in the alternate court as he could obtain in the chosen forum. Courts differ on whether this fact should prevent dismissal. In the federal courts, differences in remedy bar dismissal only if they effectively deny plaintiff any rights in the alternate forum. Piper Aircraft v. Reyno, 454 U.S. 235 (1981).

        b. Conditional dismissal: A court that is considering whether to grant a *forum non conveniens* dismissal often cannot ascertain whether the alternate forum will hear the dispute. Lack of personal jurisdiction or expiration of the statute of limitations may prevent plaintiff from bringing her claim before the new court. To deal with these problems, courts often impose *conditions* on the dismissal. For example, the court may grant defendant's motion to dismiss only if defendant agrees not to challenge lack of personal jurisdiction in the new forum.

    2. Factors: Courts consider different factors when deciding whether to grant a *forum non conveniens* dismissal. The factors considered in federal court are fairly typical.

        a. Private factors: Private factors are those related to the individual litigants, such as:

            i. where the ***underlying events occurred***;

            ii. where the ***witnesses*** and ***physical evidence*** are located;

            iii. the comparative overall ***costs*** of litigating in the two places;

            iv. whether it would be possible to ***compel witnesses to testify*** in the forum chosen by plaintiff (especially an issue when witnesses are located in other nations);

            v. ***language*** issues; and

            vi. whether a judgment by the chosen court would be ***enforceable*** in the place ***where defendant's assets are located***.

        b. Public factors: Public factors relate to the court system and include:

            i. ***choice of law questions***, including familiarity with and ease of determining the law that will govern the case;

            ii. the ***policy implications*** of the case in the more convenient forum;

            iii. the ***backlog*** in the court chosen by plaintiff;

            iv. the ***burden*** on the court system and on citizens who may be called upon to sit on a jury.

★   **Example:** The Supreme Court's decision in Piper Aircraft v. Reyno, 454 U.S. 235 (1981), is a good illustration of how these factors are applied. *Piper* involved a plane crash in Scotland. The decedents and all the heirs were residents of Scotland. The executor sued the American manufacturers of the plane and the propeller in a U.S. court. The Supreme Court indicated that the lower court should have granted a *forum non conveniens* dismissal. Considering the private factors, the Court noted that the wreckage and other witnesses were in Scotland, making Scotland a more convenient place. For the public factors, the Court noted that Scots law would govern and that Scotland had the predominant concern with the dispute. That Scots law would make it more difficult for plaintiff to recover was held not to prevent dismissal.

3. **Discretion:** A court has considerable *discretion* as to whether to dismiss an action based on *forum non conveniens*.

C. **Timing of *forum non conveniens* motion:** There are no fixed time limits for moving for a *forum non conveniens* dismissal. As a general rule, the longer the case remains in the original court, the less likely it is the court will dismiss.

VI. TRANSFER OF VENUE IN THE FEDERAL COURT SYSTEM

A case filed in one federal district can sometimes be transferred to a more convenient district. The governing statutes distinguish between transfers from a court *where both personal jurisdiction and venue are proper* and from a court where one or both of these is lacking.

A. **Overview of transfer:** Transfer in the federal court system is governed by three statutes: *28 U.S.C. §§1404, 1406, and 1631.* Which statute applies depends on the circumstances of the particular case.

1. **Federal courts only:** The transfer provisions *apply only in federal court.* State courts cannot use the federal law. In addition, a federal court may transfer the case only to *another federal court*, not to a state or foreign court. Although many states allow transfer of venue from one court within that state to a different court in that state, *nothing allows a state court to transfer a case to a federal court, a court of a different state, or a foreign court.* If a state court determines that an action could more conveniently be litigated in a different state or nation, its only option is a *forum non conveniens* dismissal.

2. **Transferee court must have jurisdiction and venue:** Although the transfer statutes allow transfer even when the original court lacks personal jurisdiction or venue, the *transferee* court must ordinarily be a court in which the case "could have been filed," i.e., where *both personal jurisdiction and venue are proper.* However, *under §1404 only*, if all parties *consent* to a particular district, the court may also transfer to that district even if it lacks jurisdiction or venue.

B. **Transfers from a court with venue and personal jurisdiction — §1404:** Section 1404 allows a court that has venue and personal jurisdiction to transfer a case to another federal district "[f]or the convenience of parties and witnesses, in the interest of justice. . . ."

1. **Transferor court must be proper:** Section 1404 applies only if the court hearing the case has both personal jurisdiction and venue. If either is lacking, the court must turn to §1406.

2. **Who may move:** Either party may seek a §1404 transfer. In a case involving multiple plaintiffs or defendants, *only one party* needs to bring the motion. The party requesting transfer has the burden of showing the alternative forum is more convenient.

3. **No time limit:** There is no time limit for making a motion under §1404. Such motions can be, and often are, granted well into the process of litigation as developments make it clear that another forum would be more convenient.

4. **Factors**: Section 1404(a) does not require transfer. Instead, the **court has considerable discretion** as to whether to transfer the case. Courts hearing a §1404(a) motion consider many of the same factors that enter into a *forum non conveniens* determination. These factors can also be grouped into *private* and *public factors*.

   a. **Private factors:** The private factors measure the interests of the litigants and include:

      i. the **convenience of the witnesses**, which many courts consider the most important factor;

      ii. the **convenience of the parties**;

      iii. **where the claim arose**;

      iv. the location of **physical evidence**, such as business records or real property; and

      v. in a case involving a contract, any **forum selection clause** in the contract will be considered as evidence of what the parties thought would be a convenient forum.

★ **Example:** In Atlantic Marine Construction Co. v. United States Dist. Ct., 134 U.S. 568 (2013), the litigants had a contract with a forum selection clause. Defendant moved to transfer under §1406, arguing the clause rendered venue improper. The Court disagreed, holding that venue was proper under the federal venue statutes without regard to the clause. However, because the chosen forum was not a federal court, defendant could not use §1404. Instead, the Court held, defendant should have used *forum non conveniens* to ask the court to dismiss based on the clause.

   b. **Public factors:** The public factors consider the interest of the court system:

      i. the comparative ease of **enforcing the judgment** in the transferor and transferee courts;

      ii. whether the judges in each district are likely to be **familiar with the governing law**;

      iii. any considerations of relative **judicial economy**; and

      iv. any **local interest** in deciding issues at home.

   c. **Plaintiff's choice strongly considered:** Courts emphasize that plaintiff's initial choice of forum is to be given considerable weight in the §1404 decision. Therefore, if the balance of factors is even relatively close, the court may well choose not to transfer.

5. **Governing law:** In a *diversity case*, a §1404 transfer *does not change the substantive law* that will be used to decide the dispute. Therefore, the transferee court will apply the same law that would have been applied by the transferor court. This rule applies regardless of which party moves for transfer. Thus, a plaintiff may select an inconvenient court to gain advantage of a favorable rule such as a longer statute of limitations and then move to transfer the case to a more convenient forum. Ferens v. John Deere Co., 494 U.S. 516 (1990).

C. **Transfer from improper court:** If the court currently hearing the case lacks either personal jurisdiction or venue, transfer under §1404 is impossible. However, transfer may still be possible in these cases under *28 U.S.C. §1406(a)*. Another statute, *28 U.S.C. §1631*, authorizes transfer from one federal court to another in specialized cases where only certain courts have subject matter jurisdiction.

1. **§1406(a):** Section 1406(a) provides that if venue is improper, the court "shall dismiss, or if it be in the interest of justice, transfer" the case.

   a. **Personal jurisdiction irrelevant:** By its terms, §1406(a) applies whenever the court lacks venue. Whether the court has personal jurisdiction is irrelevant. A party can use §1406(a) even when the court lacks *both* personal jurisdiction and venue.

   b. **Transferee court must be proper:** The transferee court *must have both personal jurisdiction and venue*. Transfer *to* a court that lacks either is forbidden. Unlike under §1404, the parties cannot consent to transfer to an otherwise improper forum.

   c. **Justice, not convenience:** Section 1406(a) is not designed to make litigation more convenient. Rather, it gives the court that lacks venue an alternative to outright dismissal. Section 1406(a) allows for a transfer only if, under the circumstances of the case, transfer is more just than dismissal for lack of venue. The main situation in which a court will deem transfer "just" is when the *statute of limitations expired* after plaintiff filed in the transferor court.

   d. **Either party may transfer:** As under §1404(a), either party may seek transfer under §1406(a). However, as a practical matter, it is usually plaintiff who avails himself of §1406. If defendant discovers that the chosen court lacks personal jurisdiction or venue, she will usually move to dismiss rather than transfer. The party seeking transfer has the burden of establishing that the conditions for transfer are satisfied.

   e. **Governing law:** Unlike §1404(a), the transferee court does not automatically apply the law that the transferor court would apply, but instead applies the law that would be applied by the courts of the state in which the *transferee* court sits.

2. **Transfer when subject matter jurisdiction lacking §1631:** Section 1631 provides that a court lacking jurisdiction "shall, if it is in the interest of justice, transfer such action" to any federal district in which the action could be heard. Although the statute speaks ambiguously of "jurisdiction," it applies only when a court lacks subject matter jurisdiction.

Quiz Yourself on VENUE

16. Pan World Airlines is a new airline that specializes in "long-haul" international flights. Pan World's main offices are in Pittsburgh, Pennsylvania (Western District of Pennsylvania). However, it operates most of its flights out of the international terminal in the Cleveland, Ohio (Northern District of Ohio) airport.

    Because Pan World's routes involve great distances, standard airplanes are not really suitable for its needs. Pan World therefore negotiates a deal to have planes custom-built for its operations. Pan World enters into a contract with Boeing, Inc., a Delaware corporation with its main facilities in Seattle, Washington (Western District of Washington); Joan Jett, a mechanical engineer who resides in Seattle, and AtomicJet, Inc., a small, specialized jet engine manufacturer, incorporated under New Mexico law and based in Los Alamos, New Mexico. This contract was negotiated and signed entirely in Chicago, Illinois (Northern District of Illinois).

Under this contract, AtomicJet agrees to produce a special engine in its factory in Los Alamos. AtomicJet will then ship those engines to Boeing's Seattle plant. Once the engines arrive, Jett will undertake the delicate task of mounting the engines to the planes. Finally, Boeing will fly the completed planes to Cleveland.

AtomicJet never ships the engines to Boeing. Frustrated, Pan World decides its only course is to sue. Pan World sues Boeing, Jett, and AtomicJet in a federal district court in the Western District of Pennsylvania.

The federal court has subject matter jurisdiction. Personal jurisdiction also exists in Pennsylvania over Boeing and Jett because Boeing is subject to jurisdiction throughout Pennsylvania, and Pan World is able to serve Jett while she is passing through the state. AtomicJet, however, is not subject to personal jurisdiction anywhere in the United States except for the District of New Mexico.

Defendants file a timely objection to the district court's venue. How should the judge rule on the venue objection? _____

17. Same facts as Problem 16, except Pan World sues the three defendants in a Pennsylvania *state* court. Defendants promptly remove the case to the Western District of Pennsylvania. After removal, defendants file a timely motion to dismiss for lack of venue. How should the court rule? _____

18. Brigid, a first-year law student in Ohio, purchased a notebook computer to help her in her studies. Two hours into her Civil Procedure exam, however, Brigid's computer crashes. Brigid cannot recover any of her work and, as a result, fails the exam.

The ill-fated notebook was purchased in the neighboring state of Indiana from Chip Douglas, a resident of Indiana. The notebook was manufactured by Pathway Computers, Inc., a South Dakota corporation. Pathway's engineers designed the computer in South Dakota. However, the unit was manufactured at one of Pathway's factories in the Eastern District of Louisiana.

Brigid decides to sue both Pathway and Chip Douglas. Her complaint alleges the computer was negligently assembled by someone on the assembly line, causing it to malfunction at the crucial moment. Brigid files her suit in the federal district court for the District of South Dakota. Pathway immediately files a timely motion to dismiss the action for lack of venue. How should the court rule on the motion? _____

19. Same facts as Problem 18, except Brigid sues in a federal court in the Southern District of Ohio, where venue is clearly satisfied. After two months, Brigid moves under 28 U.S.C. §1404 to transfer the case to the Eastern District of Louisiana. Her reason for requesting the transfer is that she wants to inspect the manufacturing facility. Moving the case would present no hardship for Pathway and Chip. Defendants nevertheless contest Brigid's motion, arguing in the alternative that it was filed too late and that it should be denied on the merits.

How is the court likely to rule on the motion to transfer? _____

20. Edna is enjoying her "golden years." Immediately after retiring, Edna left her home in chilly Vermont and moved to southern Florida. Although Florida weather agrees with her most of the time, Edna does miss the fall foliage. Therefore, Edna signs up for an October bus tour of New Hampshire. The bus company is located in Florida and maintains its fleet of buses there. All 50 passengers on the bus reside in Florida.

While driving on a New Hampshire back road, the bus inexplicably runs into a tree. Other than the passengers, no witnesses are present. The bus driver is killed, and a number of the passengers, including Edna, are seriously injured. All of the injured passengers are taken to Florida to recover. When Edna recovers, she sues the bus company in a New Hampshire state court, alleging negligence.

You are the attorney for the bus company. Although there is personal jurisdiction and venue in New Hampshire, your client does not want to litigate in that state. First, it prefers to litigate closer to home.

More important, while New Hampshire would allow punitive damages in this case, Florida not only would disallow punitive damages but also would cap each victim's pain and suffering at a modest $10,000. Under their respective choice of law rules, Florida and New Hampshire courts would each apply local law to decide this case.

What is the best way for your client to proceed in getting the case out of the New Hampshire court? Is it likely to succeed? _____

Answers

16. The court should grant the motion to dismiss. The case is governed by §1391(b). Under §1391(b)(1) (where all defendants reside), venue is not proper in any district. Two defendants reside in the Western District of Washington, but AtomicJet resides only in the District of New Mexico. Because AtomicJet is a corporation, its residence is any district where it is subject to personal jurisdiction, and the facts specify that the District of New Mexico is the only district in which it is subject to personal jurisdiction. Because *none* of the defendants reside there, the Western District of Pennsylvania is not a proper venue under (b)(1).

    Under §1391(b)(2), venue is also proper wherever a substantial portion of the events or omissions giving rise to the claim occurred. However, no acts or omissions relevant to this case occurred in the Western District of Pennsylvania, so that district is not a proper venue under (a)(2). The acts and omissions involved the contract, which was made in the Northern District of Illinois, and to be performed in the District of New Mexico, Western District of Washington, and Northern District of Ohio. Any of these districts would be a proper venue under (b)(2).

    Section 1391(b)(3) does not apply because there is at least one proper venue under (b)(1) or (b)(2) (those listed just above). Therefore, the Western District of Pennsylvania is not a proper venue. Plaintiff should have filed in Illinois, New Mexico, Washington, or Ohio.

17. The court will deny the motion to dismiss. If a case is properly removed under §1441, venue is automatically proper in the federal court. §1390(c).

18. The court should grant the motion. Venue in South Dakota is improper under §1391(b)(1) because defendants do not reside in the same state. Under §1391(b)(2), venue is proper wherever a substantial portion of the events or omissions giving rise to the cause of action occurred. Note, however, that Brigid is claiming a manufacturing defect, one caused by the negligent acts of a worker. Therefore, the design of the product, which admittedly occurred in South Dakota, is not an event or omission that counts. However, the Eastern District of Louisiana would be a proper venue under this provision.

    Because there is a proper venue under §1391(b)(2), §1391(b)(3) is not applicable.

    Note that it does not matter that the challenge in this case was filed by Pathway, the party who *does* reside in the chosen forum. Venue is still improper.

19. This problem actually has several subissues. First, is the motion timely? Section 1404 has no fixed deadline. However, it allows transfer only if it is in the "interest of justice." If Brigid has waited too long, the court may deny the motion. However, it is unlikely either defendant has suffered any prejudice from the two-month delay here.

    Second, a court may transfer under §1404 only to a district where the case could be brought (unless all parties consent to the new forum, which is not the case here). The Eastern District of Louisiana is a proper venue. Under §1391(b)(2), a substantial portion of the events and omissions—the assembly of the computer—took place there (recall that the claim is for a manufacturing defect).

Even though the Eastern District of Louisiana is a proper venue, the court would likely deny the request for transfer. The transfer is proper only if it is for the convenience of the parties and the witnesses. Brigid does not need to move the entire case to Louisiana in order to inspect the factory; she can just take a trip to that state. And the problem states that there is no real advantage to either defendant in moving. The only fact that might change this is if many of the witnesses were from Louisiana. Convenience to the witnesses is one of the most important considerations under §1404.

20. The best way to proceed is to move for a *forum non conveniens* dismissal. Note that transfer under §1404 will not work because this is a state court.

In evaluating the *forum non conveniens* request, the court will consider both private and public factors. Here, the private factors strongly favor dismissal. It is more convenient to the parties to litigate in Florida. Witnesses and business records, such as any maintenance records on the bus, are also likely to be located in Florida. The overall cost of litigation is probably less in Florida, too. The only factor pointing toward New Hampshire is that the "event" (the accident) occurred there. But since there are no witnesses in that state, that factor is of little importance. It would be slightly more difficult to enforce a New Hampshire judgment in Florida than it would a Florida judgment, but that difference is insignificant.

The public factors have little effect here. There are no choice of law issues, as each court would apply its own law. For the same reason, the New Hampshire court will have no difficulty applying its own law. The only potential issue is the difference in recovery. However, if New Hampshire follows the federal approach, it will not consider that factor. Florida law does allow recovery, merely not as much.

Taken together, then, the public and private factors suggest that a *forum non conveniens* motion is likely to succeed.

Exam Tips on
VENUE

Venue is not particularly difficult. But precisely because it is fairly straightforward, venue issues are often overlooked by students in Civil Procedure exams.

- ☞ **How to spot venue issues:** Venue issues can be presented in a fairly subtle fashion. You may encounter, for example, a party who "does not like the location" of the case or one who simply "wants to obtain dismissal" of the case.

- ☞ Unless you studied state venue rules, venue issues typically arise on an examination mainly when a case is in a federal court. On the other hand, *forum non conveniens* issues can arise in state courts.

- ☞ In applying the venue statutes, remember that §1391(b)(1) applies only if ***all*** defendants reside in the same state. Even if all defendants reside in the same state, venue is not proper in all districts in the state, but only in a district where at least one defendant resides.

- ☞ Do not forget that special rules apply to ***corporate*** and ***alien defendants***.

- ☞ Recall that a corporation is deemed to reside in every district in its ***state of incorporation***, regardless of whether it has any physical presence in that state.

☛ If a question involves a motion to dismiss for lack of venue, you should always consider whether the motion was *timely*. The rules governing how to raise the venue objection are covered in Chapter 7, Part IV.

☛ If a question deals with *forum non conveniens*, be sure to consider the availability of *transfer of venue*. If the case is in a federal court, and the more convenient forum is another federal district, the court will never use *forum non conveniens*, but will instead transfer under §1404. Therefore, *forum non conveniens* is likely to be a factor only when the better forum is a foreign court or when the forum is a state court.

   ☞ Also recall that the *grant of a forum non conveniens* motion results in *dismissal* of the case, not transfer.

☛ **Transfers:** Recall that there are actually *three* transfer statutes, which apply in different situations.

CHAPTER 4

SUBJECT MATTER JURISDICTION

ChapterScope

This chapter deals with the subject matter jurisdiction of the *federal district courts* in civil cases. Federal courts may adjudicate only certain categories of disputes. The limits on federal subject matter jurisdiction come from the U.S. Constitution, federal statutes, and the courts.

- **Two main categories:** There are two main categories of federal subject matter jurisdiction: *federal question* and *diversity of citizenship*. Although there are other federal question and diversity statutes, most cases arise under either the general federal question statute (28 U.S.C. §1331) or the general diversity statute (28 U.S.C. §1332).

- **Independent of personal jurisdiction:** Subject matter and personal jurisdiction are *separate requirements* that must be satisfied for a court to hear a case. Moreover, they are almost completely independent. Merely because a court has subject matter jurisdiction in no way implies that it has jurisdiction over the parties.

- **Exclusive and nonexclusive jurisdiction:** A case that qualifies for diversity jurisdiction almost always can be filed in either state or federal court. A case that qualifies for federal question jurisdiction usually can be filed in either court; however, some federal claims can be heard only by the federal courts.

- **Supplemental jurisdiction:** If a court has subject matter jurisdiction over some claims in a case, it may be possible for it to obtain subject matter jurisdiction over other claims that do not independently qualify for jurisdiction under the supplemental jurisdiction statute. Whether supplemental jurisdiction exists turns on the factual relationship between the various claims as well as other factors.

- **Removal jurisdiction:** If a case that qualifies for federal jurisdiction is filed in state court, defendant may be able to remove it to federal court.

I. BASIC PRINCIPLES

A. **Meaning of *subject matter jurisdiction*:** *Subject matter jurisdiction* is the authority to adjudicate and decide a case. If the court lacks subject matter jurisdiction, any party (including plaintiff) may move to have the action dismissed.

B. **Jurisdiction needed for every claim:** Most lawsuits involve multiple claims. A federal court must have jurisdiction over *every claim* in the case.

C. **Independent of personal jurisdiction:** Subject matter jurisdiction and personal jurisdiction are separate and independent requirements. Even if the court has jurisdiction over the parties, it cannot enter a binding judgment if it lacks jurisdiction over the subject matter (and vice versa).

D. **State courts:** Although this chapter deals almost exclusively with the federal courts, subject matter jurisdiction is also an issue in the state courts. For example, it is common for divorces and child custody cases to be heard by specialized state courts. However, every state has one court that can hear every case not specifically delegated to some other court.

E. **Constraints on federal subject matter jurisdiction:** Federal jurisdiction is limited by the U.S. Constitution, federal statutes, and a few court-created doctrines. Most actual disputes, however, involve the wording of the statutes.

   1. **Constitutional limits:** Federal courts are courts of *limited jurisdiction*. Article III, §2, of the U.S. Constitution lists nine categories of federal jurisdiction. Unless a case falls into one of these categories, it is unconstitutional for a federal court to hear it.

   2. **Statutes:** Article III itself does not grant jurisdiction to the lower federal courts. Instead, it is up to Congress to allocate jurisdiction to the district courts. Although many federal statutes allocate jurisdiction, a basic Civil Procedure course focuses primarily on the general statutes, 28 U.S.C. §§1331 and 1332, as well as supplemental jurisdiction (§1367) and removal (§1441).

F. **Domestic relations and probate exceptions:** Cases involving purely family matters such as divorce, child custody, and the probate of wills are considered within the exclusive purview of the state courts. A federal court will not hear these cases, even if the statutory requirements are met. Although the exception originally was considered to apply only in diversity cases, more recent decisions make it clear that the exception also applies in federal question cases. However, the domestic relations exception is limited to cases directly involving *divorce, alimony, and child custody*.

   Example: In Marshall v. Marshall, 547 U.S. 293 (2006), plaintiff brought various fraud and tortious interference claims against defendant, claiming defendant had caused her deceased husband to change his will. Although these claims would affect the will, the court held that the probate exception did not apply.

II. CHALLENGING SUBJECT MATTER JURISDICTION

Because subject matter jurisdiction is such an important limit on the authority of the federal courts, it may be challenged in a number of ways. Many of these modes of challenge are unique to subject matter jurisdiction.

A. **Any party may challenge:** Because subject matter jurisdiction is so fundamental, it can be raised by *any party* to the action. Fed. R. Civ. P. 12(h). Challenges to personal jurisdiction and venue, by contrast, can be raised only by defendants and other parties joined against their will.

B. **Court may raise *sua sponte*:** In addition, a court can raise its lack of subject matter jurisdiction *sua sponte*, without need for a motion. The parties cannot vest a court with jurisdiction by consent.

C. **No time limits:** Unlike virtually every other defense or objection, there are no time limits on challenging subject matter jurisdiction. The court or the parties can raise the issue at any time during the lawsuit. Moreover, the parties or the appellate court can raise lack of subject matter jurisdiction on appeal, even though it was not raised before.

   Example: *P* sues *D* in federal court. The trial court enters judgment for *D*, and *P* appeals. On appeal, *P* argues for the first time that the trial court had no subject matter jurisdiction. If *P* is correct, the judgment of the trial court will be vacated, even though *P* originally chose the trial court.

III. FEDERAL QUESTION JURISDICTION

Federal question jurisdiction allows the federal district courts to hear cases involving federal and constitutional claims.

A. Constitutional authorization: Article III, §2, of the U.S. Constitution gives federal courts the authority to hear "all Cases, in Law and Equity, arising under this Constitution, the Laws of the United States, and Treaties. . . ." Two basic policies underlie this provision.

  1. State court hostility: The framers feared state courts might prove hostile to enforcing federally created rights.

  2. Uniform interpretation: Allowing litigation to take place in the unitary federal court system would help ensure that laws of national scope were interpreted uniformly.

B. Statutory enablement: Congress gave the federal courts jurisdiction over federal questions in several different statutes, including:

  1. 28 U.S.C. §1331: Section 1331 is the "general" federal question statute. Most of the discussion in this part relates to §1331.

  2. Other statutes: Although they are usually not discussed in a basic Procedure course, there are several other more specialized federal question statutes, including:

  a. 28 U.S.C. §1334: This statute gives the federal district courts jurisdiction over certain matters connected with a *bankruptcy*.

  b. 28 U.S.C. §1338: Section 1338 gives the district courts *exclusive* jurisdiction over *patent, plant variety protection,* and *copyright infringement* claims, and *concurrent jurisdiction* over *trademark* claims.

  c. 28 U.S.C. §1343: This is a special provision that relates to cases arising under various federal *civil rights* laws.

C. Overview of §1331: The language of §1331 closely parallels Article III, §2: "The district courts shall have original jurisdiction of all civil actions arising under the Constitution, laws, or treaties of the United States."

  1. No amount in controversy requirement: There is no minimum amount in controversy in §1331. Federal jurisdiction exists regardless of how small plaintiff's claim is.

  Note: Until 1980, §1331 did contain an amount in controversy requirement. Therefore, many older cases discussing §1331 discuss the issue.

  2. Not exclusive: Federal jurisdiction under §1331 is concurrent, not exclusive. Most federal questions may be litigated in either state or federal court.

  a. Exceptions: In certain situations, a federal statute creating a claim also specifies that only federal courts may hear the claim. In other situations, such as actions under the antitrust laws, the courts imply that federal jurisdiction is exclusive from the nature of the federal statutory scheme.

  b. Exclusivity under other jurisdictional statutes: Some of the special jurisdictional statutes that apply to specific federal claims provide for exclusive federal jurisdiction. See, e.g., §1333 (admiralty and maritime).

      c. **Most cases litigated in federal court:** Although state courts retain the power to hear most federal questions, most plaintiffs elect to bring federal claims in federal court because of shorter dockets, greater federal sympathy to the claim, or other reasons.

   3. **Burden:** A plaintiff who wishes to invoke §1331 must include a statement in her federal complaint alleging that the requirements of the statute are satisfied.

 D. **Sources of "federal" questions:** Section 1331 enumerates three separate categories of "federal questions": cases arising under the national Constitution, cases arising under federal law, and cases arising under treaties.

   1. **Constitution:** A party whose constitutional rights are violated may in some cases bring an action directly under the U.S. Constitution. If the Constitution itself is the source of plaintiff's claim, federal courts have subject matter jurisdiction to hear the case.

   2. **Federal law:** Most federal question cases involve actions brought under federal law.

      a. **Statutes:** The overwhelming majority of cases arise under statutes enacted by Congress. A cause of action can be set forth *expressly* in the statute, or in some cases may be *implied* by a court from the language and context of the statute. Either is sufficient for federal jurisdiction.

      b. **Federal common law:** In addition to claims created by Congress, a limited body of federal judge-made substantive law exists. Claims arising under this federal common law may be heard in federal district court under §1331.

   3. **Treaties:** Treaties with other nations are negotiated at the federal level. If a treaty provides legally enforceable claims to plaintiff, the federal courts may hear the claim under §1331. Most treaties, however, do not create claims themselves but are instead implemented by federal statute.

 E. **"Arising under":** Section 1331 requires that the claim "arise under" one of the above sources of federal law.

   1. **Federal law creates right:** In the simple case, plaintiff seeks recovery based on a right specifically granted by federal law. For example, if a federal statute creates a cause of action and plaintiff's complaint invokes that federal cause of action as the basis for recovery, the case satisfies §1331.

      a. **Invoking federal jurisdiction:** In order to invoke federal jurisdiction, plaintiff need only allege a claim based on a federal statute, the Constitution, or a treaty. Whether plaintiff ultimately prevails on that claim is irrelevant. The court does not lose jurisdiction merely because it decides that the federal law does not apply to plaintiff's situation.

      b. **Claim must be substantial:** However, the *federal claim must be substantial*. If plaintiff's federal claim is frivolous, there is no federal question jurisdiction.

   2. **State law with federal element:** Sometimes a plaintiff seeks recovery on a state claim that includes as one of its elements an issue governed by federal law. Although that federal element may make the case look like a federal question, the analysis is more complicated. Two recent Supreme Court decisions illustrate the analysis.

★   a. *Grable:* In Grable & Sons Metal Prod., Inc. v. Darue Eng. & Mfg., 545 U.S. 308 (2005), the Court found that the federal element turned the state law claim into a federal question.

      i. State claim: The state claim in *Grable* was a suit to recover land that had been sold due to nonpayment of federal taxes. In most cases, state law determines ownership of land.

      ii. Federal element: The party seeking possession argued that the IRS had not given the notice required by federal law in connection with the sale. Thus, to determine if the sale was proper, and if the buyer had acquired title, the Court had to construe federal law.

      iii. Why a federal question: The Court held that the federal issue involved was "substantial" and could be resolved by a federal court without encroaching too greatly on the authority of the state courts.

   b. *Empire Healthchoice*: One year later, the Court distinguished *Grable* in Empire Healthchoice Assur., Inc. v. McVeigh, 547 U.S. 677 (2006), finding that the federal element in question did not turn the case into a federal question.

      i. State claim: In *Empire Healthchoice*, a health insurance company had paid benefits to a federal employee for certain injuries. After the employee obtained compensation from the person who caused those injuries, the insurer sued to recover the funds it had paid. This claim arose under the insurance contract and was accordingly a state law claim.

      ii. Federal element: Health insurance for certain federal employees is highly regulated by federal statute. That federal law authorized the insurance contract at issue in the case.

      iii. Why *not* a federal question: The Court held the case did not qualify as a federal question because the federal element was not nearly as important as in *Grable*. In *Grable*, the acts of a federal agency (the IRS) directly caused the sale of the land and, therefore, the claim. Moreover, the issue implicated a ***federal sovereign interest*** (collection of taxes). In *Empire Healthchoice*, by contrast, the direct cause of the dispute was the employee's settlement of a state law case. The Court also indicated that *Grable* involved a "pure" issue of law, while the issue in *Empire Healthchoice* was heavily fact dependent.

F. Well-pleaded complaint rule: The "arising under" language in §1331 has been interpreted to require plaintiff to present the federal question ***on the face of plaintiff's complaint***. However, merely including a federal issue in the complaint does not suffice. Instead, the well-pleaded complaint rule asks whether the federal element is ***necessary to plaintiff's case***.

   1. Anticipating a defense: A common situation in which a plaintiff fails to meet the well-pleaded complaint rule is when the complaint both asserts a state law claim and mentions (and then tries to negate) a federal defense to that claim.

★   **Example:** The Supreme Court's decision in Louisville & Nashville R.R. v. Mottley, 211 U.S. 149 (1908), sets out the well-pleaded complaint rule. Two people sued to enforce a lifetime pass a railroad had granted to them. The complaint sought an order of specific performance for the pass. Plaintiffs also alleged in their complaint that the railroad's reasons for refusing to enforce the pass violated both federal law and the Constitution. The Supreme Court held that the complaint failed to present a federal question. All plaintiffs needed to allege in order to recover was the existence of a contract (the pass) and breach, which were purely state law issues. *Why* defendant breached the contract was not an essential element of plaintiff's claim.

   2. Declaratory judgments: In some cases, a party does not seek damages or other affirmative relief but merely a declaration of the relative rights of the parties. This form of relief, called a *declaratory judgment*, is often intended to preempt a later lawsuit.

a. A federal statute creates the right to seek a declaratory judgment in federal court. 22 U.S.C. §2201. However, because a declaratory judgment is a form of ***remedy*** rather than a substantive claim, a suit seeking a declaratory judgment does not necessarily arise under federal law.

b. To determine if a declaratory judgment case is a federal question, a court ***looks behind the declaratory judgment*** claim to the essential nature of the lawsuit. The case is a federal question only if the lawsuit that is being preempted would itself qualify for federal question jurisdiction.

> **Example:** During a financial crisis, Congress passes a law that limits "golden parachutes" for corporate executives who lose their position. The new law provides that no executive may receive severance pay in excess of $1 million. Marnie Payoff, the CEO of a large corporation, has a contract providing for a golden parachute of $10 million. Marnie sues the corporation for a declaratory judgment, claiming the new federal law violates the U.S. Constitution. Marnie's claim is not a federal question. The dispute between Marnie and the company is merely an acceleration of a state law claim, namely, the suit for breach of contract that would occur if Marnie were to lose her position and sue for severance pay.

3. **Not constitutional:** The well-pleaded complaint requirement is not a constitutional requirement, merely an interpretation of what Congress meant in §1331. Congress may give the federal courts jurisdiction over any case in which the court actually interprets a right or duty created by federal law. In fact, other federal jurisdictional statutes do not require that the federal question appear in the complaint.

Quiz Yourself on FEDERAL QUESTION JURISDICTION

21. A federal statute limits the interest rate lenders can charge on consumer loans to 18 percent. If a loan exceeds this limit, the statute relieves the borrower of its obligation to repay the loan. Lender loans $10,000 to Borrower, which Borrower agrees to repay at 25 percent interest. When Borrower defaults, Lender sues Borrower in federal court. Lender alleges in his complaint that the loan agreement is valid notwithstanding the federal statute. Lender argues the loan was not a consumer loan because Borrower borrowed the money to establish a home business. Borrower moves to dismiss for lack of subject matter jurisdiction. How should the court rule? _____

22. Doug Dreeler was recently convicted for trafficking in illegal narcotics in violation of federal law. In addition to levying a hefty fine on Doug, the federal government invokes a federal criminal forfeiture statute to seize Doug's house. The government conducts a forfeiture sale and sells the house to Parker.

    When Parker visits his newly purchased home, he discovers that Doug is still living there. Parker sues to evict Doug from the house. Parker brings this case in a federal district court, relying on federal question jurisdiction. In his complaint, Parker does not claim that the federal forfeiture laws give him a right to sue Doug for eviction. Nevertheless, Parker alleges that federal law is crucial to his case, for it is only because of the federal forfeiture that Parker is now the owner of the home.

    Doug moves to dismiss for want of a federal question. How should the court rule? _____

Answers

21. The court should dismiss for lack of subject matter jurisdiction. In order to qualify for federal question jurisdiction, a federal question must appear on the face of Lender's well-pleaded complaint. Here, all Lender needs to allege to recover is the loan and Buyer's default. He does not need to tell the court why Borrower defaulted. Lender's anticipated federal defense does not create federal question jurisdiction.

22. The court should deny the motion. Parker's complaint does contain a federal element (federal law provides that he is now the owner of the house). Moreover, this federal element is similar to the federal element in the *Grable* case, as it turns on whether the federal government rightly seized and sold property. Seizure of property under the criminal law is an important sovereign function, much like the collection of taxes in *Grable*.

IV. DIVERSITY JURISDICTION

Diversity jurisdiction allows federal courts to hear certain actions between people who live in different states or nations.

A. Constitutional authorization: Article III, §2, of the U.S. Constitution allows the federal courts to exercise jurisdiction over "Controversies . . . between Citizens of different states . . . and between a State, or the Citizens thereof, and foreign States, Citizens, or Subjects."

B. Statutory enablement: Congress implemented this constitutional authorization in 28 U.S.C. §1332, the general diversity statute.

  1. Not exclusive statute: Section 1332 is not the only diversity statute. For example, 28 U.S.C. §1335 (discussed in Chapter 14) allows a court to hear an interpleader case when the parties are from different states.

  2. Rationale for diversity: One purpose of diversity jurisdiction is to protect out-of-state parties from discrimination by state courts. Admittedly, federal district judges are ordinarily selected from members of the bar in the state where they will serve. But because federal judges are appointed by the President and confirmed by the Senate, and hold life tenure, they are in theory less susceptible to local pressures than are state judges.

C. Overview of §1332

  1. Basic statutory requirements: Section 1332 contains *two basic requirements*. Unless both are satisfied, the federal court cannot hear the case.

     a. Diversity: First, the suit must involve plaintiffs and defendants who are "citizens of different states" or "citizens or subjects of a foreign state."

     b. Amount in controversy: In addition, the case must involve an "amount in controversy" in excess of $75,000.

  2. Not exclusive: Cases that meet the requirements of §1332 *may be litigated in either state or federal court*. Federal jurisdiction in diversity cases is concurrent, never exclusive. Plaintiff has discretion to decide whether to file his case in state or federal court. However, as discussed in Part VI of this chapter, if plaintiff files a case satisfying the requirements of §1332 in state court, defendant may be able to remove the case to federal court.

3. **When diversity determined:** Diversity *must exist at the commencement* of the action. Post-commencement events, such as a move by one of the parties, do not affect the existence of diversity. Similarly, should the court determine during the proceedings that plaintiff will recover less than $75,000, or even lose, the court does not lose jurisdiction over the action.

4. **Burden of establishing:** A plaintiff must include a statement in her federal complaint alleging that the requirements of diversity are satisfied. Fed. R. Civ. P. 8(a)(1). If jurisdiction is challenged, plaintiff also bears the burden of proving diversity exists.

5. **Exceptions to diversity:** In certain cases, a court will refuse to exercise jurisdiction even though the dispute seems to fit directly within §1332.

   a. **Abstention:** In certain cases involving important and/or unclear issues of state law, a federal court may abstain from hearing the action in order to give state courts the chance to resolve the issue. The complex subject of abstention is beyond the scope of this work.

   b. **Collusive joinder:** If parties are improperly or collusively joined to create diversity jurisdiction, 28 U.S.C. §1359 directs the court not to exercise jurisdiction. See Subpart I of this section.

D. **Complete diversity requirement:** Section 1332 has been interpreted to require "complete diversity" between plaintiffs and defendants. This requirement is met only if no plaintiff is a citizen of the same state as any defendant.

   Example: Five plaintiffs sue three defendants in a federal court, bringing purely state law claims. Four of the plaintiffs are from Maine, while one is from Florida. Two of the three defendants are from Oregon, and one is from Florida. Regardless of the amount in controversy, the suit cannot proceed as structured in federal court because the complete diversity requirement is not satisfied.

   1. **Source of rule:** The complete diversity requirement stems from the old case of Strawbridge v. Curtiss, 7 U.S. (3 Cranch) 267 (1806). Nevertheless, as Congress has never acted to override that interpretation, the requirement remains in force.

   2. **Application in multiparty case:** A case may involve multiple plaintiffs and multiple defendants. In some situations, a plaintiff may not have filed claims against one or more defendants.

★   a. **"Complete diversity":** *Even if no claim* has been filed by a particular plaintiff against a particular defendant, those two parties *must still be of diverse citizenship* for the case to satisfy the "complete diversity" rule. Caterpillar, Inc. v. Lewis, 519 U.S. 61 (1996).

   Example: *P1* and *P2* sue *D1* and *D2* in a federal district court. Both plaintiffs state a claim against *D1*, but only *P1* sues *D2*. *P1* is a citizen of Alpha, *D1* is a citizen of Beta, and *P2* and *D2* are citizens of Gamma. The federal court cannot hear the case, even though *P2* has filed no claim against *D2*.

   b. **§1332(a)(3) exception in case involving aliens:** This exception is discussed in Part G.4 of this section.

   3. **Not a constitutional requirement:** The complete diversity rule is *not* mandated by the Constitution. In fact, Article III, §2, requires only "minimal diversity," i.e., where only one plaintiff is diverse from any defendant. Other diversity statutes such as 28 U.S.C. §1332(d) and §1335 allow for jurisdiction even absent complete diversity.

   4. **Realignment of parties.** If plaintiff has placed a party on the wrong side of the suit—for example, listing someone as a defendant even though that person's interests are more closely

aligned with the plaintiff—the court may realign the parties. If realignment destroys complete diversity, the court will dismiss the case.

E. **"Citizenship" of individuals and domicile:** Section 1332 speaks in terms of "citizens" of different states. In the United States, however, citizenship is usually measured on the national rather than the state level. Courts look to the *domicile* of a party in determining whether that party is a citizen of a state.

1. **Basic test:** In order to be a "citizen of a state" under §1332, a person must be *both* a *citizen of the United States* and be *domiciled in a state*.

   a. **District of Columbia, Puerto Rico, and federal territories:** Section 1332 treats the District of Columbia, Puerto Rico, and federal territories as states for purposes of diversity jurisdiction. 28 U.S.C. §1332(e).

   b. **U.S. citizens domiciled abroad:** A U.S. citizen who is domiciled in another country *cannot sue or be sued in federal court under diversity jurisdiction*, for that person will never qualify as a citizen of a state under §1332. Nor is that person a citizen or subject of a foreign state since he is a U.S. citizen. In essence, the U.S. citizen domiciled abroad falls into a diversity jurisdiction "gap."

   ★ **Example:** In Redner v. Sanders, 2000 WL 1161080 (S.D.N.Y. 2000), the court determined that plaintiff, a U.S. citizen, had established a domicile in France. Because plaintiff was neither a citizen of a state nor a citizen of France, he could not sue defendant in federal court based on diversity jurisdiction.

2. **Domicile:** Although similar, *domicile and residence are not the same*. Domicile is a more permanent connection than residence.

   a. **Test:** The test for domicile is *actual residence plus the intent to remain*. Courts often look for the place where the person keeps "his or her true, fixed, home and principal establishment, and to which he or she has the intention of returning whenever absent."

   b. **Single domicile:** Every person has one and only one domicile.

      i. **Birth:** A person acquires a domicile at birth. This is typically the domicile of her parents, not the location of her birth.

      ii. **Change of domicile:** A person retains his current domicile until it is changed. A minor keeps the domicile of his parents as they move. Once a person attains the age of majority, she can change domicile voluntarily. Most courts, however, recognize a change in domicile only when a person both *acquires a new residence* and *has the intent to remain at that place*.

      Example: Peregrine, a domiciliary of Michigan, moves to West Virginia. While living in West Virginia, she does not intend to remain in that state. Nine months later, Peregrine moves to Texas, where she also does not intend to remain. While residing in Texas, Peregrine thinks fondly back to her days in West Virginia and decides she will move back to that state as quickly as she can and make the state her permanent home. Peregrine is still a Michigan domiciliary, even though she no longer resides there. Although her present intent is to make West Virginia her home, she did not hold the intent and the actual residence at the same time. However, as soon as she moves back to West Virginia, she will change her domicile (assuming that her intent does not change again in the meanwhile).

   c. **Intent relevant to domicile:** A person need only intend to make a state his current home in order to acquire a domicile there. He need not intend to live there for the remainder of his life.

      i. **Proving intent:** The intent to make a place a home is usually measured by objective criteria. Thus, if a person registers to vote, obtains a new driver's license and automobile tags, opens a new bank account, and sells her residence in the prior state, courts are more likely to find a bona fide change in residence. Where a person votes is often especially powerful evidence.

      ii. **Students:** Courts are hesitant to conclude that someone who moves to a state to attend school has acquired a new domicile, even if the other objective criteria are met.

         Note concerning state law residency requirements: Domicile is used to determine whether a party meets the diversity requirements of 28 U.S.C. §1332, a federal statute. The federal law is independent of state laws governing residency requirements for in-state tuition or welfare benefits. Thus, although many of the factors may be the same, whether a student qualifies for in-state tuition is irrelevant in determining whether that same student is a domiciliary of that state for purposes of diversity jurisdiction.

      iii. **Spouses and children:** Historically, spouses were deemed to have the same domicile. This old rule has been almost completely rejected. Children, however, are still considered to have the domicile of their parents. In cases where the parents live in different states, a child has the domicile of the spouse with primary custody.

   d. **Moving prior to suit:** On occasion, a person who is domiciled in the same state as a prospective defendant will move to another state prior to filing suit. He will then file the action in federal court, alleging diversity. Because diversity is measured as of the time the action is filed, a genuine move is sufficient to create diversity, even if the party's motive for moving is to create diversity.

F. **Citizenship of corporations and other special parties:** The concept of domicile is of little use in determining the citizenship of a legal person such as a corporation. For these entities, different tests apply.

   1. **Corporations:** Section 1332(c) defines the citizenship of a corporation. A corporation is a citizen of *both* the state that *incorporated it* and the state in which it has its *principal place of business*.

      a. **Dual citizenship:** Note that under this section, a corporation that has its principal place of business in a state other than its state of incorporation has two citizenships. If any adverse party is a citizen of *either* of these states, diversity jurisdiction is unavailable.

         Example: *P*, a citizen of Missouri, sues *D*, a corporation incorporated in Utah with its principal place of business in Missouri. Diversity jurisdiction is unavailable because *P* and *D* are both citizens of Missouri.

      b. **State of incorporation:** *Incorporation* is the legal act by which the corporation is created. This almost always happens under the law of a particular state. Therefore, a corporation usually has only one state of incorporation.

   ★ c. **Principal place of business:** No matter how widely diversified its operations are, a corporation has only one principal place of business. Courts previously used different tests to determine principal place of business, but the Supreme Court ruled in 2010 that a corporation's principal place of business was its ***nerve center***, "where the corporation's high level officers direct, control, and coordinate the corporation's activities." Hertz Corp. v. Friend, 130 S. Ct. 1181, 1186 (2010).

2. **Partnerships and other unincorporated associations:** Section 1332(c) does not apply to partnerships, limited liability companies, and other noncorporate associations such as labor unions and clubs. These entities do not have their own citizenship. In an action by or against one of these entities, one must consider the citizenship of ***all of the partners or members of the organization***. If any of these partners or members is from the same state as an adversary party, diversity jurisdiction is unavailable.

    a. **LLCs:** Courts differ on how to determine the citizenship of a limited liability company or "LLC." Some courts treat them as corporations, others as partnerships.

3. **Insurance companies:** In a direct action suit against an insurance company under a policy of liability insurance, §1332(c)(1) treats the insurance company as a citizen of (a) the state in which the insured is a citizen, (b) the insurance company's state of incorporation, and (c) the state where the insurance company has its principal place of business. Note that this rule has several limitations. First, it applies only when the corporation is ***sued***, not when the insurance company is a plaintiff. Second, it applies only when a third party sues the insurance company directly under a liability insurance policy (a "direct action"), not when the insured sues the insurance company. Third, the rule does not apply if the insured is also named as a defendant in the action.

4. **Representatives:** When a person dies and leaves an estate, the representative of the estate may sue or be sued to help wrap up the affairs of the deceased. In these cases, §1332(c)(2) specifies that the actual citizenship of the representative is to be ignored, and the representative is deemed to have the same citizenship as the deceased. That section also provides that the guardian or other legal representative of an infant or incompetent is deemed to have the same citizenship as the infant or incompetent. This provision prevents a party from obtaining federal jurisdiction over a dispute that is for all practical purposes between parties from the same state by the simple expediency of appointing a representative or administrator from another state.

5. **Trusts:** A trust is a legal entity with the power to sue and be sued. In most cases, the ***citizenship of the trustee*** is used to measure diversity.

G. **Alienage jurisdiction:** In addition to suits between people from different U.S. states, §1332(a)(2) allows a federal court to hear suits between a U.S. citizen and "Citizens or Subjects" of foreign states. This alienage jurisdiction is generally subject to the same rules as ordinary diversity, but has a few of its own quirks.

1. **"Citizen or subject" of a foreign state:** A foreign *state* refers to a foreign *nation*. A *subject* signifies a citizen of a nation ruled by a monarch.

2. **Domicile usually irrelevant:** In the case of alienage jurisdiction, a person need only be a citizen or subject of the foreign nation. Where the person is *domiciled* is not relevant, even if the person is domiciled in the United States. However, under §1332(a)(2) (as amended in 2011), diversity jurisdiction does not extend to an action between a citizen of a state and an alien who has been granted **permanent resident alien status** by the U.S. government and who is domiciled in that same state.

3. **Dual citizens:** When a person is a citizen of both the United States and a foreign nation, only the U.S. citizenship is counted. Thus, dual U.S.-foreign citizens cannot qualify for alienage

jurisdiction. Coury v. Prot, 85 F.3d 244, 247-248 (5th Cir. 1996). However, if a dual citizen is domiciled in a state different from that of all adverse parties, he can use ordinary diversity jurisdiction.

4. **Mixing U.S. citizens and foreign citizens:** 28 U.S.C. §1332(a)(3) creates a special rule for cases involving both citizens of states and foreign citizens. Although the complete diversity requirement still applies among the U.S. parties, as long as every U.S. plaintiff is diverse from every U.S. defendant, diversity jurisdiction is possible.

   Example: *P1* and *P2* sue *D1* and *D2* in a federal court. *P1* is a citizen of Missouri. *D1* is a citizen of Ohio. *P2* and *D2* are citizens of Indonesia. Assuming the amount in controversy is satisfied, diversity exists.

5. **Actions involving only aliens not covered:** Neither Article III, §2, nor §1332 allows federal courts to hear a suit that involves only foreign citizens, even if they are from different nations.

   Example: *P*, an Iranian citizen, sues *D*, a subject of Denmark, on a claim that arose in Florida. Although *P* and *D* are from different countries, diversity jurisdiction is unavailable because both *P* and *D* are citizens or subjects of a foreign state and therefore outside §1332.

H. **Amount in controversy:** The second main requirement of §1332 is that the suit must involve an amount in controversy of more than $75,000.

   1. **Increases:** Congress periodically increases the amount in controversy requirement.

   2. **Sums included:** Most damages are included in calculating the amount in controversy, including punitive damages. However, *interest* and *court costs* are *not included*.

      a. **Some interest allowed:** The statute excludes only interest imposed as a penalty for nonpayment, *not interest ordinarily required by contract*. For example, suppose *P* loans $70,000 to *D* at 10 percent interest, to be paid after one year. *D* defaults. The $7,000 in accumulated interest *would be included* in the amount in controversy (and would push the case over the amount in controversy requirement).

      b. **Attorneys' fees:** If plaintiff requests fees it is entitled to recover by contract or statute, the fees are included in the amount in controversy.

   3. **Measured by complaint:** The amount in controversy is measured by the sum sought in *plaintiff's complaint*. Additional amounts sought by defendant in, for example, a counterclaim ordinarily do not count in determining whether the requirement is met. On the other hand, a minority of courts hold that the amount of a *compulsory counterclaim* (see Chapter 14, Part I.B.2) can be aggregated with plaintiff's complaint to satisfy the amount in controversy.

      a. **Legal certainty rule:** The amount alleged in the complaint controls unless it appears to a *legal certainty* plaintiff will recover less than $75,000. St. Paul Mercury Indemnity Co. v. Red Cab Co., 303 U.S. 283 (1938). Thus, although the party invoking federal jurisdiction has the burden of demonstrating the amount in controversy requirement is met, the legal certainty rule makes this burden fairly easy to meet in practice.

         i. **Request is upper limit:** If plaintiff asks for *less* than $75,000, however, the requirement is not met even if it is quite likely plaintiff will ultimately recover more than $75,000. (As discussed in Chapter 7, Part III, a court may give plaintiff more than it asked for in the complaint.)

      b. **Actual recovery irrelevant:** As long as the complaint satisfies the legal certainty rule, the court's jurisdiction is not affected by the fact that it eventually awards less than $75,000.

However, if plaintiff recovers less than $75,000, the court has the discretion to deny costs to plaintiff and award costs to defendant. 28 U.S.C. §1332(b).

4. **Nonmonetary relief:** The amount in controversy requirement can be satisfied even if plaintiff seeks only an injunction or other nonmonetary relief. In these cases, the court must place a value on the relief sought. Courts vary in the approaches used, considering the *value to plaintiff*, the *cost to defendant of complying with the order*, or the *cost or value to the party invoking federal jurisdiction*. Some courts find the requirement satisfied if *any of the tests* are met.

5. **Aggregation:** If a plaintiff brings one or more claims of less than $75,000, issues of aggregation arise.

   a. **Single claim greater than $75,000:** As long as plaintiff has one claim that itself seeks an amount in excess of $75,000, the requirement is satisfied for all plaintiff's claims. Aggregation is unnecessary in such a case.

   b. **Single plaintiff, single defendant, multiple claims that are each less than $75,000:** A single plaintiff may aggregate all her claims against a single defendant, regardless of whether the claims are related in any way. The amount in controversy is satisfied if the sum of claims equals or exceeds $75,000.

   c. **Multiple plaintiffs:** Multiple plaintiffs *ordinarily may not aggregate* their claims. However, if plaintiffs present a joint claim, aggregation is possible.

      Example 1: *P1* and *P2* are passengers on a bus that is involved in a collision. Because both are diverse from *D*, the bus company, *P1* and *P2* would like to join and sue *D* in federal court. *P1* and *P2* each have damages of $50,000. *P1* and *P2* cannot aggregate their claims to meet the amount in controversy requirement because their claims are separate and distinct.

      Example 2: In the prior example, suppose that the bus hits and completely destroys a luxury car worth $100,000. The car is owned jointly by *P3* and *P4*, each of whom owns an undivided 50 percent interest. If they sue together, *P3* and *P4* meet the amount in controversy.

   d. **Multiple plaintiffs, one claim greater than $75,000:** If one of the plaintiffs has a claim in excess of $75,000, and the claims of the other plaintiffs are factually related to that claim, the parties may be able to use *supplemental jurisdiction* to bring the entire case into federal court. Supplemental jurisdiction is discussed in Part V of this chapter.

   e. **Multiple defendants:** A plaintiff suing multiple defendants meets the amount in controversy if each defendant is potentially liable for an amount in excess of $75,000, even if that liability is joint and several.

   f. **Class actions:** The amount in controversy presents a special problem in class actions, which is explored in Chapter 15.

I. **Attempts to skirt the requirements of §1332:** On occasion, a party may attempt to get a case into, or keep a case out of, federal court by manipulating the diversity requirement. Whether these attempts work may depend on whether the party is trying to *create* or to *destroy* diversity. Congress and the courts are considerably less solicitous of attempts to bring to federal court a case that should not be there.

   1. **Manufacturing diversity:** 28 U.S.C. §1359 denies a federal court jurisdiction over "a civil action in which any party, by assignment or otherwise, has been *improperly or collusively . . . joined* to invoke the jurisdiction of such court."

a. **Assignments: §1359 is usually applied in cases involving assignment of claims.** A party with a claim against a nondiverse party might try to manufacture diversity by transferring that claim to someone from another state. Although a good faith assignment is respected, a sham assignment defeats diversity.

Example: *D* owes $100,000 to *C* based on a contract between the parties. *C* wants to sue *D* on this claim in federal court. However, *C* cannot do so because she and *D* are both citizens of Georgia. *C* "assigns" the contract to *P*, a citizen of South Carolina, for the sum of $1 plus 95 percent of whatever *P* recovers from *D*. Although *P* is diverse from *D*, a federal court will not exercise jurisdiction over this case because the assignment is a collusive attempt to manufacture diversity jurisdiction.

b. **Omitting parties:** If a defendant is obligated to several plaintiffs on the same basic claim, it is ordinarily acceptable for only those plaintiffs who are diverse from defendant to sue. In certain rare cases, however, a missing plaintiff is deemed a *necessary party* under Fed. R. Civ. P. 19. If joinder of the party would destroy diversity, the court may decide that the case must be dismissed. The necessary party rule is covered in Chapter 14, Part II.D.

2. **Destroying diversity:** A party who desires to keep his case out of federal court may take steps either before or during litigation to keep the case in state court. Note that situations involving attempts to destroy diversity usually arise when a defendant attempts to *remove* a case from state court to federal court, which is discussed in Part VI of this chapter.

a. **Assignments:** Because §1359 covers only attempts to *invoke* federal jurisdiction, it does not apply when a party who is diverse from defendant assigns a claim to a nondiverse party in anticipation of litigation. Such an assignment will be honored, even though it destroys diversity.

b. **Adding nominal defendants:** If a plaintiff sues multiple defendants, the complete diversity rule defeats diversity if any one of the defendants is from the same state as plaintiff. However, if plaintiff has no real claim against a certain defendant, the court ignores that defendant in determining whether diversity exists.

Example: After he was banned from baseball, Pete Rose brought an action against the Commissioner of Baseball, the Cincinnati Reds, and Major League Baseball. Rose, a citizen of Ohio, sued in state court. Defendants tried to remove the action to federal court, even though both the Reds and Major League Baseball were also citizens of Ohio. The court allowed the removal, reasoning that because Rose had no real claim against either the Reds or Major League Baseball, those parties were merely nominal or formal defendants whose citizenship could be ignored for purposes of diversity. Rose v. Giamatti, 721 F. Supp. 906 (S.D. Ohio 1989).

Quiz Yourself on
DIVERSITY JURISDICTION

23. Jessica and Bob, both citizens of Kentucky, enter into a contract in which Bob agrees to sell Jessica a painting for $1,000. Before delivery, Bob discovers the painting is worth $100,000. Bob feels cheated and refuses to deliver the painting to Jessica.

Two days after Bob's breach, Jessica suddenly sells her house in Kentucky and buys a new house in Indiana. She moves all of her possessions to the new home and establishes a new bank account with an Indiana bank. However, because her car registration will not expire for several months, Jessica decides to take a chance and continue driving using her Kentucky plates. Jessica does not bother to register to vote in Indiana because it is not an election year.

After moving, Jessica sues Bob in a federal district court for $99,000 for breach of contract, based on diversity jurisdiction. Bob moves to dismiss for lack of subject matter jurisdiction. At the hearing on Bob's motion, Jessica frankly admits her sole motive for moving was to allow her to sue in federal court. How will the court rule on Bob's motion to dismiss? _____

24. Same facts as Problem 23, except Jessica does not move to Indiana. Instead, she establishes a new corporation called Jessi Corp. in Indiana. The corporation's principal place of business is also in Indiana. Jessica is the corporation's sole shareholder and its chief executive officer. Jessica assigns her rights under the contract with Bob to Jessi Corp. for no consideration.

Jessi Corp. sues Bob in federal district court for $99,000 for breach of contract, invoking diversity jurisdiction. Bob moves to dismiss for lack of subject matter jurisdiction. How should the court rule on Bob's motion to dismiss? _____

25. Eileen recently fulfilled her lifelong dream of skydiving. Unfortunately, her instructor never mentioned that parachutes do not deploy automatically but require the user to pull a cord. Because of this little miscommunication, Eileen suffered serious injuries.

Eileen sues Free Fall, Inc., the company that operates the skydiving operation and provided the faulty instructions. Eileen brings her case in federal district court based on diversity. She seeks $500,000 in damages. Eileen is a citizen of Ethiopia who moved to the United States two years ago. Last year, she obtained permanent residency papers from the government and applied for U.S. citizenship. However, she still must wait several years before being awarded citizenship. In the meanwhile, Eileen made a new permanent home for herself in Pennsylvania.

Free Fall is a Florida corporation with its headquarters in Georgia. It has large skydiving schools in a number of states. Free Fall's operation in Pennsylvania is the largest of its skydiving schools.

Free Fall moves to dismiss for lack of subject matter jurisdiction. How will the court rule?

_____

26. Old McDonald is an experienced farmer who works a large farm in Nebraska. His cousin Seb Urban has traveled from his home in Cleveland to visit McDonald. McDonald and Seb indulge in a bit too much liquid corn squeezings and decide it would be a "grand idea" for Seb to take McDonald's huge combine out for a spin. Seb has no idea how to operate a combine. Seb loses control of the combine and drives it into the home of McDonald's neighbor Clarabelle.

Clarabelle sues in federal court to recover for the extensive damage to her home. However, because she and McDonald are both citizens of Nebraska, Clarabelle does not name McDonald as a defendant. Instead she sues Seb and All Farm Insurance, McDonald's liability insurance carrier. Seb is a citizen of Ohio. All Farm is an Illinois corporation with its principal place of business in Illinois. Clarabelle asks for $150,000 in damages.

Seb moves to dismiss, arguing that the requirements for diversity are not satisfied. How will the court rule? _____

27. Lender sues Borrower for default under a loan agreement. The parties are citizens of different states. Lender's complaint asserts Borrower owes him $60,000 in outstanding principal, plus $14,000 in past-due interest under the loan agreement. In addition, Lender claims he is entitled to recover $1,500 in court costs. Borrower moves to dismiss, arguing the requirements of diversity are not satisfied. How will the court rule? _____

28. While driving her husband Ward to the office one morning, June Cleaver is involved in an accident with Eddie Haskell. Both June and Ward are injured. June and Ward join as plaintiffs and sue Eddie in federal court. Eddie is diverse from both June and Ward. June seeks $50,000 in damages and Ward seeks $40,000. Eddie moves to dismiss for lack of diversity jurisdiction. How will the court rule? _____

Answers

23. The court will probably deny Bob's motion because the case likely qualifies for diversity jurisdiction. First, the amount in controversy is met. Although the contract price is only $1,000, under contract law Jessica may recover the full benefit of her bargain with Bob. The painting is worth $100,000. Therefore, Jessica's claim for $99,000 (the difference between the $100,000 value and the $1,000 that she did not have to pay) is clearly a colorable claim.

The more difficult issue is Jessica's domicile. Viewed objectively, it appears Jessica has indeed changed her domicile to Indiana. She bought a house and opened a bank account in that state. Her failure to register to vote immediately is easily explainable. And although she has kept her Kentucky auto tags, her intent in so doing is merely to save money, not to keep a connection with Kentucky. Therefore, it appears Jessica has established an Indiana domicile.

Jessica's *motive* for changing domicile is irrelevant. Her motive does not make her move a "collusive act" for purposes of §1359. The parties are accordingly diverse.

24. The court should dismiss the action. The new corporation is a citizen of Indiana because it was incorporated there and has its principal place of business in that state. However, the entire arrangement— establishing the corporation and assigning the contract rights to it for no payment—is merely a collusive attempt to manufacture diversity jurisdiction, and the federal court accordingly will disregard it under §1359. The corporation is Jessica's alter ego. If it recovers damages, the benefit will inure to Jessica. Therefore, the action is one between Jessica and Bob, both of whom are citizens of Kentucky.

25. The court will deny the motion to dismiss. The amount in controversy is not an issue since it far exceeds the $75,000 threshold. The real issue is citizenship of the parties.

Eileen is an alien because she does not have U.S. citizenship. However, because she has been granted permanent resident alien status with a domicile ("permanent home") in Pennsylvania, §1332(c)(2) would not allow diversity jurisdiction in an action between her and another citizen of Pennsylvania.

Free Fall is a corporation and is therefore a citizen of both its state of incorporation and its principal place of business. If *either* of these states is Pennsylvania, diversity is defeated. Free Fall's state of incorporation is clearly Florida. Its principal place of business is Georgia, its nerve center (*Hertz*). Therefore, Eileen is diverse from Free Fall, and diversity jurisdiction is present.

26. The court will grant the motion to dismiss because the complete diversity requirement is not satisfied. Clarabelle is clearly diverse from Seb. With respect to All Farm, although the citizenship of a corporation is usually measured by the state of incorporation and principal place of business, §1332(c)(1) sets out a special rule for liability insurance companies. Because Clarabelle is bringing a direct action against the insurance company, but not against the insured (McDonald), the insurance company is also deemed to be a citizen of the same state as the insured. McDonald is clearly a citizen of Nebraska. All Farm is accordingly also a citizen of Nebraska in this action. Because the complete diversity rule requires that Clarabelle be diverse from all defendants, she cannot satisfy the requirements of diversity jurisdiction in this case.

It does not matter that it is Seb, the diverse defendant, who makes the motion to dismiss. Any party may challenge subject matter jurisdiction at any time.

27. The court will dismiss. The parties are of diverse citizenship, so the only issue is the amount in controversy. Plaintiff must assert a right to recovery in excess of $75,000, exclusive of interest and costs. Therefore, the costs will not be included in the calculation. However, the $14,000 in interest will be included. The "interest" to which §1332 refers does not include interest owed pursuant to an agreement of the parties. Nevertheless, because the total amount is $74,000 ($60,000 in principal plus $14,000 in interest), the amount in controversy requirement is not satisfied.

28. The court will grant the motion to dismiss because the amount in controversy is not met. Each of the plaintiffs here suffered an individual injury of less than $75,000. Plaintiffs could aggregate their claims only if they asserted some sort of joint claim. Neither Ward nor June has any ownership interest in the injuries suffered by the other. That they are husband and wife does not change this. Thus, the amount in controversy is not satisfied for either claim.

V. SUPPLEMENTAL JURISDICTION

If a district court can exercise jurisdiction over at least one claim in the case, it may also be able to exercise jurisdiction over other claims that do not themselves qualify for federal jurisdiction under §1331 or §1332. Jurisdiction over these other claims is called supplemental jurisdiction and is governed by 28 U.S.C. §1367.

A. Overview and terminology: Supplemental jurisdiction is possible only when at least one claim independently qualifies for federal subject matter jurisdiction under some statute other than 28 U.S.C. §1367. Courts often refer to this claim as the *federal claim*.

   1. Diversity or federal question: The "federal" claim may be either a diversity or a federal question claim.

   2. Diversity more restricted: The supplemental jurisdiction statute contains an important limitation that applies when the federal claim is a diversity claim. See §1367(b), which is discussed below.

B. History: For many years, supplemental jurisdiction was a court-created doctrine not explicitly authorized by statute. In 1990, Congress codified the doctrine for the district courts in 28 U.S.C. §1367.

   1. Pre-1990 law: The judge-made doctrine did not use the term *supplemental* jurisdiction. Instead, it distinguished between two separate forms of jurisdiction, *pendent* and *ancillary*.

   2. Current statute: §1367 eschews the old terms *pendent* and *ancillary* in favor of the single term *supplemental jurisdiction*. The several technical distinctions between ancillary and pendent jurisdiction no longer exist.

C. Applying §1367: Application of §1367 is a *two-step process*. The first is to determine if the state and federal claims have a sufficient *factual relationship* to qualify. Second, even if a relationship exists, supplemental jurisdiction may still be precluded under one of the *exceptions* in §1367(b) or (c).

   1. Relationship test: The basic analysis for whether the state and federal claims are sufficiently related is whether the two "*form part of the same case or controversy* under Article III of the United States Constitution." 28 U.S.C. §1367(a).

★   a. **Constitutional grounding:** The logic behind supplemental jurisdiction is discussed in United Mine Workers v. Gibbs, 383 U.S. 715 (1966). In that case, the Court noted that Article III of the Constitution gives the federal courts jurisdiction not over "*claims*," but instead over "*cases*." The Court reasoned that the concept of a "case" was broader than that of an individual claim. A "case" comprises all claims arising from a "***common nucleus of operative fact***." Therefore, Article III allows federal jurisdiction over the entire case, not merely over the federal question or diversity claims.

   b. **"Common nucleus" standard:** Although §1367(a) does not use the phrase "common nucleus of operative fact," the legislative history for §1367 shows that Congress intended to codify the common nucleus standard.

   c. **"Same case or controversy":** Two or more claims comprise the same Article III case if they arise out of the same basic set of facts. Claims involving many of the same witnesses or other evidence are more likely to satisfy the test. Similarly, claims that stem logically from the same core transaction or occurrence are likely to qualify under §1367(a).

★   **Example**: In In re Ameriquest Mortgage Co. Mortgage Lending Practices Litigation, 2007 U.S. Dist. LEXIS 70805 (N.D. Il.), the court found that a federal truth in lending claim and a state law fraud claim arose out of a common nucleus of operative fact, satisfying the basic requirement of 28 U.S.C. §1367(a).

2. **Exceptions:** Section 1367 sets out two main exceptions. First, §1367(b) greatly limits the use of supplemental jurisdiction in certain cases where jurisdiction over the federal claim(s) is based *solely on diversity*. Second, §1367(c) lists a number of situations where a court may, in its *discretion*, refuse to exercise jurisdiction.

   a. **Diversity exception—§1367(b):** In cases where jurisdiction over the federal claim(s) is based solely on diversity, §1367(b) denies supplemental jurisdiction over *claims brought by plaintiffs against parties joined under certain listed rules*.

      i. **Based solely on diversity:** The exclusion applies only when §1332 is the *only* basis for jurisdiction over the federal claim. If any of plaintiff's claims qualify for jurisdiction under §1331 or any other jurisdictional statute, §1367(b) does not apply.

         Example: *P* sues *D1* and *D2* in a federal court. *P*'s claim against *D1* qualifies for both diversity and federal question jurisdiction. There is no independent basis for jurisdiction over the claim against *D2*. If the two claims arise from a common nucleus of operative fact, the federal court will have jurisdiction over both. Because jurisdiction over the claim against *D1* is not based *solely* on diversity, §1367(b) does not prevent a federal court from exercising supplemental jurisdiction over the state law claim against *D2*.

      ii. **By plaintiffs:** Section 1367(b) bars only claims by plaintiffs. The reference to "plaintiff" in §1367(b) applies only to those parties *captioned as plaintiff* in the original or amended complaint.

         (a) **Counter- or cross-claims:** Thus, §1367(b) never bars counterclaims or cross-claims by defendants.

         (b) **Third-party claims:** When a defendant impleads a third-party defendant, the rules refer to the defendant as the "third-party plaintiff." See Chapter 14. A defendant/third-party plaintiff is *not considered a plaintiff* under §1367(b).

iii. **Listed rules:** Section 1367 bars only state law claims made *against* parties who are *made parties under Fed. R. Civ. P. 14, 19, 20, or 24*, or who seek to *intervene as plaintiffs under Fed. R. Civ. P. 24*, as well as claims made *by* parties who intervene as plaintiffs under Fed. R. Civ. P. 24 or who are joined as involuntary plaintiffs under Fed. R. Civ. P. 19.

(a) **Most situations are barred:** The listed Federal Rules of Civil Procedure cover the vast majority of claims that a plaintiff can make, including claims by plaintiffs against multiple defendants (Fed. R. Civ. P. 20).

★ (b) **Situations not covered by the exception:** In Exxon Mobil Corp. v. Allapattah Servs., Inc., 545 U.S. 546 (2005), the Supreme Court held that supplemental jurisdiction is available in a case where multiple plaintiffs sue a defendant in diversity, but not all plaintiffs satisfy the amount in controversy requirement.

(I) However, the Court also indicated the holding would have been different if there had not been complete diversity. A case lacking complete diversity would not have met the threshold requirement of §1367(a), because it would not have been a case over which the district court had original jurisdiction.

(II) The Court also noted that claims by multiple plaintiffs were not barred by §1367(b), reasoning that plaintiffs join voluntarily, and are accordingly not "joined" as required by §1367(b).

(III) *Exxon Mobil* also allowed use of supplemental jurisdiction in a class action where the requirements for complete diversity are met, but not all of the members had claims in excess of $75,000. The rules governing calculating diversity in class actions are discussed in Chapter 15, Part IV.

(c) **Single plaintiff/single defendant cases:** Note that it is unnecessary to consider supplemental jurisdiction in cases involving a single plaintiff and a single defendant when jurisdiction is based on diversity. If *P* has one claim against *D* that can make it to federal court because of diversity, all other claims can be *aggregated* with that claim. Unlike in supplemental jurisdiction, the claims need not be related in any way. Moreover, *none* of the claims need to meet the $75,000 threshold. All that matters is that the *total amount* of the claims exceeds $75,000. The rules governing aggregation are summarized in Part IV.H.5 of this chapter.

b. **Discretion exception:** Section 1367(c) allows a federal court to refuse to exercise supplemental jurisdiction over a state claim if the state claim *raises a novel or complex issue of state law* or *substantially predominates* over the federal claim, if the district court *dismisses all federal claims*, or for any *other compelling reason*.

i. **Predominance:** Predominance is not measured only—or even primarily—in terms of dollars. Thus, if the state claim is factually complicated and will take the overwhelming majority of the court's time and attention, the predominance factor may be satisfied.

★ **Example:** The court in Szendrey-Ramos v. First Bancorp, 2007 U.S. Dist. LEXIS 74896 (D.P.R. 2007), found the state law claims predominated over the federal claims. Plaintiffs had brought a number of complex state claims, which required extensive factual analysis.

ii.   **Other compelling reason**: Because the enumerated factors exhaust the situations where a federal court might desire not to hear the state claim, few courts have dismissed under the catchall provision.

c.   **Procedure if exceptions apply:** If either §1367(b) or (c) applies, the court will dismiss *only the state law claim* in question. It will retain jurisdiction over the remaining claims in the case.

d.   **Extension of limitations period:** If the court dismisses a state law claim, §1367(d) extends the limitations period for that claim. The limitations period is tolled while the case is in federal court, and for 30 days after dismissal, unless a longer period is provided in state law. This provision affords plaintiff the chance to refile the dismissed claim in state court.

Quiz Yourself on
SUPPLEMENTAL JURISDICTION

29. Professor Hord has developed a bad reputation because she checks books out of the library but never returns them. As a result, other library patrons are unable to complete their own research projects.

Matters reach a head when Professor Smith receives a grant for a research project. Unable to find the books he needs, Professor Smith cannot complete the project and is forced to return the $50,000 grant. Smith complains to Professor Buch, the law librarian. A quick investigation confirms what the parties already suspected, namely, that the books in question were squirreled away in Professor Hord's office.

Smith and Buch join as plaintiffs and sue Hord in federal court. Smith and Buch are both citizens of different states than Hord. Smith brings a claim under the state law of conversion, arguing that Hord's actions damaged him in the amount of $50,000. Buch, by contrast, brings a claim under the Federal Overdue Book Act, a federal statute that provides a cause of action for librarians against patrons who do not return books on time. Buch seeks the $1,000 statutory damages provided in the statute.

Hord moves to dismiss Smith's claim for lack of subject matter jurisdiction. How will the court rule? _____

30. Same facts as Problem 29, except Buch does not sue under the Federal Overdue Book Act. Instead, Buch brings his own state law conversion claim. The grant that Smith received provided not only $50,000 to Smith but also provided a separate fund of $100,000 to the school library. The entire $150,000 had to be returned to the granting agency. Buch claims that Hord's actions damaged the library in the amount of $100,000. Hord moves to dismiss Smith's claim for lack of subject matter jurisdiction. How will the court rule? _____

31. Dora Sell sues Ray O'Vack in federal district court. Dora has two claims against Ray. The first is a claim for battery, for which Dora seeks $100,000 in damages. The second is a completely unrelated breach of contract claim, for which Dora seeks $10,000 in damages. Although Dora and Ray are diverse, Ray moves to dismiss the contract claim for lack of subject matter jurisdiction. How will the court rule? _____

32. Manufacturer and Supplier have a long-term contract under which Supplier provides a vital part to Manufacturer. Supplier announces it has received a better offer from Competitor and will no longer honor its contract with Manufacturer. Manufacturer sues Competitor in federal district court, alleging two claims. The first is a claim under the federal antitrust laws. The second is a state law claim for tortious interference with contract. Competitor immediately moves to dismiss the antitrust claim, arguing that the antitrust laws do not apply to this situation. The court agrees and dismisses the antitrust claim. Now, because Manufacturer and Competitor are both citizens of Wyoming, Competitor moves to dismiss the tortious interference claim for lack of subject matter jurisdiction. How will the court rule? _____

Answers

29. The court will deny the motion to dismiss. Buch v. Hord clearly qualifies as a federal question. Although there is no independent basis for jurisdiction over Smith v. Hord (no federal question and no diversity because of the amount in controversy), the court may exercise supplemental jurisdiction over Smith's claim. For purposes of §1367(a), the two claims arise out of a common nucleus of operative fact, namely, Hord's actions in checking out and refusing to return the books. That the parties suffered different injuries from that underlying conduct does not affect the result.

The exception set out in §1367(b) does not apply here because jurisdiction over the "federal" claim (here, Buch v. Hord) is not based on diversity. Nor is the court likely to refuse to exercise jurisdiction under §1367(c). The state law claim is not terribly complex, nor is there anything in the facts to suggest it raises any novel issues. Even though the state claim far outweighs the federal in terms of damages, it will not substantially predominate at trial because it is relatively straightforward.

30. The court will deny the motion to dismiss. The facts here are similar to the *Exxon Mobil* case. Buch v. Hord qualifies for diversity jurisdiction. As before, Smith v. Hord does not qualify of its own right—not because the parties are not diverse, but because the amount in controversy is not satisfied. However, the Smith v. Hord claim will qualify for supplemental jurisdiction under these circumstances. The requirements of §1367(a) are satisfied (the analysis is the same as in Problem 32), and because §1367(b) does not mention claims by plaintiffs who join under Rule 20, that subsection is not a bar.

Incidentally, because the facts specify that the $100,000 is a separate fund, there is no possibility that the parties can aggregate their claims.

31. The court will deny the motion to dismiss. There is diversity jurisdiction over the battery claim. The contract claim cannot qualify for jurisdiction independently because the amount in controversy is not satisfied. However, Dora can aggregate the two claims. A single plaintiff may aggregate all claims she has against a single defendant, regardless of whether the claims are related. Because aggregation clearly works, there is no need to consider supplemental jurisdiction (which would not work anyway because the "same Article III case" requirement of §1367(a) is not met).

32. The court will probably dismiss the tortious interference claim. The only way that claim could be before the court is if it happens to qualify for supplemental jurisdiction. Section 1367(a) is satisfied because the federal and state claims arose from the same operative facts. Section 1367(b) is not an issue because jurisdiction over the federal (antitrust) claim was not based on diversity. However, the court may well exercise its discretion to dismiss the state claim under §1367(c)(3), which allows dismissal if the court has dismissed all of the federal claims. Although dismissal is in the court's discretion, a court is likely to dismiss where, as here, the federal claim was dismissed so early in the lawsuit.

VI. REMOVAL OF CASES FROM STATE COURT TO FEDERAL COURT

Plaintiff's initial choice of a state court is not set in stone. In some cases, a defendant may remove a case filed in state court to federal court.

A. Transfer distinguished: Removal should be distinguished from *transfers* under 28 U.S.C. §§1404 and 1406. Transfers are a discretionary change in venue from one federal court to another. **Removal**, by contrast, is a **matter of right** and moves the case from **state court to federal court**.

B. Governing law: In most cases, 28 U.S.C. §1441 provides the standard for removal. However, there are also specialized removal statutes, such as §§1442, 1442a, and 1443, which apply in particular cases. This discussion focuses only on §1441.

C. Nonremovable cases: Section 1445 forbids removal in certain categories of cases, even if the requirements of §1441 are satisfied. For example, a case arising under the **workers' compensation** laws of a state cannot be removed.

D. Application of §1441: Section 1441 provides that the defendant in a state law case may remove a case "of which the district courts of the United States have original jurisdiction."

   1. Entire case: The case must be removed as a whole. If one or more of the claims in a multiclaim case do not fit within §1441, removal is impossible.

   2. Defendants: *Only defendant may remove* a case.

      a. Plaintiffs: *Plaintiffs may not remove*, even if defendant has filed a counterclaim.

      b. Meaning of *defendant*: *Defendants* include all those who are **actually parties** to the suit and are **directly adverse** to plaintiff.

      c. Multiple defendants: In a case involving multiple defendants, **all defendants** who have been **served** must join the notice of removal. §1446(b)(2)(A). If even one defendant does not wish to remove, the case must stay in state court.

   3. District courts have original jurisdiction: The state court action must be one that could have been filed in federal court. In other words, the federal court must have **federal question, diversity, or supplemental jurisdiction** over all claims in the case.

   4. Removal based on federal question: Determining whether a state court case presents a federal question generally works exactly as it would had the action been filed originally in federal court. The court applies the **well-pleaded complaint rule** to determine if the complaint states a federal question.

      a. Forgoing all federal claims: A plaintiff is free not to assert her federal claims and file a complaint relying solely on state law. If plaintiff forgoes all federal claims, the case ordinarily cannot be removed as a federal question.

      b. Exceptions to well-pleaded complaint rule: Two exceptions to the well-pleaded complaint rule ordinarily come up only in the context of removal. In these situations, plaintiff has filed a complaint that appears to rely solely on state law. Nevertheless, the case can be removed. Both of these exceptions rarely arise.

         i. Complete preemption: Under the doctrine of preemption, a federal law overrides contrary state law. A federal law usually preempts only a specific state law. However, sometimes federal policy is so strong that federal law supplants all state laws on the subject. For example, the Federal National Bank Act preempts state law usury claims against federally chartered banks, so that any usury claims are federal rather than state claims and may accordingly be removed. Beneficial National Bank v. Anderson, 539 U.S. 1 (2003).

    ii. **"Artful pleading" doctrine:** In some cases, a plaintiff may desire to keep her case out of federal court even though it involves a federal right. If the complaint is couched purely in terms of state law but in fact contains a disguised federal claim, the case can be removed as a federal question.

  c. **When determined:** Whether the state court case presents a federal question is determined at the *time of removal*, not when the case is filed. Therefore, if plaintiff amends a complaint by substituting a federal claim for the original state law claim, the case can be removed as a federal question.

5. **Removal based on diversity:** With two significant exceptions, diversity in a removal case is treated just as in a case originally filed in federal court. The exceptions are the *home-state removal bar of §1441(b)* and the *time* at which diversity must be met.

  a. **§1441(b)(2):** This section prohibits removal based on diversity "if any of the . . . defendants is a citizen of the State in which [the state] action is brought."

    Example: Plaintiff, a citizen of Wisconsin, brings a state law action in Michigan state court against *D1*, a citizen of Missouri, *D2*, a citizen of Montana, and *D3*, a citizen of Michigan. All claims are based on state law. Removal is impossible because *D3* is a citizen of Michigan.

    i. **Rationale:** Diversity jurisdiction exists to help thwart state court prejudice against outsiders. A defendant sued in a state court in his home state need not fear such prejudice. Although plaintiff in such a case might face discrimination, plaintiff could have filed the case in federal court.

    ii. **Possibly waiveable:** A few courts treat the home-state removal bar requirement as a nonjurisdictional issue, which can be waived. Thus, if plaintiff does not file a timely objection to removal by a defendant sued in her home state, these courts will hear the case notwithstanding §1441(b).

  b. **Time for determining diversity:** In removal cases, diversity must exist in the state court case *both when the case was filed and at the time of removal*. This differs from the timing rule that applies to federal question removal.

    i. Therefore, if plaintiff adds a nondiverse party after the complaint was filed but before removal, removal is impossible. Similarly, a defendant cannot remove merely because the court dismisses the claims of all nondiverse plaintiffs.

    ii. **Exception 1:** However, the general timing rule does not apply to *postfiling acts by a plaintiff that create diversity*. For example, if plaintiff voluntarily dismisses his claims against all nondiverse defendants in the state court action, the case can be removed if it meets the other requirements for removal.

    iii. **Exception 2:** In addition, if a case in which the parties are not diverse is *improperly removed* but the district court fails to remand, any judgment rendered by the district court is valid provided that diversity *did* exist *at the time judgment was entered*. Caterpillar, Inc. v. Lewis, 519 U.S. 61 (1996).

6. **Removal based on supplemental jurisdiction:** Many cases involve several claims for relief, such as multiple claims by plaintiff and/or counterclaims by defendant. Unless federal question and/or diversity jurisdiction exist for every claim in the case, it is necessary to consider supplemental jurisdiction when defendant attempts to remove. Determining whether supplemental jurisdiction exists works exactly as it would had the case been filed originally in federal court.

7. **Removal of separate and independent claims:** When plaintiff's case involves state law claims that are "separate and independent" from the federal claims, *§1441(c)* may allow removal of the *federal* claims in the case.

   a. **Applies only in federal question cases:** Section 1441(c) is explicitly limited to cases where one of the claims is a federal question.

   b. **Not supplemental jurisdiction:** Section 1441(c) requires that the state and federal question claims be separate and independent. Thus, it covers cases *not covered by supplemental jurisdiction*.

   c. **Remand of nonfederal claims:** After the case is removed, the federal court is required to sever all nonremovable claims, and remand them to the state court from which the action was removed.

E. **Place to which case removed:** Section 1441(a) specifies that defendant removes to the federal district court "for the district and division embracing *the place where such action is pending*." Therefore, if the case is in a state court in Louisville, Kentucky, defendant will remove to the federal district court for the Western District of Kentucky, Louisville division. *Venue is automatically proper* in the designated district. There is no need to apply §1391. §1390(c).

F. **Procedure in removal:** Most procedural requirements for removal are set out in *28 U.S.C. §§1446 and 1447*. These requirements are strictly followed.

   1. **Notice:** A defendant starts the removal process by filing a *notice of removal* with the appropriate district court. The notice must contain a brief statement of the grounds for removal. In addition, defendant must attach copies of all state court pleadings.

      a. **Not a motion or petition:** Note that the party does not "request" removal from either the state or federal court. Filing the notice itself results in removal, subject to the federal court's authority to remand the case if the requirements for removal are not met.

      b. **Copy to state court:** After filing the notice with the federal court, defendant must promptly file a copy of the notice with the state court. Defendant also must give notice to all adverse parties in the case.

   2. **Timing:** The notice must be filed in federal court within *30 days* after defendant receives *notice* she is a defendant in a state court case that could have been filed in federal court.

      a. **Original complaint states removable case:** If the original case filed by plaintiff is removable, the notice must be filed within 30 days of the *earlier of* (i) the date defendant receives a copy of the complaint, or (ii) if state law does not require the complaint to be served on defendant, the date defendant is served with a summons.

      b. **Case made removable by amendment or order:** If the original case was not removable, but the case becomes removable because of an amendment to the pleadings or plaintiff's dismissal of one or more parties, the notice must be filed within 30 days of the date defendant receives the order or amended pleading.

   c. **One-year limit:** Section 1446(c)(1) sets out an important limit for diversity cases. A diversity case cannot be removed more than one year after it was originally commenced, even if the amendment or order making it removable does not occur more than a year later. However, the one-year bar does not apply if plaintiff has acted in bad faith to prevent defendant from removing the action.

      Example 1: *P* sues *D1* and *D2* for $500,000 each, alleging only state law claims. *P* and *D1* are diverse, but *P* and *D2* are from the same state. Thirteen months after serving defendants with the summons, *P* dismisses the claims against *D2*. Even though the case now meets the requirements for diversity, *D1* cannot remove. However, if the court finds that *P* joined, and later dismissed, *D2* in bad faith, *D1* will be able to remove.

      Example 2: *P* sues *D1* and *D2* for $500,000, alleging only state law claims. *P* and *D1* are diverse, but *P* and *D2* are from the same state. Thirteen months after serving defendants with the summons, *P* amends the complaint to add a federal question against *D2*. The federal question claim and state law claim arise from a common nucleus of operative fact. Defendants can remove based on the federal question if they file the notice within 30 days after receipt of the amended complaint.

   d. **Multiple defendants:** In a case involving multiple defendants, the 30-day period begins to run for each defendant when that defendant is served. §1446(b)(2)(B). If a particular defendant's 30-day period has expired, that defendant may consent to a notice of removal filed by a later-served defendant, in which case the case may be removed. §1446(b)(2)(C).

  3. Procedure after removal: Section 1446 governs the procedure after removal.

   a. **When removal effective:** Removal is effective *when the copy of the notice is filed with the state court* and given to all adverse parties. 28 U.S.C. §1446(d).

   b. **State court loses jurisdiction:** Once the state court receives its copy of the removal notice, §1446(d) directs it to proceed no further with the case. Proper removal strips the state court of its jurisdiction over the matter. Any subsequent orders it issues have no effect.

   c. **Objections to removal:** Objections to the procedure by which the case is removed must be filed within *30 days* following filing of the notice of removal. Objections to the *subject matter jurisdiction* of the federal court, however, are not subject to this rule and can be made at any time.

   d. **Remand:** If the federal court determines removal was improper, it will remand the case to the state court.

Quiz Yourself on
SUBJECT MATTER JURISDICTION

33. Peter is employed by a partnership comprising Donna and Doug. After he is fired, Peter sues Donna and Doug for violation of federal labor laws. Peter files his case on May 1 in a state court. He serves both defendants the same day. Donna files a timely notice of removal to the federal court in the district and serves copies on the other parties and the state court. Peter wants to object to removal. Where should Peter object? Assuming Peter objects properly, how will the court rule? _____

34. Same facts as Problem 33. On July 1, before the court rules on Peter's objection, the parties file an amended notice that both Donna and Doug sign. Peter objects to the new attempt to remove. How will the court rule? _____

35. While crossing the street at a marked intersection, Adam is struck and seriously injured by a vehicle driven by Don Gage. Don is a paramedic who was rushing to an accident scene at the time. Adam sues Don in a California state court for negligence, seeking $60,000 in damages. Don answers by citing a new federal statute that creates an immunity for fire, EMS, and police personnel who cause injuries in the line of duty. Don then files a timely notice of removal. Adam objects. Will the federal court hear the case? _____

36. Same facts as Problem 35, except Adam's claim is $160,000. Adam is a citizen of Nevada, while Don is a citizen of California. Don files a timely notice of removal, and Adam objects. How will the court rule? _____

37. Barney and Floyd, two citizens of North Carolina, are embroiled in a bitter dispute. Barney is upset with Floyd for two reasons. First, Floyd, the town barber, recently took out an advertisement in the local paper stating that getting a haircut from Floyd would help a person get the "woman of your dreams." Barney got a haircut but not a date.

Barney's second claim relates to the town choir. Barney, who fancies himself a budding opera singer, was crushed when Floyd beat him out for a spot in the choir.

Unable to resolve the matter amicably, Barney sues Floyd in a North Carolina state court. His complaint contains two counts. Count One, involving the haircut, is a claim for false advertising under 15 U.S.C. §1125(a). His second claim is a state law claim for intentional infliction of emotional distress, based on the choir fiasco.

Floyd files a timely notice of removal. Barney objects to removal. How will the court rule? _____

38. Da Vinci has just invented a better mousetrap. However, Da Vinci is reluctant to market the product. A few years ago, Edison obtained a patent on his own mousetrap. Da Vinci is worried that if he markets his invention, he will infringe Edison's patent. To protect himself, Da Vinci sues Edison in federal district court, requesting a declaratory judgment that Da Vinci's trap is sufficiently dissimilar so that it does not infringe Edison's patent. Da Vinci and Edison are both citizens of Maine.

Later, Da Vinci changes his mind. Unable to get the court to agree to a voluntary dismissal, Da Vinci argues the court should dismiss the case for lack of subject matter jurisdiction. Edison protests because he wants the question resolved once and for all in the federal court. What will be the ultimate outcome of the jurisdictional issue? _____

39. Mari-Elise, a trial attorney, is a certified coffee addict. One day, while in the middle of trial in federal court, Mari-Elise decides she needs another cup. She accordingly leaves the courtroom during a brief recess in the trial to seek her next fix. Unfortunately, the only coffee shop is in the courthouse cafeteria, located in the basement of the federal court building. Because of the distance involved and the long queue at the coffee shop, Mari-Elise does not return to the courtroom until after the judge has resumed the case. Furious at Mari-Elise's delay, the judge holds her in contempt of court and levies a hefty fine.

Mari-Elise sues Cup-o-Joe, the company that owns the coffee shop, for negligence. Mari-Elise alleges that Cup-o-Joe was negligent in placing its coffee shop so far from the courtroom. Cup-o-Joe's answer points out that a federal statute prohibits the sale of coffee in federal buildings in any location other than the basement.

Cup-o-Joe then files a timely notice of removal. Mari-Elise contests removal. She correctly points out that she is a citizen of Pennsylvania, while Cup-o-Joe is an Indiana corporation with principal place of business in Pennsylvania. Mari-Elise also argues that her state law negligence claim does not constitute a federal question. Did Cup-o-Joe properly remove the case? _____

40. Refer to the facts of Problem 39. Perry Grynn is another coffee addict. Like Mari-Elise, Perry was late to court because of the remote location of the Cup-o-Joe coffee shop. Perry brings his own action against Cup-o-Joe in a federal district court, basing jurisdiction on diversity.

At the time of his injury, Perry was a citizen of Indiana. One year before filing suit, however, he accepts a new position in the state of New Mexico. Perry views this new position as a temporary job, and while he resides in New Mexico for several months, he does not intend to remain.

Two weeks before filing his suit, Perry moves again, this time to Pennsylvania. As he is driving through Kentucky on the way to his new Pennsylvania home, Perry realizes that New Mexico was not all that bad. He immediately decides that he wants New Mexico to be his permanent residence. Once he reaches his new home in Pennsylvania, Perry calls his old employer in New Mexico and convinces him to give Perry his old job back. Perry packs his belongings and prepares to return to New Mexico. The day before moving back to New Mexico, he files his suit in a Pennsylvania federal court against Cup-o-Joe. He serves process that same day.

After Perry's move, Cup-o-Joe moves to dismiss for lack of subject matter jurisdiction. How will the court rule on Cup-o-Joe's motion? _____

41. Reva, a law student, is notoriously late for class. Determined to change her ways, Reva vows to get to class earlier. On the very first day of her new vow, however, Reva finds herself running late. Therefore, rather than circle around the private property that sits between the bus stop and the law school, Reva cuts across the property. While crossing the property she steps in a bear trap and is seriously injured.

Reva sues Gary, the crotchety old man who owns the land, for negligence and battery. Because she and Gary are diverse, and because her damages far exceed $75,000, Reva brings her case in federal court relying on diversity jurisdiction.

Gary files an answer containing a counterclaim. In his counterclaim, Gary seeks damages for Reva's trespass to his property. Under governing state law, however, Gary can recover no more than $10 for this trespass.

Reva immediately moves to dismiss the counterclaim for lack of subject matter jurisdiction. How will the court rule? _____

42. ACME Foods produces the nation's most popular children's cereal, which it sells under the brand name Sugarsweet®. ACME advertises its product extensively on television. However, it does not use the Internet in its marketing efforts.

ACME is shocked to discover that one of its competitors, XYZ, Inc., registered the domain name *www.sugarsweet.com*. XYZ uses this Web site to tell consumers how its products are far superior to Sugarsweet.

ACME immediately sues XYZ in a state court. ACME has two claims. The first is a claim under the federal "cybersquatting" statute, which allows someone with a famous mark such as ACME's Sugarsweet to prevent others from registering that mark as a domain name. The second is a common law unfair competition claim.

XYZ files a timely notice of removal. Although the parties are not diverse, XYZ points out that one of the claims arises under a federal law, the cybersquatting statute. ACME contests removal, preferring to have the action heard in state court. How will the court rule? _____

43. Frostbite Lending Company, a small state bank located in Fairbanks, Alaska, specializes in making "subprime" loans to risky borrowers. Frostbite protects itself from the high risk associated with these loans by charging exorbitant interest rates. Two of Frostbite's borrowers join as plaintiffs in a federal

court action to cancel their respective loans, claiming the loans violate state usury laws. One of these plaintiffs—Alice—is a citizen of Alaska, like Frostbite. The other plaintiff—Cal—is a citizen of California. Each plaintiff seeks an amount in excess of $75,000.

Frostbite immediately moves to dismiss Alice's action for lack of subject matter jurisdiction. While Alice acknowledges that her action alone does not meet the requirements for diversity, she claims her joinder with Cal allows the court to exercise supplemental jurisdiction over his claim. Will the court dismiss Alice's action for lack of subject matter jurisdiction? _____

Answers

33. Peter should file his objection in the federal court to which defendant attempted to remove. Section 1446(d) provides that once a copy of the notice of removal is filed with the state court, the state court "shall proceed no further" with the case. Therefore, Peter must ask the federal court to remand the case.

    The federal court will remand the action to state court because it was not properly removed. In a case involving multiple defendants, all defendants must join in the notice of removal.

34. The federal court will remand the action to state court. Although all defendants removed, the amended notice was filed too late. Section 1446(b) requires that the notice be filed within 30 days following defendants' receipt of the complaint setting out the federal question. Because the complaint was filed and served on both defendants on May 1, the notice would have to have been filed by the end of May.

35. The federal court will remand the case. A case may be removed under §1441(a) only if it could have been filed originally in federal court. Because of the amount in controversy, this case could go to federal court only as a federal question under §1331. However, for the case to qualify as a federal question, a federal claim must appear on the face of the complaint. Adam's complaint states only a state law claim. The interposition of the federal defense does not turn the case into a federal question.

36. The federal court will remand the case. As modified, the case could have been brought in federal court only on the basis of diversity. However, §1441(b) bars removal solely on the basis of diversity by a defendant who is sued in her home state. Because Don is a California citizen sued in a California state court, he cannot remove.

37. Removal of the federal false advertising claim will be allowed, but the state claim will be decided by the state court. The false advertising claim can be removed as a federal question. The state law claim cannot be removed on the basis of diversity because the parties are both citizens of North Carolina. Nor is it a federal question. Moreover, because the claims are unrelated, removal based on supplemental jurisdiction is not possible.

    However, precisely because the claims are unrelated, removal is possible under §1441(c). Floyd's federal claim is a federal question. Section 1441(c) accordingly allows Floyd to remove the case. However, once the case is removed, §1441(c) requires the federal court to remand the *state* claim to state court.

38. There are two issues here: whether Da Vinci, as plaintiff, may challenge jurisdiction and whether the court actually has jurisdiction.

    Da Vinci clearly can raise the issue. Subject matter jurisdiction can never be waived and can be raised by any party, or the court itself, at any time.

    However, the court will not dismiss the case. Although there is no diversity, the case presents a federal question. A court analyzes a declaratory judgment by determining what action would occur if plaintiff had not filed for declaratory relief. Here, absent a declaratory judgment, Edison would eventually sue

Da Vinci for infringement of his patent. That action could be heard in a federal court as a federal question (in fact, it could *only* be in federal court because federal jurisdiction in patent infringement cases is exclusive under 28 U.S.C. §1338). Therefore, Da Vinci's suit for declaratory judgment likewise presents a federal question.

39. Removal is not proper under these facts. In order to remove a case, the case must be one that could have been filed by plaintiff in a federal court. Mari-Elise could only file her case in federal court if it would qualify for diversity or federal question jurisdiction. Diversity is clearly not met because the parties are from the same state (the corporation has two citizenships here, one of which is the same as Mari-Elise's).

Nor does Mari-Elise's negligence claim involve a federal question. The basic claim arises under state law. Admittedly, the court may need to interpret the federal law dealing with coffee shop siting in order to resolve the claim, as that law may provide Cup-o-Joe a defense. A state law claim that incorporates federal law as an element may sometimes qualify as a federal question. In order to qualify as a federal question, however, the underlying federal law must be sufficiently important, as well as a central part of the dispute. Here, the federal law is not an important element of the dispute between the parties. The case is similar to *Empire Healthchoice* in that it involves an operative act that was undertaken by a private party.

40. The court will dismiss the case for lack of subject matter jurisdiction. The case does not involve a federal question. Nor are Perry and Cup-o-Joe diverse. Perry is probably still a citizen of Indiana, which is one of the states of which Cup-o-Joe is a citizen (because Indiana is the state of incorporation). He did not become a New Mexico citizen when he moved there, for the facts specify that while there he never intended to remain. Without the intent to remain, he did not become a New Mexico domiciliary.

His later change of plans also did not establish a New Mexico domicile. To become a domiciliary of a state, one must both reside there and have the intent to remain at the same instant. When Perry changed his mind, he was in route to Pennsylvania. Because he decided to live in New Mexico before he established residence in Pennsylvania, he never became a Pennsylvania domiciliary. Moreover, Perry had not returned to New Mexico when he filed his suit. Diversity is measured when the suit is commenced. Although he became a New Mexico domiciliary *after* filing the case, on the crucial date—the date of filing—he had not yet become a New Mexico domiciliary.

Because he did not change his domicile, Perry keeps his original domicile of Indiana. Therefore, he is not diverse from Cup-o-Joe.

41. The court will keep the counterclaim. Every claim in a federal case, including counterclaims, must qualify for federal jurisdiction. There is no independent jurisdiction over the counterclaim. Trespass is not a federal question. Although the parties are diverse, the amount in controversy is not met for the counterclaim (and defendants cannot aggregate a counterclaim with plaintiff's claim).

However, supplemental jurisdiction will be available for the counterclaim. The counterclaim involves the same Article III case as Reva's claim, as both claims derive from a common nucleus of operative fact. Her act of trespassing across the property not only gave rise to her claim but also Gary's counterclaim. Therefore, §1367(a) is satisfied.

Section 1367(b) is not a bar. Although this is a case in which jurisdiction over the federal claim is based solely on diversity, Gary's counterclaim is not a claim by a plaintiff and is therefore not affected by §1367(b).

Nor will §1367(c) be a problem. The federal claim, not the state claim, predominates here. The state claim is relatively straightforward and will not occupy much of the court's time.

42. Removal will be allowed. A defendant may remove a case that could have been filed in federal court. The cybersquatting claim presents a federal question. Although the unfair competition claim is not a federal

question and does not qualify for diversity because the parties are not diverse, it could be brought along with the cybersquatting claim using supplemental jurisdiction. (In truth, the party probably would not rely on §1367, the general supplemental jurisdiction statute, but instead invoke §1338(b), a specialized statute that applies to unfair competition claims. The cybersquatting law is part of federal trademark law. However, the analysis under each statute is basically the same.)

The two claims are sufficiently related to comprise the same Article III case under §1367(a). Both claims arise out of XYZ's registration of the Web site. Section 1367(b) is not an issue because, although this is a claim by a plaintiff, jurisdiction over the federal claim is based on federal question, not diversity. Nor is it likely that a court would exercise discretion to dismiss the common law claim.

Because supplemental jurisdiction would allow both claims to be filed in federal court, XYZ can remove under §1441(a). The facts specify the notice of removal was timely.

43. The federal court will dismiss Alice's case. Supplemental jurisdiction is not available. Although the claims arguably arise from a common nucleus of operative fact, the Court's ruling in *Exxon Mobil* would bar the use of supplemental jurisdiction. According to that case, two nonfederal question claims do not constitute "the same Article III case" unless all of the plaintiffs are diverse from the defendant(s). Here, complete diversity is not present. Note that this case is distinguishable from the facts of *Exxon Mobil* itself. In that case, there was complete diversity, but not all plaintiffs satisfied the amount in controversy.

Exam Tips *on*
SUBJECT MATTER JURISDICTION

☛ Questions involving subject matter jurisdiction are likely to arise mainly in actions brought in, or that are being removed to, *federal courts*.

   ☞ One important exception is a situation where the federal courts have *exclusive jurisdiction*. If a claim over which the federal courts have exclusive jurisdiction is brought in state court, the state court must dismiss. Such actions may also be removed to federal court, even though the state court lacked jurisdiction.

☛ **Analytical hierarchy:** When dealing with a question of federal subject matter jurisdiction, always consider diversity and federal question jurisdiction first. Only if these fail do you need to consider the considerably more difficult issue of supplemental jurisdiction.

   ☞ One common situation where students fall into the trap of unnecessarily discussing supplemental jurisdiction is one involving *aggregation* of claims to meet the amount in controversy. Remember that a single plaintiff may aggregate all claims she has against a single diverse defendant, regardless of whether the claims are related in any way.

☛ Recall that defects in subject matter jurisdiction *cannot be waived*. Challenges to subject matter jurisdiction may be made at any time, by any party, and by the court itself.

☛ Do not overlook the court-created *domestic relations* and *probate* exceptions to federal jurisdiction.

☛ **Federal question jurisdiction:** The two most difficult issues in federal question jurisdiction are the "well-pleaded complaint" rule and determining when a claim "arises under" federal law.

   ☞ Applying the *well-pleaded complaint rule* requires a consideration of both the substantive law and the rules governing pleading. In essence, you must consider what plaintiff needs to plead in order to state a claim under that particular theory of relief. Any unnecessary information plaintiff includes will not be considered.

☞ *Declaratory judgment* claims present special problems in applying the well-pleaded complaint rule. If faced with such a claim, try to determine who would sue whom if the declaratory judgment had not been brought. If that later claim would qualify for federal question jurisdiction, the declaratory judgment claim will, too.

☛ **Diversity jurisdiction:** The most confusing issues in diversity jurisdiction are the complete diversity rule, determining the citizenship of the parties, and the amount in controversy.

☞ In a multiparty case, always check to ensure there is *complete diversity*.

☞ When dealing with individual litigants, be prepared to discuss their *domicile*. One's domicile need not be the same as one's current residence.

☞ Do not forget the special rules that apply to corporations, liability insurance carriers, representatives, and permanent resident aliens. For example, a corporation often has two citizenships. Recall that if either of these is the same as the citizenship of an opposing party, there is no diversity jurisdiction.

☞ Make sure you have a handle on the many technical points that go into the *amount in controversy*, such as what types of interest may be included, how a court will ascribe a value to a specific remedy such as an injunction, and the rules governing *aggregation of claims*.

☞ If the parties are engaged in manipulative behavior to try to get the case into federal court, you should discuss §1359. That statute, however, deals only with attempts to manufacture, not defeat, jurisdiction.

☛ *Supplemental jurisdiction* augments federal question and diversity. As noted above, consider supplemental jurisdiction for a claim only after you rule out federal question and diversity.

☞ Supplemental jurisdiction replaced the older judge-made doctrines of ancillary and pendent jurisdiction. You should not mention the older doctrines.

☞ When applying the "same Article III case" test of §1367(a), use the "common nucleus of operative facts" approach of the Supreme Court's *Gibbs* decision. If the two claims arise from the same core event or series of events, the claims may comprise the same Article III case even if they do not share all that many facts.

☞ The diversity exception of §1367(b) is particularly difficult for many students. The exception applies only to claims by plaintiffs, only to claims against parties joined under the listed rules, and only if jurisdiction over the federal claim is based solely on diversity.

☞ Make sure you fully understand the rationale of the Supreme Court's *Exxon Mobil* decision. That rationale allows supplemental jurisdiction when not all plaintiffs meet the amount in controversy, but *not* when one or more of the plaintiffs is not diverse from a defendant.

☞ Do not forget to apply the discretionary exceptions of §1367(c). Recall, though, that a court usually refrains from dismissing a state law claim under §1367(c) unless it clearly falls into one of the listed categories.

☛ Removal from state court to federal is usually proper only when the case could have been brought originally in a federal court. Therefore, every removal question also requires you to consider federal question, diversity, and possibly supplemental jurisdiction.

☞ Be sure to consider the timing and procedural issues involved in removal.

CHAPTER 5

THE *ERIE* DOCTRINE

ChapterScope

The *Erie* doctrine plays a major role in defining the nature and role of the federal courts in the United States. The doctrine ensures that state courts get to establish the common law rules in tort, contract, property, and other areas of substantive law.

■ The basic command of *Erie* is that the **federal courts must follow state substantive law**, except when a valid federal statute or rule applies, or in certain areas of special federal prerogative.

■ *Erie* has its roots in the **Rules of Decision Act**, 28 U.S.C. §1652. However, the doctrine is also grounded in the U.S. Constitution.

■ A federal court is not always required to defer to state law.

■ If a *federal statute* provides the substantive law for a case, the federal court will apply the federal law, not state law. Therefore, *Erie* applies mainly (but not exclusively) in **diversity cases**.

■ A federal court also has the **inherent power** to enact its own rules of **procedure**.

■ The **Federal Rules of Civil Procedure** are a special case. Although drafted by the Supreme Court (and accordingly "judge-made law"), the Federal Rules are authorized by the **Rules Enabling Act**, 28 U.S.C. §2072. Because of the delegation from Congress, courts use a **different test** in cases involving the Federal Rules than in cases involving ordinary judge-made procedural rules.

■ Finally, there is a limited body of **substantive federal common law**, which overrides state law just as federal statutes do.

■ When a federal court is required by *Erie* to apply state law, it must determine the current state of the law by evaluating state court precedent.

I. OVERVIEW OF *ERIE*

The *Erie* doctrine evolved through a series of Supreme Court cases. Before exploring the genesis, it may help to take a brief look at the doctrine as it exists today.

A. Three categories of *Erie* issues: *Erie* cases fall into three basic categories. The analysis of each differs significantly.

1. **No federal positive law:** The first category involves cases, like *Erie* itself, where there is **no federal positive law** (that is, no statute or written rule) on the subject. In these cases, the **Rules of Decision Act** (28 U.S.C. §1652) applies. Part III of this chapter explores this category.

   a. In these cases, the federal court is deciding **whether to ignore state law** and instead decide the issue based on federal precedent or the judge's opinion of how the issue should be resolved.

b. Cases in this category are resolved by determining whether ignoring state law and applying a contrary federal rule would be *likely to cause forum-shopping for a different outcome*, i.e., affect a party's decision whether to litigate in state or federal court. If forum-shopping is likely, state law must be applied.

2. Federal rules: The second category of *Erie* cases encompasses those that involve a *Federal Rule of Civil Procedure* or other federal rule created under the *Rules Enabling Act* (28 U.S.C. §2072). This situation is discussed in Part IV of this chapter.

    a. Although the Federal Rules of Civil Procedure are judge-made law, they are different for purposes of *Erie*. Congress delegated part of its lawmaking authority to the Supreme Court in §2072.

    b. Analysis of a Federal Rule of Civil Procedure or other Rules Enabling Act rule turns on whether the rule in question can rationally be characterized as a rule governing procedure, and whether the rule unduly abridges, enlarges, or modifies substantive rights. If the Federal Rule of Civil Procedure *is procedural*, and *does not abridge, enlarge, or modify* a substantive right, it applies in lieu of state law.

3. Federal statute: The third category of *Erie* cases includes those that involve a federal statute. Because *Erie* is not a limit on Congress, a federal statute will always be applied, provided it is constitutional and really governs the situation at hand. This situation is discussed in Part V of this chapter.

B. Conflicts: In all three categories of *Erie* cases, it is important to ensure the federal "law" actually conflicts with state law.

II. THE *ERIE* DECISION

The Supreme Court decided *Erie* in 1938. However, the roots of the opinion are much older.

★ **A. Historical background:** *Erie* stems from the 1789 *Rules of Decision Act* and the Supreme Court's interpretation of that act in Swift v. Tyson.

    1. Rules of Decision Act: The Rules of Decision Act (hereinafter RODA) provided that "the *laws of the several states*, except where the constitution, treaties, or statutes of the United States shall otherwise require or provide, shall be regarded as the rules of decision" in the federal courts. RODA remains in effect, with slight modifications. It is codified at *28 U.S.C. §1652*.

    2. *Swift*: The Supreme Court's most important pre-*Erie* interpretation of RODA was Swift v. Tyson, 41 U.S. 1 (1841). The basic holding of *Swift* was that federal courts were *not bound by RODA to follow state judicial opinions* on most legal issues. Instead, a federal court could make an independent interpretation of what the common law rule was on the particular subject.

        a. Rationale: *Swift* turned on the meaning of the word "laws" in RODA.

            i. To the Court, the term included only *state statutes* and *local common law* such as rules governing real property. By contrast, *court decisions interpreting the general common law* were not "state laws" within the meaning of RODA.

            ii. *Swift*'s interpretation of RODA was based on a particular view of the nature of the common law that was to dominate legal thinking for decades. To the Court, the common law *did not trace its origins to any individual state*. Instead, it was a body of unwritten law that applied in all common law nations. The decisions of a particular state court *did not create* the law, but rather merely *interpreted* this body of general law. That interpretation did not bind other courts interpreting the same general rule.

    b. Creation of federal common law: Although the federal courts after *Swift* were not bound to follow state courts, they were bound to follow rulings of the federal courts of appeal and Supreme Court. As federal courts continued to interpret the common law, there developed a body of precedent called *federal common law*, which applied in the federal courts only.

★ **B.** *Erie*: The Supreme Court revisited RODA in Erie Railroad v. Tompkins, 304 U.S. 64 (1938). *Erie* not only overturned *Swift*'s interpretation of RODA but also replaced its view of a "general" common law with an entirely different paradigm.

    1. Facts: Plaintiff in *Erie* was hit by a train while walking along the tracks of defendant railroad in Pennsylvania. He sued the railroad in a federal district court based on diversity jurisdiction, claiming the railroad had acted negligently by leaving the door to one of the cars open.

    2. Clash of laws: Under Pennsylvania law, plaintiff could recover only upon a showing of "wanton" negligence because he would be considered a trespasser on the railroad's right-of-way. Plaintiff, however, argued the federal court should apply the "general" or federal common law rule, which required the railroad to act with ordinary care.

    3. Holding: The Supreme Court held that the lower court was obligated to apply Pennsylvania's wanton negligence standard.

    4. Rationale: The Court *overturned* its earlier holding in *Swift*, finding that the reference to "laws" in RODA included not only state statute law but also *state judicial opinions* interpreting the common law.

        a. View of common law: The *Erie* Court rejected the idea that there was a "general" common law that applied with equal force in all common law jurisdictions. Instead, the court indicated that each sovereign state created *its own common law*.

        b. Federal courts and common law: The Court also held that federal courts, unlike state courts, had *no power to create general common law*. Therefore, RODA required the federal courts to follow the common law rules set out by the state courts.

★ **C. Constitutional underpinnings of** *Erie*: The Court in theory could have reached its holding solely on the basis of RODA. However, the Court made it clear the result in the case was dictated by the *U.S. Constitution*.

    1. Applicable provision: The constitutional basis for the holding is not entirely clear. The best interpretation is that the holding is based on core principles of *federalism* reflected in Article I, Article III, and the Tenth Amendment.

    2. Constitutional argument: The Court began its constitutional discussion (in Part III of the opinion) with the premise that "*there is no federal general common law.*"

        a. Limits on Congress: It then noted that although Congress clearly has the power to pass laws on specific subjects, it did not have the power to supplant the *entire body of state common law* with federal statutes. If it did, Article I of the Constitution, which carefully delineates Congress's powers, would be rendered meaningless.

b. **Limits on federal courts:** Allowing federal courts to enact their own common law rules in every diversity case would give the federal government a back-door way to exercise legislative power over many subject areas reserved to the states.

III. APPLYING *ERIE* IN THE ABSENCE OF FEDERAL POSITIVE LAW

Erie suggests that a federal court has no power to make law. Although the Court quickly backed off from that blanket rule, it struggled with how to define the sorts of rules that fell under *Erie*'s mandate.

★ **A.** *Guaranty Trust* **and the "procedural" exception:** Seven years after *Erie*, the Supreme Court recognized an important exception in Guaranty Trust Co. v. York, 326 U.S. 99 (1945). Most first-year courses concentrate on this "procedural" exception.

  1. **Statute of limitations vs. laches:** Because *Guaranty Trust* was a case in equity (a suit for breach of a trustee's fiduciary duty is equitable), the court of appeals held the trial court should have applied the traditional equitable doctrine of laches when determining if the action was brought too late. By contrast, the courts of New York (the state in which the federal district court sat) would have applied the state statute of limitations even when the action was in equity. Under the New York law the action would be barred, whereas under laches it could proceed. The Supreme Court held the federal court had to apply the state statute of limitations and dismiss the action.

  2. **Procedural exception:** Although finding statutes of limitations within the scope of *Erie*, *Guaranty Trust* is better known for its discussion of what sorts of rules do *not* fall within *Erie*'s command. The Court held *Erie* applied only to matters of **substance, not procedure**. A federal court is **free to ignore state procedural rules** and rely on the customs and practices used in federal court.

  3. **Outcome determinative test:** The Court noted that the law at issue in the case itself—a statute of limitations—was usually considered a rule of procedure in other contexts. However, the Court held it is a substantive rule for *Erie*. The Court ruled that any rule that could **affect the outcome** should be considered **substantive** under *Erie*. A state statute of limitations can clearly change the outcome, as it prevents the court from even hearing the case.

  4. **Problem with analysis:** The problem with the outcome determinative test is that virtually any procedural matter can change the outcome of a case. Therefore, the test would require federal courts to apply many state rules that seem clearly procedural.

     Example: The fee for filing a case in federal district court is $100. The state filing fee is $120. Under the outcome determinative test, the federal court would have to charge $120. If a party walked into state court and tried to pay only $100, the clerk would not accept the complaint, and plaintiff would stand no chance of recovery. For a federal court to accept the same complaint and hear the case clearly could change the outcome. And yet such a rule is clearly "procedural."

 B. Redefining *procedure*: *Guaranty Trust*'s outcome determinative test proved unworkable in practice. The Court struggled to develop a workable test for twenty years.

★ 1. ***Byrd*:** Byrd v. Blue Ridge Electric Cooperative, 356 U.S. 525 (1958), held that a federal court did not have to follow a state law that required a certain issue to be decided by the judge. Instead, the federal court could follow the federal practice of having a jury decide most issues in the case.

   a. **Judge vs. jury:** The Court acknowledged that whether a judge or jury decided the case could affect the outcome. However, it noted the likelihood of a different outcome was not great.

   b. **Federal interest:** Moreover, the Court noted a ***strong federal interest in using juries*** whenever possible, as evidenced by the Seventh Amendment to the U.S. Constitution. (Note that the Court did *not* find that the Seventh Amendment actually required a jury in the case; if it had, the Amendment would have required a jury notwithstanding *Erie*.)

   c. **State practice not bound up with right:** On the other hand, the state rule requiring a judge was neither "tied up" with the state right, nor reflected a strong state interest, but was merely a historical practice.

   d. **Holding:** Applying these considerations, the Court held the federal court could use a jury, even though the difference in laws was slightly outcome determinative.

   e. **Current relevance:** Although the Supreme Court's *Hanna* test, discussed just below, provides a more workable way to deal with most procedural issues, the *Byrd* balancing test has never been disavowed. It continues to apply to judge-jury questions and is often invoked by the lower courts on other issues.

★ 2. ***Hanna* and forum-shopping:** In Hanna v. Plumer, 380 U.S. 460 (1965), the Court held that Fed. R. Civ. P. 4, rather than state law, controls how process may be served. Although the case was decided based on the Rules Enabling Act, discussed in Part IV of this chapter, *dictum* in the decision also supplied a new test for determining whether ordinary judge-made rules are procedural.

   a. **Rationale:** The *Hanna* Court stated that *Erie* had "twin aims": discouraging ***forum-shopping*** and avoiding ***inequitable administration of the laws***. Therefore, a federal court should not be required to apply state law whenever the outcome might differ, but only when the difference in outcome would contravene one of the aims of *Erie*.

   b. **New test:** Thus, a federal court must apply state law only when failure to do so would ***likely result in forum-shopping between state and federal courts*** because of the likelihood of a ***different outcome***.

      i. **Forum-shopping:** By restricting *Erie* to cases where forum-shopping is likely, the test allows a federal court to apply its own procedural customs even though there is a chance the outcome would differ. A federal court must apply state law only if the likelihood of a different outcome is so great that plaintiff will base her choice of forum on the different rules.

      ii. **Irrelevant which court preferred:** Under the *Hanna* test, it is irrelevant whether the litigant would prefer state or federal court. In either case, state law applies.

      iii. **Different outcome:** *Erie* is concerned with forum-shopping only when it is motivated by the hope for a ***different outcome*** based on a ***difference in applicable laws***. Other motivations for forum-shopping do not matter.

Example: The filing fee in federal court is $100, while in state court it is $10,000. Although this difference is likely to cause forum-shopping and is based on a difference in laws, the federal court need not charge the state fee. Any forum-shopping that occurs will not be designed to procure a more favorable outcome.

  c. **Applying the test—an example:** Today, the *Hanna* test covers most cases involving federal judge-made law. The following example illustrates how the test applies.

    i. **Facts:** *P* sues *D* in a federal court in State *X*. *P*'s complaint alleges a state law fraud claim. *P* argues that two laws of State *X* should apply in the federal proceeding.

      (a) First, *P* argues that *X*'s law governing ***burden of persuasion*** should apply to the case. *X* requires plaintiff to prove fraud merely by a ***preponderance of the evidence***. All other states, by contrast, require a party suing for fraud to prove the fraud by ***clear and convincing evidence***, a much more difficult standard.

      (b) Second, *P* argues that the federal court should schedule an ***immediate trial***, following *X*'s procedural rule requiring fraud claims to be put before all other claims on the trial docket.

    ii. **Decision:** The federal court must follow the state burden rule, but not the scheduling rule.

      (a) If the burden rule is not followed, it could lead to forum-shopping for a different outcome. A plaintiff might be more inclined to sue in state court if it is easier for her to prove her case in that court. (Note that it does not matter that *this* particular plaintiff chose federal court, where the burden is higher.)

      (b) Differences in how a case is put on the trial docket might also lead to forum-shopping since a plaintiff usually wants his claim wrapped up as quickly as possible. However, this is not forum-shopping *for a different outcome*. Therefore, the federal court need ***not follow the state rule***.

C. Choice of law: When a state court hears a dispute that has connections to multiple states, it does not necessarily apply its own law. The court instead engages in a choice of law analysis to determine which state's law applies. This analysis relies on the state's ***choice of law rules***, which are typically rules established by precedent. Choice of law rules differ significantly from state to state.

  1. ***Erie* and choice of law:** In Klaxon Co. v. Stentor Electric Manufacturing Co., 313 U.S. 487 (1941), the Supreme Court held that a state's choice of law rules are ***substantive***. Therefore, a federal court will decide a case not necessarily under the law of the state in which it sits, but under the law that ***would be applied*** by the courts of the state in which it sits. The *Klaxon* rule survives *Hanna*. Day & Zimmerman, Inc. v. Challoner, 423 U.S. 3 (1975).

  Example: A federal district court in Maine is hearing a diversity case brought by a Quebec plaintiff against a Maine defendant. The action arises out of a breach of contract that was to be performed in Quebec. Maine state courts would apply Quebec law to determine if defendant's act breached the contract. Contract law is clearly substantive because applying different rules on the issue of breach could result in forum-shopping. Therefore, the federal court must likewise apply Quebec law.

  2. **State jurisdiction irrelevant:** The rule of *Klaxon* applies even if the state in which the federal court sits could not hear the case because of lack of personal jurisdiction over some defendants. Griffin v. McCoach, 313 U.S. 498 (1941).

D. Judge-jury determinations: Although the Supreme Court has dealt with relatively few cases falling into the first *Erie* category, it has faced one issue—whether a judge or jury decides a particular issue in a case—twice.

    1. *Byrd*: *Byrd* is discussed on page 85. Although one could argue that the *Byrd* balancing test has been replaced by the *Hanna* test, lower courts still sometimes invoke *Byrd*.

★   **2. *Gasperini*:** Gasperini v. Center for Humanities, Inc., 518 U.S. 415 (1996), is a post-*Hanna* decision that deals with how a jury verdict would be **reviewed**. The state law allowed the **court of appeals** to overturn the verdict if it "**deviates materially** from what would be reasonable compensation." Federal courts, by contrast, apply a much more stringent standard. The Supreme Court held that the federal court had to use the **state law standard**. However, the **trial court**, not the court of appeals, would apply the state standard.

        a. The Court held that the difference in standards for reviewing jury awards would be *likely to cause forum-shopping*. Therefore, the federal court had to apply the state standard.

        b. However, the Court also held that because of the **Reexamination Clause of the Seventh Amendment**, the court of appeals could not apply the state standard. On the other hand, because trial judges at common law could review the substance of verdicts, the Court held the **trial judge should apply** the state law standard.

Quiz Yourself on APPLYING ERIE *TO JUDGE-MADE LAW*

44. Texas is well known for its state pride. To instill even more patriotism, the Texas legislature enacts a statute that requires all attorneys appearing before a court to wear a Texas flag lapel pin. If an attorney does not wear the pin, the court may not hear his argument.

Sam Houston, a Texas attorney, is ready to try his first solo case in federal court. Although he has meticulously prepared his witnesses and arguments, he forgets to wear his Texas flag lapel pin to the federal court. Opposing counsel therefore objects when Sam stands up to present his case. Federal courts have no policies dealing with lapel pins. Will the federal court let Sam proceed? _____

45. The state of Tranquility has suffered a series of fires in its courts, which destroyed irreplaceable records. To deal with this problem, the Tranquility High Court enacts a new rule requiring all documents filed with the court to be submitted on fireproof paper. Although this limits the threat of fire, fireproof paper costs $4 per sheet.

Penny Pincher is considering bringing a case under a federal statute. Because her case is very complex, she anticipates having to file at least 10,000 sheets of paper during the proceeding. Although Penny can sue in either federal or state court, she is inclined to pick federal court to minimize her litigation costs. If Penny does sue in federal court, can she use ordinary paper instead of the fireproof paper? _____

46. Wolverine, Inc., manufactures snowblowers. Wolverine is a small Michigan corporation that is located entirely in, and sells all of its product in, that state.

Courtney is Wolverine's best salesperson. As a reward, Wolverine pays for Courtney to attend a major snowblower manufacturer's convention in Pristine Beach, Florida. While at the convention, Courtney has slightly *too* good a time at one of the free cocktail receptions. Courtney gets out the sample snowblower that she brought with her to the convention and uses it to inflict serious damage on the pristine beaches in front of one of Pristine Beach's finest hotels.

The hotel, a Florida corporation, decides to sue. Because Courtney is currently behind bars and unlikely to be able to pay a judgment, the hotel sues Wolverine. The hotel brings the suit in a federal district court in Michigan, basing subject matter jurisdiction on diversity.

Wolverine is glad it is located in Michigan rather than Florida. Unlike Florida law, Michigan law does not impose liability on an employer for a tort like that committed by Courtney. Wolverine therefore moves to dismiss the case. Will the case be dismissed? _____

Answers

44. The federal court will let Sam argue. True, the Texas rule is outcome determinative in the sense that Sam cannot prevail if he cannot address the court. Nevertheless, pure "outcome determination" is no longer the test. Now the test is whether the difference in rules would likely lead to forum-shopping. No reasonable attorney would base her choice of federal or state court on whether attorneys must wear a Texas flag lapel pin.

45. There are two issues in this problem. First, the case is not exempt from the *Erie* doctrine merely because the action arises under federal law. Although *Erie* issues arise most commonly in diversity cases, they can also arise in federal question cases.

    Second, the federal court will not require fireproof paper. True, the difference in laws might well cause forum-shopping—indeed, it looks as if Penny is actually engaged in forum-shopping. However, because the forum-shopping is not for a different outcome, it should not cause the court to apply state law.

46. This is an *Erie* question with a choice of law twist. First, the federal court clearly must follow state law on the basic issue of whether an employer can be liable for the intentional torts of an employee. To refuse to follow state law would generate forum-shopping.

    But which state's law? The Michigan federal court, under *Klaxon*, is required to apply the law that would be applied by the courts of the state in which it sits. Although the court sits in Michigan, the Michigan state courts might apply Florida law, given that plaintiff is from the state, defendant's employee acted in the state, and the harm occurred there. Without knowing Michigan's choice of law rules, it is impossible to predict the outcome.

IV. CLASHES BETWEEN THE FEDERAL RULES AND STATE LAW

The second category of *Erie* case involves situations where the Court must decide whether to apply a Federal Rule of Civil Procedure or similar written court rule. The analysis applied in these cases is significantly different from that applied in cases involving judge-made rules.

   A. **Federal rules defined:** Most of the cases involving this branch of the analysis have dealt with the *Federal Rules of Civil Procedure*. However, the same basic analysis also applies to the *Federal Rules of Appellate Procedure* and *Bankruptcy Rules*.

1. **Common source of rules:** All of these rules share one crucial feature. They were *promulgated by the Supreme Court* pursuant to a *delegation of power from Congress.*

    a. **Rules Enabling Act:** Congress clearly has the constitutional authority to regulate the procedure in the federal courts. However, Congress delegated a large portion of this authority to the Supreme Court in the Rules Enabling Act (REA), *28 U.S.C. §2072.*

    b. **Process:** Pursuant to 28 U.S.C. §2074, the Court must transmit proposed rules to Congress. Congress may reject rules created under the REA. But unless Congress takes action within the specified period, the rule takes effect on the following December 1.

2. **Supremacy:** When the Court creates a federal rule under this delegated power, the rule overrides state law under the Supremacy Clause, just as a federal statute would. 28 U.S.C. §2072(b). However, the federal rules only apply in federal court, and do not preempt state procedural rules for state courts.

★ **B. Overview of analysis:** Hanna v. Plumer, discussed in Part III above, sets out the analysis for dealing with a clash between a federal rule and state law. Because *Hanna* involved this very situation, this portion of the opinion is *not dictum.*

    1. **"Valid" and "applicable":** At its core, the analysis of a federal rule is logically the same as the analysis that applies to a federal statute: If the rule is *valid* and *applicable*, it *automatically applies*. However, because of restrictions that Congress has placed on the federal rules, determining whether a federal rule is "valid" is more complicated.

    2. **Three-step analysis:** Basically, *Hanna* sets out a three-step analysis. First, you must determine that the rule *actually applies*. Second, the state law and federal rule must actually *conflict*. Finally, you must ensure the federal rule is *valid under the REA.*

C. Determining the applicability of a federal rule: The first step in an *Erie* analysis involving a federal rule is to make sure the rule actually governs the situation before the Court. Although the federal rules are not to be read narrowly to avoid a conflict with state law, in some cases the Court seems to have read a rule more narrowly than the text would dictate.

    1. *Walker:* In Walker v. Armco Steel Corp., 446 U.S. 740 (1980), the Court faced an alleged clash between Fed. R. Civ. P. 3, which indicates a case is "commenced" when the complaint is filed, and a state statute that provided an action was not "commenced" for purposes of the statute of limitations until service occurred. The Court held Rule 3 does not govern when a case commences for purposes of statutes of limitations, but is merely an internal timing rule for applying other federal rules. Therefore, the Court applied the state law because no Federal Rule of Civil Procedure was in conflict.

★   2. *Semtek:* Semtek International, Inc. v. Lockheed Martin Corp., 531 U.S. 497 (2001), also interprets a federal rule quite narrowly. At issue in *Semtek* was *Fed. R. Civ. P. 41(b)*, which deals with the effect of an *involuntary dismissal*.

        a. The trial court had dismissed the case based on the state *statute of limitations*.

        b. Under Fed. R. Civ. P. 41(b), most involuntary dismissals operate as "an adjudication on the merits." This is a term of art that usually indicates the claimant is barred from bringing its claim again.

        c. Plaintiff sued again in a state court in a different state. This second state had a longer statute of limitations.

d. The Supreme Court held the claim was not barred. The Court suggested Fed. R. Civ. P. 41(b) might exceed the REA if it barred a substantive law claim. Instead, the Court held that the law of the state in which the original federal court sat would be used to determine if plaintiff's claim is barred. Most states do not treat a statute of limitations dismissal as a bar to bringing the action in a jurisdiction with a longer limitations period.

e. The full reach of *Semtek* is unclear. The main impact of the case, however, will be on "substantive" dismissals such as the statute of limitations, where state law is most likely to differ from the Rule 41(b) standard. For most procedural dismissals, such as dismissals for failure to cooperate in discovery, state law is likely to produce a result similar to that suggested by the language of Fed. R. Civ. P. 41(b). Note, however, that many states hold that a dismissal for failure to state a claim does not preclude plaintiff from suing again, a result at odds with pre-*Semtek* federal precedent.

D. Does the federal rule clash with state law? The next step in the analysis is to determine whether a true conflict exists between the federal rule and state law. If there is a way the court can apply *both federal and state law*, there is no conflict, and the court will apply both rules.

★   **Example:** In Burlington Northern R.R. v. Woods, 480 U.S. 1 (1987), the Court dealt with an alleged conflict between a Federal Rule of Appellate Procedure and state law. State law required a defendant who lost an appeal to pay a penalty of 10 percent of the original judgment. Fed. R. App. P. 38 gives a federal appellate court authority to award a sanction only in the case of a "frivolous" appeal. However, under the federal rule, the sanction is not fixed, and the court has the discretion to award nothing. Plaintiff argued the two rules did not conflict because a federal court could always award a 10 percent penalty, and then award additional costs if it found the appeal frivolous. The Court disagreed, found that the rules conflicted, and held the federal rule applied under the *Hanna* test.

E. Determining the validity of a federal rule: The last, and most difficult, step in dealing with a federal rule is to determine if the rule is valid. A federal rule is valid if it *fits within the authority delegated* by Congress to the Supreme Court *in the REA.*

   1. Limits established by REA: The REA does not give the Supreme Court unfettered discretion. Instead, the act places two key limits on the Court's power to create rules.

      a. Limit 1: The Court may enact only general rules of *practice and procedure* and *rules of evidence*.

      b. Limit 2: The rule cannot abridge, enlarge, or modify any substantive right.

   2. Presumption of validity: However, because a federal rule is promulgated by the Supreme Court itself and is approved by Congress, *Hanna* indicates there is a presumption the rule is valid under the REA. Therefore, unless the federal rule *clearly* is not a rule of procedure or clearly affects substantive rights, it will be found to satisfy the twin requirements of that act.

      a. Many courts cite Justice Harlan's concurrence in *Hanna*, which suggests that under the *Hanna* test a federal rule is valid as long as it is "*arguably procedural.*"

      b. In fact, the Supreme Court has never actually found a rule invalid under the REA, although in *Semtek* it expressed some doubts concerning Fed. R. Civ. P. 41(b). The overwhelming majority of courts of appeal similarly uphold the federal rules.

      c. Other bases for invalidity: On the other hand, a federal rule is not valid merely because it satisfies the REA. A rule could also be invalid because it violates the Constitution or conflicts with a federal statute. These situations usually are outside the scope of most first-year Procedure courses.

3. **Forum-shopping irrelevant:** Although the analysis of a federal rule and the analysis of judge-made law both speak in terms of *procedure*, that term *has a very different meaning* in the two contexts. When analyzing a federal rule, it is *irrelevant whether the difference in laws would lead to forum-shopping*. Even if the difference in laws makes the state or federal forum more appealing, the federal court can apply a federal rule as long as it arguably regulates procedure and does not significantly abridge, enlarge, or modify a substantive right.

4. **Examples:** The following examples illustrate application of the analysis for a federal rule.

Example 1: *P* sues *D* in federal court for injuries sustained when *D*'s herd of pygmy goats trampled *P*. Although *P* could obtain personal jurisdiction over *D* under state law, *P* prefers to use *in rem* jurisdiction by seizing the goats, because the value of the herd is more than sufficient to satisfy *P*'s claim. Under state law, *P* could use *in rem* jurisdiction in this case. However, *Fed. R. Civ. P. 4(n)* provides that *in rem* jurisdiction is available only when a plaintiff cannot obtain *in personam* jurisdiction. *P* argues the federal court must follow the state rule and allow him to use *in rem* jurisdiction in this diversity case.

Outcome: The federal court will apply Fed. R. Civ. P. 4(n) and deny *P*'s request to use *in rem* jurisdiction. The federal rule here governs service of process and the court's jurisdiction, subjects that clearly fall within the realm of "procedure" under the REA. Nor does the rule in any way abridge *P*'s right because *P* can still recover for the harm using *in personam* jurisdiction.

Example 2: *P* sues *D* in federal court, alleging a state law claim for discrimination based on gender. Although *P* has suffered $200,000 in damages, *P*'s complaint asks for damages in the amount of $600,000. *P* relies on a recent (and purely hypothetical) amendment to Fed. R. Civ. P. 54(c), which provides that, "In a case alleging discrimination based on gender or race, the final judgment shall grant the party three times the damages to which he was otherwise entitled." State law allows only ordinary damages.

Outcome: The hypothetical *federal rule is invalid*, and cannot be applied in federal court. The rule clearly *enlarges* the underlying substantive right. Therefore, even if it is "arguably procedural" because it involves damages, it is invalid under the second limitation in the REA.

V. FEDERAL STATUTES

Cases involving federal statutes are in many ways the easiest category of *Erie* case. The *Supremacy Clause* of Article VI of the U.S. Constitution provides that federal law takes precedence over state law. Therefore, if a federal court is faced with a true conflict between a valid federal statute and a state statute or common law rule, *Erie* is *not an issue*. The federal law applies.

A. **Is statute valid?** Of course, a federal law takes precedence only if it is constitutional.

B. **Does statute apply?** A federal statute automatically applies only if it actually covers the issue before the court. It is important to isolate the actual issue before the court in order to determine whether the statute applies.

★ **Example:** An informative example of this sort of analysis is the Court's opinion in Stewart Organization, Inc. v. Ricoh, 487 U.S. 22 (1988). *Ricoh* was a contract dispute. Defendant moved under 28 U.S.C. §1404 to transfer venue to New York, citing a *forum selection clause* that provided that all disputes under the contract had to be heard in New York. Plaintiff resisted transfer, relying heavily on an Alabama law declaring such clauses invalid. The Court held that the real issue in the case was whether to grant a transfer under §1404. The federal statute clearly applied to that issue. Moreover, in determining whether to grant a §1404 transfer, the lower court should consider the forum selection clause. Regardless of whether the clause was "enforceable," it could be considered as evidence of whether the parties thought New York was a convenient and fair place to hear the case.

C. **Does statute clash with state law?** The final step in the analysis is to determine whether the statute and state law truly conflict. If there is a way the court can apply *both federal and state law*, there is no conflict, and the court will apply both rules.

Quiz Yourself on
APPLYING ERIE WHEN THERE IS A FEDERAL RULE OR STATUTE

47. Wendy Worker, a longtime employee of X, Y & Z, is fired one week before her sixty-fifth birthday. Wendy suspects X, Y & Z fired her because of her age, which would violate state law. Nevertheless, although Wendy *suspects* her age was the reason she was fired, she does not have sufficient evidence to prove that at trial. Hugh Mannresources, the Director of Personnel for X, Y & Z, knows the truth. Although Wendy has tried to speak about the matter with Hugh, he steadfastly refuses to answer any questions. Without Hugh's information, Wendy is certain she cannot prevail in the case.

    Wendy eventually sues X, Y & Z in a federal district court in Wyoming, basing jurisdiction on diversity of citizenship. Wendy chooses federal court over state court because of their different discovery rules. Under Wyoming law, a party cannot force a person who is not a party to the case to provide information in the discovery process, although the party can call the person as a witness at trial. Fed. R. Civ. P. 30, by contrast, allows a party to depose a nonparty witness such as Hugh. If a witness refuses to answer a proper question, the court can hold the witness in contempt.

    When Wendy notices Hugh's deposition, X, Y & Z objects, arguing the Wyoming law must apply. Who will prevail? _____

48. Same basic facts as Problem 47. Wendy serves X, Y & Z by serving a general agent. Immediately after receiving service, X, Y & Z moves to dismiss the action. X, Y & Z cites a Wyoming law that clearly states a partnership is not a "person" in the eyes of the law. Therefore, unlike corporations, Wyoming does not allow a partnership to sue or be sued. Anyone who was injured by partnership activity must instead sue one or more partners individually.

    Wendy disagrees with X, Y & Z's contention. Wendy points out that Fed. R. Civ. P. 4(h) allows a person to serve process on a general partnership by serving one of the general agents. She argues this language clearly authorizes suit against X, Y & Z in federal court, even though she acknowledges she cannot sue in state court.

    Who is correct? _____

49. Peggy Pedestrian is seriously injured when she is struck by an automobile driven by Dan Dangerous. Peggy sues Dan in a Vermont federal court based on diversity. Dan immediately tries to implead Neverpay Insurance Company, his liability insurance carrier, as a third-party defendant.

Neverpay objects to Dan's attempt to drag it into this suit. Neverpay cites a provision of Vermont law that prevents an insured from joining its insurance company as a party to a suit. The Vermont statute was passed because of the fear that if the insurance company is named as a party, the jury is more likely to be sympathetic to plaintiff and award excessive damages. Nevertheless, Vermont will allow the insured to sue the insurance company in a separate action, provided that action is not commenced until *after* the suit against the insured is complete.

Dan maintains he may sue Neverpay in a federal court. He points to Fed. R. Civ. P. 14, which specifically allows him to implead Neverpay because Neverpay "is or may be liable" to Dan.

Will Dan's claim against Neverpay be allowed in the case? _____

50. Couch Potato, a serious television fan, purchases a new diet drug called Faddiet from Impulse Buying Network (IBN), a cable television shopping network. Couch has IBN ship the product from its warehouse in the State of Confusion to Couch's humble abode in the State of Tranquility. When Faddiet fails to work as promised, Couch sues IBN in federal court under Tranquility's false advertising laws. Jurisdiction is based on diversity.

IBN immediately moves to dismiss the action, citing a Tranquility law providing that a retailer selling a product manufactured by another is not liable for any defects in the product. In response, Couch cites a federal statute providing that a retailer that sells products in interstate commerce is vicariously liable for defects in the product.

Should the federal court dismiss Couch's suit? _____

Answers

47. Wendy will prevail. This is a clash between a federal rule and a state law. Under *Hanna*, the federal rule will apply as long as it can rationally be deemed procedural and does not abridge, enlarge, or modify any substantive rights. Fed. R. Civ. P. 30 almost certainly meets that standard. It is "procedural" because it is designed to deal with what happens in the process of litigation, as opposed to dealing with the rights of the parties outside court. Nor does the process change Wendy's legal right to recover. (One could make a colorable argument that Hugh has a sort of "substantive right" under state law not to be forced to testify, which the federal rule "abridges." But that argument is weak because Wendy can force Hugh to testify *at trial* even under state law.)

    Note the clear evidence of forum-shopping here. However, that is irrelevant under the Federal Rules of Civil Procedure analysis.

48. This time X, Y & Z will prevail. A court almost certainly would find ***no conflict*** between Fed. R. Civ. P. 4(h) and the Wyoming rule. Rule 4(h) merely deals with how service will occur *if* the party is able to sue a partnership. It nowhere states that a party *can* sue a partnership.

    Note that if a court were to adopt Wendy's interpretation, Rule 4(h) might be invalid. Creating liability against an entity where no liability existed at state law would arguably involve the creation of a new substantive right.

49. The federal court should hear the claim against Neverpay. Fed. R. Civ. P. 14 satisfies the test under the REA. Although it may appear at first glance that the federal rule creates a new substantive right, in truth it merely allows for the merger of what would be two separate lawsuits in state court. The legal rules that determine whether the insurance company is liable do not change in any way.

That the Vermont rule is supported by strong policy concerns does not change the result. Vermont's concerns relate to the fairness of the litigation process, not to the substantive rights themselves.

50. The court should not dismiss Couch's suit. This is a clash between a federal statute and state law. In that case, the federal statute controls as long as it is valid and can be read actually to cover the situation. The federal statute is clearly valid (Congress can regulate interstate commerce, and the law does not violate any individual human rights), and governs Couch's case.

VI. FEDERAL SUBSTANTIVE COMMON LAW

Part III of this chapter discussed federal *procedural* judge-made law. However, a limited body of federal judge-made law exists that is *clearly substantive* in nature.

A. **Where substantive federal common law exists:** Although the cases defy easy characterization, the Supreme Court has found federal common law to exist in cases where there is a strong and unique federal interest, such as those in which the *federal government is a party, admiralty and maritime* cases, and cases involving *international relations*.

B. **Characteristics of modern federal common law:** The substantive federal common law that exists today differs in certain significant respects from the pre-*Erie* body of federal precedent. First, federal common law presents a *federal question. Federal common law claims* can accordingly be heard in federal court regardless of whether the parties are diverse. Illinois v. City of Milwaukee, 406 U.S. 91 (1972). Second, federal substantive common law applies not only in federal courts but also in *state courts*.

Quiz Yourself on
THE ERIE *DOCTRINE*

51. Randy Risktaker is a precocious youth who lives in a small Iowa town. One day, Randy and his friends decide to engage in one of the rites of passage for young men in the country, namely, tipping cows. Tipping cows involves going up to a sleeping cow and pushing it over. Tipped cows suffer nothing more than a slight surprise.

Randy and his friends travel to Nebraska in search of prey. Randy, however, does not choose wisely. Instead of a sleeping cow, Randy tips a wide-awake bull. The bull does not take kindly to Randy's advances and causes Randy serious injuries.

Randy sues Fannie Farmer, the owner of the bull, for negligence in a federal district court in Nebraska. Fannie moves to dismiss based on Nebraska's pleading rules. Under Nebraska law, a plaintiff cannot recover unless he pleads that he did *not* assume the risk. Because Randy did not include that in his pleadings, Fannie argues, the court should dismiss his case.

Randy counters by brandishing his copy of Fed. R. Civ. P. 8(c). That federal rule lists "assumption of risk" as an "affirmative defense." If something is an affirmative defense, defendant has the burden to raise the issue in the pleadings. If defendant fails to raise the issue in the pleadings, the court cannot hear evidence on the issue.

Will the court dismiss Randy's case? _____

52. Same basic facts as Problem 51, but assume the court lets Randy's case proceed to trial. Fannie and Randy both present evidence to the jury concerning assumption of risk. When the evidence is complete, the judge prepares to issue jury instructions. The proposed instructions state that Randy has the burden of proving, by a preponderance of the evidence, that he did not assume the risk.

Randy objects to the proposed instruction. He notes that in every other state that recognizes the defense of assumption of risk, defendant has the burden of showing, by a preponderance of the evidence, that plaintiff assumed the risk. Although there is no federal statute or rule on point, Randy argues the federal court need not consider itself bound by the idiosyncratic state law standard on burden of proof.

Will Randy prevail on his objection? _____

53. Several weeks after undergoing surgery, Patient develops a severe infection. Patient sues Surgeon for medical malpractice in federal district court. Suspecting Patient's infection was caused by postsurgery events rather than the surgery itself, Surgeon moves for a physical exam of Plaintiff under Fed. R. Civ. P. 35. That rule would clearly allow an exam under these circumstances. However, Patient objects, citing a state privacy law that protects people from being forced to undergo medical exams. Although that right can be waived, Patient never explicitly waived his state law protection.

Will the federal court order Patient to submit to the physical? _____

54. Priscilla Procrastinator recently bought a painting from Dan Dealer. Soon after the painting is delivered, Priscilla discovers it is a worthless forgery. However, Priscilla does not sue Dan until 363 days after delivery. Priscilla files her breach of contract action in federal court, based on diversity.

Priscilla serves Dan three weeks after filing the complaint. Dan immediately moves to dismiss based on the statute of limitations. Under state law, a party suing for breach of contract must commence the action within one year of the breach. Moreover, state law is clear that an action is not "commenced" until service occurs on defendant. Because service on Dan did not occur until after one year had expired, Dan claims the action is barred.

Although Priscilla concedes that Dan has correctly stated state law, she points out she filed her action in *federal* court. And Fed. R. Civ. P. 3 clearly provides that an action is commenced when the complaint is filed with the court. Because filing occurred within a year of the breach, Priscilla is confident she can proceed with her suit. Will Priscilla or Dan prevail? _____

55. After losing his shirt in a risky stock purchase, Investor sues Accountant for misrepresentation. Investor brings this action in a federal district court, basing jurisdiction on diversity. Soon after the action is commenced, Accountant moves for an order requiring Investor to file a bond in the case. Accountant cites a recently enacted federal statute requiring anyone who sues an accountant for fraud or misrepresentation to file a bond in an amount equal to ten times the amount of the claim. If plaintiff eventually loses the suit, the accountant receives the amount of the bond as compensation for the inevitable damage to reputation caused by a fraud allegation. By its explicit terms, the statute applies to all claims, including state law claims. Must Investor file the bond in this diversity case? _____

Answers

51. Randy's case will not be dismissed. The issue here involves a clash between a Federal Rule of Civil Procedure and a state rule of procedure. In this situation, the federal rule will control as long as it is procedural and does not abridge, enlarge, or modify the underlying substantive right. Fed. R. Civ. P. 8(c) clearly passes this test. The rule does not change the substantive law in any material way. Assumption of the risk is clearly a defense under Nebraska law. All Rule 8(c) does is to determine *who* must initially raise the issue to make it an issue for trial.

52. Randy's objection will be denied. Because there is no federal positive law on point, this question is governed by the "likely to cause forum-shopping" test. Here, ignoring the state law would be quite likely to cause forum-shopping. The burden of proof concerns who wins a close case. Therefore, a party might be likely to select the forum that made it easier for him to win.

53. This presents a difficult clash between a Federal Rule of Procedure and state law. First, one must determine if this can rationally be considered a rule of procedure. Here, the answer is yes: A rule that deals with discovery is a rule of procedure.

The second part of the analysis is whether the federal rule would abridge, enlarge, or modify a substantive right. The answer is probably no, although the question is difficult. The state law does look much like a substantive right. However, that right can be waived. By suing in federal court—a system that authorizes exams of this sort—plaintiff effectively waived his state law protection. Thus, application of the federal rule does not abridge his rights. See Sibbach v. Wilson, 312 U.S. 1 (1941).

54. There is no conflict between the federal and state rules. In fact, this is almost exactly like Walker v. Armco Steel, discussed in Part IV.C. The Court in that case held there was no conflict because Fed. R. Civ. P. 3's definition of when a case is commenced was not meant to apply to statutes of limitations. Because Rule 3 does not apply, the case involves a clash between state law and federal judge-made law. The court should apply state law if the difference between the state and federal laws could induce forum-shopping. It is highly likely that a plaintiff would choose federal court if that court used a rule that made it easier to satisfy the statute of limitations. Therefore, the federal court must follow the state law.

55. Investor will be required to file the bond. The question involves a clash between a federal statute and state law. True, the federal law may cause forum-shopping and could easily be deemed to create a substantive right. But Congress, unlike the courts, has the power to create substantive law. Although this statute may not be wise, it is within Congress's constitutional powers and therefore must be applied.

Exam Tips on
THE ERIE *DOCTRINE*

Erie issues can be among the most difficult questions on a Civil Procedure exam. But do not let that prospect frighten you. The keys to dealing with an *Erie* problem are knowing how to spot an issue and figuring out which of the tests applies.

☛ **Spotting an *Erie* issue:** *Erie* issues can be very difficult to spot on a law school examination, not because your professor is trying to be sneaky (well, not *necessarily*), but instead because of the nature of the *Erie* problem itself.

   ☞ Remember that *Erie* is an issue **only in federal court**.

   ☞ Most of the discussion of *Erie* in a first-year course focuses on when a federal court must follow a state "procedural" rule. This means that *Erie* issues may arise in connection with virtually any topic you discuss in Civil Procedure. What may look like a relatively straightforward question of pleading or discovery may actually have an *Erie* issue lurking in the background.

☞ One tip for spotting an *Erie* issue is when the question involves a suit in federal court but, for some reason, ***specifies what the state law rule is on a particular matter***. After all, *Erie* only matters if state law and federal law differ.

☞ Sometimes a question ***gives you only a state rule*** on a topic. However, if you studied the corresponding Federal Rule of Civil Procedure or other federal law on that topic, you should apply the federal law and determine if *Erie* applies. For example, if a question tells you that the state rules absolutely prevent a party from amending its pleadings, and you studied pleading during that particular term, you should also consider the Fed. R. Civ. P. 15 rules dealing with amendments.

☞ If the problem gives you a state law but there is no corresponding federal rule that you can think of, there is still an *Erie* problem. In this case, the real issue is ***whether the federal court must apply the state law***. To refuse to apply the state law, as a practical matter, means that the federal court is applying a "federal" judge-made rule that is the opposite of the state law.

☛ **Beware of the "false conflict":** Once you have found the *Erie* issue, take a second look at the state and federal rules on the subject. ***Make sure the rules actually conflict.*** If application of the state and federal rules does not make a difference, there is no conflict, and an *Erie* analysis is technically unnecessary. However, unless the case falls squarely within one of the Court's earlier decisions or the lack of any conflict is absolutely clear, ***be very hesitant before basing your entire answer on a finding of "no conflict."*** If you are wrong in that conclusion, you will have left out the lion's share of the analysis.

☛ **Do not forget precedent:** The Supreme Court has decided a number of *Erie* cases. If the case involves the same issue as one of those cases, the decision controls. There is no need to reinvent the wheel.

☛ **Categorizing the *Erie* issue:** Categorize any question not squarely dealt with by precedent using the three categories set out in this chapter. The analysis differs depending on the type of issue. You may find it helpful to create a flow chart, checklist, or other device to help you remember the different analyses that apply in each situation.

☛ **Federal statutes:** If the *Erie* problem involves a federal statute, the analysis is relatively simple: If the federal statute is valid and really applies to the situation, then it controls.

☞ Unless you have had a course in Constitutional Law, you do not have the tools to determine whether an act of Congress is "valid." However, if the law is blatantly invalid—for example, if it impermissibly discriminates on the basis of race—then the possibility of invalidity should at least be mentioned.

☛ **Federal rule crafted under Rules Enabling Act:** If the case involves a Federal Rule of Civil Procedure or other rule enacted under the REA, your task is to determine whether the rule fits within the powers Congress gave the Supreme Court in the Rules Enabling Act.

☞ Again, make sure the rule conflicts.

☞ In determining whether the rule can ***reasonably be characterized as procedural***, ask yourself whether the rule is concerned with what goes on ***during the litigation*** or what went on ***outside the litigation***.

☞ After that, consider the real impact of the rule. Does it change the legal parameters of the claim or defense, or make it significantly easier for one party to win? If so, the federal rule is invalid.

☞ ***When in doubt, conclude that an existing federal rule is valid.*** The Supreme Court has made it clear that the federal rules have a presumption of validity.

☛ If you conclude (reluctantly) that a federal statute or Federal Rule of Civil Procedure is invalid or does not apply, do not automatically conclude that state law governs. Instead, determine whether the federal court is required to follow state law even without any federal positive law to the contrary. This is governed by the "likely to cause forum-shopping" analysis.

☛ **Federal judge-made law:** If the issue is a clash between a judge-made federal rule and state law, or if the problem simply gives you a state law and the issue is whether the federal court must apply it, your task is to determine whether the ***difference*** between federal and state laws would ***likely cause forum-shopping for a different outcome***.

    ☞ *Try to avoid using the phrases "substantive/procedural" and "outcome determinative"* in the analysis. The "likely to cause forum-shopping" analysis is how a court determines whether a rule is substantive.

☛ **Judge-jury determinations:** Because of *Byrd* and *Gasperini*, questions involving judge and jury are not governed by the "likely to cause forum-shopping" analysis. If your question deals with those sorts of issues, apply the analysis in those cases instead.

CHAPTER 6

AN OVERVIEW OF LITIGATION

ChapterScope ────────────────────────────

This chapter presents a conceptual overview of litigation. Details of the litigation process, and alternatives to that process, are reserved until later chapters.

▪ Before filing a case, an attorney considers what *remedies* might be available.

  ▪ Generally, *equitable* remedies are available only if *legal* remedies are somehow inadequate.

▪ Certain remedies may be available while the case is still pending.

  ▪ If necessary to preserve the status quo, a party may be able to obtain a *preliminary injunction* or *temporary restraining order*.

  ▪ In addition, a party may be able to have certain assets of the defendant *seized* during the case to ensure those assets remain available to satisfy a judgment.

▪ Modern litigation is expensive. *Attorneys' fees* comprise the lion's share of litigation costs. Under the so-called *American rule*, each party pays its own attorneys' fees. However, the default American rule is increasingly being replaced by statutes and rules authorizing fee-shifting.

I. REMEDIES

Generally speaking, a remedy is a statement by the court indicating one party's responsibilities toward the other. Remedies can be broadly divided into three main categories: *substitutionary, specific*, and *declaratory*.

A. Substitutionary remedies: A substitutionary remedy attempts to *replace* what plaintiff lost with something that is the rough equivalent. The most common substitutionary remedy is *damages*. However, there are different types of damages.

  1. Generally: Although there are significant differences between the various forms of substitutionary remedies, all share certain basic features.

    a. Nature of money judgment: A judgment awarding damages is *not an order to pay*. Failure to pay does not subject the judgment debtor to contempt of court. Instead, the judgment merely states that defendant is liable in that amount to plaintiff.

    b. Enforcement: If the judgment debtor does not pay, the judgment victor can use the judgment to *seize assets* of the judgment debtor.

      i. The assets are then *sold* at a sheriff's sale (or equivalent), and the proceeds used to satisfy the judgment.

      ii. However, the victor cannot reach all the debtor's property with a judgment. Every state provides that certain property is *exempt* from execution, either in whole or up to a certain dollar amount.

iii. A judgment creditor may also be able to obtain other assets of the judgment debtor. For example, it may be possible to **garnish** funds owed by a third party to the judgment debtor, such as **wages** or **bank accounts**. Garnishment of wages, however, is severely limited by federal law and many states' laws.

c. **Delay in enforcement:** In federal court, a party may neither execute on a judgment nor bring another proceeding to enforce it (such as garnishment), until **14 days** after entry. Fed. R. Civ. P. 62(a). This gives the judgment loser the chance to file a motion for a new trial or to lodge an appeal. The judgment loser may also obtain an order staying enforcement during the course of an appeal. However, in the latter case the party will usually be required to file a **supersedeas bond** to protect the judgment winner.

2. **Compensatory damages:** Compensatory damages are money intended to compensate the injured party for the harm it suffered. Because it is often impossible for a defendant to undo the injury, the court assigns a value to the injury and awards damages to plaintiff in that amount.

a. **Caveat:** *The substantive law limits the types of damages that can be recovered.* For example, tort plaintiffs often cannot recover purely economic loss. Similarly, a plaintiff suing for breach of contract cannot recover for emotional distress caused by the breach.

b. **No double recovery:** In addition, the court must be careful not to award a **double recovery**.

Example: In a case involving destruction of a machine, plaintiff is entitled to the market value of the machine, the transaction costs required to obtain a replacement, and any lost profit during the period between destruction and replacement. However, plaintiff is not entitled to receive the profits it would have earned from the machine after replacement because that would constitute a double recovery. Once the machine is replaced, plaintiff is able to earn those profits itself.

c. **Mitigation:** A plaintiff is usually required by the substantive law to take reasonable steps to mitigate her damages.

3. **Liquidated, statutory, and multiple damages:** In cases where it is difficult for a party to prove its injury, the party may be entitled to liquidated, statutory, or multiple damages.

a. **Liquidated damages:** Parties who enter into **contracts** often specify an amount as **liquidated damages**. As long as the amount specified is not clearly unreasonable, plaintiff need not prove actual injury but can recover the amount agreed upon by the parties.

b. **Statutory damages:** Similarly, statutes sometimes provide a *fixed amount* of *statutory damages* that a party may recover in case of a violation.

c. **Multiple damages:** Other statutes provide for **double or treble damages**.

4. **Punitive damages:** As the name implies, punitive damages are meant as a form of punishment. Thus, they are not compensatory or substitutionary in nature. There are constitutional limits on punitive damages.

a. **When available:** Punitive damages are usually available only in tort cases and only when defendant acted **intentionally** or **willfully**.

b. **Calculation:** Punitive damages are designed to **deter similar conduct in the future**. How large the punitive damages award must be in order to be an effective deterrent varies depending on defendant's wealth.

c. **Constitutional limits:** In recent years, the U.S. Supreme Court has imposed several important limits on punitive damages awards. These limits stem from the ***Due Process Clause*** of the Fourteenth Amendment, which prevents a state from depriving anyone of property without affording due process of law. "Property" includes money.

   i. **Limits on amount:** The Due Process Clause prevents ***grossly excessive*** punitive damages awards. Whether an award is grossly excessive turns on how maliciously or reprehensibly defendant acted, the type of harm suffered by plaintiff (merely economic versus personal injury), and a ***comparison of punitive damages with the actual damages*** suffered by the victim. If punitive damages are out of proportion, the award is excessive. State Farm Mutual Automobile Insurance Co. v. Campbell, 123 S. Ct. 1513 (2003).

   ii. **Limits on procedure:** A state must also ensure meaningful judicial review is available for a jury award of punitive damages. Honda Motor Co. v. Oberg, 512 U.S. 415 (1994).

   iii. **Limits on how damages calculated:** Juries cannot base a calculation of punitive damages on harm to *nonparty* victims. Phillip Morris USA v. Williams, 127 S. Ct. 1057 (2007).

B. **Specific remedies:** In the second major category of remedies, the court orders a party to act or refrain from acting in a certain way.

1. **Enforcement:** Unlike damages, a judgment awarding a specific remedy usually results in a ***court order***. Violation of that order may subject the party to ***contempt of court***.

2. **Types of specific remedies:** There is a wide array of specific remedies. The most common specific remedy is the ***injunction***. Other common specific remedies include specific performance, accounting, ejectment, mandamus, replevin, rescission of a contract, and restitution.

3. **Equity:** Most, but not all, specific remedies originated in equity and are today still considered equitable in nature.

   a. **Exceptions:** However, not all specific remedies are equitable. Examples of "legal" specific remedies are ejectment and replevin.

   b. **Nature of equitable remedies:** Historically, there were crucial differences between equitable and legal claims and remedies. Today, however, only two important differences remain.

      i. **Defenses:** A party seeking equitable relief is subject to various equitable defenses such as ***laches, estoppel***, and ***unclean hands***. These defenses usually do not apply in cases seeking legal relief.

      ii. **Hierarchy of remedies:** Historically, a party could obtain equitable relief only if she could show her ***legal relief was inadequate***. This standard ***remains in force***. However, courts today are more willing to find damages inadequate and, accordingly, to grant equitable relief.

      Example: In Lucy Webb Hayes Natl. Training School v. Geoghegan, 281 F. Supp. 116 (D.D.C. 1967), a hospital sued the husband of a patient, requesting an order requiring the husband to move his wife from the hospital. The court held that the legal remedy of damages was inadequate, as it would result in the wife staying in the hospital as long as the husband was willing to keep paying.

4. Injunctions: The most common specific remedy is the injunction.

   a. Types: Injunctions may be *mandatory* or *prohibitory* in nature. A mandatory injunction orders defendant to undertake certain acts; a prohibitory injunction orders defendant to refrain from certain acts.

   b. Factors considered: In addition to determining whether the legal remedy is adequate, a court considers the following in determining whether to grant an injunction:

   i. a *balance of the hardship* to defendant if the injunction were ordered and the hardship to plaintiff if the injunction were denied, and

   ii. the public interest.

   Example: In eBay Inc. v. MercExchange, L.L.C., 547 U.S. 388 (2006), the Supreme Court, rejecting considerable lower court precedent, held that the balancing and public interest analyses must be applied, even in actions under federal statutes like the patent laws.

C. Declaratory relief: The declaratory judgment is a unique remedy. It does not require the loser to pay money or take specific action. Instead, it merely states the rights of the parties.

Example: *P* has built a new factory and is ready to begin manufacturing a new and better mousetrap. However, *D* has a patent that covers mousetraps similar to the one *P* plans to manufacture. *P* fears that if she builds the trap, *D* will sue her for infringement. *P* may bring a suit asking for a declaration that her trap does not infringe *D*'s patent. If *P* prevails, *D* will be barred by claim preclusion (see Chapter 13) from suing *P* for making that particular trap.

1. Statutory source: 28 U.S.C. §2201 allows federal courts to grant declaratory judgments.

2. Special problems: Declaratory judgments present special problems with respect to federal question jurisdiction and jury trials. Those issues are discussed in Chapters 4 and 10, respectively.

II. PROVISIONAL REMEDIES

A court typically grants a remedy at the conclusion of the case. However, a party may sometimes obtain relief before the case is resolved. Because the merits of the case have yet to be considered, a party must make a strong case to be awarded a provisional remedy.

A. Nature: Provisional remedies are *always specific relief.* A plaintiff who seeks damages must wait until a final judgment, no matter how badly she needs the funds. (A court may compensate for this delay by adding an award for interest on the judgment.) In addition, provisional remedies are by nature *temporary.* Once the court considers the matter more fully, the provisional remedy will be replaced by any final remedy.

B. Primary types: The three primary provisional remedies are the *preliminary injunction*, the *temporary restraining order*, and the *pretrial attachment* of property for security.

1. Preliminary injunction: A preliminary injunction is an injunction granted during the pendency of a case. Its primary purpose is to *preserve the status quo* so that any final relief granted by the court can be effective.

a. **Standard:** The standard for a preliminary injunction is more rigorous than that for a final injunction. Courts typically require the party requesting a preliminary injunction to prove several things.

    i. **Likely to prevail:** The requesting party must prove it is likely to prevail on the merits of the case. Ordinarily the court holds a hearing where it considers the evidence and the legal merits of plaintiff's claim.

    ii. **Irreparable injury:** The requesting party must run the risk of suffering irreparable injury if relief were delayed until the end of the case. In essence, the party must show a strong need to issue the injunction *now*, instead of after the trial.

    iii. **Balance of the hardships:** The party must show it would be harmed more by denial of the preliminary injunction than the other party would be harmed by the injunction.

    iv. **Public interest:** The injunction must be in the public interest.

b. **Sliding scale:** A strong showing of one of these factors may compensate for a weak showing on one or more of the others.

    i. **Balance of hardships.** In cases where the balance of hardships (Part iii above) is *strongly in favor of the party requesting relief*, a number of courts modify Part i's analysis to allow a preliminary injunction as long as the party demonstrates there are *serious questions*; i.e., that the party has a "fair" chance of winning the case on the merits.

    ii. **Likelihood of prevailing.** Similarly, if a party is very likely to prevail, many courts do not require a strong showing of irreparable harm.

★   iii. **Need for evidence on all elements.** However, a party may still need to have some evidence on each of the four factors. Winter v. Natural Resource Defense Council, Inc., 555 U.S. 7 (2008).

c. **Bond:** The requesting party must usually file a bond as a condition to granting a preliminary injunction. The bond helps ensure that the enjoined party can recover any damages it may suffer as a result of a wrongfully issued preliminary injunction.

2. **Temporary restraining order:** Like a preliminary injunction, a temporary restraining order (TRO) is a form of *specific relief* granted early in the case. However, there are important differences between TROs and preliminary injunctions.

Note on terminology: The term *temporary restraining order* does not mean the same thing in all courts. Some courts use the terms *TRO* and *preliminary injunction* interchangeably. This discussion focuses on the definition used in the federal courts.

a. *Ex parte*: A TRO is typically issued *without notice to the other party*. In some cases, however, the party is given notice, but the court holds an immediate and relatively cursory hearing because of the urgency of the matter.

b. **Showing irreparable injury:** The irreparable injury requirement is much more rigorous for a TRO than it is for a preliminary injunction. The requesting party must show that he would suffer irreparable injury *if he had to take the time to use the regular preliminary injunction process*. Thus, a TRO is available only if the situation is so urgent that even the preliminary injunction process would fail to protect the requesting party.

    c. Limit on term: The TRO is an emergency order that is intended to preserve the status quo until a hearing can be held on a preliminary injunction. Therefore, its term is extremely limited. In federal court, a TRO cannot exceed *14 days* unless the court explicitly extends it. Fed. R. Civ. P. 65(b)(2).

  3. Pretrial attachment: A plaintiff typically must wait until he receives a final judgment before he may reach defendant's property. In certain situations, however, a plaintiff may have defendant's property seized at the outset of the case and held by the court.

    a. When available: The purpose of pretrial seizure is to prevent defendant from disposing of the property during the course of the case. Seizure can be very useful in a case where plaintiff asks for damages and is worried defendant will dispose of its nonexempt assets during the case.

    b. Limitations: Even though pretrial seizure is for a limited time (the duration of the case), it constitutes a "deprivation" of defendant's property within the meaning of the Fourteenth Amendment to the U.S. Constitution. Therefore, defendant is entitled to *due process of law*.

★   **i.** *Fuentes*: The Supreme Court's landmark decision in Fuentes v. Shevin, 407 U.S. 67 (1972), held the Due Process Clause limits pretrial seizures. In that case, the Court struck down a state law that allowed a creditor to repossess property sold on credit without prior notice to the debtor. The law allowed the creditor to file an application making only cursory allegations that he was entitled to the property. The sheriff would then seize the property. The debtor received no prior notice, either of the suit or the seizure. That the creditor was required to file a bond was not sufficient protection to satisfy the Due Process Clause.

      ii. Factors: However, pretrial seizure is not always unconstitutional. The Supreme Court's decision in Connecticut v. Doehr, 501 U.S. 1 (1991), held that a court must consider *three factors* in determining whether a state's pretrial attachment procedure is constitutional.

        (a) Strength of defendant's interest: This factor considers how strong a right defendant has in the property and how great an impact the deprivation would have on that interest.

        (b) Strength of plaintiff's interest: The court compares the parties' interests. Other things equal, if plaintiff has a *preexisting interest in the property*—such as a mortgage or security interest—the seizure is more likely to be upheld.

        (c) Risk of a wrongful deprivation: Finally, the court must consider whether the state's attachment process creates a high risk of erroneously depriving defendant of its property.

          1. Timing: A key element in this factor is *when the hearing will occur*. Even if no preseizure hearing is available, a *prompt postseizure hearing* may save the procedure.

          2. Strength of plaintiff's showing: Another important factor is *how strong a showing plaintiff must make to the court*. The procedure likely will be held invalid if plaintiff is required to make only conclusory statements.

          3. Who decides: Similarly, *who makes the decision* is an important issue. If the decision about whether to allow seizure is made by the clerk instead of a judge, it is much more likely the procedure will be held unconstitutional.

4. **Bond required:** Finally, the procedure should require plaintiff to file a bond to compensate defendant for any harm it suffers because of a wrongful seizure.

Quiz Yourself on
REMEDIES AND PROVISIONAL REMEDIES

56. Alpha sues Beta for breach of contract. The court enters judgment for Alpha, finding Beta liable for $30,000 in damages. After repeated requests, Beta refuses to pay. Alpha petitions to have Beta held in contempt of court. Will Alpha succeed? _____

57. During a frenzied poker game, Summers and Winters suspect Dan Dealer is dealing from the bottom of the deck. When their suspicions prove correct, Summers and Winters take Dealer "out back" and beat him up. Dealer responds by suing the two for battery. Because battery is an intentional tort, Dealer seeks both compensatory and punitive damages.

   The parties stipulate that Summers and Winters played an equal role in planning and carrying out the beating. However, the evidence also shows that Summers is five times as wealthy as Winters. The jury awards Dealer $5,000 in compensatory damages, plus punitive damages of $2,000 from Winters and $20,000 from Summers. Summers challenges the jury verdict, raising two arguments. First, he argues that punitive damages cannot exceed the amount of compensatory damages. Second, he contends that even if the $20,000 figure might be acceptable standing alone, it is unfair for him to be held liable for more punitive damages than Winters given that the parties played an equal role in the beating. Will the jury verdict stand? _____

58. Emma Employee is an engineer with HiTech, Inc., a company that produces cutting-edge electronics. When she took the job, Emma signed a confidentiality agreement that prevents her from disclosing certain company secrets.

   Because of her considerable talents, Emma is recruited by a number of other companies. She eventually takes a position with another firm in a different field. Worried that Emma will try to impress her new employer by revealing HiTech's secrets, HiTech asks for and receives a temporary restraining order that prevents Emma from taking her new job "until such time as the underlying issues in this dispute are resolved at a full trial."

   Emma objects to the long term of the order. She points out that it may take years for the case to reach trial, by which time her new employer will have rescinded its offer. At the very least, Emma argues, she should be entitled to appear at a hearing to challenge the need for pretrial relief. Is Emma likely to prevail on her objection? _____

Answers

56. The court will not hold Beta in contempt. Unlike a specific remedy, a money judgment is not an order, and is accordingly not punishable by contempt.

57. The jury verdict is proper. First, although punitive damages cannot be completely out of proportion to compensatory damages, the amount of compensatory damages is not an absolute ceiling on punitive damages. A 4:1 ratio is not excessive.

Second, that Summers is required to pay ten times more punitive damages than Winters for the same behavior is not grounds to challenge the verdict. Punitive damages are intended to have a deterrent effect. It clearly takes more to deter someone with considerable assets than it takes to deter a poorer person. Moreover, even though Summers is only five times as wealthy as Winters, the jury could conclude that a $10 penalty would have the same deterrent effect as a $1 penalty would have on the less well-to-do Winters.

58. Emma is almost certain to prevail on her objection. A temporary restraining order (TRO) is an emergency order issued without notice to the affected party. Because of this lack of notice, a TRO lasts only until such time as the parties can attend a hearing to debate whether the TRO should be converted to a preliminary injunction.

    Note, too, that if this action is in *federal* court, Fed. R. Civ. P. 65(b)(2) limits the term of the TRO to 14 days.

III. ATTORNEYS' FEES

Litigation is expensive. The costs required to conduct a case—filing fees, the costs of service, and copying charges—may prove substantial. However, *attorneys' fees* typically comprise the vast majority of litigation expenses.

A. **American rule:** The traditional "American rule" requires *each party to pay its own attorney*. Under the English rule in the United Kingdom, by contrast, the loser pays at least a portion of the victor's fees.

B. **Funding attorneys' fees:** Because many litigants cannot afford an attorney at an hourly rate, the legal system allows various methods of funding the high costs of litigation.

   1. **Insurance:** From defendant's perspective, insurance often helps solve the problem. A *liability insurance policy* requires the insurance company to pay not only for liability but also for the *costs of defense*. In many cases, the duty to pay for the attorney is more valuable than liability coverage.

   2. **Contingent fees:** The contingent fee arrangement allows plaintiffs who cannot otherwise afford an attorney to obtain representation.

      a. **Percentage of recovery:** Under a contingent fee arrangement, the lawyer's fee is a *percentage of any recovery*. Although the percentage varies from lawyer to lawyer and from case to case, it is usually in the range of 20 to 50 percent of the recovery. Attorneys commonly use a "sliding scale," under which the percentage is relatively low if the case is settled before filing or in the very early stages, and increases as the case goes through discovery and to trial and appeal.

      b. **Ethical issues:** An attorney may have an ethical obligation to advise a client of fee options, including the relative advantages and disadvantages of contingent fees.

   3. **Pro bono and public interest lawyers:** Individual attorneys may provide representation on a *pro bono* basis. Organizations such as Legal Aid also provide representation to low-income or otherwise disadvantaged litigants.

   4. **Litigation finance:** Banks are increasingly willing to loan money to plaintiffs or counsel to help fund litigation, and take repayment from the proceeds of the case.

C. **Fee-shifting:** Although the American rule is the default rule in U.S. courts, in practice there are many situations where a party's fees are paid by another party.

   1. **Contractual fee-shifting:** Contracts today often require the ***breaching party to pay*** the attorneys' fees of the other party. A few require the ***loser to pay*** the winner's fees, which may deter wrongful breach of contract claims.

   2. **Statutory fee-shifting:** When a legislature creates a cause of action, it often provides for payment of the winner's attorneys' fee. Such provisions are especially prevalent in civil rights statutes and other statutes that allow suit against government.

      a. **Limits:** Recovery is almost always limited to a "reasonable" fee.

★   b. **Prevailing party:** A fee-shifting statute that awards fees to a "prevailing party" applies only when a party obtains a court judgment in its favor. Thus, a plaintiff who *settles* may not use the statute to recover fees from defendant. Buckhannon Board and Care Home, Inc. v. West Virginia Department of Health and Human Resources, 532 U.S. 598 (2001).

      c. **Fed. R. Civ. P. 68 and settlements:** If a plaintiff rejects a formal settlement offer made by defendant, but at trial ultimately recovers less than the amount offered, Fed. R. Civ. P. 68 requires plaintiff to pay any costs incurred by defendant after the offer. In most cases, these costs do *not* include attorneys' fees. However, where plaintiff sues under a statute that shifts fees, costs under Fed. R. Civ. P. 68 do include ***plaintiff's attorneys' fees***. Marek v. Chesney, 473 U.S. 1 (1985). Therefore, plaintiff will be denied fees incurred after the date of the offer.

Quiz Yourself on
AN OVERVIEW OF LITIGATION

59. Chris and Pat live next to each other in the suburbs. When Pat announces she is going to start raising pot-bellied pigs, a popular pet, on her property, Chris sues Pat for nuisance. Chris asks the court both to enjoin Pat from operating a pig ranch and to compensate Chris for any decrease in property value that would result from being next to a pig ranch. Assuming Chris wins on the merits, will she be granted all the relief she requests? _____

60. Tenant leased an apartment from Landlord for two years. The apartment had a unique solar-powered water heater. Unfortunately, the water heater failed while Tenant was living in the apartment. Tenant repaired the water heater at his own expense. Because he had paid for the repairs, Tenant took the water heater with him when he moved out at the end of the lease.

    Claiming that all fixtures must remain in the apartment, Landlord demands that Tenant return the water heater. Tenant refuses. Landlord therefore sues Tenant. Because it is no longer possible to buy a solar water heater that is compatible with the apartment, Landlord asks the court to grant a mandatory injunction requiring Tenant to return the original water heater to Landlord. Assuming Landlord wins the case, is the court likely to grant an injunction? _____

61. Same facts as Problem 60, except assume Tenant has not yet moved out of the apartment. Tenant is preparing to take the water heater with him when he leaves. In fact, Tenant has paid an extra fee to the moving company for the additional trouble involved in moving the heater. However, Tenant is worried Landlord will sue him for taking Landlord's property. Tenant wants to enlist the aid of the court system

to confirm that he may take the water heater. Is there anything Tenant can do, other than taking the heater and subjecting himself to a suit by Landlord?   _____

62. Lender has just sued Borrower for failure to repay a loan. Because the loan is not secured by any collateral, Lender is worried whether she will get paid if she has to wait until trial. Therefore, she asks the court to issue an order to the sheriff to seize enough of Borrower's assets to repay the loan. The motion includes an affidavit in which Lender states she is "really worried" Borrower will not repay. In addition, Lender asks that the assets be seized without notice to Borrower, in case Borrower should attempt to hide the assets. Is the court likely to grant Lender's request?   _____

63. Donna operates a Burger Queen franchise in Walla Walla, Washington. When Burger Queen comes up with a new marketing campaign, Donna finds the scheme trite and refuses to display the marketing materials in her restaurant.

Burger Queen sues Donna in federal court for breach of the franchise contract, seeking $50,000 in damages. In addition, Burger Queen asks the court to require Donna to pay its attorneys' fees. A clause in the contract clearly requires the franchisee to pay for the franchisor's attorneys' fees in any action brought to enforce the franchise agreement. However, Burger Queen is not required to pay the franchisee's attorneys' fees if Burger Queen is sued for breach.

Donna objects to the request for attorneys' fees, arguing the contract provision violates the American rule that prevails in the U.S. courts. Is Burger Queen likely to recover its attorneys' fees?   _____

64. Same facts as Problem 63. Donna makes a formal written offer to settle the case for $10,000. Burger Queen rejects the offer, and the case proceeds to trial. At trial, Burger Queen wins a judgment of $5,000. Burger Queen then asks the court to award it the $9,000 in court costs it incurred in litigating the case. Is Burger Queen likely to recover these costs?   _____

Answers

59. Chris will be awarded either damages or an injunction, but not both. If Chris obtains an injunction, her property will not decrease in value. Therefore, an award of both an injunction and damages would constitute a double recovery.

60. Even if Landlord wins, she will not receive an injunction. An injunction is a form of equitable relief. To obtain equitable relief, Landlord must demonstrate the available legal remedies are insufficient. The legal remedy of damages may not be sufficient here because it is impossible to buy a new water heater. However, the legal remedy of replevin, which would require Tenant to return the property, provides exactly the relief Landlord seeks.

61. Tenant may be able to sue for a declaratory judgment. Tenant has a demonstrable fear of being sued in the future and needs a court's decision in order to determine whether to carry through with his planned course of action.

62. Lender's request will be denied. Prejudgment attachment of a defendant's assets complies with due process only if the seizing party has a significant interest in the property and takes steps to minimize the risk of a wrongful deprivation. Lender has no security interest or other legal interest in Borrower's property (the facts specify the loan is unsecured). Although this sort of preexisting interest is not absolutely necessary, without such an interest Lender must make a very strong showing that Borrower will dispose of the property before final judgment. Lender's affidavit comes nowhere close to meeting

this rigorous standard, because it does not assert any facts suggesting Borrower plans to dispose of the property.

Lender's request to have the attachment occur without notice to Borrower compounds the problem. Due process usually requires a hearing prior to the deprivation. Only if the party seeking seizure makes a very strong showing of potential harm will seizure without notice be upheld. Again, Lender has not come close to making such a showing.

63. If Burger Queen wins the case, it is likely to recover its attorneys' fees. The traditional rule that each party pays its attorney can be changed by mutual agreement, such as this contract. Nothing requires that the agreement be two-sided; a term like that in the hypothetical contract, where only the franchisee has to pay the franchisor's fees, is valid.

64. Burger Queen may recover some of its costs, but not all. Donna's offer qualifies as a settlement offer under Fed. R. Civ. P. 68. Burger Queen rejected the offer, but ultimately recovered less than Donna's offer. As a result, it is not entitled to recover any costs it incurred after the date of the offer.

Exam Tips on *AN OVERVIEW OF LITIGATION*

☞ There are important differences between ***legal*** and ***equitable*** remedies. Equitable relief is not available unless the legal remedy is inadequate. Thus, if an exam question asks whether a party is entitled to equitable relief, you should discuss whether damages or some other legal remedy would solve the problem.

   ☞ Unfortunately, the only way to know which remedies are legal and which are equitable is to learn them by rote.

☞ When calculating ***damages***, you need to draw on the knowledge acquired in your other substantive law courses. For example, although a party can recover expectation damages for breach of contract, she cannot recover punitive damages or damages for emotional distress.

   ☞ In addition, when calculating damages, always make sure a party is not getting compensated twice for essentially the same harm.

☞ ***Punitive damages*** are only available in exceptional cases, such as intentional torts. They are not available for breach of contract, even if the breach is purposeful.

☞ Recall that a court considering whether to grant an ***injunction*** considers not only the private interests of the parties but also the ***public interest***.

☞ When dealing with provisional remedies, be sure you understand the difference between a ***preliminary injunction*** and the more drastic ***temporary restraining order***.

☞ If a question involves ***pretrial attachment*** of a defendant's assets, make sure you address the due process limits on such attachment.

☞ ***Attorneys' fees***: Do not forget that although the American rule is the default rule, it can be—and often is—changed by statute or by agreement of the parties.

CHAPTER 7

PLEADING

ChapterScope

Pleading is the means by which parties advise the court and each other of the claims and defenses they plan to assert at trial. This chapter focuses on the pleading system used in the *federal courts*. Although the Federal Rules of Civil Procedure pleading rules have been adopted by many states, other states have significantly different systems.

- The two main pleadings in a case are the *complaint* and the *answer*.

  - The *complaint* is the paper filed by plaintiff that describes the underlying event and sets out the claim or claims for which plaintiff seeks to recover.

  - The *answer* contains a party's response to allegations made by another party. Under the Federal Rules of Civil Procedure, answers are filed not only in response to the complaint but also in response to counterclaims, cross-claims, and other claims for relief. In addition to admissions, denials, and defenses, an answer may also include a *counterclaim*.

- In some cases, a party may be required to respond to the answer with a *reply*.

- The Federal Rules of Civil Procedure also allow the parties to bring *motions*. A motion differs from a pleading in that it focuses narrowly on one or a few issues.

- **Stating a claim:** Under the Federal Rules of Civil Procedure, a complaint need not satisfy any magical litany in order to state a claim. For most claims, the Federal Rules of Civil Procedure simply require a *short and plain statement of the claim*. Although this was historically a very low threshold, recent Supreme Court cases seem to require more factual detail.

  - In addition, the rules require considerably more detail for certain issues such as *fraud*.

  - A party pleading a claim must also set out a *demand for relief*.

- **The answer:** The rules governing answers are somewhat more complicated than those governing complaints. Basically, an answering party can respond to a claim by *admitting* all or part of what the claimant says, *denying* what the claimant says, and/or alleging an *affirmative defense*.

  - A *denial* must directly respond to the allegations in the claim. Failing to deny an allegation in the claim or filing an ineffective denial is treated as an admission.

  - Logically, an *affirmative defense* concedes that the facts as presented by claimant are correct, but alleges additional facts that relieve the answering party from liability.

- Fed. R. Civ. P. 11 attempts to ensure truthful and good faith pleadings. Under this provision, the party or the party's attorney must *sign* all pleadings and motions. By signing, the person makes certain representations.

- Pleadings may be *amended*. Depending on the circumstances, the party seeking to amend may have to obtain *court permission*.

I. HISTORICAL DEVELOPMENT OF PLEADING

The law of pleading has changed significantly over the years. The history of pleading involves *three distinct stages*.

A. Common law pleading: The common law pleading system evolved in England over several centuries. This system was highly formulaic, fairly arcane, and contained traps for the unwary.

   1. Law, not facts: The common law pleading system focused on pleading legal theories, not the underlying facts. Pleadings comprised pro forma allegations, and provided very little factual information about the underlying dispute.

   2. Historical significance: Although common law pleading has been abandoned by all U.S. jurisdictions, it still affects modern pleading, albeit indirectly. The common law writs evolved into the modern common law causes of action. The nature of many tort, contract, and property claims was defined by the writs.

B. Code pleading: Code pleading, which is still in force in several states, represented a *fundamental change* from the basic notions underlying common law pleading.

   1. Purpose: Code pleading was built on the premise that the purpose of pleadings was to *give notice* to the other side of what the party was alleging.

   2. Facts, not law: Code pleading required the pleader to make "a statement of the *facts* constituting the cause of action, in *ordinary and concise language*." In fact, a complaint can be held insufficient in a Code pleading state if it states *legal conclusions* instead of simply setting out the facts leading to that conclusion.

C. Pleading under the Federal Rules of Civil Procedure: The remainder of this chapter discusses the third main category of pleading, which is the system provided in the Federal Rules of Civil Procedure. This system is often called *notice pleading*.

   1. Purpose: As with Code pleading, the purpose of pleading under the federal rules is to give other parties notice of what claims and defenses are being raised.

   2. Both facts and law: Unlike Code pleading, however, the Federal Rules of Civil Procedure do allow a party to make some legal conclusions. The pleading need only provide adequate notice of the underlying event and the claims or defenses arising from it.

II. FEDERAL RULES OF CIVIL PROCEDURE PLEADING—OVERVIEW

Under the common law pleading system, pleadings could continue through many stages. The Federal Rules of Civil Procedure reject this approach and allow only a limited number of pleadings. All other issues are raised by motion.

A. Pleadings allowed: *Fed. R. Civ. P. 7(a)* is quite specific concerning what pleadings are allowed.

   1. Pleadings between plaintiff and defendant: In a lawsuit involving one plaintiff and one defendant, *Fed R. Civ. P. 7(a)* allows only a *complaint*, one or more *answers*, and, if the court orders it, a *reply* to an answer.

    a. Complaint: The complaint is the document filed by plaintiff that specifies all claims he has against defendant.

    b. Answer: Defendant responds to the complaint by filing an answer. Defendant's answer responds to all of plaintiff's claims. Defendant may also file one or more counterclaims in the answer, in which case plaintiff must file its own answer to the counterclaim. Note, however, that a party responding to a claim may raise certain defenses by motion rather than in an answer.

    c. Reply: A reply is a response to another party's answer. However, a reply occurs only when the court orders it. Fed. R. Civ. P. 7(a)(7).

  2. Pleadings in cases involving additional parties: As Chapter 14 discusses, many cases involve additional parties. In these cases, *Fed. R. Civ. P. 7(a)* allows the parties to allege their claims and defenses in additional pleadings.

B. Form of pleadings: Fed. R. Civ. P. 10 requires pleadings to fit a basic format.

  1. Case information: Every pleading must contain a *caption* indicating the *name of the court*, the *title* of the action (which in the case of the complaint must include the names of all parties, but in subsequent pleadings need only state the first plaintiff and the first defendant), the *file number* assigned to the case, and a designation of the *type of pleading* involved.

  2. Disclosure statement: In cases involving nongovernmental corporations, Fed. R. Civ. P. 7.1(a) adds a disclosure requirement. The corporation's first pleading must include two copies of a disclosure statement revealing any parent corporation and any publicly held corporation that owns 10 percent or more of its stock.

  3. Separating allegations: *Fed. R. Civ. P. 10(b)* requires parties to divide their claims and defenses into separate paragraphs. However, Rule 10(b) is *rarely enforced* in actual practice. It is extremely unusual for a complaint or answer to be held defective because of a party's failure to divide material into separate paragraphs, counts, or defenses.

    a. Separate claims: Claims and defenses must be made in *numbered paragraphs*. The contents of each paragraph must be limited to a single set of circumstances.

    b. Separate transactions: If a party includes multiple claims based on separate transactions or occurrences, or separate defenses, each such claim or defense must be *stated separately*, at least if a separate statement would make the pleading clearer. Separate claims are usually referred to as Count I, Count II, and so on.

    c. Adoption by reference: Parties making multiple claims may avoid repeating the same facts for each claim by adopting allegations of a prior paragraph by reference. Fed. R. Civ. P. 10(c).

  4. Exhibits: *Fed. R. Civ. P. 10(c)* allows a party to attach written documents, such as contracts, as exhibits to the pleadings.

C. Motions: All requests to the court other than pleadings are made by motion.

  1. Requirements: *Fed. R. Civ. P. 7(b)* sets out certain requirements concerning motions. A motion:

    a. Must be *in writing* unless it is made during a hearing or at trial,

    b. Must *state with particularity* the grounds on which it is based,

    c. Must state *the relief sought,* and

    d. Must be *signed* in accordance with Rule 11 or, for discovery motions, Rule 26(g).

  2. Hearing: The court typically will hold a *hearing* on the motion as soon as it is feasible.

III. FEDERAL PLEADING—CLAIMS FOR RELIEF

Although the rules significantly relax the technical requirements for stating claims, *Fed. R. Civ. P. 8 and 9* nevertheless establish certain standards.

A. Applies to all claims: The rules discussed in this section apply not only to plaintiff's complaint but also to *counterclaims, cross-claims,* and *third-party claims*. However, courts are split as to whether the same standard applies to *affirmative defenses*. To simplify matters, the following discussion is phrased only in terms of plaintiff's complaint. All references to the *plaintiff* and to the *complaint* should be read to apply equally to counterclaims, cross-claims, and third-party claims.

B. Contents of complaint: A complaint contains three basic components (Fed. R. Civ. P. 8(a)):

  1. a short and plain statement of the *basis for subject matter jurisdiction,*

  2. a short and plain statement of the plaintiff's *claim*, and

  3. a demand for judgment setting out the *relief* plaintiff seeks.

C. Jurisdiction: Plaintiff must allege the basis for the court's jurisdiction over all claims.

  1. Federal question: If jurisdiction is based on a federal question, the complaint typically cites the federal statute or constitutional provision involved.

  2. Diversity of citizenship: If jurisdiction is based on diversity of citizenship, the complaint will state the citizenship of the parties and specify that the amount in controversy exceeds $75,000.

  3. Supplemental jurisdiction: If jurisdiction is based on supplemental jurisdiction, the complaint should indicate the claim in the suit to which the claim in question is supplemental and specify that the claim in question forms part of the same Article III case as that other claim.

D. Statement of the claim: The "short and plain statement" standard of Fed. R. Civ. P. 8(a) is not difficult to satisfy in most cases.

  1. Basic standard: A claim is sufficient as long as it provides defendant *adequate notice* of plaintiff's claims and of the basic situation or situations from which those claims arise.

  Note on Federal Forms: For many years, the federal rules contained an appendix of Forms. A pleading that complied with the relevant Form was deemed per se sufficient. However, the Supreme Court abolished the Forms in 2015, possibly because some did not comply with the recent Supreme Court cases discussed in this section.

  2. Pleadings construed to do justice: *Fed. R. Civ. P. 8(d) and (e)* reinforce this principle. Rule 8(d)(1) provides that all averments shall be "simple, concise, and direct." Rule 8(e) provides that all pleadings are to be construed "as to do *justice*."

  3. Legal conclusions: The pleading may include legal conclusions, such as "the parties entered into a contract." On the other hand, plaintiff may be required to indicate that it has facts to support its legal conclusions.

★   **Example 1:** The Supreme Court's decision in Bell Atlantic Corp. v. Twombly, 550 U.S. 544 (2007), indicates how the Court is increasingly requiring plaintiffs to include some facts in the complaint. Plaintiffs in that case sued for an antitrust violation. Their complaint stated that "on information and belief" defendants had entered into a contract or conspiracy in restraint of trade. The Court held the complaint insufficient under Fed. R. Civ. P. 8. The Court held that in order to be sufficient, the complaint must include "enough factual matter (taken as true) to suggest that an agreement was made."

★   **Example 2:** The Court's 2009 decision in Ashcroft v. Iqbal, 556 U.S. 662 (2009) elaborates on this standard. That case involved an action against federal government officials, alleging they were behind plaintiff's torture. The Court held plaintiff had alleged no facts that made it plausible to conclude that the defendants had actually intended to subject the plaintiff to torture. After *Iqbal*, it appears that parties pleading a claim must include sufficient facts to allow the court to infer plaintiff's claim is ***plausible***.

4. **Legal theories:** A plaintiff need not explicitly state the legal theory on which she relies. As long as plaintiff states sufficient facts, she can later argue any legal theory that provides a cause of action under those facts. Therefore, for example, if plaintiff alleges defendant was driving with his eyes closed, those facts would state a claim for negligence.

5. **Interplay between pleading and discovery:** One key feature of the Federal Rules of Civil Procedure is the interplay between pleading and discovery. Information missing from the complaint—such as how defendant was negligent or the full injuries suffered by plaintiff—can be fleshed out in the process of ***discovery***.

6. **Inconsistency:** A party may assert alternative, or even inconsistent, grounds for relief. Fed. R. Civ. P. 8(d)(3).

E. **Elevated pleading standards:** Although the short and plain statement standard applies to the vast majority of claims, the Federal Rules of Civil Procedure require greater specificity for certain issues.

1. **Fraud and mistake:** A party asserting fraud or mistake must state the ***circumstances*** constituting fraud or mistake ***with particularity***. Fed. R. Civ. P. 9(b). Note that this elevated standard applies not only to claims, but to any allegation of fraud, including those in the answer.

   a. **General allegation insufficient:** Therefore, a general allegation that defendant "fraudulently" caused plaintiff to sign the contract is not sufficient. Plaintiff needs to describe in detail the representations made by defendant, when they were made, and how they were incorrect.

★   **Example:** Stradford v. Zurich Insurance Co., 2002 WL 31027517 (S.D.N.Y. 2002), demonstrates how the higher standard of Fed. R. Civ. P. 9(b) applies. The court held the fraud claim in that case insufficient because it did not specify the content of the allegedly fraudulent statement.

   b. **Other issues in case:** Other issues in a fraud or mistake case, namely ***malice***, ***intent***, ***knowledge***, and any ***other conditions of mind***, are ***not subject to the higher standard***, but may be alleged generally like other matters under Fed. R. Civ. P. 8(a).

2. **Special damages:** A party who claims any items of special damage must state those items specifically. Fed. R. Civ. P. 9(g). The concept of special damages applies to two situations. The first where claimant has an injury that would not be reasonably expected. If a party seeks to

introduce evidence on any such special injuries at trial, it needs to allege the injuries specifically in the claim. Second, some claims—particularly those involving defamation—include special damages as an element of the claim. In this latter situation, special damages can be thought of as "actual" damages.

3. **Other issues:** Although courts sometimes apply heightened pleading standards for other issues, the Supreme Court in Leatherman v. Tarrant County Narcotics Intelligence & Coordination Unit, 507 U.S. 163 (1993), held that courts may not apply a heightened standard to a civil rights claim against a municipality, as such claims are not mentioned in Fed. R. Civ. P. 9.

F. **Pleading special matters:** While Fed. R. Civ. P. 9(b) and (g) raise the bar on fraud, mistake, and special damages, other provisions of Rule 9 simplify pleading of other matters.

   1. **Capacity and authority:** A claimant does not need to allege that it has the capacity and authority to sue or that defendant has the capacity and authority to be sued. Fed. R. Civ. P. 9(a)(1)(A) and (B). Note, however, where a party is suing or being sued in a *representative* capacity, the pleading may need to discuss capacity to assert *jurisdiction*.

   2. **Conditions precedent:** When a claim turns on the satisfaction of one or more conditions precedent, plaintiff may allege generally that all conditions have been met. Fed. R. Civ. P. 9(c).

   3. **Official documents and acts:** If plaintiff's claim turns on an official document or act, she need only allege that the document was issued or the act performed legally. Fed. R. Civ. P. 9(d).

   4. **Judgment of other court:** If plaintiff invokes a judgment rendered by another court, he need not allege that the rendering court had jurisdiction. Fed. R. Civ. P. 9(e).

G. **Prayer for relief:** Fed. R. Civ. P. 8(a)'s third requirement is "a demand for the relief sought, which may include relief in the alternative or different types of relief." Thus, plaintiff *must specify the remedy* he would like the court to grant.

   1. **Different types allowed:** A plaintiff may seek several different types of relief, even on a single claim. The rule even allows plaintiff to seek *alternate and inconsistent forms of relief.* For example, a plaintiff who claims a defendant fraudulently induced her to enter a contract could ask the court to rescind the contract or, in the alternative, to reform it to correspond to the parties' true agreement.

   2. **Prayer nonbinding:** Even though the Federal Rules of Civil Procedure require a demand for relief, the *court is not limited to the demand* when it determines the actual relief to which plaintiff is entitled. Fed. R. Civ. P. 54(c). A court may even grant damages in excess of that sought by a plaintiff. The only exception is a default judgment, where the demand for relief does constrain the court. Fed. R. Civ. P. 54(c).

Quiz Yourself on
THE COMPLAINT

65. Captain's prize possession is his luxurious 60-foot yacht. One day, Captain arrives at the marina just in time to see Tennille sailing away in the yacht. Captain wants to sue Tennille for conversion in a federal district court, relying on diversity jurisdiction. However, Captain is unsure whether diversity jurisdiction exists. May Captain file a complaint that says nothing about diversity, thereby putting the burden on Tennille to raise lack of jurisdiction in her answer? _____

66. Same facts as Problem 65. Captain files a complaint in federal district court. His complaint alleges diversity jurisdiction exists. The remainder of his complaint is short and to the point, stating merely:

> 2. On August 9, 2016, defendant Tennille converted to defendant's own use property owned by plaintiff. The property converted consists of a 2002 model year Nautilus 60-foot yacht.

> 3. The property is worth $100,000.

> Wherefore, plaintiff demands judgment against defendant in the sum of $200,000 in compensatory and punitive damages, interest, and costs.

Tennille brings the proper motion to challenge the complaint. Tennille accurately points out that conversion is an intentional tort. Tennille accordingly alleges that Captain's complaint is insufficient because it says nothing about Tennille's intent. Is the complaint sufficient? _____

67. Same facts as Problems 65 and 66, except assume the complaint set out in Problem 66 is sufficient to state a claim for conversion. At trial, Captain plans to introduce evidence not only concerning the value of the yacht but also showing that Captain lost his job as a nightclub singer at a club on a nearby island because he had no means of transport. As the complaint is currently worded, will Captain face any difficulties introducing that evidence? _____

68. Same facts as Problems 65 and 66, except Captain also includes the following paragraph in his complaint:

> 4. In the alternative, defendant Tennille breached an oral lease between plaintiff and defendant, dated on or about January 1, 2016, in which defendant agreed to pay plaintiff $20,000 within three weeks following every occasion on which she used the yacht.

Tennille files the proper motion to contest paragraph 4. She correctly points out that the paragraph sets out a new and different cause of action, which should be labeled as a second count. Tennille argues the complaint is defective because it fails to distinguish the separate counts. Is she likely to prevail on this argument? _____

69. Same as Problems 65, 66, and 68, except instead of challenging the complaint for failure to divide the allegations into counts, Tennille argues the complaint is deficient because of a fatal inconsistency. Tennille correctly points out that the second and fourth paragraphs are logically inconsistent: If she could take the boat provided she paid for it later, she could not have committed conversion. Is the complaint deficient because of this inconsistency? _____

70. Borrower sues Lender in federal court for breach of a commitment to make a real estate loan. Borrower attaches a copy of the commitment contract to the complaint. This contract explicitly states that Lender was not obligated to make the loan until after Buyer produced a title opinion letter stating the property was free of all liens. In his complaint, however, Borrower alleges only that "all conditions precedent set out in the contract are satisfied." Lender challenges the complaint, arguing that Borrower needs to describe the condition and to state how it was met. Is Lender correct? _____

Answers

65. No. A complaint in a federal action must specify the basis for subject matter jurisdiction. Fed. R. Civ. P. 8(a)(1).

66. Although cursory, the complaint is sufficient. It provides defendant notice of the claim against her, and the underlying facts.

67. Tennille could successfully object to the evidence about the lost gig. This harm is an example of special damages, which Fed. R. Civ. P. 9(g) requires Captain to plead specifically. By failing to plead such damages specifically, Captain may be barred from proving them at trial.

68. Tennille is not likely to prevail. Although the rules do specify that separate legal claims should be set out as separate counts, courts rarely force parties to comply.

69. The inconsistency does not make the complaint improper. Fed. R. Civ. P. 8(d)(3) explicitly allows a party to allege inconsistent theories.

70. Lender is not correct. Fed. R. Civ. P. 9(c) provides it is sufficient for a complaint to state simply that all conditions precedent are satisfied. If Lender thinks the condition is not satisfied, it is Lender's responsibility to raise that issue in the answer.

IV. FEDERAL PLEADING—DEFENDANT'S RESPONSE TO THE COMPLAINT

A party responds to a claim in two basic ways. The ***answer*** is the party's required response, in which the party deals with all allegations in the claim. However, before filing the answer, the party may make one or more ***motions*** challenging specific issues. Answers and motions may be filed not only by defendant but also by other parties in responses to counterclaims, cross-claims, and the like.

A. Pre-answer motions: Defendant may raise certain procedural issues by motion.

    1. General considerations concerning pre-answer motions: *Fed. R. Civ. P. 7(b)(1)* provides that a party seeking any form of relief from a court may request that relief by motion.

        a. Examples: Thus, if defendant wishes to ***challenge the judge*** because of bias or to have the case ***transferred to a different venue*** under 28 U.S.C. §1404, she would make the request by motion, which might occur either before or after the answer.

        b. Motion as alternative to answer: In addition, however, ***Fed. R. Civ. P. 12*** allows a defendant to raise certain ***defenses and objections***—matters usually raised in the answer—in a pre-answer motion. Rule 12(b) allows defendant to move for ***dismissal*** of the case, while Rules 12(e) and (f) ask plaintiff to ***correct*** deficiencies in the complaint.

        c. Multiple defenses and objections allowed: The rule also allows defendant to include all defenses and objections in a single motion.

    2. Rule 12(b) defenses: Fed. R. Civ. P. 12(b) allows defendant to make certain listed defenses by motion. These motions are often referred to by their Rule 12 notation; e.g., a motion to dismiss a complaint for failure to state a claim is often called simply a Rule 12(b)(6) motion. Rule 12(b) allows the following to be raised by motion:

   a. lack of *subject matter jurisdiction* (Fed. R. Civ. P. 12(b)(1)),

   b. lack of *personal jurisdiction* (Fed. R. Civ. P. 12(b)(2)),

   c. improper *venue* (Fed. R. Civ. P. 12(b)(3)),

   d. insufficient *process* (Fed. R. Civ. P. 12(b)(4)),

   e. insufficient *service* of process (Fed. R. Civ. P. 12(b)(5)),

   f. *failure to state a claim* upon which relief can be granted (Fed. R. Civ. P. 12(b)(6)), and

   g. *failure to join a party* as required by Rule 19 (Fed. R. Civ. P. 12(b)(7)).

3. The Rule 12(b)(6) defense: The substance of all the other Rule 12(b) defenses is covered elsewhere. Only the Fed. R. Civ. P. 12(b)(6) motion presents considerations unique to this chapter.

   a. Standard: When considering a Fed. R. Civ. P. 12(b)(6) motion, the court determines if the complaint, on its face, "fails to state a claim upon which relief may be granted."

   b. When complaint "fails to state a claim": A complaint can be defective in two basic ways.

★

      i. Facts: First, plaintiff may have left out allegations concerning one crucial element of a given claim. Given the "notice pleading" approach of Fed. R. Civ. P. 8(a), however, these cases are relatively rare. In addition, a complaint can be defective if it does not contain "enough facts to state a claim to relief that is plausible on its face." Bell Atlantic Corp. v. Twombly, 550 U.S. 544 (2007). The plausibility standard applies mainly to factual conclusions in the complaint.

★

      ii. Law: In the alternative, plaintiff may have fully set out the facts, but those facts do not allow plaintiff to recover under any legal theory. For example, in Haddle v. Garrison, unpublished, Docket No. 96-00029-CV-1 (S.D. Ga. 1996), the trial court granted defendant's Fed. R. Civ. P. 12(b)(6) motion because under the facts alleged in the complaint, the law would not allow plaintiff to recover. When the case was appealed to the U.S. Supreme Court, however, the Court held that a cause of action would exist under federal civil rights laws. As a result, the Court reversed and held the complaint stated a claim. Haddle v. Garrison, 525 U.S. 121 (1998).

   c. Conversion to summary judgment: If a Fed. R. Civ. P. 12(b)(6) motion includes facts not set forth in the pleadings, the court treats the motion as one for *summary judgment*. Fed. R. Civ. P. 12(d); see Chapter 9, Part VII.

   d. Effect of granting a Rule 12(b)(6) motion: Before dismissing, a court will ordinarily grant plaintiff *leave to amend* the complaint to allow it to cure the defect. However, in federal court, a Rule 12(b)(6) dismissal for failure to state a claim is a dismissal *on the merits* unless the court specifies otherwise. Fed. R. Civ. P. 41(b); Federated Department Stores v. Moitie, 452 U.S. 394, 399 n. 3 (1981).

      i. A dismissal on the merits prevents plaintiff from bringing any claim against the same defendant based on the same underlying set of facts.

      ii. Some states do not treat a dismissal for failure to state a claim as a dismissal on the merits, even if the state rules otherwise mirror the federal rules.

4. Other challenges to ambiguous or objectionable complaints: Other provisions in Fed. R. Civ. P. 12 allow defendant to challenge a complaint because it is ambiguous or includes objectionable material.

a. Rule 12(e) motion for a more definite statement: If a party is served with a *pleading to which a responsive pleading is allowed*, but that pleading is so *vague or ambiguous* that the party cannot reasonably prepare a response, the party may move for an order requiring the pleader to provide additional information or clear up the ambiguity.

   i. Must be specific: The motion must specify the vague or ambiguous portions of the pleading.

   ii. Rarely used: In practice, *parties rarely use Fed. R. Civ. P. 12(e)*. If a claim is truly too vague to allow the party to frame an answer, the party usually simply moves to dismiss under Rule 12(b)(6) for *failure to state a claim*.

b. Rule 12(f) motion to strike: Fed. R. Civ. P. 12(f) allows a party to move to strike portions of a pleading that are *redundant, immaterial, impertinent*, or *scandalous*.

   i. Timing: The motion must be made *before the movant files a responsive pleading* or, if no responsive pleading is allowed, within *21 days* of service of the pleading.

   ii. Redundant or superfluous material: Courts *rarely grant* a Rule 12(f) motion merely because a pleading contains some redundant or superfluous material. However, if the party served with the pleading faces a *considerable burden* responding to the immaterial information, the court may order the extra material to be stricken.

   iii. Dismissing portions of complaint: Fed. R. Civ. P. 12(f) may also be used to dismiss some, but not all, of the counts in a complaint. A few courts do not allow a Rule 12(b)(6) motion to be used in these situations. In these courts, the Rule 12(f) motion can be used to strike the improper counts.

   Example: *P* sues *D* for unfair competition and negligent infliction of emotional distress. Although governing law recognizes unfair competition, it does not recognize negligent infliction. Depending on the court's practice, *it may dismiss* the negligent infliction claim either under Rule 12(b)(6) or Rule 12(f).

   iv. Scandalous allegations: With respect to scandalous allegations, courts strike only when the scandalous allegation is of *marginal or no relevance* or when the allegations are worded in a particularly *inflammatory way*.

5. Timing of pre-answer motions and waiver of defenses: *Fed. R. Civ. P. 12(g)* and *12(h)* set out strict time deadlines governing when the Federal Rule 12 defenses and objections must be raised. A party must raise certain matters no later than the answer, and even earlier in some cases. Defenses and objections not raised in time are *waived*.

a. If pre-answer motion filed: *Fed. R. Civ. P. 12(g)(1)* allows a party who raises a Rule 12 defense or objection by pre-answer motion to *join all Rule 12 defenses* and objections available to that party.

   i. However, if a party raises any Rule 12 defense or objection by pre-answer motion but *omits* a defense of *lack of personal jurisdiction, improper venue, insufficiency of process*, or *insufficiency of service of process*, the party *waives* the omitted defense. *Fed. R. Civ. P. 12(h)(1)(A)*.

(a) ***Fed. R. Civ. P. 12(g)(2)*** precludes the party from raising the matter by a ***second pre-answer motion***.

(b) **Rule 12 objections:** Note that a pre-answer motion can result in a waiver under Fed. R. Civ. P. 12(g) and (h) if it raises a defense or objection listed in ***any subsection of Fed. R. Civ. P. 12***, not only the items listed in Fed. R. Civ. P. 12(b). Therefore, for example, a defendant who files a pre-answer motion to strike (Fed. R. Civ. P. 12(f)) must include any defenses based on personal jurisdiction, venue, and service, or those defenses are lost.

(c) **Non-Rule 12 objections:** However, there are also objections that a party may make prior to the answer that do not involve Fed. R. Civ. P. 12. For example, a party need not include the Rule 12(b)(2)-(5) defenses in a motion to disqualify a judge for bias. Similarly, while a motion to dismiss for lack of venue under Rule 12(b)(3) triggers the rule, a motion to *transfer* venue under 28 U.S.C. §1404 does not.

ii. This strict waiver rule ***does not apply to lack of subject matter jurisdiction, failure to state a claim***, and ***failure to join a party under Rule 19***. Similarly, there is no waiver of the Rule 12(e) and (f) motions for a more definite statement and to strike. Even if a party raises a pre-answer motion asserting a different Rule 12 defense, the party preserves these defenses and objections.

Example 1: Defendant files and serves a pre-answer motion to dismiss the case for lack of subject matter jurisdiction. The court denies the motion. Defendant now wants to raise ***insufficiency of service*** and ***failure to state a claim upon which relief can be granted*** in his answer. Defendant has lost the service defense by failing to include it in the pre-answer motion. Fed. R. Civ. P. 12(h)(1). However, he can still raise the failure to state a claim defense. Fed. R. Civ. P. 12(h)(2).

Example 2: Defendant files and serves a pre-answer motion to disqualify opposing counsel based on a conflict of interest. The court denies the motion. Defendant now wants to raise the defenses of ***insufficiency of service*** and ***failure to state a claim upon which relief can be granted***. Defendant can still raise both defenses, either by pre-answer motion or in the answer. Although she did file a pre-answer motion, that motion ***did not raise any Rule 12 defenses or objections*** and therefore is not a "motion under this rule" within the meaning of the first sentence of Fed. R. Civ. P. 12(g)(2).

b. **If no pre-answer motion:** If defendant does not file a pre-answer motion based on Rule 12, he must object to personal jurisdiction, venue, insufficiency of process, and insufficiency of service no later than the ***answer*** or in an ***amendment as of right to the answer***.

Example 1: *P* sues *D*. *D* files a pre-answer motion claiming that *P*'s complaint fails to state a claim on which relief can be granted. That request is denied. *D* then challenges personal jurisdiction in her answer. *D* will be deemed to have waived her personal jurisdiction challenge. Failure to include the defense in the pre-answer motion prevents defendant from raising the defense, either in the answer or by another motion. Fed. R. Civ. P. 12(g).

Example 2: *P* sues *D*. *D* brings no pre-answer motions. *D* files a timely answer but forgets to include the defense of lack of venue. The time period for amending the answer as of right (see Fed. R. Civ. P. 15(a)) has expired. *D* has waived his venue challenge. Fed. R. Civ. P. 12(h)(1).

B. The answer: Regardless of whether defendant files a pre-answer motion, defendant must also respond to the complaint by filing an answer (unless, of course, the court grants defendant's motion to dismiss). Unlike a motion, the answer must deal with all plaintiff's allegations. The answer may include claims against plaintiff or other defendants.

1. **Rules not limited to defendant:** The rules discussed in this section apply not only to defendant's answer to the complaint but also to the answers filed by various parties to a counterclaim, cross-claim, or third-party claim. However, to simplify matters, the following discussion is phrased only in terms of defendant's answer. All references to the *defendant* and to the *answer* should be read to apply equally to answers filed by these other parties.

2. **Time for filing the answer:** *Fed. R. Civ. P. 12(a)* requires defendant to file an answer within a certain time period. The period varies depending on the defendant and whether plaintiff asked defendant to waive service.

   a. **Default rule—21 days:** In most cases, defendant must *serve* its answer within *21 days* of the date she was served with the summons and complaint. Fed. R. Civ. P. 12(a)(1)(A)(i).

   b. **Effect of waiver of service:** However, a defendant who agrees to plaintiff's request to *waive service* has more time to respond. If the request was sent to defendant *in the United States*, a defendant who waives service has *60 days* following the date the request was sent to answer. This period is extended to *90 days* if the request was sent to defendant *outside the United States*. Fed. R. Civ. P. 12(a)(1)(A)(ii).

   c. **United States as defendant:** The United States, a federal agency, or a federal officer or employee, has *60 days* to answer. Fed. R. Civ. P. 12(a)(2). The 60-day rule also applies to federal officers sued in an *individual capacity* in connection with duties performed on behalf of the federal government. Fed. R. Civ. P. 12(a)(3). The waiver of service rules do not apply to the United States, so there is no extension of this time period as there is in the case of other defendants.

   d. **Effect of motions:** If a party files a *pre-answer motion under Fed. R. Civ. P. 12*, the time to answer is extended.

      i. In most cases, defendant is required to answer within *14 days* after the party receives notice of the *court's denial* of the motion. Fed. R. Civ. P. 12(a)(4)(A). Of course, if the court *grants* a motion to *dismiss* the entire action, defendant is not required to file an answer.

      ii. If the court grants a motion for a more definite statement, the answer must be filed within *14 days* of the date the *more definite statement is served*. Fed. R. Civ. P. 12(a)(4)(B).

3. **Denials and admissions:** The basic rule dealing with how defendant responds to the allegations of plaintiff's complaint is *Fed. R. Civ. P. 8(b)*. This rule requires defendant to "*admit or deny* the allegations asserted against it."

   a. **Effect of failure to deny:** The consequences of failing to deny something in the complaint can be quite severe. Pursuant to Fed. R. Civ. P. 8(b)(6), *failure to deny an allegation* made in a pleading constitutes an *admission* of the matter in question.

      i. **Responsive pleading required:** Failure to deny operates as an admission only when *a responsive pleading is required*. If no responsive pleading is required to a particular pleading, all averments in that pleading are automatically ***deemed denied***. Fed. R. Civ. P. 8(b)(6). For example, if defendant includes an affirmative defense such as statute of frauds, and plaintiff is not required to respond to defendant's answer, plaintiff will automatically be deemed to deny the statute of frauds defense.

    ii. **Exception:** Defendant is not required to deny averments relating to the ***amount of damages***. Thus, a defendant can contest the amount of damages at trial even if it did not deny the damages demand in its answer.

b. **Lack of knowledge:** All averments in a pleading must be made in good faith and be grounded in fact. Thus, Fed. R. Civ. P. 8(b) could pose a problem for a defendant who does not have enough information to deny in good faith something alleged in the complaint. If defendant fails to deny, it might be deemed to admit the matter. ***Rule 8(b)(5)*** avoids this problem by allowing a defendant to plead that it "***lacks knowledge or information sufficient to form a belief about the truth of an allegation.***"

    i. **Specificity required:** Defendant must specifically state it lacks knowledge or information about the particular allegation.

    ii. **Effect:** A response alleging lack of information is ***treated as a denial***. Thus, the issue remains in controversy for purposes of discovery and trial.

    iii. **Information and belief:** A variation on this theme is a ***denial based on information and belief***: In this situation, defendant strongly suspects something but does not have first-hand knowledge. Like the denial based on lack of information, it operates as a denial.

        (a) The denial based on information and belief is ***not explicitly authorized*** by the Federal Rules of Civil Procedure. Instead, it is a vestige of prior practice that still lingers on today.

        (b) In truth, there is no longer any need for a denial based on information and belief. If a party has a good faith belief that an averment is false, it may deny the matter outright consistent with the requirements of Rule 11 (discussed below in Part VII). If it does not have enough information to make a good faith denial, it can simply plead lack of information.

c. **Denials must meet substance of complaint:** All denials must "fairly respond to the substance of the allegation." Fed. R. Civ. P. 8(b)(2). A denial that fails to meet this standard is called an ***ineffective denial***. An ineffective denial is treated as a failure to deny and may accordingly constitute an ***admission*** of the matter in question under Fed. R. Civ. P. 8(b)(6).

    i. **Partial denials:** If defendant in good faith intends to deny only part of an averment, it must specify which portions it denies.

★

    Example: Paragraph 4 of plaintiff's complaint states simply that defendant "hit and kicked me." Defendant denies paragraph 4. In truth, defendant did kick plaintiff but did not hit plaintiff. Because the denial does not specify which portion of plaintiff's allegations are actually being denied, the ***denial is ineffective***. See Zielinski v. Philadelphia Piers, Inc., 139 F. Supp. 408 (E.D. Pa. 1956) (it is an ineffective denial for defendant simply to deny plaintiff's allegations that defendant "owned, operated, and controlled" a forklift when defendant owned the forklift, but did not operate and control it).

    ii. Objection permitted: The rules allow a party to *object* to the form of a denial. Fed. R. Civ. P. 12(h)(2).

    iii. Caveat: Fed. R. Civ. P. 8(e), which provides that pleadings should be ***construed to do justice***, applies to the answer as well as the complaint. Therefore, courts are not likely to treat an ineffective denial as an admission unless defendant intended to mislead plaintiff or unless plaintiff has irreversibly relied to its detriment on the misleading denial. In the prior example, most courts would allow defendant to amend the response.

  d. General denials: A general denial is when defendant denies ***every allegation of the entire complaint***.

    i. Rarely appropriate: Although the general denial was often used in the past, it is rarely proper in modern practice. For example, if the complaint correctly states plaintiff's residence, defendant cannot in good faith use a general denial, even if everything else in the complaint is false. Nevertheless, Fed. R. Civ. P. 8(b)(3) explicitly allows a defendant to make use of a general denial when she in good faith wants to controvert everything in the complaint, including plaintiff's allegations of jurisdiction.

    ii. General denial with exceptions: Although a true general denial is rare, parties sometimes file an answer in which they deny everything in the complaint *except* for certain items that they explicitly admit.

    iii. "Backup" general denial: In addition, defendants often include a general denial as a backup to their individual admissions or denials. Thus, after admitting certain matters and denying others, an answer typically closes with a statement such as "every other allegation in Plaintiff's complaint not specifically admitted or denied above is denied."

  e. Alternative and inconsistent denials: Just as a plaintiff may make inconsistent claims, a defendant may make alternative and inconsistent denials.

  Example: *P* sues *D* for breach of contract. In its answer, *D* first denies there is a contract between the parties. *D* then alleges that even if there is a contract, *D* did not breach. Although logically inconsistent, these alternative denials are acceptable.

4. Defenses: A defendant may also respond to the complaint by setting forth one or more defenses. A *defense* is a legal reason why plaintiff is not entitled to the relief it requests. Logically, defendant argues that even if the facts alleged by plaintiff are true, plaintiff cannot recover.

  a. Defenses and denials can be mixed: Answers often include both denials and defenses. Therefore, in a breach of contract case, a defendant could both deny that the parties ever entered into an agreement and, in the alternative, argue that the agreement was not enforceable because of the statute of frauds.

  b. Types of defenses: Conceptually, there are two basic categories of defenses.

    i. Ordinary defenses: An ordinary defense considers only the complaint and argues that plaintiff may not recover because of a procedural, legal, or pleading defect. All the ***Fed. R. Civ. P. 12(b) defenses*** fall in this category.

ii. **Affirmative defenses:** An affirmative defense usually involves the introduction of *new facts* that, when coupled with the facts alleged by plaintiff, prevent plaintiff from recovering.

   (a) **Types of affirmative defenses:** *Fed. R. Civ. P. 8(c)* contains a list of affirmative defenses.

   (b) **Additional affirmative defenses:** The list in Rule 8(c) is *not exclusive*. Thus, while *comparative negligence* is not listed in Fed. R. Civ. P. 8(c), it is treated as an affirmative defense.

★

   Example: The Supreme Court's decision in Jones v. Bock, 549 U.S. 199 (2007), applied this reasoning to a case involving exhaustion of administrative remedies. A federal statute required prisoners to exhaust administrative remedies before bringing a federal suit challenging prison conditions. Even though exhaustion is not listed in Fed. R. Civ. P. 8(c), the Court held it was an affirmative defense that should be raised by defendant, not an element of plaintiff's case.

   (c) **Plaintiff can supply facts for affirmative defense:** Although a defendant usually alleges new facts when pleading an affirmative defense, in some situations plaintiff itself will provide the necessary facts. Suppose, for example, plaintiff is suing defendant for a contract for the sale of goods with a purchase price of $800. Because the sales price exceeds $500, that contract falls within the statute of frauds. If plaintiff's complaint specifies the contract was *oral*, plaintiff in essence has supplied all of the facts necessary to allege defendant's affirmative defense.

c. **Rules do not "create" defenses:** Merely because a defense is listed in Fed. R. Civ. P. 8(c) does not mean it exists as a matter of substantive law. Many states, for example, have abandoned the defense of assumption of the risk. In an action in federal court governed by the law of one of these states, a defendant cannot invoke that defense.

d. **Burden of pleading:** If neither plaintiff nor defendant raises a particular issue in their pleadings, that issue usually cannot be litigated at trial (the main exceptions are subject matter jurisdiction and an issue raised at trial by one party without objection by the other). In that case, the party who does *not have the "burden of pleading"* on that issue automatically prevails on the issue.

   i. **Who has burden of pleading:** Determining which party has the burden of pleading an issue is sometimes fairly difficult.

   ii. **Rules 8(c) and 12(b):** Fed. R. Civ. P. 8(c) and 12(b) help resolve the burden of pleading issue for many common issues. By providing that certain issues are defenses, those rules clearly put the burden of pleading the issue on defendant. Thus, unless defendant pleads the affirmative defense of contributory negligence in the answer, defendant cannot argue the question at trial (except in the rare case discussed in 4.b.ii.(c) above where plaintiff provides the necessary facts).

   iii. **Court decides:** For issues not mentioned in those rules, the court must determine who bears the burden of pleading. Although there is no mechanical test used in these cases, courts consider several factors:

   (a) whether the *facts necessary to establish the defense* are more likely to be known by one party than the other;

(**b**) if the underlying claim arises under a statute, whether the ***language of the statute*** treats the issue as part of the claim or as an exception; and

(**c**) whether ***analogous issues*** are usually treated as elements or defenses.

    iv. **Burden of production distinguished:** The burden of pleading must be distinguished from the burden of production. The burden of production determines who must introduce evidence on that issue at trial. It is an issue in summary judgment and judgment as a matter of law. See Chapters 9 and 11.

C. Heightened pleading standards, special matters: Courts are split as to whether the plausibility standard of Fed. R. Civ. P. 8(a) applies to defenses. However, most agree the heightened pleading standards discussed in Part III.E and the special rules discussed in Part III.F apply equally to defenses and denials. For example, a defendant who wants to defend a breach of contract claim based on fraud must allege the ***circumstances*** constituting fraud with particularity. Fed. R. Civ. P. 9(b). With respect to capacity, Rule 9(a) specifies that the party ***challenging*** capacity must raise the issue by a ***specific denial***.

D. Counterclaims, cross-claims, and third-party claims: In addition to denials and defenses, defendant may also file claims against plaintiff or codefendants. A claim against plaintiff is called a ***counterclaim***, while a claim against a codefendant is called a ***cross-claim***. In addition, defendant may be able to ***implead*** additional parties to the action. The rules governing when counterclaims, cross-claims, and impleader claims are allowed are discussed in Chapter 14. The standards governing how a party states a claim in a counterclaim, cross-claim, and impleader claim are identical to the standards that apply to plaintiff's complaint.

Quiz Yourself on
RESPONDING TO THE COMPLAINT

71. Alpha sues Beta in federal court for breach of contract. Beta does not file a pre-answer motion. Beta's answer alleges that the chosen court does not have personal jurisdiction over her. Alpha argues Beta waived the jurisdiction defense by failing to raise it in a pre-answer motion. Did Beta waive the defense of lack of personal jurisdiction? _____

72. Same facts as Problem 71, except Beta does file a pre-answer motion to strike one paragraph in Alpha's complaint, alleging the paragraph is scandalous. The court grants the motion. Beta raises personal jurisdiction for the first time in her answer. Has Beta waived the defense of lack of personal jurisdiction? _____

73. Pedro sues Dante in federal court, alleging two separate claims. Pedro's first claim is for intentional infliction of emotional distress, based on Dante's breach of a contract between the two. Pedro's second claim is for fraud, based on certain other financial dealings between the two.

Dante is sure that Pedro cannot recover on either claim. Under applicable law, a party cannot recover for emotional distress arising from a breach of a contract. Although the law of the jurisdiction does recognize fraud claims, Pedro fails to plead the circumstances surrounding the fraud with sufficient particularity, as Fed. R. Civ. P. 9(b) requires. What motion or motions should Dante bring to challenge the complaint? _____

74. Client sues Attorney for malpractice. Client has the summons and complaint served on Attorney on Friday, December 4, 2015. Attorney files no pre-answer motions. When is Attorney's answer due? If, on the other hand, Attorney files a pre-answer motion, does the due date for the answer change? _____

75. Professor Jones sues Student Smith for defamation, based on an article in the school newspaper criticizing Jones's classroom teaching. This article was signed with Smith's name. In paragraph 3 of his complaint, Jones alleges, "An article written by defendant Smith appeared in the February 2016 version of *The Docket*, the law school's newspaper. This article defamed plaintiff by falsely alleging he was 'boring' and 'pompous.' These false allegations greatly harmed plaintiff's reputation."

In truth, it was another student, not Smith, who wrote the article. Smith rather enjoys Jones's classes. Although Smith did read the article, she has no idea whether the statements harmed Jones's reputation. Nevertheless, because paragraph 3 is false when read as a whole, Smith's answer states simply, "Defendant denies paragraph 3 of the complaint." Is this a proper way for Smith to deal with paragraph 3? _____

76. Same facts as Problem 75, except Smith deals with paragraph 3 of the complaint as follows: "Defendant denies she wrote the article referenced in paragraph 3. In the alternative, if defendant did write the article, defendant denies the statements in the article were false."

Jones argues that because the statements in Smith's answer are inconsistent, Smith's denial is ineffective. Will Jones prevail? _____

77. Lender sues Guarantor in federal court for breach of a contract in which Guarantor agreed to guarantee a loan from Lender to Borrower. Guarantor moves to dismiss for failure to state a claim. Guarantor correctly notes that under governing law, a guaranty contract must be in writing. Guarantor further notes that the complaint nowhere states the contract was in writing, nor did Lender attach a copy of the contract to the complaint. Will the court grant Guarantor's motion? _____

Answers

71. Beta did not waive the defense. Nothing requires Beta to bring a pre-answer motion. Because Beta did not file a pre-answer motion, she can raise personal jurisdiction for the first time in her answer. Fed. R. Civ. P. 12(h)(1)(B).

72. Now Beta has waived the defense. Note that Fed. R. Civ. P. 12(g) applies whenever a party files a pre-answer motion "under this rule" (Rule 12). A Rule 12(f) motion to strike, although not listed in Fed. R. Civ. P. 12(b), is a motion under Rule 12. By failing to include the personal jurisdiction defense in this motion, Beta has waived it. Fed. R. Civ. P. 12(g).

73. A single Fed. R. Civ. P. 12(b)(6) motion will take care of both claims. The defense of "failure to state a claim" applies both when a party states a claim that is not recognized at law (the emotional distress claim) and when the party's allegations do not meet the requirements of the pleading rules (the fraud claim). Note, however, that the court is likely to give Pedro leave to amend the fraud claim, assuming Pedro can allege facts sufficient to meet the heightened pleading standard.

74. Because the facts specify Attorney was "served" (as opposed to a request for waiver of service), Attorney has 21 days to answer. Fed. R. Civ. P. 12(a)(1)(A)(i). Under Fed. R. Civ. P. 6, this period includes intervening weekends and holidays. Therefore, the answer is due on Friday, December 25, 2015. However, because this date is the Christmas Day holiday, the due date is delayed until the next day the court is open, namely, Monday, December 28, 2015.

If Attorney files a pre-answer motion, the due date for the answer may be changed. If the court dismisses, the case is over and no answer is required. If the court denies the motion to dismiss, Attorney in most cases has 14 days from notice of the court's ruling. If the court requires a more definite statement, the answer is due 14 days after the more definite statement is served.

75. Smith's denial is ineffective because it fails to meet the substance of what was alleged. Smith should deny only the statement about authorship.

    In theory, an ineffective denial constitutes an admission. In a case like this, however, the court is very likely to allow her to amend her answer. If she did not write the article, she should not be forced to act as if she did for purposes of trial.

76. The answer is fine. Just as a plaintiff may plead in the alternative, a defendant may defend in the alternative.

77. The court will deny the motion. Guarantor is arguing the statute of frauds. Fed. R. Civ. P. 8(c)(1) explicitly indicates that statute of frauds is an affirmative defense. Therefore, the burden of pleading falls on Guarantor. Guarantor has the burden of pleading the contract was *not* in writing; Lender need not specify it was in writing.

V. AMENDMENTS TO THE PLEADINGS

Flexibility is the hallmark of federal pleading. That flexibility is also apparent in the rules allowing amendment. A pleading can be changed to cure a defect in the original, to incorporate new information acquired since the original, or to incorporate events that occurred after the pleading was filed. In some situations, however, the party must obtain permission to amend.

A. **When permission of the court is required:** *Fed. R. Civ. P. 15(a)* allows a party to amend its pleading *once* without obtaining court permission (which the rule calls "as a matter of course"), as long as the amendment occurs within certain time limits.

  1. **If responsive pleading required:** If the pleading is a *complaint, an answer with a counterclaim, a cross-claim,* or *a third-party complaint*, the party must amend within *21 days* following *service* of the earlier of (a) the responsive pleading, or (b) a Rule 12(b), (e), or (f) motion. Note this time limit is based on *actual service* of the responsive pleading or motion, not the deadline for service. Even though defendant is allowed 21 days to answer a complaint, defendants often answer before or (with the court's permission) after the 21-day deadline.

  2. **If no responsive pleading required:** For all other pleadings, the party must amend within *21 days after the pleading is served*.

  3. **Obtaining court permission:** If a party desires to amend after these deadlines or to amend a second time, she must obtain the other party's consent or permission of the court. However, Fed. R. Civ. P. 15(a)(2) indicates that leave to amend shall be freely given "when justice so requires." In practice, courts are extremely accommodating. Leave to amend is denied only if the other party can show *prejudice* by the amendment or the defect in the original pleading was the result of *inexcusable neglect or carelessness* on the part of the pleader.

★   **Example:** In Beeck v. Aquaslide 'N' Dive Corp., 562 F.2d 537 (8th Cir. 1977), defendant discovered several months into the case that it had not produced the slide that had harmed plaintiff. Defendant therefore asked to amend its answer to deny that it made the slide. By the time defendant made this discovery, the statute of limitations had expired, which meant plaintiff could not sue the actual manufacturer. Notwithstanding this hardship to plaintiff, the court allowed the amendment. Given that defendant had not acted in bad faith, the court held that only plaintiff should suffer from the parties' joint mistake concerning the identity of the manufacturer.

4. **Amending during or after trial:** A party may amend its pleadings during, or even after, trial, with the court's permission. ***Fed. R. Civ. P. 15(b)***.

B. **Relation back of amendments:** ***Fed. R. Civ. P. 15(c)*** allows some amendments to relate back to the date of the original pleading.

1. **Affects statute of limitations:** Relation back is important when a party wants to add new claims after the statute of limitations has expired. If the original pleading was timely, and the amended pleading adding the new claims relates back, the new claims may not be barred by the statute of limitations (unless the limitations period on the new claims is shorter).

2. **Relation back unrelated to need for court permission:** Whether an amendment relates back has ***nothing to do with whether the party needs to obtain the court's permission*** to amend. Fed. R. Civ. P. 15(a) and 15(c) are completely separate questions.

3. **When amendments adding claims relate back:** An amendment relates back when:

   a. the applicable statute of limitations allows amendments to relate back; or

   b. the claim or defense set out in the amended pleading arose out of the ***conduct, transaction, or occurrence*** set out in the original pleading.

4. **When amendments changing parties relate back:** A more demanding standard applies if the amendment changes the party against whom a claim is asserted or renames that party. An amendment changing or renaming the party relates back only if:

   a. the amended complaint meets the standard discussed just above in Fed. R. Civ. P. 15(c)(1)(B) for relation back of claims, and

   b. the party being brought in by amendment acquires ***sufficient notice*** about the existence of the lawsuit within the ***specified time***.

      i. **Formal notice of the lawsuit is not required:** "Notice" in this context is not the same as service. It is sufficient if the party learns of the action by word of mouth or other informal means.

      ii. **Sufficiency of notice:** Notice is sufficient if it is ***received early enough to prevent prejudice*** to the party in preparing its defense and if it ***contains enough information*** so that the party is aware or should be aware that he would have been named a defendant in the original action if a mistake had not been made as to that party's identity.

      iii. **Timeliness: The party must receive** notice before the Fed. R. Civ. P. 4(m) deadline for serving the summons and complaint. This deadline is typically ***120 days after the complaint is filed***, but may be extended by the court. Note that the time period turns on the ***deadline for service***, not when service is actually effected.

      Example: *P* and *D* are neighbors who share a common driveway between their houses. Late one evening, a large rental truck runs into *P*'s house while backing out of the driveway, causing extensive damage. *P* thinks he saw *D* driving the truck. *P* therefore sues *D* in a federal court. The complaint is filed and served 10 days before the statute of limitations expires on the claim.

Two months later, *D*'s twin sister calls *P*. In this conversation, the sister admits that she, not *D*, was driving the truck. The sister had just learned of the lawsuit from *D* and felt obligated to confess to *P*. The sister also admits she did not have a license to drive a truck of this size but that the rental company rented to her anyway.

Because *D* did not know her sister was driving the truck, *D* is not liable to *P* under governing law. Therefore, *P* immediately files and serves an amended complaint that substitutes *D*'s sister for *D* as defendant. Moreover, the complaint adds the truck rental company as an additional defendant, claiming the rental company is also liable for renting a truck to a person without the proper license. The rental company admits it knew of the accident on the day it happened and of *P*'s lawsuit on the day it was filed. The sister and the rental company both move for summary judgment, claiming that the limitations period has expired. *P*'s claim against the sister does relate back, but the claim against the rental company is barred by the statute of limitations. The sister received notice within 120 days following service, and it is clear she knew she should have been a defendant. Note that *P* need not show the sister was "hiding" her guilt; the amendment relates back even though the sister came forward. With respect to the rental company, however, the requirements of Fed. R. Civ. P. 15(c) are not satisfied. Even though the company knew of the lawsuit, there was no "mistake concerning the identity of the proper party." *P* knew, or could have determined, the name of the rental company prior to filing suit.

C. **Other changes to the pleadings:** Rule 15 also authorizes amendments to conform the pleadings to the evidence and supplemental pleadings.

1. **Amendments during and after trial to conform to the evidence:** During trial, if a party attempts to introduce evidence on matters outside the pleadings, the other parties may object. However, if a party fails to object, he is deemed to have ***impliedly consented*** to litigation of the issues raised in the evidence. In addition, a party may ***expressly consent*** to litigation of matters outside the pleadings.

   a. If a party consents, Fed. R. Civ. P. 15(b)(2) provides that any issues raised are treated as if they were raised in the pleadings, and allows a party to amend its pleadings to make them conform to the newly raised issues.

   b. Even if a party objects to the introduction of the evidence, the issue may end up forming part of the trial. Fed. R. Civ. P. 15(b)(1) provides that a court ***should freely permit an amendment*** to the pleadings at trial if it will help resolve the merits of the action, unless the late amendment would cause the other parties ***undue prejudice***.

2. **Supplemental pleadings:** A party may also be allowed to supplement its original pleadings to set forth new matters. Fed. R. Civ. P. 15(d).

   a. **Amendments distinguished:** Supplemental pleadings set forth facts that ***arise after the original pleading was filed***. Amended pleadings, in contrast, deal with facts that existed at the time of the original pleading.

   b. **Court permission:** Supplemental pleadings ***always require court permission***. However, leave to amend is freely given.

Quiz Yourself on
AMENDMENTS TO THE PLEADINGS

78. Reva, a stellar law student, is upset to learn that Jeff, the class entrepreneur, secretly copied her detailed Civil Procedure outline. After months of negotiating with Jeff prove fruitless, Reva sues Jeff in federal court for copyright infringement, asking for $5,000 in damages.

Three months after serving the complaint, Reva discovers that on the same day Jeff copied her Procedure outline, he also copied her Contracts outline. She wants to amend her complaint to add a second claim for copyright infringement. However, given that Jeff has not yet filed or served an answer, she is unsure how to amend. In addition, she is unsure whether the amendment will be effective. The statute of limitations on the infringement claims expired three weeks after the original complaint was filed.

How may Reva amend her complaint? Given that the statute of limitations has expired, will the amendment do her any good? _____

79. Same facts as Problem 78, except that at the same time Reva learns about the Contracts outline, she also discovers that Jeff had set up a kiosk in the law school lobby two weeks after Reva filed her suit. From this kiosk Jeff sold copies of Reva's Civil Procedure outline to other students. Because these acts cause further harm to Reva, she wants to modify her complaint to ask for additional damages. How can she modify her complaint? _____

Answers

78. This problem raises two questions: how to amend and whether the amendment relates back. These are separate questions, governed by different standards.

Fed. R. Civ. P. 15(a)(1) allows Reva to amend her complaint once as a matter of course within 21 days after Jeff answers. Because the problem indicates Jeff has not answered, Reva may amend without obtaining either the court's or Jeff's permission.

Of course, if the claim is barred by the statute of limitations, amending does Reva little good. However, Fed. R. Civ. P. 15(c) allows an amendment to a pleading to relate back to the date of the original pleading. If the amendment relates back to the date of her original complaint, the claim for copying the Contracts outline is not time-barred.

There is no indication the applicable statute of limitations allows the claim to relate back. Under Fed. R. Civ. P. 15(c)(1)(B), however, the claim relates back as long as it arises out of the same conduct, transaction, or occurrence as the claim set out in the original pleading. Technically, there are two basic occurrences here: Jeff's copying of the Civil Procedure outline and his copying of the Contracts outline. Nevertheless, because these happened on the same day and were probably caused by the same basic motivation, the two claims probably arise from the same conduct. Reva accordingly should be able both to amend and to survive any statute of limitations challenge.

79. The events in question occurred *after* the complaint was filed. Therefore, Reva needs to file a supplemental complaint pursuant to Fed. R. Civ. P. 15(d). Note that the court must approve the supplemental pleading, although approval is almost certain here.

VI. MOTION FOR JUDGMENT ON THE PLEADINGS

Once pleading is complete, *Fed. R. Civ. P. 12(c)* allows any party to move for judgment on the pleadings.

A. Timing: A motion for judgment on the pleadings may be filed only *after all pleading is complete*, but early enough so as not to *delay the trial*.

B. Standard: The court considering the motion accepts all facts alleged in all the pleadings as true (unless those facts fail the plausibility standard discussed in Part III.D of this chapter). If the court concludes one party is entitled to judgment as a matter of law, it will grant the motion and render judgment.

C. When used: The motion for judgment on the pleadings is most commonly used by a *claimant* against a party who has *failed to defend* against that person's claim. In a way, it is the logical counterpart to the Fed. R. Civ. P. 12(b)(6) motion for failure to state a claim.

   1. Failure to defend: *Fed. R. Civ. P. 12(h)(2)* allows a party to raise "failure to state a legal defense to a claim" at any stage of the proceedings and lists the motion for judgment on the pleadings as one of the means by which the objection can be raised.

   Example: *P* sues *D* for both battery and negligence. *D*'s answer denies all allegations of negligence but says nothing about the battery claim. Because failure to deny constitutes an admission, *P* can move for a judgment on the pleadings on the battery claim since *D* in effect has admitted the battery. (Of course, the court may allow *D* to amend her answer if the failure to deny was an oversight.)

   2. Conversion to summary judgment: If a party moving for judgment on the pleadings introduces matters outside the pleadings, the court treats the motion as one for *summary judgment*.

VII. ETHICAL LIMITATIONS ON PLEADINGS, MOTIONS, AND OTHER ARGUMENTS

Fed. R. Civ. P. 11 sets out strict standards designed to ensure honesty and accuracy in pleadings and written motions.

A. Signing requirement: Fed. R. Civ. P. 11(a) requires certain documents to be *signed*.

   1. Documents governed: The requirement applies to *most documents* the parties file with the court, including *pleadings and motions*.

   a. Unfiled documents: Although Fed. R. Civ. P. 11(a) does not explicitly limit the signing requirement to papers filed with the court, other language in the rule makes it clear that only filed papers are covered. Therefore, the rule does not apply to correspondence between the parties and internal memoranda.

   b. Discovery not included: The provisions of Fed. R. Civ. P. 11 do not apply to discovery, including motions filed with the court to compel or object to discovery requests. Fed. R. Civ. P. 11(d). Note, however, that *Fed. R. Civ. P. 26(g)* establishes a separate signing requirement for discovery.

2. **Who must sign:** Each paper must be signed by at least one ***attorney*** of record for the party. If the party is not represented, the party signs the paper.

3. **Required information:** In addition to the signature, the signer must provide her address, email address, and telephone number.

4. **Effect of failure to sign:** If a party submits a paper subject to the signing requirement without the required signature, the court will strike the paper.

B. **Representations made to court:** The crux of Fed. R. Civ. P. 11 is its ***implied certifications***, set out in Fed. R. Civ. P. 11(b). The certification rule overlaps, but is separate from and in addition to, the signing requirement of Fed. R. Civ. P. 11(a). Whenever an attorney or unrepresented party ***presents a matter to the court***, he is deemed to have certified things concerning that matter. If these certifications are not accurate, the party is subject to sanctions.

1. **Acts constituting certification:** A party is deemed to make the Rule 11 certifications when he ***presents*** a paper to the court. A paper is presented when it is:

   a. ***signed***,

   b. ***filed with the court***, or

   c. ***advocating*** the contents of the paper to the court in oral presentation. Most courts limit advocacy to an attorney who continues to advocate orally matters set out in a filed paper, not to matters first raised at oral argument.

2. **Certifications made:** An attorney or unrepresented party who presents a matter to the court in any of the ways described just above certifies that:

   a. she has conducted an ***inquiry*** into the matter that is ***reasonable under the circumstances***, and

   b. that the following are true to the best of the person's knowledge, information, and belief:

      i. the pleading, motion, or other paper is not being presented for any ***improper purpose*** (*improper* explicitly includes harassment and delay);

      ii. all legal arguments in the paper are supported either by ***existing law*** or by a ***nonfrivolous argument*** to extend, modify, or reverse existing law;

      iii. all factual contentions are either currently supported by evidence, or are likely to be supported by evidence after further investigation or discovery (provided the currently unsupported contentions are specifically identified); and

      iv. all ***denials*** of factual contentions are either currently ***supported by evidence***, or are reasonably based on ***belief*** or ***lack of information*** (provided the currently unsupported denials are specifically identified).

      Example 1: *P* sues *D* in federal court for trademark infringement. After *D* wins the case, he brings a motion for Rule 11 sanctions against *P* based on two items in *P*'s complaint. First, *P* alleged that *D* earned $250,000 in profits from infringing *P*'s mark. Although this allegation turned out to be correct, *P* merely made up this number without any background investigation. Second, *P*'s legal argument as to why *D*'s acts constituted infringement had previously been explicitly rejected by the court of appeals for that circuit, even though they were later accepted in seven other federal circuits. *P* is subject to sanctions for the factual allegation, but not the legal one. With respect to the facts, *P* wrongfully certified that she had conducted a reasonable background investigation. That her allegation turned out to be true does not matter. The legal allegation, by contrast, could be supported by a good faith argument for reversing existing law in the circuit, based upon the views of the other circuits.

★ **Example 2:** The Eighth Circuit's decision in Walker v. Norwest Corp., 108 F.3d 158 (8th Cir. 1996), involves an example of a pleading that makes claims not supported by the law. Plaintiffs sued several defendants in federal court, relying on diversity jurisdiction. The complaint alleged that plaintiffs were citizens of South Dakota and that one of the defendants was a citizen of Minnesota. The complaint did not specifically state the citizenship of the other defendants. However, plaintiffs did allege that some of the other defendants "resided" in South Dakota. The court imposed sanctions because plaintiff's allegations of diversity jurisdiction were not supported by the law. (Recall that the complete diversity rule used in diversity cases requires that no defendant can be from the same state as any plaintiff.)

★ **Example 3:** Christian v. Mattel, Inc., 286 F.3d 1118 (9th Cir. 2003), by contrast, deals with the *factual* inquiry required by Rule 11. Plaintiff sued defendant, claiming defendant's Barbie doll infringed the copyright in plaintiff's doll. The facts, however, clearly showed that defendant had copyrighted its Barbie doll before plaintiff obtained its copyright. Because copyright infringement requires proof of copying, plaintiff was not entitled to recover. The court held sanctions on plaintiff would be appropriate, especially because plaintiff could easily have discovered defendant's copyright date by examining the back of Barbie's head.

C. **Sanctions:** If any of the certifications prove untrue, Fed. R. Civ. P. 11(c) allows a party to move for the imposition of *sanctions*. However, the rule contains a *safe-harbor provision* giving the offender the opportunity to cure her error in certain situations. *Sanctions are never required.* Moreover, the rule limits a court's discretion concerning the type of sanction.

   1. **Process:** Sanctions may be imposed either following motion by the party or on the court's own initiative. In all cases, however, the person to be sanctioned must be afforded *notice* and an *opportunity to be heard*.

      a. **By motion:** *Fed. R. Civ. P. 11(c)(2)* allows a party to move for sanctions.

         i. **Service:** The party first *serves* the motion on the offending party.

         ii. **Safe harbor:** However, unlike the vast majority of other motions, a motion for Rule 11 sanctions is *not immediately filed* with the court. The motion may be filed only if the offending party does not withdraw or correct the challenged paper within *21 days* following service of the motion or other period established by the court.

         iii. **Costs and fees:** The court may award costs and reasonable attorneys' fees to the party who prevails on a motion for sanctions.

      b. **Court's initiative:** The court may also impose sanctions on its own initiative. *Fed. R. Civ. P. 11(c)(3)*.

         i. Before imposing sanctions, the court must issue an *order to show cause* why sanctions should not be imposed.

         ii. The *safe-harbor provision does not apply* to sanctions imposed on the court's own initiative.

   c. Order: An order imposing sanctions must specifically describe the offending conduct and justify the sanctions imposed. ***Fed. R. Civ. P. 11(c)(6)***.

2. **Persons subject to sanctions:** The court may impose sanctions on the ***individual attorneys*** who violated the rule, their ***law firm***, and a ***party***. However, there are limits on a court's power to sanction a party.

   a. A court may sanction a party only if she either violated the rule herself or was responsible for the violation. ***Fed. R. Civ. P. 11(c)(1)***.

   b. Monetary sanctions cannot be imposed against a ***represented party*** for violating the provision dealing with improper ***legal*** contentions. ***Fed. R. Civ. P. 11(c)(5)(A)***.

3. **Sanctions allowed:** The rule limits sanctions to whatever "***suffices to deter repetition***" of such conduct in the future. Thus, a sanction may be ***punitive***. Fed. R. Civ. P. 11(c)(4) allows for the following sanctions:

   a. ***nonmonetary*** sanctions, which the Advisory Committee notes suggest may include an order striking pleadings or issuance of a reprimand;

   b. a ***penalty***, which must be paid to the ***court*** instead of the other party; and/or

   c. in a case where a ***party moved*** for sanctions, an order requiring the offending party to reimburse the movant for costs and attorneys' fees ***caused by the violation***. However, costs and fees are available only when needed for ***effective deterrence***.

4. **Determining appropriate sanction:** The ***Advisory Committee notes*** indicate a court has ***considerable discretion*** in determining an appropriate sanction. However, they also suggest certain factors to consider in determining an appropriate sanction:

   a. whether the violation was ***willful*** or merely negligent;

   b. whether the offending party ***intended to injure*** the other party;

   c. whether the offending person has had ***legal training***;

   d. whether there was a ***pattern*** of offending conduct, in this case or in others;

   e. whether the wrongful activity ***pervades*** an entire pleading or motion or only a particular claim or defense; and

   f. the effect the violation had on the process of litigation, including a consideration of any ***added time or expense***.

Quiz Yourself on PLEADING

80. While attending a fireworks show, Spencer Spectator is seriously injured when a shell detonates too close to the ground. Spencer sues Charlie Cherrybomb, who organized the pyrotechnics display, in federal court. Although Charlie organized the show, others actually set off the fireworks.

   Spencer's complaint reads (other than the caption and signature) as follows:

1. Jurisdiction in this case is based on 28 U.S.C. §1332.

2. On or about July 4, 2012, at a fireworks show at the Woodford County Fairgrounds in Eureka, Illinois, Plaintiff was seriously injured by an explosion caused by fireworks.

3. Defendant Cherrybomb owed a duty to Plaintiff by virtue of the fact that Defendant organized the fireworks show in question.

4. Defendant Cherrybomb breached that duty by failing to act as a reasonable person would under the circumstances.

5. Defendant's negligent acts caused Plaintiff's extensive injuries.

6. As a result of Defendant's negligence, Plaintiff suffered serious burns, causing him great pain, and requiring him to incur over $20,000 in medical expenses.

Wherefore, Plaintiff demands judgment against Defendant in the sum of $100,000 together with costs.

Charlie feels that both the jurisdictional and substantive allegations in Spencer's complaint are worded too vaguely. What motion or motions should Charlie bring to challenge the allegations?

_____

81. Same facts as Problem 80. Suppose Charlie first objects to subject matter jurisdiction by filing a pre-answer motion to dismiss for lack of jurisdiction. The court denies the motion. In his answer, Charlie raises the defense of failure to state a claim, based on the allegations concerning negligence. Will the court hear Charlie's defense of failure to state a claim? _____

82. Same facts as Problems 80 and 81, except assume the court finds Charlie raised both defenses in timely fashion. Is Charlie likely to prevail on either his challenge to the jurisdictional allegations or his argument that Spencer has not stated a claim? _____

83. Karen shows cairn terriers at dog shows. When she learns that a champion cairn is expecting puppies, Karen contacts the owner, Breeden, to see if Breeden might be interested in selling. Karen and Breeden enter into a contract in which Karen agrees to pay $2,000 for her choice of one puppy from the litter.

Shortly after the birth, Karen goes to visit the new litter. In one glance, she realizes that the mother had been fooling around, quite possibly with the local English bulldog. The puppies clearly are not purebred cairn terriers.

Karen sues Breeden for rescission of the contract. She wants to argue that the contract is voidable because of a mutual mistake of fact as to whether the puppies would be purebred cairns. The relevant portions of Karen's complaint read as follows:

2. On or about March 5, 2016, Plaintiff and Defendant entered into a contract. This contract provided that Plaintiff would pay $2,000 to Defendant. In return, Defendant promised Plaintiff that Plaintiff could have her choice of one puppy from a litter to be delivered by Toto2, a dog belonging to Defendant.

3. Said contract is invalid because of a mutual mistake of fact concerning the pedigree of the puppies.

Wherefore, plaintiff demands that the aforementioned contract between Plaintiff and Defendant be rescinded, and the parties restored to their position before the agreement.

Breeden moves to dismiss for failure to state a claim. Although she acknowledges that mutual mistake is a basis for rescission, she claims that Karen's complaint is too vague. How will the court rule? _____

84. Same facts as Problem 83, except that rather than suing to rescind the contract, Karen simply refuses to pay or accept possession. Breeden sues Karen in federal district court for breach of contract. Karen files an answer that denies both that there was a contract and that she breached.

Several weeks after the pleadings are closed, Karen files a motion for judgment on the pleadings. In this motion, Karen points out that Breeden's complaint did not specify the contract was in writing. The statute of frauds requires that contracts for the sale of goods for a price in excess of $500 be in writing. Will Karen prevail? _____

85. Snidely Whiplash was seriously injured in an automobile collision at an intersection. After talking to the other driver, Snidely strongly suspects the traffic light at the intersection was malfunctioning. Snidely therefore sues City in a federal district court. Snidely claims that (a) the light did not work properly, (b) City was negligent in failing to make sure that the light worked properly, and (c) as a result, Snidely was involved in an accident and suffered $100,000 in damages.

City is now preparing its answer. It is prepared to admit that Snidely was involved in an accident but to deny that it was in any way negligent. However, City really has no idea whether the light was malfunctioning on the date in question. City engineers have inspected the light since the accident, and although it is working fine now, this brand of light has a history of malfunctioning. In addition, while City realizes Snidely suffered some harm it has no idea whether he really suffered damages of $100,000. Therefore, City is thinking about simply not responding to Snidely's allegations concerning the light and his damages. Does City run any risk if it fails to respond to those allegations? _____

86. Hatfield and McCoy are neighbors who do not get along. One day McCoy comes home to find his house burned to the ground. McCoy is sure Hatfield intentionally set the blaze. McCoy's suspicions are confirmed when he sees footprints leading from Hatfield's house to McCoy's and back again. McCoy therefore sues Hatfield for $200,000 in damages. McCoy's complaint specifically alleges that Hatfield intentionally set the fire. Furious at these allegations, Hatfield refuses to speak to McCoy. Instead he immediately files a motion for sanctions under Fed. R. Civ. P. 11. Will the court impose sanctions on McCoy? _____

Answers

80. Charlie should bring a motion to dismiss setting forth two objections: lack of subject matter jurisdiction based on the jurisdictional allegation, and failure to state a claim for the remainder of the complaint.

81. The court will consider the motion to dismiss for failure to state a claim. Fed. R. Civ. P. 12(g) does provide that if a party brings a pre-answer motion based on any grounds listed in Rule 12, he must include those defenses set out in Rule 12(h)(1) or they are waived. Failure to state a claim is not included within Rule 12(h)(1) and therefore is not waived. Fed. R. Civ. P. 12(h)(2) explicitly allows a party to raise the defense of failure to state a claim in a pleading.

82. Charlie is correct when he argues that the allegations concerning jurisdiction and the cause of action are insufficient. However, he is not likely to prevail on either motion.

The jurisdictional allegation is not sufficient. Although Spencer has alleged the basis for jurisdiction, he has supplied the court with no facts that would allow it to determine whether jurisdiction is met. At the very least, Spencer should have alleged the parties' citizenships.

Although it is a closer case, the allegations of negligence are also insufficient. The federal rules use "notice" pleading, under which plaintiff need only give defendant a general idea of the claims. However, the Supreme Court decisions in *Twombly* and *Iqbal* require Spencer to include enough facts from which it would be plausible to infer his claim is true. Spencer has not done this. Given that Charlie only organized the show, the actual negligence could have been committed by the people who set off the fireworks. Spencer has not set out enough facts to make it plausible to conclude Charlie was responsible.

Nevertheless, it is unlikely the court will dismiss on either ground. Instead, it will probably give Spencer leave to amend.

83. The court should grant Breeden's motion to dismiss. Karen's complaint is sufficiently detailed to survive the general "notice pleading" standard of Fed. R. Civ. P. 8(a). However, Rule 9(b) requires that a party alleging fraud *or mistake* must set out the circumstances surrounding the fraud or mistake with particularity. Karen needs to provide more details concerning what the parties assumed when entering into the contract, and how those expectations were not met.

84. Karen will not prevail. Statute of frauds is an affirmative defense. Fed. R. Civ. P. 8(c)(1). Karen therefore has the burden of pleading the contract was *not* in writing.

85. Under Fed. R. Civ. P. 8(b)(6), failure to deny an averment constitutes an admission, except for averments as to the amount of damage. Therefore, if the City does not respond, it may be deemed to have admitted the light was not working properly. However, it will not have admitted that Snidely suffered $100,000 in damages. (Note that many courts will find that the City admitted that Snidely suffered *some* harm, but let the City contest the *amount* of harm.)

The City does have another option. Because it truly has no way to determine with certainty whether the light was working, it can plead that it is without knowledge or information sufficient to form a belief. That plea of lack of knowledge is treated as a denial. Fed. R. Civ. P. 8(b)(5).

86. The court will not impose sanctions. McCoy probably violated Fed. R. Civ. P. 11. He really has no factual support leading him to conclude that Hatfield intentionally set the blaze. Fed. R. Civ. P. 11(b)(3). The footprints do not show that Hatfield set the fire since any number of alternate explanations are possible.

However, the court will not impose sanctions because Hatfield did not comply with the safe harbor provision. Hatfield should have served McCoy with his motion pointing out the problem. Only if McCoy refused to withdraw the allegation within the 21-day period would Hatfield be entitled to file the motion and obtain an order for sanctions.

 Exam Tips on
PLEADING

☞ Most pleading questions involve the Federal Rules of Civil Procedure. Questions concerning common law or Code pleading are relatively rare, unless you are in a Code pleading state.

☞ Be sure to keep the difference between *pleadings* and *motions* distinct in your mind.

    ☞ Pleadings are the general documents setting out all the parties' claims and substantive defenses.

    ☞ Motions, by contrast, are more specific requests to the court. They typically deal with procedural requests. However, certain defenses such as lack of jurisdiction or venue may also be raised by motion.

☞ The word "motion" should never be used as a verb. A party "moves" for relief, not "motions" for relief.

☛ **The complaint:** The basic "short and plain statement" standard of the federal rules is relatively easy to satisfy. As long as the complaint gives defendant notice of the claims and the underlying facts giving rise to those claims, it is sufficient.

☞ The notice pleading standard applies not only to the complaint but also to most other affirmative claims for relief, such as counterclaims and cross-claims.

☞ Be sure to discuss the Supreme Court's "plausibility" standard, which requires the pleading to contain some factual support for claimant's conclusions.

☞ Look out for questions involving the *heightened pleading standards* set out in Fed. R. Civ. P. 9, such as claims for fraud, mistake, and special damages.

☛ **Motions by defendant:** Defendant may raise certain objections to the complaint by motion.

☞ Students dealing with motions often overlook the issue of *timing*. You must thoroughly understand the Fed. R. Civ. P. 12(g) and (h) rules governing when certain defenses can be raised.

☞ Recall that Fed. R. Civ. P. 12(g) comes into play whenever a party raises a defense or objection mentioned *anywhere in Rule 12*. Its use is not restricted to defenses listed in Fed. R. Civ. P. 12(b). A Rule 12(f) motion to strike, for example, triggers Rule 12(g).

☛ When dealing with a *Rule 12(b)(6)* motion, ask yourself two questions.

☞ Is the claim stated in sufficient detail under the standards of Fed. R. Civ. P. 8 and 9? Courts usually give leave to amend if the problem is one of insufficient detail.

☞ Is claimant trying to recover under a legal theory recognized by the substantive law? Even if the complaint is meticulously detailed, if the law does not recognize the claim a Rule 12(b)(6) motion is appropriate.

☛ **The answer:** The rules governing the answer are much more detailed, and in some ways less forgiving, than those governing the complaint. The *same rules* also *apply to the reply.*

☞ If a question mentions dates, be sure to consider whether the answer was filed on time.

☞ The most important criterion to recall in framing an answer is that failure to deny—which includes an ineffective denial—can be deemed an admission, except for allegations concerning the amount of damages.

☞ Recall that if a party does not know whether a particular allegation is true, she may be able to plead *lack of information*, which is treated as a denial.

☞ Make sure you know which issues are *affirmative defenses*. If something is an affirmative defense, defendant has the burden of initially pleading it. Fed. R. Civ. P. 8(c) contains a partial list of affirmative defenses.

☛ **Amendments:** There are two key issues in amendments, which must be kept separate. The first is whether a party needs court permission to amend. The second is whether an amendment adding claims or changing parties relates back. Merely because the court gives permission does not mean the amendment relates back.

☛ **Ethical limitations:** Recall that under Fed. R. Civ. P. 11, an attorney (or in some cases a party) who presents a motion or pleading to a court makes a number of certifications concerning the factual and legal matters alleged in that motion or pleading.

☞ When dealing with Rule 11 sanctions, do not forget the *21-day safe-harbor provision*, during which the party may withdraw the offending presentation.

☞ Recall that any monetary *penalties* for Rule 11 violations are paid to the court, not to the other party.

CHAPTER 8

DISCOVERY

ChapterScope ━━

This chapter deals with discovery, the process by which a party gathers information from others to help her prepare for trial. It discusses only discovery in the *federal courts.* Although many states pattern their discovery rules after the Federal Rules of Civil Procedure, others use significantly different methods.

■ The federal rules recognize *six primary methods* of discovery.

■ *Mandatory disclosures*, under which each party is required, even without a request, to disclose certain information to the other, such as the names of eyewitnesses and copies of contracts and other key documents, as well as witnesses and experts to be called at trial;

■ *Depositions*, where a witness is questioned under oath by one or more of the parties;

■ *Interrogatories*, which are written questions another party must answer in writing;

■ *Inspection* of tangible property or documents (including electronic files);

■ *Requests for admission* of facts or the application of law to fact; and

■ *Physical and mental examinations* of parties.

■ *Most of these methods* apply only as *between the parties*. Only depositions and requests for inspection can be used to obtain information from nonparties.

■ Parties can often discover facts even though those facts *could not be used as evidence* at trial. As long as the information might lead to facts that could be introduced, it can be discovered.

■ There are limits on a party's ability to discover certain types of information, including *work product*, information protected by a *privilege*, and *trade secrets*.

■ A party may be required to *supplement* prior discovery to correct errors.

■ Discovery usually proceeds without oversight by the court. Other than physical and mental examinations, a party *need not obtain the court's permission* before seeking discovery.

■ However, the party usually needs to obtain a *subpoena* from the court to compel a nonparty to provide information.

■ Federal courts, and many state courts, must hold a *pretrial conference*, which narrows down the case by weeding out uncontested issues and anticipating discovery battles.

I. OVERVIEW OF DISCOVERY

A. **Increased emphasis on discovery:** Pleading and discovery work in concert. Parties usually must disclose only a few basic facts in the pleadings. Discovery allows parties to learn more about the other party's claims or defenses.

B. Mandatory disclosures: Traditionally, discovery reflected the adversarial nature of litigation. A party had to ask for information to obtain it. Today, the federal rules, and the rules of some states, also require parties to *disclose* certain basic information *without a request* from the other side. Parties must disclose information at the beginning of the case and again on the eve of trial.

C. Discovery methods: Once the initial mandatory disclosure is complete, parties may obtain information through various discovery methods. Each method has advantages and disadvantages.

D. Broad scope: To help discovery achieve its aims, the rules place very few limits on what parties can discover. Fed. R. Civ. P. 26(b) allows discovery of most information that is *relevant* and *not privileged*.

E. Certification of discovery: The party or her attorney must sign all mandatory disclosures and discovery requests and responses. The signature certifies the disclosure, request, or response is both proper and not unduly burdensome.

II. SCOPE OF DISCOVERY

Fed. R. Civ. P. 26(b)(1) sets out the general standard for determining whether information can be discovered. A party can discover information relating to "any *nonprivileged* matter that is *relevant* to any party's claim or defense . . . ."

A. Applies to ordinary discovery: This standard applies to all situations in which *a party seeks information* from someone else. It technically does *not apply to mandatory disclosures*. However, most information that must be disclosed under Rule 26(a) also meets the standard.

B. Relevance: The first step in determining whether information is discoverable is to determine whether it is relevant. Relevance is a low threshold.

   1. *Relevance* **defined:** Information is relevant as long as it may help a party prepare his case. It need not be evidence the party will use at trial.

   2. Relevance to any party's claim: The Fed. R. Civ. P. 26(b)(1) standard was *narrowed* by an amendment in 2000. The prior provision allowed discovery of any information relevant to the subject matter of the action. Under the new standard, it must be relevant to a claim or defense of a party.

★   **Example 1:** In Favale v. Roman Catholic Diocese of Bridgeport, 233 F.R.D. 243 (D. Conn. 2005), plaintiff sued her ex-employer, alleging negligent hiring and negligent supervision of plaintiff's supervisor. Plaintiff sought discovery of any treatment the supervisor may have received for anger and other psychological conditions. The court denied discovery, finding the information irrelevant. Plaintiff's complaint, which sought recovery for sexual harassment instead of harm caused by anger, limited the scope of relevancy.

   a. Any party: The information can be relevant to the claim or defense of any party, not merely the party requesting it.

   b. Good cause: Information that is relevant to the subject matter of the action but not to a party's claim or defense can be discovered, but only if the party obtains a *court order* upon a showing of *good cause*.

3. **Need not be admissible at trial:** Fed. R. Civ. P. 26(b)(1) further provides: "Relevant information need not be admissible at the trial if the discovery appears ***reasonably calculated*** to lead to the discovery of admissible evidence." Therefore, a party must disclose information that cannot be used at trial.

   a. **Background information:** The rule allows discovery of background information that plays no role at trial, such as a witness's telephone number.

   b. **Information precluded as evidence:** More significantly, however, the rule allows a party to discover information, such as hearsay evidence, that the Federal Rules of Evidence specifically prevent from being admitted at trial.

      Example: *P* is injured when his toaster bursts into flame. *P* sues *D*, the manufacturer of the toaster. *P* serves interrogatories on *D*, asking *D* to disclose any "changes in the design of the toaster" made after the accident. *D* had redesigned the toaster after the accident to use a more heavy-duty power cord. However, evidence of the design change could not be introduced at trial. *D* must nevertheless disclose the design change. Even though the information is not admissible, it may help *P* determine what was wrong with the toaster. *P* can use other evidence at trial to prove that the original power cord was dangerous.

4. **Financial information:** A plaintiff may want information concerning defendant's assets to decide whether it is economically worthwhile to seek a money judgment against that defendant. Such information is generally ***not discoverable*** because it is irrelevant to whether plaintiff is entitled to a judgment. However, there are exceptions.

   a. **Punitive damages:** Punitive damages consider a party's net worth since the amount necessary to "punish" a defendant varies depending on defendant's wealth. Therefore, a plaintiff who seeks punitive damages can discover defendant's assets.

   b. **Insurance:** In the ***initial mandatory disclosures***, a party must disclose to the other side any ***liability insurance coverage*** that may cover the claim being litigated.

5. **Proportionality and privacy limits:** Not all relevant, non-privileged information can be discovered. The federal rules impose a proportionality requirement. Courts also will limit discovery of very private information that is of marginal relevance in the case.

   a. **Proportionality:** Fed. R. Civ. P. 26(b)(2)(C) allows a court to limit or bar discovery if the discovery sought is "unreasonably cumulative or duplicative, or can be obtained from some other source that is more convenient, less burdensome, or less expensive," or if "the burden or expense of the proposed discovery outweighs its benefit."

      i. Similarly, Fed. R. Civ. P. 26(c) allows a court to issue a protective order against discovery that would cause "undue burden or expense."

      ii. For ***electronically stored information***, Fed. R. Civ. P. 26(b)(2)(B) allows a party to refuse to turn over information from sources that are not reasonably accessible because of undue burden or cost.

      ★ **Example:** In Price v. Leflore County Detention Center, 2014 WL 3672874 (E.D. Okla.), plaintiff, whose son died while incarcerated in defendant prison, sought discovery of all complaints about failure to provide medical treatment filed by other prisoners during the prior ten years. The court refused plaintiff's motion to compel. It found the information was of scant relevance to plaintiff's case, and very difficult for defendant to compile, as it would require review of every prisoner file.

b. Privacy: Fed. R. Civ. P. 26(c) allows a court to grant a protective order in situations where disclosure of information in discovery would cause "annoyance," "embarrassment," or "oppression."

    i. Proper court: The person seeks the order from the district court where the action is pending. In the case of a deposition, the person may in the alternative obtain an order from the district court where the deposition is taking place.

    ii. Informal discussion as prerequisite: The movant must certify that she *conferred or attempted to confer* with the other affected parties in an attempt to resolve the discovery dispute without court intervention. Fed. R. Civ. P. 26(c)(1).

    iii. Reasonableness standard: Discovery by its very nature can be annoying and burdensome. A court will grant a protective order only if the annoyance, embarrassment, oppression, burden, or expense is "unreasonable" under the circumstances of the case.

★   **Example:** Rengifo v. Erevos Enterprises, Inc., 2007 WL 894376 (S.D.N.Y.) deals with private information. Plaintiff sued his employer for unpaid overtime. Defendant sought to discover plaintiff's immigration status, social security number, and authorization to work in the United States. Even though defendant agreed not to disclose the information to others, the court denied discovery, finding the information highly private and of little litigation value to defendant.

    iv. Trade secrets: A trade secret is secret information, such as a chemical formula, list of ingredients, industrial process, or customer list, that affords the person who possesses it a competitive advantage.

        (a) Relevance and harm: A trade secret can be *highly relevant*. For example, a party who becomes ill after consuming a food product would very much like to know the secret ingredients in that product. However, if the information falls into the hands of a competitor, any commercial advantage to the manufacturer would be lost.

        (b) Ways to protect: Courts often exercise considerable creativity in dealing with trade secrets. For example, the court may conduct an *in camera inspection* of the secret, where the information is provided to the court but not to the requesting party. The court then distills the information and provides the requesting party only what it needs.

C. Privileges: Even if it is relevant, information cannot be discovered if it is protected by a privilege. Privileges protect information from being disclosed *by a particular source*. The party may still obtain the information from other sources.

Example: *P* sues *D* for injuries sustained in an automobile accident. *P* deposes *D*'s attorney, and asks what *D* told the attorney about the accident. *P* cannot discover the information because it is protected by the attorney–client privilege. However, *P* can discover what *D knows* by other means, including by asking *D* directly. The information is not immune from discovery merely because it was relayed to the attorney.

1. Common privileges: The law of privileges varies from state to state. However, certain privileges are recognized in many states.

    a. Self-incrimination: The privilege against self-incrimination allows a person to refuse to admit a criminal act by that person, provided the person still could be prosecuted for the crime. The privilege is guaranteed by the U.S. Constitution, and therefore applies equally in all courts.

    b. Attorney–client: The attorney–client privilege gives a past or present client the right to prevent an attorney from disclosing information pertaining to the legal representation.

    c. Doctor–patient: The doctor–patient privilege gives a past or present patient the right to prevent a doctor, and in some states hospitals and other medical practitioners, from disclosing information relating to treatment.

    d. Priest–penitent: The priest–penitent privilege gives a person the right to prevent a religious official from disclosing information relayed in confidence.

    e. Spousal: The spousal privilege gives a person the right to prevent a spouse from disclosing information relayed in confidence.

  2. Governing law in federal court: Federal Rule of Evidence 501 provides that when a federal court hears a case governed by state law, the federal court uses state law to determine the existence and scope of any privileges.

  3. Privileges absolute: Unlike the work product and expert "privileges" discussed below in section D, a true privilege is an ***absolute bar*** to discovery of the information. A privilege prevents disclosure regardless of how badly the other side needs the information from the protected source. Thus, in the prior example, *P* could not obtain the information from the attorney even if *D* had slipped into a coma.

  4. Waiver: However, privileges can be waived. One way a party can waive its privilege is by introducing evidence of the protected communication.

  5. Claiming privilege: A party cannot withhold information based on a claim of privilege unless he makes the claim ***expressly*** and provides enough of a ***description*** of what is being withheld to allow the requesting party to determine if the privilege applies. Fed. R. Civ. P. 26(b)(5)(A).

D. Work product: The work product exception, set out in ***Fed. R. Civ. P. 26(b)(3)***, covers documents and tangible things prepared ***in anticipation of litigation***. These items may only be obtained upon a showing of ***need***.

★ **1. History:** Although now codified into the Federal Rules of Civil Procedure, the work product doctrine was originally a court-created exception. The Supreme Court explicitly recognized the doctrine in Hickman v. Taylor, 329 U.S. 495 (1947). Although *Hickman* applied only to items prepared by ***attorneys***, the rule has been extended to other representatives.

  2. Purposes of work product rule: *Hickman* established that the limited exception for work product serves two purposes.

    a. First, it prevents one side from ***free-riding*** on the work of another party. By encouraging each side to prepare its own case, the rule helps ensure the adversary system works as intended.

    b. Second, the rule helps to minimize the number of situations in which the ***attorney will be called as a witness***. Testimony by a party's attorney is a particular problem in litigation.

  3. Overview of Rule 26(b)(3): To understand the current work product rule, it is crucial to understand that Rule 26(b)(3) was written against the backdrop of *Hickman*.

    a. Work product is discoverable only when specifically allowed in the rule.

b. As a result, information that meets the general characteristics of work product but is not listed in Rule 26(b)(3) ***cannot be discovered even on a showing of need***. Most significantly, the rule mentions only documents and tangible things. Information that is ***nontangible***—such as what an attorney heard when interviewing a witness or what an insurance agent recalls seeing when investigating the scene of an accident—does not fall within the exception and ***cannot be discovered*** at all.

4. Work product defined: Fed. R. Civ. P. 26(b)(3) allows discovery of documents and tangible things that are otherwise discoverable that were ***prepared in anticipation of litigation or for trial*** by the ***party or the party's representative***.

   a. Documents and tangible things: The rule does not define "document" or "tangible thing." Courts generally interpret the term loosely and protect letters, notes taken during an interview, photographs, and tapes.

   b. Otherwise discoverable: The material must be ***relevant*** and ***not privileged***, as required by Fed. R. Civ. P. 26(b)(1).

   c. In anticipation: The material must have been prepared in anticipation of a litigated dispute.

   i. The case need not actually be underway when the item is prepared. Once the underlying event giving rise to the litigation has occurred, materials prepared in anticipation of a later lawsuit are protected.

   ii. The protection does not extend to documents prepared in the ***ordinary course of business***, such as the personnel records of a business or the medical records of a hospital, which would have been prepared regardless of whether litigation occurs.

   d. Representatives: The rule explicitly includes as representatives a party's "attorney, consultant, surety, indemnitor, insurer, or agent." Other representatives may also fall under the rule.

5. When work product can be discovered: A party may discover work product only by demonstrating ***substantial need*** for the information and that the same basic information cannot be acquired ***from another source*** without undue hardship.

   a. Need: The information should be important to the party seeking it. Work product that merely verifies evidence the party already has cannot be discovered, unless the party's evidence is weak or ambiguous.

   b. Other sources: In addition, if the party with the information obtained it from another source, and that source is accessible to the party seeking the information, the party seeking the information must go to the primary source. However, if the party cannot obtain the information from the other source because of ***substantial cost*** or because the primary source is a witness who is ***hostile*** to the party, he may be able to obtain it from the other party.

   Example: *P* is injured while hiking with his friend *W* on *D*'s land. Shortly after the injury, *D* interviews *W*. *P* sues *D* and files a Rule 34 request for production of *D*'s notes of the interview. If *W* is still available, *D* should not be required to turn over the notes. *P* can interview or depose his friend and obtain the information directly, and accordingly has no need for *D*'s notes.

c. Exception: A person need not show need to discover the *person's own statement* concerning the action. A person (regardless of whether she is a party) may obtain a copy of her own statement from the other side's representative *without showing need*.

d. Mental impressions: When ordering discovery of work product, a court must protect against disclosure of the *mental impressions, conclusions, opinions, or legal theories* of the attorney or representative. Fed. R. Civ. P. 26(b)(3)(B). To the extent work product information reveals these matters, the court will order it to be turned over only if there is no other way for the requesting party to obtain the information.

Example: In the prior example, suppose *D* taped the interview with *W*. In addition, *W* signed a written statement setting forth in *W*'s own words what *W* saw. *W* is unavailable, and *P* seeks both the tape and the statement. *D* refuses. The court should order disclosure of the statement but not the tape. The tape may reveal *D*'s legal strategies in the selection and order of the questions. And once *P* has the statement, he does not need the tape to discover what *W* saw.

E. Expert information: *Fed. R. Civ. P. 26(b)(4)* governs discovery of information and opinions held by experts. The rule draws a clear distinction between experts who *may testify at trial* and those who were *employed only for trial preparation*.

1. *Expert* **defined:** An expert is someone with *specialized knowledge* in a particular subject area who *gives an opinion* based on facts presented to her or which she obtains by investigation.

Example: *X* is a police investigator who specializes in arson. *X* wakes up one night to find his neighbor's house on fire. *X* watches the house burn down. After her insurance company refuses to pay, the neighbor sues. The insurance company calls *X* as a witness. Even though *X*'s perception of the fire will be affected by his expertise in arson, *X* is not testifying as an expert if he simply describes what he saw that night. However, *X* would be testifying as an expert if asked to give his opinion as to how the fire started.

2. **Testifying expert:** The *mandatory disclosure* rules require a party to provide detailed information about experts who may testify at trial. Fed. R. Civ. P. 26(a)(2). *Rule 26(b)(4)(A)* allows a party freely to *depose* anyone identified as a testifying expert.

3. **Nontestifying expert:** If the expert will not testify, the facts she knows and the opinions she has formed are usually *not discoverable*. Other parties may discover that information only upon a showing of need. *Fed. R. Civ. P. 26(b)(4)(D)*. When discovery is allowed, it must be by *deposition* or *interrogatories*.

a. Given that other experts in the field are usually available, this standard is very difficult to meet. However, a party can show need in a case where the underlying facts are no longer available for other experts to examine.

Example: The requesting party in Thompson v. The Haskell Co., 65 Fair Empl. Prac. Cas. (BNA) 1088 (M.D. Fla. 1994), was able to show need. A crucial issue in that case was a party's mental state *at a particular time*. Because the mental state could well have changed, the other party was allowed to discover the opinions of a nontestifying psychologist who examined the party during the crucial period.

b. **Exception:** Although a physician or other medical professional is technically an expert, the report prepared following a *Rule 35 physical or mental examination* can be obtained without a showing of need under the circumstances set out in that rule. See Part IV.G of this chapter.

4. **Costs:** A party who seeks discovery from an expert is usually required to pay a reasonable fee to the expert providing the information, as well as the expert's costs. Fed. R. Civ. P. 26(b)(4)(E). In the case of nontestifying experts, the party must also pay a fair portion of the fees and expenses initially paid by the party who retained the expert.

Quiz Yourself on
SCOPE OF DISCOVERY

87. Graffiti, Inc., manufactures a line of spray paints. During the past two years, several consumers have been seriously injured when cans of Graffiti paint exploded during use. Two consumers, Albert and Betty, join as plaintiffs and sue Graffiti in federal court. Before the answer, Albert serves a set of interrogatories on Graffiti. Graffiti refuses to answer. Is Graffiti justified in refusing to respond to the interrogatories? _____

88. Same facts as Problem 87. Albert alleges a design defect, arguing the company designed a defective spray mechanism. Betty, by contrast, relies on a theory of manufacturing defect, claiming one of the employees was careless in assembling the can. Graffiti denies liability to either plaintiff.

Several months into the case, Albert serves two timely discovery requests. First, he sends interrogatories to Betty, asking her to reveal any information she has that might indicate a problem with the manufacture of the can. Betty objects to the relevance of these questions. Second, Albert notices the deposition of Caleb. Caleb is another victim of an exploding Graffiti spray paint can. Caleb has sued Semi Conscious Co., a trucking company, in state court. Caleb claims the problem with the can arose when Semi transported the cans in trucks that were too hot, causing stress to the delicate components of the spray valve. At the deposition, Albert asks Caleb to disclose any information he has about problems in the transport of the spray paint cans. Caleb also objects to the relevance of the questions. Is Albert entitled to receive the information he wants from Betty and Caleb? _____

89. Same facts as Problem 87. Several months into the case, Graffiti serves a timely set of interrogatories on Albert. One of the interrogatories asks Albert to describe in detail the circumstances under which he was using the spray paint can. Albert is reluctant to answer the question, for in truth Albert was using the can to paint graffiti on the walls of the local law school. Vandalism is a felony in that state, and the statute of limitations has not yet expired. Must Albert answer the question? _____

90. After years of experimentation, Sarah discovers a cure for the common cold, comprising a complex mixture of herbs and other natural ingredients. Only Sarah knows the ingredients. Because it is herbal, Sarah was not required to obtain FDA approval for the product. Nor does the law require her to list the ingredients. Sneezy, who suffers from frequent colds, brings a product liability suit against Sarah after suffering a severe allergic reaction to her product. Sneezy is allergic to several different herbs and asks Sarah to disclose the ingredients in her product. If Sarah objects, is it likely that Sarah will be required to disclose all the ingredients? _____

91. Ali and Frazier are involved in a serious fight, in which both suffer significant injuries. Ali hires Ann Attorney to sue Frazier. Before filing the case, Ann interviews Ali, Frazier, and Leonard, a third party who happened to be watching as the two pugilists fought. She obtains written statements from all three. After the case is commenced, Frazier serves timely interrogatories on Ali, asking Ali to turn over copies of any statements made by Frazier, Ali, and Leonard. Will Ali be required to turn over the statements taken by Ann? _____

92. Author sues Publisher for copyright infringement based upon Publisher's unauthorized publication of a book that is somewhat similar to Author's manuscript. In preparation for trial, Author retains two experts, Fitzgerald and Hemingway. Author concludes that Fitzgerald will make a much better witness and therefore decides to have only Fitzgerald testify at trial. Publisher wants to depose both Fitzgerald and Hemingway to obtain their opinions. Will Publisher succeed? _____

Answers

87. Graffiti's refusal to respond is justified. Fed. R. Civ. P. 26(d)(1) provides parties may not use interrogatories or other methods of discovery until after the parties meet in the discovery conference. The conference will occur after pleading is complete.

88. Albert may receive the information he wants from Betty, but probably not from Caleb. Neither request is relevant to Albert's claim or any defense to his claim. Because he claims a design defect, information about the manufacture or transport of the product is not relevant. However, Fed. R. Civ. P. 26(b)(1) allows a party to obtain information that is relevant to the claim or defense of *any party*, not merely the claims and defenses of the requesting party. Therefore, because the information is clearly relevant to Betty's claim and Betty is a party, Albert can discover it.

Because Caleb is not a party, Albert is not automatically entitled to information that relates only to Caleb's claim. However, the information is relevant to the subject matter of the case. Therefore, Albert could petition the court to allow him to discover that information. However, it is unlikely Albert can show good cause. Given that he is relying only on the design defect theory and that Graffiti is not asserting the defect arose in transport, Albert really has no need for information about transport.

89. Albert need not answer the question. Although the information is clearly relevant, it is privileged. The U.S. Constitution provides a privilege against self-incrimination, under which a party cannot be required to admit a crime if prosecution is still possible.

90. If Sarah seeks a protective order, it is likely the court will not order full disclosure. The information sought is clearly both relevant to Sneezy's claim and not privileged. However, that information qualifies as a trade secret because it affords Sarah a competitive advantage.

Trade secrets are not completely protected from disclosure. Here, the facts indicate Sneezy knows that he has allergies to certain herbs. Therefore, the court might allow him to discover only whether those herbs are present. Second, the court might have Sarah submit the information to the court, not to Sneezy, to control the amount of unnecessary information Sneezy can learn.

91. Frazier may obtain his own statement, but not those of Ali or Leonard. This problem raises issues of work product and privilege. The written statements collected by Ann are clearly documents prepared in anticipation of litigation. Frazier may obtain Leonard's statement only upon a showing of need. Frazier does not seem to be able to show need. He clearly already knows Leonard's name and, accordingly, can conduct his own interview. Frazier can obtain a copy of the statement only if Leonard is not available or refuses to cooperate. Although Frazier's statement is also work product, Fed. R. Civ. P. 26(b)(3)(C) explicitly allows a party to obtain a copy of his own statement without showing need. Ali's statement goes beyond work product—it is protected by the attorney–client privilege. Therefore, Frazier cannot obtain it under any circumstances. However, Frazier can depose Ali and obtain the information directly.

92. Publisher can clearly depose Fitzgerald but probably cannot depose Hemingway. Because Fitzgerald is an expert who will be testifying at trial, Fed. R. Civ. P. 26(b)(4)(A) allows Publisher to depose him. However, because Hemingway is not testifying, Publisher can obtain information from him only by showing need. Since Publisher already has access to Fitzgerald, it really does not need to talk to Hemingway.

III. SEQUENCE OF DISCOVERY

Discovery typically begins early in the case and may continue until shortly before the trial. Discovery usually proceeds in a particular order.

A. Discovery conference: *Fed. R. Civ. P. 26(f)* requires the parties to meet "as soon as practicable" to discuss the claims and defenses that have been filed and whether settlement is possible. If no settlement is reached, the parties are required to prepare a "discovery plan" for the case.

   1. Discovery plan: The discovery plan covers the *subjects* on which discovery is to be had, the *timing and form* of mandatory disclosures and discovery, any agreement the parties may reach that either *limits* discovery or *relaxes limits* prescribed by the rules, and any orders the court should issue to facilitate the discovery process.

   2. Prerequisite to discovery: Unless the action is one in which mandatory disclosures need not be made, the parties agree, or a court orders otherwise, a party may not engage in discovery until after the discovery conference. Fed. R. Civ. P. 26(d)(1).

B. Initial disclosures: Shortly after the discovery conference, the parties make the initial mandatory disclosures required by Fed. R. Civ. P. 26(a).

C. Party-initiated discovery: Once the initial disclosures are complete, the parties may serve discovery requests on each other and on third-party witnesses. This phase may take months or even years in a complex case.

D. Pretrial disclosures: As the case nears trial, the parties again make certain mandatory disclosures of expert witness information and other evidence to be offered at trial.

IV. DISCOVERY METHODS

The Federal Rules of Civil Procedure require parties to turn over certain information to other parties. In addition to these mandatory disclosures, the rules allow parties to obtain information from other parties, and in some cases nonparties, through a variety of means.

A. Mandatory disclosures: The mandatory disclosure rules require parties to turn over, without being asked, information that is typically sought as a matter of course in discovery. There are *two main stages* of mandatory disclosures.

1. **Background and overview:** The mandatory disclosure provisions of *Fed. R. Civ. P. 26(a)* radically change the tradition of litigation as an adversarial process. Many state rules do not include mandatory disclosure requirements.

2. **Initial disclosures:** *Rule 26(a)(1)* requires parties to turn over listed items.

   a. **Timing:** The initial disclosures must be made within *14 days* following the discovery conference unless the parties agree otherwise or the court extends the time. Fed. R. Civ. P. 26(a)(1)(C).

   b. **What must be disclosed:** *Fed. R. Civ. P. 26(a)(1)(A)* **requires the parties to disclose** the following information:

      i. the name and, if known, the contact information of any person *likely to have discoverable information* (such as an eyewitness) that the party *may use to support its claim or defense* in any way *other than impeachment*;

      ii. the *subject of the information* known by those people;

      iii. a copy or description of all *documents, electronically stored information, and tangible things* (for example, a written contract) that the party *may use to support its claim or defense* in any way *other than impeachment*;

      iv. a computation of *damages*, together with supporting documentation; and

      v. any *liability insurance policy* that may apply to the claim or claims.

   c. **"May use" and "impeachment":** Under i and iii above, a party must disclose only those people and documents she *may use to support her claim or defense, unless* these items will be used *solely for impeachment*.

      Example 1: Use: *P* sues *D* for injuries sustained in an automobile collision at an intersection. *P* claims *D* ran a red light. Before filing suit, *P* interviewed an eyewitness to the collision. This eyewitness told *P* in the interview that *P*, not *D*, ran a red light. *P* need not disclose this witness to *D* because *P* will not call the witness at trial (unless *P* is a fool).

      Example 2: Impeachment: *P* sues *D* for breach of an oral contract. *D* denies the parties have a contract. *P* is in possession of a letter *D* wrote to a friend, in which *D* admits she in fact did enter into an oral contract with *P*. *P* plans to use this letter at trial only if *D* takes the witness stand and denies a contract. *P* need not disclose the letter to *D*. Because using the letter to contradict *D*'s testimony constitutes use for purposes of impeachment, the rule does not require *P* to disclose the letter.

   d. **Exempted proceedings:** *Fed. R. Civ. P. 26(a)(1)(B)* exempts certain proceedings from the initial disclosure requirement.

3. **Pretrial disclosures:** Rules 26(a)(2) and (a)(3) require the parties to disclose additional information as the date for trial draws near.

   a. **Expert testimony:** The party must disclose the *identity* of any person who may testify as an *expert*. If the person is retained or employed specifically to provide expert testimony, or is an employee whose duties regularly involve giving expert testimony, the party must also include a *report* signed by the expert witness describing the person's qualifications as an expert, the opinions the expert will give and the grounds for those opinions, all information considered by the expert in forming the opinion, any exhibits the expert may use, the amount of compensation the expert will receive for testifying, and a list of all other cases during the past four years in which the person has testified as an expert. Fed. R. Civ. P. 26(a)(2)(B)(i)-(vi).

b. **Lay witnesses:** The party must disclose the name and, unless already provided, the contact information for all witnesses the party may call at trial, other than witnesses used solely for purposes of impeachment. The disclosure must differentiate between witnesses a person plans to call and those he may call depending on the circumstances. If the party will present a witness's testimony by means of a deposition, the party must so indicate and provide transcripts of the portions of the deposition that apply. Fed. R. Civ. P. 26(a)(3)(A)(i) and (ii).

c. **Tangible evidence:** The party must identify documents and other tangible evidence that may be used at trial, except for items to be used solely for impeachment. The disclosure must differentiate between evidence the person plans to use and that which he may use depending on the circumstances. Fed. R. Civ. P. 26(a)(3)(A)(iii).

d. **Timing:** These disclosures must be made at least *30 days before trial* in the case of lay witnesses and tangible evidence, and *90 days* in the case of experts, unless the court otherwise specifies.

B. **Overview of methods of obtaining information from others:** Other than the mandatory disclosures, all formal discovery in a case proceeds by a party requesting information or admissions from others. The federal rules provide various means of obtaining this information.

1. **When discovery may commence:** *Rule 26(d)(1)* provides that discovery cannot commence until *after the discovery conference*. (The only exception is the Rule 27(a) pretrial deposition, discussed below.) This limit can be waived by stipulation of the parties or by order of the court.

2. **Choice of methods:** A party may usually obtain discovery using whatever method he deems most effective. The Federal Rules of Civil Procedure generally do not mandate the use of one type or another. The most important exception is the *physical or mental exam*, which is available only if the information cannot be obtained by alternate means. See Part G.

3. **Informal information gathering not barred:** Nothing in the discovery rules limits a party's ability to gather information by informal means, such as independent investigation or witness interviews. Informal information gathering may occur before the case is filed and can continue while the case proceeds. In many cases, most "discovery" is of this informal type.

C. **Depositions:** Taking a deposition resembles questioning a witness at trial. The witness is placed *under oath*. One or more of the parties poses questions to the witness, which the witness answers. The entire proceeding is *transcribed*.

1. **Who may be deposed:** A deposition is one of the few discovery devices that may be used against *nonparties*. The person who answers the questions is called the *deponent*.

2. **Limit on availability:** A party usually does not need the court's permission to conduct a deposition. However, exceptions exist. First, leave of court is required if the deponent is *in prison*. Second, a party needs either leave of the court or a stipulation signed by all parties if the deponent has *already been deposed* or if the proposed deposition would result in *more than 10 total depositions* by the party and those aligned with the party. Fed. R. Civ. P. 30(a)(2).

3. **How initiated:** A party initiates a deposition simply by giving *reasonable notice* to all other parties. The notice specifies the time and location of the deposition, as well as the name of the deponent.

a. **Party deponent:** If the person to be deposed is a party, the notice places a duty upon the party to appear at the deposition and submit to questioning. A party may be required to travel to a distant location, including other states, for purposes of providing deposition testimony. However, if the location or timing is too burdensome, the party deponent may petition the court for *a protective order* under Fed. R. Civ. P. 26(c). Protective orders are discussed in Part II of this chapter.

b. **Nonparty deponent:** If the person to be deposed is not a party, the notice does not obligate the person to appear. In these cases, the party should also obtain a *subpoena* requiring the witness to appear at the time and place specified in the notice of deposition. *Fed. R. Civ. P. 45* sets forth detailed rules governing subpoenas.

   i. **Issuing court:** The subpoena must be issued by the district court in the *district where the deposition* is to be conducted. Fed. R. Civ. P. 45(a)(2)(B).

   ii. **Location of deposition:** On motion of the witness, the court will quash or modify the subpoena if it requires the witness to travel to a place *more than 100 miles* from where that person resides, is employed, or regularly conducts business in person, or if it subjects the person to an undue burden. Fed. R. Civ. P. 45(c)(3)(ii) and (iv).

   iii. **Service:** Fed. R. Civ. P. 45(b)(2) provides a subpoena may only be served:

      (a) anywhere in the district *where the subpoena was issued*;

      (b) anywhere *within 100 miles* of the place *where the deposition is to be conducted* (which means service may occur outside the district where the deposition will take place);

      (c) if state law so allows, *anywhere within the state* in which the *deposition is issued*;

      (d) if a federal statute so allows, any place the *court authorizes* based on *good cause*.

   iv. **Consequences of failure to obtain subpoena:** If the party fails to obtain a subpoena and the witness does not appear for the deposition, the witness cannot be sanctioned in any way. However, the party who noticed the deposition may be required to pay the expenses and attorneys' fees of all other parties who attended the deposition. Fed. R. Civ. P. 30(g)(2).

c. **Production of documents:** The notice may also request the deponent to bring documents or tangible things to the deposition. Fed. R. Civ. P. 30(b)(2). In the case of a nonparty deponent, the subpoena may also specify that the person should bring along the document or tangible thing. Fed. R. Civ. P. 45(a)(1)(A)(iii). Such a subpoena is commonly called a *subpoena duces tecum*. See Fed. R. Civ. P. 30(b)(2).

d. **Deposing corporations and other associations:** Often, a party suspects that someone within a corporation or other association has the desired information, but is not sure *who* that person is. In this situation, *Fed. R. Civ. P. 30(b)(6)* allows the party to notice a deposition of the organization itself, describing in detail the type of information being sought.

   i. **Designated person:** The corporation or association must then *designate one or more persons* either within the organization or who agree to testify on behalf of the organization, and *inform the requesting party* about what each person will testify. The designated person then appears at the deposition and testifies as to any specified matters either known or reasonably available to the organization.

      ii. Particular person: The last sentence of Fed. R. Civ. P. 30(b)(6) makes it clear that if the party requesting information knows of a particular person in the organization who is likely to have information, the party *may forgo the above process* and simply depose that particular person by the normal process.

4. Deposition procedure: A deposition may be *held anywhere*, although it usually takes place in the offices of an attorney representing a party. However, Fed. R. Civ. P. 30(b)(4) also allows the deposition to be conducted by "remote means," which includes *telephone or video conference*.

    a. Court officer: Unless the parties stipulate otherwise (which they usually do), the deposition is conducted before an officer of the court.

    b. Oath: The deponent is placed under oath.

    c. Questioning and cross-examining: The party requesting the deposition then asks questions. Other parties may also examine the deponent.

    d. Inspection: If documents or tangible things have been produced, inspection of those items will occur.

    e. Recording deposition: The questions and answers are *transcribed* by a court reporter or by *electronic means*. The party noticing the deposition may select the means of preserving the testimony and bears the cost. Any other party, with prior notice to the deponent and other parties, may specify *additional means* of preserving the testimony.

    f. Objections: The deponent or any party may object to the content or form of a question. Objections must be made *concisely* and in a *nonargumentative* and *nonsuggestive* manner. Fed. R. Civ. P. 30(c)(2). This prevents an attorney from "coaching" the witness to provide a certain answer or to frame the answer in a particular way.

      i. However, because no judge is at the deposition to resolve the objection, the objection is *noted on the transcript*, and the *deponent usually must then answer the question* notwithstanding the objection.

      ii. An attorney may instruct a party not to answer a question only when necessary to protect a *privilege*, pursuant to a limit on discovery already imposed by the court, or if the party plans immediately to seek a *protective order*. Fed. R. Civ. P. 30(c)(2).

    g. Protective orders: Fed. R. Civ. P. 30(d)(3) allows a party to seek a protective order when a deposition is conducted in *bad faith* or in a way that unreasonably *annoys, embarrasses, or oppresses* the deponent or a party. For example, continually asking about irrelevant matters may lead to a protective order.

      i. The order must be obtained from a district judge in the district *where either the action is pending or the deposition is being taken*.

      ii. Most attorneys seek protective orders only in egregious cases.

    h. Time limit: Rule 30(d)(1) limits a deposition to a *single day of 7 hours*, unless the parties stipulate or the court specifies a longer or shorter time.

    i. Review of transcript: *If the deponent or a party requests*, the deponent may review the transcript. If the deponent would like any changes, she may sign a statement indicating the requested changes and the reasons for them. Fed. R. Civ. P. 30(e).

5. **Special depositions:** The discussion above deals with the standard oral deposition, the most common type. However, the rules also allow for two other types of depositions.

   a. **Deposition before commencement of action:** In certain situations, *Fed. R. Civ. P. 27* allows a person to depose another person even before a lawsuit is commenced.

      i. **When used:** A person might want to take such a deposition to *preserve the testimony* of an important witness who is in poor health or about to leave the country for an extended period of time.

      ii. **Petition:** A pre-action deposition always requires *court approval*. The person seeking the deposition must file a *verified petition* describing the underlying dispute, the likely adverse parties to that dispute, the information the person thinks the deponent has, and why the information needs to be obtained now rather than during the case. *Notice* must be provided to all expected adverse parties at least 21 days prior to the hearing date. Fed. R. Civ. P. 27(a)(2).

      iii. **Depositions pending appeal:** *Fed. R. Civ. P. 27(b)* also allows for depositions to be taken while a case is on appeal.

   b. **Deposition by written questions:** *Fed. R. Civ. P. 31* allows a party to conduct a deposition without showing up in person. The party instead submits *written questions*, which the person presiding at the deposition reads to the deponent. The presiding official also records the answers.

      i. **When used:** The deposition on written questions is typically used only to obtain noncontroversial background information from *nonparty witnesses*. If the witness is a party, the information can be obtained more expeditiously by use of interrogatories.

      ii. **Cross-examination:** Copies of the written questions are provided to all parties. Those parties may then submit *written cross-examination questions* to the presiding officer and other parties. Following that, the parties may serve *redirect* and *recross* questions.

D. **Interrogatories:** Interrogatories are *written questions* that the recipient answers *under oath*. *Fed. R. Civ. P. 33* governs interrogatories.

   1. **Availability:** Interrogatories may only be used against *parties*. Court approval is not necessary.

      Note: Nothing prevents a party from sending written questions to a nonparty. Although the nonparty is under no obligation to answer, if the nonparty voluntarily answers, the party is free to use the information.

   2. **Limit on number:** *Fed. R. Civ. P. 33(a)* prevents a party from serving more than *25 questions* on any other party, unless the court approves or the parties agree to more. If a given question has discrete subparts, each *subpart* counts as a *separate question*.

   3. **Answers:** Typically, the party will work with an attorney in framing the answers. The answers must be *signed* by the person. Any objections must be signed by the party's attorney.

      a. **Time to answer:** The questions must be answered within *30 days* of service unless the court orders or the parties agree otherwise. Fed. R. Civ. P. 33(b)(2).

      b. **Duty to investigate:** Unlike depositions, where the witness answers from personal knowledge, a party answering interrogatories has a *duty to investigate*. Therefore, if the answer is not personally known to the party but can be obtained from records or other sources, the party must conduct a reasonable investigation and provide any information it finds.

    c. Exception for business records: The duty to investigate can prove cumbersome, especially if the records are not organized in a way that corresponds to the questions. ***Rule 33(d)*** provides that if the answer to an interrogatory can be found in the party's business records, and the burden of finding the information is substantially the same for both parties, the party served may *specify the records* in which the answer may be found and allow the asking party to *conduct its own search* of those records.

    d. Objections: Unlike in a deposition, a party who objects to a question posed in interrogatories may refuse to answer that question and instead state with specificity why the question is objectionable. Fed. R. Civ. P. 33(b)(4). The inquiring party's recourse is to obtain a Rule 37 order compelling the served party to answer.

        i. A question is objectionable if, for example, it is overly burdensome or calls for privileged information.

        ii. However, Rule 33(a)(2) makes it clear that a question is not objectionable merely because it asks the party to apply law to fact. For example, plaintiff can ask defendant if defendant was "negligent" because that involves the application of law to fact.

E. Inspection of documents, electronically stored information, and things: *Fed. R. Civ. P. 34* allows a party to inspect *records and things* in the possession of another party.

    1. When available: Rule 34 can be used only against *parties*. Even if the party is not in actual possession of the item, he must make it available for inspection if it is possessed by someone *under that party's control*.

    Note: Obtaining records and things from nonparties: Although Rule 34 is available only against parties, it is also possible to inspect physical evidence controlled by a nonparty. *Fed. R. Civ. P. 45(a)(1)(C)* allows the party to obtain a subpoena requiring the nonparty to produce and permit inspection of tangible items or to permit inspection of premises. The subpoena authorizing inspection may be issued in conjunction with a deposition of the nonparty, but no deposition is necessary.

    2. Procedure: A party seeking inspection of tangible items under Rule 34 serves a *request* upon the party in possession or control of the item. The request must describe the items to be inspected and specify a reasonable time and place for the inspection to occur. The other party then files a *response* within 30 days, indicating whether the inspection will be allowed or if there are any objections.

    3. Other parties: Rule 34 does not require that the request be served on parties other than the one possessing or controlling the item in question.

    4. Duty to preserve information: A party anticipating litigation may have an incentive to destroy damning documents. Courts have dealt with this by imposing a duty on parties to preserve documents. This duty, however, creates special issues in the case of data stored electronically.

★   **Example:** Zubulake v. UBS Warburg LLP, 220 F.R.D. 212 (S.D.N.Y. 2003), demonstrates the issues that can arise with respect to electronic data. The court found UBS violated its duty to preserve certain important information when it erased its backup tapes. However, because plaintiff could not show the information would have helped her win the case, the court refused to sanction UBS.

F. Requests for admission: *Fed. R. Civ. P. 36* allows a party to ask another party to admit certain matters. If the other party does not either object to or effectively deny the matter, the matter may be *deemed admitted* for purposes of trial.

1. When available: Requests for admission may only be used against *parties*. A party will typically use the device near the end of discovery to weed out matters in the pleadings that have been resolved by discovery, and thereby pare down the case for trial.

Note: Although technically a discovery device, requests for admission are conceptually more like *pleadings*. They resemble a second round of pleadings that help the parties determine what issues remain in dispute.

2. What may be requested: A party may request anything within the scope of discovery, including *opinions and the application of law to fact*. A party may ask another party to confirm a particular document is genuine, for example, that a particular item is indeed a deceased party's last will. A party may not object to a request to admit merely because it involves an issue that constitutes the crux of the case or because the matter is something that "should be proved at trial."

3. Process: A party seeks an admission by serving a *request* on the other party. Unlike depositions and interrogatories, there is no limit on the number of requests that may be served.

a. Response: The party served with the request may

i. *admit* the matter is true;

ii. *deny* the matter, if the party can deny it in good faith;

iii. state in detail reasons why the party *cannot truthfully admit or deny* the request; or

iv. *object* to the request.

b. Form of denial: A denial must "fairly respond to the substance of the matter . . . ." Fed. R. Civ. P. 36(a)(4). Moreover, a party who intends to deny only part of a statement must specify in detail which parts are admitted and which are denied. This is the same standard that applies to the answer.

c. Effect of failure to deny: A party who does not deny a request to admit, or who sets forth an ineffective denial, is deemed to have *admitted* the matter requested.

d. Use of admission: Any admission *applies only in the particular case* and has no effect in other cases.

G. Physical and mental examinations: *Fed. R. Civ. P. 35* makes it possible to force a *party* to submit to a *physical or mental examination*. Unlike all other discovery devices, a party seeking a physical and mental exam must *show good cause* and obtain a *court order*.

1. When available: A physical or mental exam may be ordered only for a *party* or person *in custody or under the legal control of a party*.

a. Custody or control: The reference to a person under custody or control refers to a ward, such as an infant or incompetent. The rights of wards are usually litigated by *guardians*.

b. Need not be adverse: The party to be examined need not be adverse to the movant. However, it is rarely possible to show good cause for examining a coparty since the requesting party will usually have no need for the information at trial.

2. **Court order required:** Unless the party to be examined consents, a party seeking an exam must obtain an order from the court *in which the action is pending*. The order is granted only if the party demonstrates the physical or mental condition is *in controversy* and if *good cause* exists for the examination.

    a. **In controversy:** The physical or mental condition of a party is *in controversy* if the condition is *relevant* to one or more claims or defenses in the case and if there is a *genuine dispute* concerning the condition.

        i. **Relevancy:** For example, if a defendant in a breach of contract case argues the contract is invalid because defendant was insane when the alleged agreement was reached, defendant's mental condition is in controversy.

★   ii. **Placing condition in controversy:** Because of the highly intrusive nature of exams, the Supreme Court in Schlagenhauf v. Holder, 379 U.S. 104 (1964), limited the ways in which a person's physical or mental condition may be placed in controversy.

            (a) A party may *place her own condition* in controversy *in the pleadings* by alleging a claim or defense that turns on that condition.

            (b) However, a party *may not place the condition of another party* in controversy *in the pleadings*. Instead, the party needs to offer an *affidavit* or other affirmative evidence tending to show the person's condition is in controversy.

            Example: *P* and *D* are injured in an automobile collision. *P* sues *D*, alleging in the complaint that *D* was negligent for failing to wear eyeglasses while driving. *D* denies both that *P* was injured and that *D* was negligent. *P*'s injury is in controversy, as *P* placed it in controversy in his complaint. However, *D*'s vision is not yet in controversy. On the other hand, if *P* finds a person with personal knowledge that *D* has bad eyesight, *P* could use an affidavit by that person to put *D*'s vision in controversy.

    b. **Good cause:** To demonstrate good cause, the movant must show that the *information cannot reasonably be obtained by other means*. For example, if the party to be examined is willing to turn over his medical records, the movant may not be able to demonstrate good cause.

    Example: Consider the prior example. The state in question has no doctor–patient privilege for optometrists. Because *P* can obtain all the information she needs from the optometrist, there is no good cause for an exam.

    c. **Violation of order:** A party who disobeys a court order to submit to an exam is subject to sanctions under *Fed. R. Civ. P. 37(b)(2)*. However, unlike other discovery orders, the court *cannot hold the party in contempt*. Fed. R. Civ. P. 37(b)(2)(A)(vii).

3. **Particulars concerning the exam:** The exam must be conducted by a *licensed or certified* examiner. The *movant* may select *where* the examination is held and must *pay all costs* associated with the examination.

4. **Examiner's report:** After the examination, the examiner prepares and delivers a *written report* to the party requesting the examination. The examined party may obtain a copy of the report on request. However, the request comes with significant cost. If the examined party requests the report, the party requesting the examination may obtain copies of *all other examinations of the examined party* involving the same condition. Fed. R. Civ. P. 35(b)(3). The examined

party ***waives any doctor–patient or similar privilege*** protecting all other reports. Fed. R. Civ. P. 35(b)(4).

Quiz Yourself on DISCOVERY METHODS

93. Roxanne hires CoverUp Roofing Co. to re-roof her house. Several days later, Roxanne comes home to find the president of CoverUp waiting at her door. The president declares the job was completed that very day. Roxanne gladly pays the president the agreed-upon fee. Later, Roxanne talks to Nozy Nabor, a retired gentleman who lives across the street. Nozy tells Roxanne he saw the president go up to Roxanne's house early that morning and ring the doorbell. When no one answered, he drove away. Suspicious, Nozy watched the house all day. Nozy is certain no roofers ever worked on Roxanne's house.

    Infuriated, Roxanne sues CoverUp for fraud. The case reaches the mandatory initial disclosure stage. Roxanne wonders whether she needs to disclose Nozy Nabor to CoverUp. She prefers to keep him a secret and surprise CoverUp with the damning proof of fraud at trial. Must Roxanne disclose Nozy? _____

94. Same facts as Problem 93. Assume Roxanne discloses Nozy in the initial disclosures. CoverUp deposes Nozy. The deposition turns out to be quite lengthy. After six full hours, Nozy declares, "If this isn't over in another hour, I'm going home—and don't even think of trying to depose me again!" Is Nozy entitled to make good on his threat? _____

95. Same facts as Problem 93, except Roxanne sues both CoverUp and the president as separate defendants. Roxanne serves interrogatories on each defendant. The set she serves on CoverUp contains 19 questions. The set she serves on the president contains 22 questions. Although three of the questions are the same, the rest are significantly different. CoverUp and the president object to the interrogatories, claiming Roxanne has exceeded the maximum allowed by the rule. How should the court rule on the objections? _____

96. Alpha runs a red light at a congested intersection, colliding with Beta and Gamma. Beta and Gamma each sue Alpha for their injuries, but in separate actions. In his case, Beta files a request for admission asking Alpha to admit he failed to maintain his brakes. Alpha responds by admitting he was negligent in maintaining his brakes. Now, Gamma attempts to use Alpha's admission in Beta v. Alpha in her case. Is the admission binding on Alpha in Gamma's case? _____

97. Bill Billionaire is 99 years old. After Bill has a brief but life-changing conversation with his postman, he asks his attorney to change his will to name the postman sole beneficiary of his vast estate. Upon hearing of Bill's plans, Bill's children bring an action to have a guardian appointed to handle Bill's affairs. The complaint claims Bill has "become insane." Later, the children ask Bill to submit to a mental examination. Bill refuses. Is there any way the children can force Bill to undergo an exam? _____

98. Rosie is seriously injured when a bone in a can of baked beans breaks her tooth. Rosie sues Barbara's Baked Beans Company, the manufacturer, for her injuries. Rosie needs to find out how the bone got in the can. She wants to depose someone who was working in the canning department on the fateful day, but does not know who has this information. How can Rosie find out what she wants to know? _____

Answers

93. Roxanne is required to disclose Nozy's name, address, and telephone number, as well as a summary of the information he knows. Fed. R. Civ. P. 26(a)(1)(A)(i) requires a party to disclose this information about any individual who has discoverable evidence the party will use at trial for purposes other than impeachment. Roxanne will probably use Nozy's testimony to prove her claims, unless she has some other means of proving no roof was put on her house and she saves Nozy for impeachment.

94. Fed. R. Civ. P. 30(d)(1) specifies that no deposition may exceed a single day of seven hours. No person may be deposed for a longer period, or asked to return another day, without the court's or the other party's permission. Nozy therefore is justified in refusing to continue the deposition past seven hours or to come back a second day. However, CoverUp may petition the court for more time.

95. The objection will fail. Fed. R. Civ. P. 33(a)(1) allows a party to "serve upon any other party no more than 25 written interrogatories. . . ." Therefore, Roxanne is entitled to serve up to 25 questions on *each defendant*. It does not matter whether the questions are the same or different.

96. No. Under Fed. R. Civ. P. 36(b), an admission is binding only in that particular case.

97. Fed. R. Civ. P. 35 allows a party to force another party to submit to a mental (or physical) examination. However, the party must obtain a court order. To obtain the order, the party must demonstrate the mental condition of the other party is in controversy and that good cause exists for the exam. The latter requirement is met, for absent a mental exam, there is no way the children can prove Bill's lack of capacity. However, on the facts, Bill's condition is not yet in controversy. A party cannot put another party's condition in controversy by the pleadings alone. Instead, the children need more proof, such as an affidavit of someone who has observed Bill's eccentric behavior on other occasions.

98. Fed. R. Civ. P. 30(b)(6) allows Rosie to notice the deposition of the company and describe the information sought. The company must designate one or more people who have knowledge of the subject matter to testify and then tell Rosie what their testimony will cover.

V. SUPPLEMENTING DISCLOSURES AND RESPONSES

In some situations, Fed. R. Civ. P. 26(e) requires a *party* to *supplement or correct* disclosures and responses.

    A. Only parties: Nonparties are never under a duty to supplement.

    B. Court-ordered supplementation: A party must supplement a mandatory disclosure or responses to discovery when ordered to do so by the court.

    C. Supplementing disclosures: Even without a court order, a party must supplement its mandatory disclosures if it learns the earlier disclosure was *incomplete or incorrect* in some *material* way and the additional or correct information has *not otherwise been made known to* the other parties through discovery or in writing.

    D. Supplementing other discovery: A party may also be required to supplement its responses to other forms of discovery.

        1. Responses covered: A party must supplement its *answers to interrogatories, response to a request for production of documents,* and *answer to requests for admission*. Note that answers to a deposition need not be supplemented.

2. **When supplementation required:** A party must supplement a response if it learns the earlier answer or response was *incomplete or incorrect* in some *material* way, and the additional or correct information has *not otherwise been made known to* the other parties through discovery or in writing.

Example: *P* and *D* are embroiled in a lawsuit in which *P* claims *D* failed to pay her for painting *D*'s house. The contract required *P* to paint *D*'s house on or before May 10. *P* has recently learned that three pieces of information she gave to *D* are incorrect. First, in her initial disclosures, *P* failed to mention the name of a witness who saw her perform the work. *P* knows, however, that *D* also found this witness in an informal conversation with the neighbors. Second, in her deposition, *P* told *D* she painted the house on May 3, when in truth she did it on May 20. Third, when *D* filed a request to admit the house was not painted by May 10, *P* refused to admit, still thinking at the time that she had performed the work on May 3. *P* must supplement her disclosures and her answer to the request to admit. Even though *D* has learned of the witness, *D* did not acquire that information by way of discovery or in writing. *P* need not supplement her answer in the deposition because depositions are not subject to the supplementation requirement.

VI. PREVENTING DISCOVERY ABUSE

Although discovery is designed to operate with little court supervision, disputes invariably arise. The rules give courts several tools to police abuse.

A. **Signing of discovery:** *Fed. R. Civ. P. 26(g)* attempts to prevent abuse by requiring all discovery documents to be *signed*. Rule 26(g) is discovery's counterpart to Fed. R. Civ. P. 11.

1. **What must be signed:** The rule requires that most mandatory disclosures and all discovery requests, responses, and objections be signed.

2. **Who signs:** At least one attorney of record must sign. If a party has no attorney, the party signs.

3. **Effect of signing:** By signing, the signer certifies she has conducted a *reasonable inquiry* and that, to the best of her knowledge, information, and belief:

   a. In the case of *mandatory disclosures*, the disclosure is *complete* and *correct* when made.

   b. In the case of other discovery requests, responses, and objections, the item is:

      i. consistent with the *rules*;

      ii. warranted by existing *law* or a nonfrivolous argument for changing existing law;

      iii. not made for any *improper purpose*, including harassment or delay; and

      iv. not unreasonably or unduly *burdensome*, considering the needs of the case, the amount in controversy, the importance of the issues, and the discovery already conducted.

4. **Violation of rule:** If the above standards are violated, the court may impose an appropriate sanction on the signer and/or the represented party.

   i. **No safe harbor:** Unlike Fed. R. Civ. P. 11, Rule 26(g) has no safe harbor provision.

   ii. **Motion not required:** No motion is necessary to obtain sanctions, although sanctions on the court's own volition are rare.

    iii. Sanctions: Although the judge has considerable discretion in determining an appropriate sanction, the rule specifically authorizes an award of expenses and ***attorneys' fees.***

  5. Rule 11 not applicable: Fed. R. Civ. P. 11 does not apply to discovery. Fed. R. Civ. P. 11(d). Therefore, Rule 26(g) is the only certification provision applicable in discovery.

B. Compelling discovery: A party served with what it considers to be an improper or overly burdensome discovery request will sometimes simply refuse to provide the information. In these situations, the requesting party may obtain an ***order compelling discovery. Fed. R. Civ. P. 37(a).*** The order itself may impose sanctions on the disobedient party. Failure to comply with the order may lead to additional sanctions.

  1. Proper court: If the person who refuses to provide information is another ***party***, the motion is filed in the court in which the ***case is pending***. If the person who refuses to provide information is a ***nonparty*** who is being deposed, the motion is filed in the court where the ***deposition is pending***. Fed. R. Civ. P. 37(a)(2).

  2. Must attempt to negotiate: A motion to compel discovery must include a certification that the movant has previously conferred in good faith or attempted to confer with the person refusing to provide information in order to resolve the matter without court intervention. Fed. R. Civ. P. 37(a)(1).

  3. Compelling disclosure or discovery: An order compelling discovery is available for all discovery ***except requests for admission*** and ***physical and mental examinations***. Of course, in the case of an exam, the party seeking the exam has already obtained an order under Fed. R. Civ. P. 35. In the case of requests for admission, failure to deny constitutes an admission.

  4. Sanctions for unsuccessful motion: If a party's motion to compel discovery is ***unsuccessful***, and the court finds the motion was ***not substantially justified***, the court may order that party and/or his attorney to pay the expenses, including attorneys' fees, of the party defending the motion. However, the court must give notice and opportunity to be heard before imposing such a sanction. ***Fed. R. Civ. P. 37(a)(5)(B).***

  5. Order, additional sanctions: If the moving party ***prevails***, the court will order the other side to cooperate in discovery and may impose ***sanctions*** in some situations.

    a. Costs and attorneys' fees on successful motion: The court may require the party or person subject to the order to reimburse the movant for costs and attorneys' fees, unless the failure to provide information was ***substantially justified*** or ***other circumstances*** make an award unjust. Fed. R. Civ. P. 37(a)(5)(A).

    b. Additional sanctions: ***Fed. R. Civ. P. 37(d)*** allows a court to impose additional sanctions on a ***party*** who refuses to provide information in certain situations.

      i. When available: Additional sanctions are available against a party who ***refuses*** to ***appear at its*** deposition or ***answer an interrogatory***, or ***refuses*** to respond to a ***request for inspection*** of documents or tangible things. The rule also applies when a party notices the deposition of an organization on certain matters, leaving it to the organization to determine the people who will testify. If the designated people fail to attend, the organization is subject to sanctions.

      ii. These additional sanctions usually accompany an order to compel discovery. However, they may also be imposed absent such an order. Therefore, if a party obtains the information from another source, it may seek sanctions against the noncooperative party even without an order compelling discovery.

   iii. Sanctions available: Fed. R. Civ. P. 37(d) allows a court to order that:

     (a) certain *matters* in the discovery request be *deemed established*;

     (b) the noncooperating party be barred from making certain claims or defenses or from introducing evidence on certain matters;

     (c) parts of the noncooperating party's *pleadings be struck*;

     (d) the *action be stayed* until the party complies; or

     (e) the *action be dismissed*; or

     (f) a *default judgment* be entered.

   iv. Proportionality requirement: Notwithstanding the broad array of listed sanctions, there is a proportionality requirement in the application of Rule 37, which prohibits use of the most severe sanctions in cases of minor transgressions.

     (a) When considering how severe a sanction to impose, courts focus on whether the sanctioned party acted in *good faith or willfully*, if the rule was *clear* or open to interpretation, and the degree to which the failure *affected the underlying case*.

     (b) Within the above restrictions, the trial judge has wide discretion in selecting which sanctions to impose. An appellate court will overturn that decision only upon a showing of *abuse of discretion*.

     ★ **Example:** The court in Security National Bank of Sioux City v. Abbott Laboratories, 2014 WL 3704277 (N.D. Iowa), discussed the importance of *deterrence* in determining appropriate sanctions. The court's sanctions included requiring the offending attorney to prepare an instructional video.

6. Sanctions for disobeying order: Violation of a discovery order exposes the violator to *additional sanctions*, even if the party was sanctioned when the order was issued.

  a. When available: Sanctions are available whenever a *party* violates a court's discovery order. The rule applies to not only an *order compelling discovery* but also an *order to take part in a discovery conference* (Fed. R. Civ. P. 26(f)) and an *order to submit to a physical or mental examination* (Fed. R. Civ. P. 35).

  b. Sanctions available: The sanctions available for violation of an order are generally the same as those set out in 5.b.iii. However, there is one crucial difference. Because the offender has violated a court order, he may also be held in *contempt of court*. Fed. R. Civ. P. 37(b)(2)(A)(vii).

   i. Contempt: Contempt is a severe sanction. Typically, the party will be required to pay a monetary fine to the court. The fine may be *levied on a daily basis*, until the party "removes the contempt" by complying with the order. In cases of especially flagrant disobedience, the party may be *jailed* until she complies.

   ii. Exception: Contempt is *not available* for refusing to submit to a *physical or mental examination*. Fed. R. Civ. P. 37(b)(2)(A)(vii).

iii. **Proportionality requirement:** The proportionality requirement also applies to sanctions imposed for violating a court order. However, because the party has been specifically directed to respond, a court is much more likely to determine that a party acted *willfully*, thus allowing for the imposition of *more severe sanctions*.

C. **Specific sanctions:** In addition to the general provisions discussed above, the discovery rules contain specific sanctions for certain discovery problems.

1. **Failure to attend depositions:** If a party who notices a deposition fails to attend, he may be required to pay the expenses and attorneys' fees of any parties who do attend. Fed. R. Civ. P. 30(g)(1). A party may also be required to pay costs and attorneys' fees of other parties if he notices the deposition of a nonparty witness but neglects to serve a subpoena on that witness, and the witness fails to attend the deposition. Fed. R. Civ. P. 30(g)(2).

2. **Failure to answer question at deposition:** A *party* or *nonparty* deponent who refuses a court order to be sworn in at a deposition or to answer a question after being sworn in may be held in *contempt of court.* Fed. R. Civ. P. 37(b)(1).

3. **Failure to disclose or supplement:** A party who omits information required by the mandatory disclosure rules (see Part IV.A) or to supplement a response as required by Rule 26(e) is subject to sanctions unless the party demonstrates the failure was *substantially justified* or *harmless.* Fed. R. Civ. P. 37(c).

   a. **Sanction:** A party who fails to disclose or supplement is *barred from introducing evidence* on that matter at trial or at any hearing on a motion. As an additional or alternate sanction, the court may order the party to pay the expenses and attorneys' fees other parties incurred in obtaining the information from other sources, together with additional sanctions.

   b. **When failure is "harmless":** A failure to disclose or supplement is deemed harmless when the information is of *little significance* to the other party in proving or defending his case or when the other party *already had obtained the information* from another source when the disclosure or supplementation should have occurred.

4. **Failure to admit:** If a party unreasonably fails to admit a matter covered by a request to admit, the requesting party may be able to recover all reasonable expenses, including attorneys' fees, it incurs in proving that matter at trial. Fed. R. Civ. P. 37(c)(2).

5. **Discovery plan:** A party who refuses to participate in the framing of the discovery plan may be required to reimburse other parties for any reasonable expenses, including attorneys' fees, they incur because of the failure to participate. Fed. R. Civ. P. 37(f).

Quiz Yourself on DISCOVERY

99. A newspaper article claims Lieutenant Smith, a local police officer, is "on the take." The article quotes an "anonymous source." Smith sues the newspaper. The newspaper answers by claiming the story is true. Smith learns the anonymous source is a senior citizen who supposedly witnessed him taking a payoff. However, Smith has also learned from several friends of this witness that the senior citizen

suffers from extremely poor eyesight. Smith asks the court for an order requiring the senior citizen to submit to an optical exam. Will the court grant the order? _____

100. Same facts as Problem 99, except that rather than ask for an optical exam, Smith serves the senior citizen with a set of interrogatories to glean what the senior citizen really saw. The senior citizen gladly obliges, sending back detailed answers. The newspaper moves for a protective order preventing Smith from using the answers in any way. The newspaper argues interrogatories may be used only against parties to the action. Will the court grant the protective order? _____

101. During a hotly contested volleyball game, Spike purposefully shoves Danny, causing serious injuries. Danny's girlfriend Dawn witnesses the event. Danny sues Spike for battery. Spike sends deposition notices to Danny and Dawn. Neither Danny nor Dawn shows up on the appointed date. What can Spike do? _____

102. Same facts as Problem 101, except Dawn attends her deposition. After being sworn in and answering a few questions, Dawn suddenly becomes defensive and refuses to answer any more. What can Spike do? _____

103. Horace Mann is a claims adjuster for an insurance company. While driving down a busy highway, Horace sees a truck change lanes and collide with three cars. All three car drivers are seriously injured. Horace stops and helps the three victims. As a trained claims adjuster, Horace also instinctively takes photographs of the crash scene. Horace, however, is not the only person who photographs the scene. A police forensics unit shows up a few minutes after Horace and also takes detailed photographs of the accident scene.

The next day, Horace discovers his company has issued a liability insurance policy covering the truck driver. Horace therefore visits all three drivers in the hospital to try to learn what happened. All three drivers give Horace written statements.

One of the car drivers soon sues the truck driver for her injuries. Horace is assigned to collect more background information concerning the case. Horace discovers the names of two bystanders who happened to see the collision. He interviews these bystanders and obtains written statements from them.

You represent the truck driver in this case. Your client asks you four questions:

a. Must he reveal Horace's name, or the names of the bystanders, in the list of witnesses disclosed in the initial disclosures?

b. If plaintiff somehow learns Horace's name, can plaintiff depose Horace about what Horace saw on the day of the wreck?

c. Can plaintiff obtain Horace's photographs of the crash scene?

d. Must your client turn over the statements Horace took from the three car drivers and two bystanders? _____

104. Attorney Albert has brought an action against Megacorp, Inc., alleging violation of employment discrimination laws. Albert's client, who is 6′ 3″ tall, alleges she was fired because of her height. Albert serves interrogatories on Megacorp. One of the interrogatories asks for the names and employment histories of all employees, present and past, who were taller than 6′. Although Megacorp does have this information in its personnel files, the files are organized on the basis of the employees' names, not their height. Therefore, to provide this information, Megacorp would need to search every one of its many thousands of employee files. Is there anything Megacorp can do to spare itself this trouble? _____

105. Dean Deponent is testifying at a deposition. When the line of questioning turns to certain intimate aspects of Dean's life—aspects Dean feels are completely irrelevant to the case—he refuses to answer. Flustered, the attorney immediately goes to the court and seeks an order compelling discovery. Will the court issue the order?   _____

Answers

99. The court will refuse the request. Under Fed. R. Civ. P. 35, only parties may be ordered to submit to physical or mental exams. The senior citizen is not a party.

100. The court will not grant the protective order. The Federal Rules of Civil Procedure merely provide that nonparties are not *required* to respond to interrogatories. If they choose to respond, the party can still use the answers. In essence, the interrogatories here are a form of informal discovery.

101. Fed. R. Civ. P. 37(d)(1)(A) requires a party who fails to attend his deposition to pay the expenses and attorneys' fees of any party who did attend. Therefore, Danny must reimburse Spike for these expenses.

Dawn, however, is not a party. Because Spike did not obtain a subpoena requiring her to attend (the problem says only that he sent her notice), she cannot be sanctioned.

102. Fed. R. Civ. P. 37(b)(1) provides a nonparty deponent like Dawn can be held in contempt for refusing to answer questions after taking the oath, but only after the court orders her to answer. Spike will need to obtain a court order.

103. This problem involves work product. Horace is a representative of the truck driver. Therefore, documents prepared by Horace may qualify for work product protection, but only to the extent they were prepared in anticipation of litigation.

   a. What Horace observed at the accident scene was not information prepared in anticipation of litigation. Horace is an ordinary witness, just like any other bystander. Therefore, his name, as well as the names of the other witnesses, must be disclosed to plaintiff.

   b. For the same reason, plaintiff is free to depose Horace.

   c. The photographs of the accident scene were not prepared in anticipation of litigation either. Therefore, they can be discovered. (Note that the discussion in the problem about the police photographs is therefore irrelevant—plaintiff can obtain the photographs of Horace even without a showing of need.)

   d. The statements Horace took from the drivers and the bystanders, by contrast, were all prepared in anticipation of litigation. Therefore, the work product rule applies. However, the statement Horace took from plaintiff must be turned over. Fed. R. Civ. P. 26(b)(3)(C) provides that a party can always obtain a copy of her own statement without showing need. With respect to the other statements, it is unlikely plaintiff can demonstrate need. As long as she has the names of the witnesses (which she should get in the mandatory disclosures), she can interview those witnesses herself.

104. The information is relevant because it may show how Megacorp has treated tall employees in the past. However, Megacorp does not have to amass the data itself. Fed. R. Civ. P. 33(d) allows it to open up its records to Albert, and let Albert seek the information. The burden on Albert of poring through the records is the same as the burden on Megacorp.

105. The court will not issue the order. Dean's refusal to answer is wrongful. If he felt the questions were improper because irrelevant, Fed. R. Civ. P. 30(c)(2) requires the witness to object, but then answer the question anyway, with the objection noted on the transcript. Dean cannot simply refuse to answer.

However, the attorney did not follow the proper procedure for an order compelling discovery. Under Fed. R. Civ. P. 37(a)(1), the party seeking the order must certify she made a good faith attempt to confer with the deponent to work out an amicable solution to the problem. The attorney made no such effort here.

Exam Tips *on* DISCOVERY

☛ Discovery follows a fairly regimented schedule. You may find it helpful to set out a timeline for the entire discovery process, which details the point at which certain events will occur.

☛ Be sure you understand the practical differences between the different types of discovery. For example, most of the discovery methods apply only to parties to the case.

☞ It is especially important to draw a clear distinction between *mandatory disclosures* and other forms of discovery.

☛ The concept of *relevance* often proves difficult. It may help to think of relevance as a two-part question: *whether* the information is relevant, and *to what* it is relevant.

☞ Whether information is relevant is a very loose standard. In order to be relevant, information need only make a given proposition more or less likely to be true.

☞ Recall that information can be relevant for discovery even though it cannot be used as evidence at trial.

☞ On the other hand, in order to be discoverable, information must be relevant to *a claim or defense in the case*. Information that tends to prove or disprove other issues cannot be discovered.

☛ *Privileged* information cannot be discovered even if it is relevant.

☞ Privileges protect the *source* of information, not the information itself.

☞ Privileges are also an issue in *work product*. If a question deals with an attempt to obtain information from an attorney, discuss both privilege and work product. If the attorney learned the information from the client, a privilege is likely to apply.

☛ **Depositions:** Unlike most other discovery devices, a deposition may be used against nonparties. A party needs a subpoena to ensure a nonparty witness's attendance.

☞ In most cases, someone being deposed must answer even objectionable questions. The objection is noted on the transcript.

☛ **Interrogatories:** Unlike in a deposition, a party answering interrogatories has a *duty to investigate* to find the information.

☛ **Examining documents and tangible things:** Recall that although Fed. R. Civ. P. 34 can be used only against parties, a party who seeks discovery of documents or tangible things from someone not a party can obtain a subpoena under Fed. R. Civ. P. 45 allowing access to and inspection of the items.

☛ **Physical and mental examinations:** Because physical and mental examinations are the only form of discovery against another party requiring court permission, make sure you discuss the "in controversy" and "good cause" issues in your answer.

    ☞ A party usually cannot put the other party's condition in controversy by the pleadings alone. Instead, the party must submit an affidavit.

    ☞ If there is some other way to obtain the information, the party cannot show good cause.

☛ **Work product:** Work product is one of the few issues in discovery that lends itself well to the examination format. Law school examinations accordingly often have work product questions, so make a special effort to master the rule.

    ☞ Work product no longer applies only to documents prepared by an attorney. Under the Federal Rules of Civil Procedure, it also applies to things prepared by the party or any representative of the party.

    ☞ Recall that something can be "prepared in anticipation of litigation" even if it was prepared before the lawsuit was even filed.

    ☞ The work product protection is a qualified privilege that can be overcome by showing need. Thus, when discussing work product, be sure to discuss whether the requesting party can acquire the same information from other sources.

    ☞ The rule governing *nontestifying experts* is very similar to the work product rule, although it is much more difficult to show need in the case of an expert.

☛ When dealing with *sanctions*, remember that a party must ordinarily attempt to negotiate with the offending party before running off to court for sanctions.

    ☞ A court will rarely impose the most severe sanctions without providing some sort of warning first. However, once the party violates an order compelling discovery, more severe sanctions are possible, at least if the violation is willful.

CHAPTER 9

RESOLUTION WITHOUT TRIAL

ChapterScope

This chapter deals with how a pending case can be resolved without a trial. It deals both with disputes already in the court system and those resolved by settlement or extra-judicial decision makers like arbitrators. Because state rules vary significantly, this chapter focuses on the *federal courts*.

■ Parties who settle a case typically enter into a settlement agreement, which may result in a *voluntary dismissal* or a *consent judgment*.

■ A *plaintiff* may also *voluntarily dismiss* his case even without a settlement. Depending on what has happened in the case, plaintiff may need the consent of the other side or a court order to dismiss.

■ Because of the costs of and limited remedies available in ordinary court litigation, parties increasingly use *alternate dispute resolution* procedures, primarily arbitration and mediation.

■ Courts have several tools to control the pre-trial process. The federal rules allow the judge to schedule one or more *pre-trial conferences* to deal with issues in the case as well as scheduling matters.

■ If a defendant fails to participate in a case after being served with process, the court may issue a *default judgment*.

■ Conversely, if plaintiff fails to prosecute the case diligently, follow governing rules, or obey court orders, the court may *dismiss* the case against plaintiff's will.

■ Either party may ask the court to issue a *summary judgment* on one or more claims in the case. If the court determines there is no genuine dispute concerning the facts, it will issue a judgment on that claim.

I. SETTLEMENT

Most disputes are resolved by *settlement*. A dispute may be settled before plaintiff files suit, while a case is pending, or even after the court enters judgment (to forestall an appeal).

A. Judicial approval usually unnecessary: The parties ordinarily do not need to notify the court or obtain court approval before settling a case. However, court approval may be required in a case involving *minors*. Moreover, *Fed. R. Civ. P. 23(e)* requires court approval before a *class action* may be dismissed or settled.

B. Termination of pending case: If a suit is underway, the settling parties must arrange to have the suit terminated. In most cases, dismissal is effected by a *voluntary dismissal* (typically by stipulation), which is discussed in Part VI of this chapter. However, the parties may have the court enter a *consent decree*.

C. **Postjudgment settlement:** Special issues arise when the parties settle a case after the trial court judgment, while the case is on appeal. The judgment loser in such a case may want to *expunge the trial court's judgment*, to prevent other parties from relying on that judgment in later litigation. However, courts are split as to whether they will honor the parties' agreement to expunge a judgment.

D. **Barring later actions:** Whether the settlement bars later actions depends on the form of dismissal.

   1. **Settlement agreement:** The settlement agreement itself typically forbids either party from suing on the claim again. Because the agreement is a contract, it binds the parties (assuming it is valid under contract law).

   2. **Voluntary dismissal:** The claim preclusion effect of a voluntary dismissal is discussed in Part VI.

   3. **Consent decree:** A consent decree is a judgment and accordingly is entitled to full *claim preclusion* effect.

★   4. **Confidentiality provision:** A settlement agreement often contains a confidentiality provision barring the parties from speaking about the underlying dispute or the terms of the settlement. Although these agreements are generally enforceable, they do not necessarily protect a party who is later subpoenaed to testify in litigation involving the same basic subject but involving a different plaintiff or defendant. Kalinauskas v. Wong, 151 F.R.D. 363 (D. Nev. 1993).

II. ALTERNATIVE DISPUTE RESOLUTION

Rather than take a dispute to court, the parties may decide—or be required by contract—to take their dispute to an arbitrator or mediator. While both arbitration and mediation use a nonjudicial third party, there are important differences.

A. **Mediation:** Mediation is a formalized attempt to reach a settlement. Unlike typical settlement negotiations, a third party, the mediator, works with the parties to help them agree how to resolve their dispute.

   1. **Mediator lacks authority:** A mediator has *no power* to force the parties to do anything. Instead, the mediator talks to the parties—sometimes together, sometimes separately—in an attempt to find common ground and provide a neutral third party's perspective.

   2. **Required mediation:** In some situations, *mediation may be required*. For example, some states require parties to a divorce to take part in mediation.

B. **Arbitration:** Arbitration also introduces a third party to the dispute. Unlike mediation, however, the arbitrator actually *renders a decision*. Arbitration is accordingly more like litigation.

   1. **Binding vs. nonbinding arbitration:** In most cases, the parties are bound by the arbitrator's decision. Sometimes, however, parties submit to nonbinding arbitration. The "decision" in nonbinding arbitration allows the parties to assess the strength of their respective cases.

   2. **Contract:** In most cases, arbitration stems from a contract in which the parties agree to submit their disputes to arbitration instead of going to court. Therefore, the agreement must be a legally enforceable contract.

★   **Example:** In Ferguson v. Countrywide Credit Industries, Inc., 298 F.3d 778 (9th Cir. 2002), the court found a lender's clause unconscionable because it was one-sided, and because a potential employee could not negotiate to change the language.

   a. **Interstate commerce:** Some states will not honor arbitration agreements as a matter of policy. However, if the underlying contract involves *interstate commerce*, the *Federal Arbitration Act*, 9 U.S.C. §§2 et seq., makes the agreement to arbitrate enforceable, regardless of whether state law honors arbitration agreements.

      i. The contract must still meet the other state law requirements for an enforceable contract.

      ii. However, if the state law interferes with the goals of the federal act, it will not be applied.

★   **Example**: In AT&T Mobility LLC v. Concepcion, 131 S. Ct. 1740 (2011), the Court dealt with a state law that treated an arbitration clause as unconscionable (and therefore unenforceable) because it barred class action suits. The Court found the state law did not apply because it conflicted with the Federal Arbitration Act's goal of streamlined dispute resolution.

   b. **Precondition:** The contract typically makes arbitration a *precondition to suing in court*. If a party attempts to forgo the arbitration process and sue in court, the other side may move for dismissal of the court case.

   c. **Limits:** Not all issues may be sent to arbitration. For example, most courts will not enforce an agreement between husband and wife to submit their divorce or any child custody issues to binding arbitration.

3. **Arbitration process:** Arbitration can be conducted by a single arbitrator or by a panel of several (typically three) arbitrators.

   a. **Flexible procedure:** An arbitrator is *not bound by the rules of procedure and evidence* to the same extent a court is. Therefore, an arbitrator may hear claims not set out in the parties' briefs. An arbitrator may also consider nonadmissible evidence such as hearsay.

   b. **Inquisitorial role:** An arbitrator is free to ask her own questions of the witnesses or ask to review documents not submitted by the parties in evidence.

   c. **Governing law:** Parties to an arbitration have some ability to *specify the law* that governs their dispute. Thus, they may agree their dispute is governed by industry custom rather than the usual law of contract.

   d. **Opinion of arbitrator:** The arbitrator typically renders a *written opinion*. Although this opinion does bind the parties in that dispute, it has little weight as precedent, even in later arbitrations involving the same parties.

4. **Judicial review of arbitration:** Although judicial review of an arbitrator's decision is available, it is extremely limited. A court *cannot review the merits* of the decision. It may only review *whether the arbitrator acted within the scope of her authority*.

★   **Example:** Ferguson v. Writers Guild of America, West, 226 Cal. App. 3d 1382, 277 Cal. Rptr. 450 (1991), shows how courts defer to arbitration. The parties in that case had agreed an arbitration panel would determine who would be named in the credits to a film. Ferguson challenged the panel's decision that he was not entitled to credit. The court refused to overturn the decision, finding the arbitrators had acted within the scope of the powers vested by the arbitration agreement. Even though some of the procedures were of questionable fairness, the court noted Ferguson had agreed to them beforehand.

Quiz Yourself on
ALTERNATIVE DISPUTE RESOLUTION

106. Digimage, Inc., makes high-end digital cameras. Digimage obtains the lenses for these cameras from Schott Glass, GmbH. One of Schott's shipments contains a number of lenses that Digimage believes do not meet the required specifications. Because the contract between Digimage and Schott requires all disputes arising under the contract to be submitted to binding arbitration, the parties hold a three-day arbitration. The arbitrator finds the lenses do not meet specifications and issues a ruling that Schott should immediately send replacement lenses.

Schott refuses to comply with this order. It claims that notwithstanding the language in the contract stating the arbitration was "binding," only a court has the power to adjudicate the rights of the parties. Is Schott correct? _____

Answer

106. Schott is not correct. Parties may agree to binding arbitration, which adjudicates their rights fully. Because the contract clearly specified the arbitration was binding, the arbitrator's decision binds Schott. Digimage may need to go to court for an order enforcing the ruling, but the court will not review the arbitrator's findings.

III. JUDICIAL MANAGEMENT OF LITIGATION

Parties complain not only about the expense of litigation but also about the time it takes to complete a case. Courts have many tools to reduce the time and cost. This discussion focuses primarily on the tools used in federal court.

A. **Dismissals and defaults:** Much delay in litigation is attributable to two causes: plaintiffs who file a suit and then do nothing to bring it to completion, and defendants who engage in dilatory tactics to delay recovery. The federal rules contain provisions designed to combat both of these problems.

   1. **Involuntary dismissal of plaintiff's case:** Fed. R. Civ. P. 41(b) allows a court to dismiss plaintiff's case if plaintiff fails to prosecute the case diligently or fails to comply with a court order. Involuntary dismissals are discussed in Part V of this Chapter.

2. **Default judgments:** When a defendant fails to defend itself, comply with a court order, or cooperate in discovery, the court may enter default judgment against that defendant. Default judgments are explored in greater depth in Part IV of this Chapter.

B. **Pretrial conference:** Fed. R. Civ. P. 16 gives a federal court discretion to order one or more pretrial conferences to discuss virtually any matter relevant to the case. A pretrial conference will result in a *pretrial order* that guides the remainder of the case. Although Rule 16 applies only to the federal courts, many states have similar provisions.

   1. **The conference:** *Fed. R. Civ. P. 16* sets forth the procedure for calling a pretrial conference. The rule leaves it to the discretion of the court whether to call a conference, but lists a number of reasons why a court might want to do so. Some federal districts have enacted local rules making a pretrial conference mandatory.

      a. **Types:** More than one conference is possible. For example, Fed. R. Civ. P. 16(b) envisions a *scheduling conference* to deal with amendments to pleadings, motions, disclosures, and discovery. Similarly, Rule 16(e) specifically authorizes a *final pretrial conference* that is to be held as close to the start of trial as reasonably possible.

      b. **Parties involved:** The conference must be attended by the *attorneys* and all *unrepresented parties*. At least one attorney for each party must have the authority to enter into stipulations and make admissions. The court may require the parties to be available by telephone or other means during the conference so the case can be settled. Fed. R. Civ. P. 16(c). Sanctions are available if a party fails to attend, be prepared for, or cooperate in a pretrial conference. Fed. R. Civ. P. 16(f).

      c. **Matters for consideration:** Virtually any issue that may arise in the pretrial or trial process is open for consideration at a pretrial conference. *Fed. R. Civ. P. 16(c)* contains a long list of items that may be discussed, including settlement, eliminating frivolous claims or defenses, stipulation of certain facts, discovery issues, and how to manage the trial.

   2. **Order:** If action is taken at the pretrial conference, the court issues an *order*.

      a. **Issuing deadlines:** An order following a scheduling conference must be issued as soon as practicable, and no later than the earlier of *90 days following the appearance of defendant* or *120 days following service on defendant*. Fed. R. Civ. P. 16(b). There is no deadline for other orders.

      b. **Parties affected:** A pretrial order *binds all parties* for the remainder of the case. Fed. R. Civ. P. 16(d).

      c. **Amendments:** The schedule set out in the scheduling order may be amended only for good cause, and with the judge's consent. Fed. R. Civ. P. 16(b)(4). An order issued after the final pretrial conference may only be amended to *prevent manifest injustice*. Fed. R. Civ. P. 16(e).

IV. DEFAULT

A party who fails to respond to a claim can be declared in default and may have judgment rendered against it. *Fed. R. Civ. P. 55* governs default judgments.

A. **Two stages:** There are two distinct stages in issuing a default judgment. The first is the *entry of default* against the party. Following that, the clerk or the court enters a *default judgment*.

B. **Entry of default:** *Fed. R. Civ. P. 55(a)* allows entry of default whenever a party *fails to plead or otherwise defend* a claim.

   1. **Not only defendants:** Although it is normally defendant who defaults, the rule applies to all parties against whom a claim is filed. Thus, a plaintiff who fails to defend a counterclaim can have a default entered against her on the counterclaim.

   2. **Who enters:** The *clerk* enters the default. Fed. R. Civ. P. 55(a). However, because the clerk does not investigate whether defendant has served an answer, the clerk usually acts only following a request by plaintiff.

   3. **Plead or otherwise defend:** Entry of default occurs after a party fails "to plead or otherwise defend." A party pleads by filing an *answer* or *reply*. The phrase "otherwise defend," however, is more ambiguous.

      a. Filing a *pre-answer motion* raising a Fed. R. Civ. P. 12 defense or objection, or a *motion for summary judgment,* clearly constitutes "defending" the action, and precludes entry of default.

      b. Whether other actions qualify as "defending" is less clear. For example, a §1404 *motion to transfer venue* does not qualify as "otherwise defending" because defendant is not challenging either the merits of the case or the court's power to hear it.

      c. A party must plead or otherwise defend within the deadline for an answer (which is usually 21 days but which can be extended, as discussed in Chapter 7). However, a court will typically deny a request for default judgment filed immediately after the time for filing an answer has expired.

   4. **Exception—sanction defaults:** The Federal Rules of Civil Procedure also allow for default judgment as a *sanction* against a party who refuses to cooperate in discovery or to obey a court order. Although sanction defaults are governed in most respects by Rule 55, there are certain differences. First, the *court*, not the clerk, *enters the default*. Second, the "plead or otherwise defend" language of Rule 55(a) does not apply.

   5. **Notice:** The *Rule does not require service* of the *entry* of default on the defaulting party. Defendant was already served with process and should realize an action is pending.

   6. **Effect of entry of default:** Entry of default has several consequences.

      a. Most *facts* alleged in the pleadings are *deemed admitted (because the party failed to deny them)*. However, the defaulting party may contest the amount of damages, unless damages are liquidated.

      b. The party is *not entitled to notice* of future proceedings in the case, except as discussed below with respect to the entry of judgment.

C. **Default judgment:** After default is entered against a party, the claimant may move for entry of the default judgment. However, the defaulting party may be entitled to notice and a hearing at which it can present evidence on certain issues.

   1. **Who enters judgment:** Depending on the circumstances, the clerk or the court may enter the default judgment.

a. **Clerk:** The clerk enters the default judgment if all the following conditions are satisfied (Fed. R. Civ. P. 55(b)(1)):

   i.   the claim is for a *sum certain*, or a sum that can be made certain by calculation;

   Example: *P* sues *D* to recover on a promissory note. The outstanding principal balance is a sum certain. If interest accrues on that principal at a defined rate, the claim is for a sum that can be made certain by calculation.

   ii. the entry of default was based on the party's *failure to appear* (which means the clerk does not enter judgment when default is imposed as a sanction);

   iii. the defaulting party is *not a minor or an incompetent person*; and

   iv. the defaulting party is *not the United States or a federal officer or agency* (Fed. R. Civ. P. 55(d)).

b. **By court:** In all other cases, the court enters the default judgment. Fed. R. Civ. P. 55(b)(2).

2. **How judgment obtained:** The claimant must *apply* to have judgment entered by the court. Again, a court rarely grants an application made immediately after the deadline for answering has expired.

3. **Hearing:** If damages are not a sum certain, or if the court feels it needs evidence to substantiate any allegations in the claim, the court schedules a hearing prior to entering judgment. Otherwise, no hearing is necessary.

   a. At the hearing, claimant *proves up the damages* by offering evidence. The defaulting party, if he attends, may counter that evidence.

   b. However, unless the court specifically asks for evidence, claimant *need not prove the other elements* of her claim. Nor may the defaulting party, if he appears, offer evidence on the merits.

   c. This rule flows naturally from the pleading rule in Fed. R. Civ. P. 8(b)(6), which provides that a party who fails to deny an allegation in a pleading is deemed to admit that allegation, *except* for allegations relating to the "amount of damages."

4. **Notice of hearing:** If the defaulting party has *appeared* in the action, Fed. R. Civ. P. 55(b)(2) requires he be *served with written notice* of the application for judgment at least *7 days* before the hearing.

   a. **Defaulting party who "appears":** A party can be declared in default for failing to plead or otherwise defend. Thus, the notice requirement applies only to a party who *appears* in the action, *but does not defend* by serving an answer or other defensive motion. A party may appear by filing a motion to extend the time for an answer, by moving for a change in venue, or, in some courts, even by sending a letter to the opposing party discussing settlement options.

   b. **When notice not required:** A party *who does not appear* does not receive notice. In addition, most courts do not require notice when the default judgment is imposed as a *sanction*. In sanction cases, the court often has previously given the party some notice of its improper acts and the possibility of default, such as an order to show cause.

5. **Limit on default judgment:** A judgment by default cannot award damages in excess of, or different in kind than, what the complaint seeks. Fed. R. Civ. P. 54(c).

D. Challenging defaults and default judgments: A party may challenge both the entry of default and the default judgment pursuant to Fed. R. Civ. P. 55(c) and 60(b).

   1. Entry: A party may have the entry of default set aside by showing *good cause* why it did not plead or otherwise defend. Examples of good cause include that the party never received service of process or suffered a serious illness.

   2. Default judgment: A default judgment may in some cases be set aside if the party against whom it was entered can show procedural irregularities or other reasons to set aside the judgment.

      a. Ordinary vs. sanction defaults: It is often said that *default judgments are highly disfavored*. However, this maxim applies mainly to judgments rendered against a party who failed to plead or defend. A default judgment rendered as a sanction is much more difficult to overturn.

      b. Procedural errors: Procedural errors *do not always require setting aside* the judgment. The court instead evaluates whether the error affected the party's ability to protect himself against default judgment.

★   **i.** However, if the procedural defect is so significant that it *denies due process*, the defect is automatically grounds for reversal. Moreover, if the procedural defect denies due process, a state cannot require the defaulting party to prove a *meritorious defense* to have the default set aside. Peralta v. Heights Medical Center, 485 U.S. 80 (1988).

         ii. Similarly, the judgment may be set aside if the rendering court lacked *subject matter* or *personal jurisdiction*. Improper venue is not grounds to set aside a default judgment.

      c. Other reasons to reopen: A party may be able to set aside a default judgment even if the court followed the dictated procedure to the letter. Here, however, the party's chances of success turn on the circumstances.

         i. No notice of action: If a party can demonstrate it never received notice of the action, a court will almost automatically set aside the default judgment. Recall that failure to receive notice does not necessarily constitute a procedural defect. As long as the claimant serves using authorized means, service is procedurally proper regardless of whether defendant actually receives the notice.

         ii. Other bases: If the party can show any of the grounds for reopening a judgment listed in Fed. R. Civ. P. 60(b), the court will set aside the default judgment. Rule 60(b) is discussed in Chapter 13, Part V.A. Although courts are normally very strict in applying this rule, the standard is more forgiving for non-sanction default judgments.

V. INVOLUNTARY DISMISSAL

Logically, the involuntary dismissal is defendant's counterpart to the default judgment. A court may dismiss plaintiff's action (or one or more claims in that action) when plaintiff fails to take an active role in the case, or as a sanction.

   A. Grounds: *Fed. R. Civ. P. 41(b)* allows a court to dismiss for two reasons.

      1. Failure to prosecute: If plaintiff fails to move the case along to completion, the court can dismiss it.

    a. Dismissal rare: Courts are reluctant to dismiss for failure to prosecute. A court typically warns plaintiff and gives him a chance to justify the delay.

    b. Prejudice: Although defendant technically need not demonstrate it is prejudiced by the delay, courts rarely dismiss for failure to prosecute if defendant is not injured or if defendant is also responsible for the delay.

  2. Failure to comply with rules or court order: Dismissals for failure to comply with the rules or a court order can be divided into two categories.

    a. Defect: The first is where there is a defect in the claimant's case, including *lack of jurisdiction*, any other *Rule 12 defense,* and *statute of limitations*.

    b. Sanction: Second, a court may dismiss a case as a sanction for violating a rule or court order during the case. However, because less drastic punishments are usually available, sanction dismissals are *relatively rare*.

B. Effect of dismissal: Fed. R. Civ. P. 41(b) also specifies the effect of a dismissal on later litigation. In many cases, the dismissal will be an *adjudication on the merits*, which prevents plaintiff from suing defendant again.

  1. Basic rule: An involuntary dismissal operates as *an adjudication on the merits* unless one of the following is true:

    a. The court dismisses for lack of subject matter jurisdiction, personal jurisdiction, or venue, or because of failure to join a necessary party under Fed. R. Civ. P. 19; or

    b. The *court specifies* in the dismissal order that the adjudication is *not on the merits*.

    c. Some dismissals never on the merits: The judge has some discretion to alter the default rule of Rule 41(b). But that discretion is only one way. Although a judge may turn a dismissal that would ordinarily be on the merits into one that is not, the judge *has no power to declare* that a dismissal for lack of jurisdiction, venue, or failure to join a necessary party is on the merits.

    Example 1: *P* sues *D* for breach of contract. The court dismisses because of *P*'s failure to prosecute the case. The order of dismissal is silent as to whether it operates as an adjudication on the merits. *P* cannot sue *D* again for the same breach.

    Example 2: Same facts as prior example, except the court dismissed for lack of venue. *P* is free to sue *D* again (in a court with venue).

★ **2. Important exception in federal courts:** The Supreme Court's decision in Semtek International, Inc. v. Lockheed Martin Corp., 531 U.S. 497 (2001), significantly limits the effect of a Fed. R. Civ. P. 41(b) dismissal by a federal court. *Semtek* is discussed in Chapter 5, Part IV.C.2.

    a. The Court in *Semtek* held that a Rule 41(b) dismissal based on expiration of the statute of limitations only bars a party from refiling in the *same federal court* that granted the dismissal.

    b. Although portions of the Court's discussion focus explicitly on statute of limitations dismissals, the Court never restricts its holding to those dismissals. It is therefore unclear whether the holding applies to dismissals on other grounds, such as failure to prosecute.

    c. If a party refiles in any other court, the preclusive effect of the dismissal is governed by the law of the state in which the federal court that dismissed the case sat. Because state rules often treat dismissals the same as Rule 41(b), the practical effect of *Semtek* may be limited to a few issues, such as statute of limitations, where Rule 41 seems to dictate a different outcome than state law.

3. **Application of rule:** The preclusion rules of Fed. R. Civ. P. 41(b) are applied strictly. For example, in federal court a dismissal for failure to state a claim upon which relief can be granted *is an adjudication on the merits*, unless the court gives leave to amend or explicitly provides in its order the dismissal is not on the merits. Federated Department Stores v. Moitie, 452 U.S. 394 (1981). In many states, by contrast, a dismissal for failure to state a claim does not operate as an adjudication on the merits.

VI. VOLUNTARY DISMISSAL

A plaintiff may voluntarily dismiss a pending action. Although such dismissals often accompany settlements, a plaintiff may also choose to dismiss for tactical reasons, such as a desire to spend more time marshaling evidence or to refile the action in a different court.

A. **How case dismissed:** A case can be dismissed in three ways, depending on the point in the case at which dismissal occurs.

1. **By notice:** If defendant has not yet served an *answer* or a motion for *summary judgment*, plaintiff may dismiss the case without approval of the court or consent of the other parties. Plaintiff effects the dismissal by filing a *notice of dismissal* with the court.

   a. Plaintiff's right to dismiss by notice is based on *actual service* of the answer or summary judgment motion, not on the time allowed for service of the answer. Thus, even if four months have expired since it served its complaint (recall that Rule 12 requires an answer within 21 days), plaintiff may still dismiss by notice if defendant has not yet served its answer or a motion for summary judgment. Conversely, if defendant answers the day after the complaint is served, plaintiff may no longer dismiss by notice.

   b. Dismissal by notice is also available for counterclaims, cross-claims, and third-party claims. In these cases, the period for dismissal by notice expires when the adverse party *serves its responsive pleading*, or, if no response is required, when *evidence* on the claim is introduced at trial or at a hearing (including a hearing on a summary judgment motion). Fed. R. Civ. P. 41(c). Note that for these claims the summary judgment *hearing*, not the prior motion for summary judgment, terminates the claimant's right to dismiss by notice.

2. **By stipulation:** A plaintiff may also dismiss by filing a *written stipulation of dismissal* signed by *all parties* who have *appeared* in the case. Dismissal by stipulation may occur at any point in the case, even during trial.

3. **By court order:** Plaintiff may also file a motion asking the court to dismiss his case. If plaintiff cannot unilaterally dismiss by notice, and one or more appearing parties refuses to sign the stipulation, dismissal by court order is plaintiff's only option. Dismissal by order may occur at any point in the case. However, if a counterclaim has been filed in the action, and the defendant who filed that counterclaim objects to the dismissal, the court cannot dismiss plaintiff's claim unless it can retain jurisdiction over the counterclaim. Fed. R. Civ. P. 41(a)(2).

B. **Effect of dismissal on refiling:** Whether plaintiff may refile its case after a voluntary dismissal depends on the type of the dismissal.

1. **By stipulation or court order:** Fed. R. Civ. P. 41(a)(1)(B) and (a)(2) provide that dismissals by stipulation and court order are *without prejudice, unless* the stipulation or order *provides otherwise.*

2. **By plaintiff:** A dismissal by notice is usually *without prejudice, unless plaintiff specifies it is with prejudice.* Fed. R. Civ. P. 41(a)(1)(B). However, a notice of dismissal is an adjudication on the merits if filed by a plaintiff who has *previously dismissed another action* involving the same claim.

   Example: *P* sues *D*. *P* dismisses the case by filing a notice of dismissal. *P* then refiles. *P* and *D* settle the second case and file a stipulation of dismissal. The stipulation, however, is silent as to whether it bars later litigation. *P* now sues *D* a third time. Although *D* can use the settlement agreement to show the affirmative defense of accord and satisfaction, *P* is not barred by Fed. R. Civ. P. 41(a) from bringing the claim. The "prior dismissal" rule of Rule 41(a)(1) does not apply because the second case was dismissed by stipulation, and the rule specifically applies only when the second dismissal is by notice.

Quiz Yourself on DEFAULTS, AND DISMISSALS

107. Porthos sues D'Artagnan in a federal district court in Virginia for injuries Porthos sustained in a duel between the two. Porthos later learns that under governing law, neither party to a duel may recover for his injuries. Before D'Artagnan files a pleading or motion, Porthos files a notice of dismissal. In this notice, Porthos explicitly indicates that he is dismissing to enable him to file the case in a different state, where the law allows recovery. D'Artagnan objects to this dismissal. Can D'Artagnan prevent Porthos from dismissing the case? _____

108. Same facts as Problem 107. Assume Porthos successfully dismisses the case by a notice of dismissal. Porthos refiles in a Tennessee federal court, where governing law allows recovery for injuries sustained in a duel. D'Artagnan moves to dismiss, arguing Porthos lost his right to sue again by voluntarily dismissing the case. Will D'Artagnan's motion succeed? _____

109. Tenant, a small business, leases its store from Landlord. Landlord sues Tenant, stating two claims. First, Landlord asks for ejectment, claiming Tenant has not paid several months of rent. Second, Landlord seeks damages for harm Tenant allegedly caused to the leased premises.

   Tenant immediately files a demand for a jury trial, which is denied. Tenant does not file an answer or take any further action in the case. Two months after the answer was due, Landlord moves for an entry of default. Will default be entered? _____

110. Same facts as Problem 109. Assume the clerk enters a default against Tenant. Can Landlord immediately collect money from Tenant, or will it have to take additional steps to have an enforceable judgment? _____

111. Passenger sues Driver in federal court for injuries sustained in a one-car accident. The court grants Driver's motion to dismiss for lack of subject matter jurisdiction. The court's order of dismissal explicitly states, "This dismissal for lack of subject matter jurisdiction is an adjudication on the merits."

A week later, Passenger sues Driver again in the same federal court. However, in his complaint Passenger states he moved to an adjacent state last week and is now a citizen of that state. Driver moves to dismiss based on the explicit language in the earlier order of dismissal. Who wins?   _____

Answers

107. D'Artagnan's objection is useless. Under Fed. R. Civ. P. 41(a), Porthos may dismiss by filing a notice of dismissal before D'Artagnan serves either an answer or a motion for summary judgment. The facts specify that D'Artagnan has not served a pleading or motion. Porthos's motives for dismissing the case are irrelevant.

108. D'Artagnan loses again. Under Fed. R. Civ. P. 41(a)(1), a dismissal by notice is without prejudice unless the notice states otherwise or plaintiff has dismissed once before.

109. The clerk should enter default in this case. Under Fed. R. Civ. P. 55, default is entered against a party who fails to plead or otherwise defend. Tenant did not file an answer and so has not pled. Although Tenant did appear by filing its demand for a jury, that demand does not constitute a defense since it does not challenge anything Landlord has alleged.

110. Obtaining a default judgment is a two-stage process. Entry of default is the first step. Getting the default judgment is the second. If damages are for a sum certain, the clerk issues the judgment. Here, however, although the rent is a sum certain (or a sum that can easily be calculated), the damages to the space are not a sum certain. Therefore, the judge must enter the judgment.

The judge will ordinarily hold a hearing at which Landlord must prove the amount of damage. Moreover, under Fed. R. Civ. P. 55(b)(2), Tenant will have to be served with written notice of the hearing. That rule requires notice to a defaulting defendant who appeared. Although Tenant failed to plead or otherwise defend, it appeared when it filed its jury demand.

111. Passenger will prevail. Fed. R. Civ. P. 41(b) explicitly says an involuntary dismissal for lack of jurisdiction is not an adjudication on the merits. The judge has no authority to convert such a dismissal into an adjudication on the merits.

VII. SUMMARY JUDGMENT

Summary judgment is a frequently sought—although much less frequently granted—way to resolve a case before trial. Summary judgment allows the court to look beyond the language in the pleadings to the actual facts supporting each side's case. The governing rule is *Fed. R. Civ. P. 56.*

A. Other procedures distinguished: Summary judgment should be distinguished from other means of resolving a case before trial.

1. Judgment on the pleadings: The *Fed. R. Civ. P. 12(c)* judgment on the pleadings allows a court to resolve a case based solely on the allegations in the pleadings. However, the court *must accept the factual allegations* in the pleadings as true. In a summary judgment motion, by contrast, the court looks at the evidence supporting the claims and defenses.

2. **Judgment as a matter of law:** A judgment as a matter of law under Fed. R. Civ. P. 50 occurs *during the trial*. A summary judgment motion, by contrast, must be made before trial commences.

B. **Procedure:** A party requests summary judgment by filing a motion. Fed. R. Civ. P. 56 governs the content, form, and timing of the motion.

   1. **Types of summary judgment:** A party may seek summary judgment on all claims in the case, or a *partial summary judgment* on one or more specific claims. Fed. R. Civ. P. 56(a) and (b). Claims include counterclaims, cross-claims, and third-party claims.

   2. **Who can move:** Either the claimant or the defending party may move for summary judgment on a particular claim. In fact, it is fairly common for *both* parties to move for summary judgment. If the facts are undisputed, summary judgment allows the court to decide the case as a matter of law.

   3. **Form of motion:** Although a party requests summary judgment by filing a specific motion under Fed. R. Civ. P. 56, Rule 12 also provides that certain other motions can be "converted" to a motion for summary judgment. If a party's motion to dismiss for *failure to state a claim* or *judgment on the pleadings* includes facts outside the pleadings, the court treats the motion as a motion for summary judgment. *Fed. R. Civ. P. 12(d)*.

   4. **Material accompanying motion:** A party moving for summary judgment usually includes supporting materials with the motion, such as affidavits, answers to interrogatories, and transcripts of depositions. The rule specifically provides all affidavits must be based on *personal knowledge*, set out facts that would be *admissible in evidence*, and show that the person making the affidavit is competent to testify on the matters covered by the affidavit. Fed. R. Civ. P. 56(c)(4). The movant also typically includes a *memorandum* explaining why summary judgment is appropriate.

   5. **Timing:** A motion for summary judgment may be filed very early in the case. Under Fed. R. Civ. P. 56(b), the motion can be filed at any time until 30 days following the close of discovery.

      a. **Response:** The opposing party has a reasonable time to respond. Fed. R. Civ. P. 56(f).

      b. **Disposition of early motions:** A motion for summary judgment presented at a very early stage of the case may present a problem for the other party. In such cases, the court may *delay the hearing* on the motion until the party has had adequate opportunity to *conduct discovery*. Fed. R. Civ. P. 56(d).

   6. **Response by opposing party:** The party opposing the motion for summary judgment may submit its own evidence supporting its side of the argument, including *affidavits* and a *memorandum* opposing the motion.

C. **Hearing:** Once the motion and supporting evidence and memoranda have been submitted, the court will typically hold a hearing. All parties may appear at this hearing and argue for or against summary judgment. Although a court may take oral testimony at the hearing, most courts rely exclusively on the material submitted by the parties.

D. **Standard for summary judgment:** Fed. R. Civ. P. 56(a) provides that the court shall grant summary judgment if there is *no genuine dispute as to any material fact* and the movant is *entitled to judgment as a matter of law*.

1. **Basic principles:** Numerous cases establish guidelines for applying this standard.

    a. **Court does not weigh evidence:** The trial judge does not weigh the competing evidence. If there is conflicting evidence, the court must deny summary judgment.

    b. **Credibility:** Similarly, the court does not determine whether the evidence is credible. Determining credibility is the province of the factfinder (jury or judge) at trial.

    c. **Favor nonmoving party:** All evidence is to be viewed in the light most favorable to the nonmoving party.

    ★ **Example:** Tolan v. Cotton, 134 S. Ct. 1861 (2014), illustrates the above guidelines. In this case, the court of appeals had affirmed the trial court's grant of summary judgment for a police officer in a case alleging the officer had used unreasonable force. The Supreme Court reversed, holding summary judgment improper. The Court indicated the court of appeals had erroneously "weighed" the conflicting evidence, and failed to view the evidence in the light most favorable to the non-moving party (plaintiff).

    d. **The problem of inferences:** If each party has direct testimony involving the crucial issue, the court's task is simple: summary judgment must be denied. The more difficult cases are where parties offer evidence that requires the factfinder to draw an inference as to the crucial fact.

    Example: *P* is trying to prove *D* was intoxicated. *P* offers direct eyewitness evidence that *D* was seen walking into a bar on the day in question. This evidence calls for an inference: namely, that defendant drank and became intoxicated.

    i. As a general rule, inferences are considered *a matter for the jury*. Therefore, a court faced with evidence calling for an inference typically denies summary judgment and lets the jury decide the question.

    ii. However, in some situations the inference is simply *too improbable* or farfetched to be allowed. In these cases, the court can grant summary judgment against the party who needs the benefit of the inference.

    Example: Consider the prior example. The eyewitness also testifies *D* left the bar 30 seconds later and was not seen reentering. It would be improper for the finder of fact to infer that *D* became drunk while in the bar. If this is *P*'s only evidence of intoxication, the court should grant summary judgment for *D*.

    iii. **Competing inferences:** In many cases, more than one inference can be drawn from the evidence. Unless all reasonable inferences favor one party, the court *should grant summary judgment* for the party without the burden of production, as discussed below. However, if one inference is much more likely than the alternative, the court may conclude it is the only viable alternative.

    Example 1: While standing in the quadrangle minding his own business, Law Professor is hit in the head with a baseball. He immediately turns in the direction from which the ball came. He sees only two people, *A* and *B*. Law Professor sues *A* for battery. *A* moves for summary judgment and should prevail. Law Professor's case requires an inference: namely, that *A, not B*, threw the ball. Because it is equally likely *B* threw the ball, it is impossible to draw the inference Law Professor needs. Without the inference, Law Professor cannot win.

Example 2: Same as prior example, except that when Law Professor turns, *B* is sleeping in the quadrangle. Now *A*'s motion will be denied. Law Professor's inference that *A* threw the ball is far more likely than the alternative inference that *B* was the culprit.

e. **Issues within the province of the jury:** Some issues are considered particularly appropriate for jury determination. One example is *negligence*. Even if the facts are clear, a court is much less likely to grant a summary judgment on the issue of whether defendant exercised reasonable care than it is on other issues in the case.

2. **No genuine issue of material fact:** Fed. R. Civ. P. 56 bars summary judgment only if there is a *genuine* issue of material fact. This standard allows the court to look beyond the pleadings and to evaluate the evidence to determine if a real dispute exists.

   a. **Various views:** Courts differ significantly in how rigorously they treat this requirement. In some states, it is virtually impossible to get summary judgment. As long as the nonmovant has some evidence supporting its side, the court will let the case go to trial even if the evidence is very weak. In other states, and in the federal courts, summary judgment is granted more frequently. Although these courts insist they are not judging credibility or weighing evidence, in truth they often do both to a limited degree.

   b. **The importance of the burden of production:** To understand how the "no genuine issue" standard is applied, it is necessary to understand the burden of production.

      i. **Burden of production:** The burden of production, sometimes called the burden of "going forth with the evidence," dictates who must introduce evidence on an issue. *If neither party offers any evidence on an issue, the party with the burden of production loses on that issue.*

         (a) *A claimant* typically bears the burden of production on *every element* of its claim. Therefore, a plaintiff suing for breach of contract must introduce evidence that a contract existed, that it was breached, and that plaintiff suffered damages as a result. Similarly, a defendant counterclaiming for battery must show an offensive contact, intent, and harm.

         (b) A party *defending against a claim* typically has the burden of production on all *affirmative defenses*. Therefore, a defendant who is defending a breach of contract action by arguing the contract was procured by fraud must introduce evidence of a false representation by plaintiff and reasonable reliance by defendant to its detriment.

         (c) **Switching burdens:** If the party with the burden of production introduces strong evidence supporting his claim or defense, the burden of production switches to the other side. If the other party fails to offer any evidence in her favor, the court may take the case from the jury and issue summary judgment.

           Example: *P* sues *D* for breach of contract. *D* denies both that a contract existed, and that it was breached. *D* does not raise any affirmative defenses. *P* introduces a deposition of *D* in which *D* admitted the contract, *D*'s breach, and *P*'s damages. The court will grant summary judgment for *P* unless *D* introduces other evidence that tends to negate at least one of the elements.

      ii. **Interrelationship of burden of production and summary judgment:** The burden of production plays a crucial role in summary judgment. Logically, there are two distinct categories of summary judgment cases.

(a) Nonmovant has the burden: If the party moving for summary judgment does not have the burden of production, the court's task is to determine *whether the other party has satisfied its burden* of production by *introducing evidence on all elements*. If it has not satisfied the burden, summary judgment will be granted.

(b) Movant has the burden: If the party moving for summary judgment has the burden of production, the court should grant summary judgment if:

(1) movant has introduced so much evidence that the burden has shifted to the other side, and

(2) nonmovant has not introduced enough evidence to meet the burden that was shifted to it.

iii. Effect of burden of persuasion: The burden of persuasion is the standard applied by the finder of fact in determining who prevails at trial. In most civil matters, the party with the burden of persuasion must prove his case by a *preponderance of the evidence*. However, for certain issues, most notably *fraud*, the burden is *clear and convincing evidence*. The burden of persuasion affects the burden of production. In a fraud case, for example, a plaintiff must produce more evidence to meet its burden of production than it would on a claim where the burden of persuasion was a mere preponderance of the evidence. Anderson v. Liberty Lobby, Inc., 477 U.S. 242 (1986).

c. Application of standard in cases where defendant moves for summary judgment: If defendant moves for summary judgment, the court must decide whether plaintiff has significant evidence supporting its claim.

Note on terminology: To simplify matters, the discussion in this part and Part d speaks in terms of plaintiffs and defendants. However, the analysis *also applies to defenses, counterclaims, and other claims*. When dealing with these other claims, *plaintiff* should be ready to refer to the party with the burden of production, while *defendant* is the party without the burden of production.

i. Every element: Plaintiff must have significant evidence on *every element of the claim*. If plaintiff lacks evidence on even one element, the court should grant summary judgment for defendant even if plaintiff has overwhelming evidence on all other elements.

ii. "Mere scintilla test": Some courts will deny summary judgment if plaintiff has any evidence in its favor. However, the *federal courts* have *rejected the mere scintilla approach* and require plaintiff to have significant evidence.

iii. Defendant's duty: Defendant has the initial responsibility, or burden, of demonstrating to the court the absence of a genuine issue of fact.

★   **(a)** The U.S. Supreme Court elaborated on this duty in Celotex Corp. v. Catrett, 477 U.S. 317 (1986). It held defendant *need not offer proof that negates plaintiff's case*. It need only show that plaintiff has failed to meet the burden of production. (On the other hand, if defendant *does* have affirmative evidence that negates an element of plaintiff's claim, it is free to introduce it.)

★   **Example:** Bias v. Advantage International, Inc., 905 F.2d 1558 (D.C. Cir. 1990), illustrates how a defendant shows the absence of facts necessary to support plaintiff's claim. Plaintiff in that case was the estate of a college basketball star. Decedent died two days after being selected in the first round of the NBA draft. The estate claimed that defendant, decedent's agent, had breached its promise to procure life insurance covering decedent. Defendant admitted it had breached this promise but countered by asserting that decedent's drug use would have made it impossible to procure a policy. Defendant supported this allegation with evidence showing that decedent used drugs regularly and that no life insurance company would issue a policy to a drug user. The court found this evidence sufficient to demonstrate no genuine issue of material fact. Moreover, because plaintiff had no real evidence suggesting to the contrary, summary judgment for defendant was appropriate.

(b) However, defendant cannot merely assert generally that plaintiff has no evidence. Instead, it must point out to the court those parts of the depositions, affidavits, and other evidence that demonstrate plaintiff has no evidence on one or more elements of its claim. Fed. R. Civ. P. 56(c)(1).

d. **Application of standard in cases where plaintiff moves for summary judgment:** A plaintiff may also seek summary judgment when she feels her evidence completely overwhelms the evidence of defendant.

i. Logically, granting summary judgment to a plaintiff presents greater difficulties. Even if defendant has no evidence, the jury could always disbelieve the evidence proffered by plaintiff and find for defendant. Nevertheless, courts do enter summary judgment for plaintiffs.

ii. For plaintiff to prevail on a summary judgment motion, it must present enough evidence to *switch the burden of production* to defendant. Plaintiff must have *substantial evidence* on *every element* of its claim. That evidence should be from neutral, unbiased witnesses. In addition, defendant must either have no conflicting evidence or evidence that is so completely overwhelmed by plaintiff's evidence that it cannot be believed. If defendant raises significant issues concerning the credibility of plaintiff's evidence, a court is less likely to grant summary judgment.

3. **Movant entitled to judgment:** The second part of the summary judgment standard is that the movant must be entitled to judgment as a matter of law. This means governing law must allow the movant to prevail on the undisputed facts. In most cases, this part of the standard presents little difficulty. Nevertheless, a summary judgment motion can serve the same role as a motion to dismiss for failure to state a claim: Even if the evidence is exactly as plaintiff claims, if the law does not favor plaintiff, a court should not grant summary judgment for plaintiff.

E. **The judgment:** A summary judgment on the entire case is a *final judgment* and is treated like a judgment rendered after a full trial.

Quiz Yourself on
RESOLUTION WITHOUT TRIAL

112. Paulette fancies herself a future Olympic equestrian. Hoping to hone her riding skills, she arranges a week-long visit to Darrell's Dude Ranch in Colorado. Once he hears that Paulette wants a challenge,

Darrell puts her on EF-5 Tornado, his meanest and most cantankerous horse. EF-5 throws Paulette into the dust, bruising both her ego and her hip. Paulette sues Darrell in federal district court for $150,000.

Before filing his answer, Darrell meets with Paulette. The two agree to settle the case for $60,000. The parties file a stipulation of dismissal, and Darrell promptly pays the $60,000. Two weeks later, Paulette sues Darrell again on the same claim. Conceding that Darrell already paid her $60,000, Paulette asks for only $90,000 in damages. Darrell promptly moves to dismiss the case. However, Paulette correctly points out that the stipulation of dismissal had no explicit language preventing Paulette from suing for the remaining money. Does the stipulation prevent Paulette from suing for the remaining $90,000? _____

113. Same facts as Problem 112, except Paulette and Darrell do not settle the case. After several months, Darrell has neither answered nor filed any papers with the court. Paulette therefore obtains an entry of default against Darrell. She now seeks a default judgment. However, she has three questions. First, she wants to know if the court will hold a hearing before entering the default judgment. Second, if the court does hold such a hearing, she is unsure whether Darrell is entitled to notice. Third, while she asked for $150,000 in damages in her complaint, she has since discovered her injuries are more extensive than she thought and that her real damages are $300,000. Therefore, she wants to know if she can convince the court at the hearing to enter judgment in the larger amount. You are Paulette's attorney in this matter. How will you advise her? _____

114. Art Luvver collects valuable paintings. After buying a masterpiece at auction, he arranges to have Van's Van Lines transport the painting to Art's home. While en route, the driver of the truck is involved in an accident with another vehicle. Both drivers perish, and the masterpiece is completely destroyed.

Art sues Van, the owner of Van's Van Lines, in federal court. Van does not bother to answer or make a motion. Instead, he immediately moves for summary judgment, alleging Art has no proof that Van's employee was in any way negligent. Under governing law, Art must prove negligence to recover. Realizing he has no evidence of negligence, Art elects to dismiss the case by filing a notice of dismissal. After dismissing, Art hopes to refile the case in another state, where the governing law would make Van strictly liable. May Art dismiss his case by filing a notice of dismissal? _____

115. Same facts as Problem 114, except Art decides not to dismiss. Instead, Art contests Van's summary judgment motion. Art first argues the motion was filed too early. Second, Art claims that even if the motion is timely, the court should not hold the hearing this early in the suit. Is Art likely to prevail on either argument? _____

116. Same facts as Problems 114 and 115. Assume the court postpones the hearing on the motion for summary judgment. Art and Van conduct discovery for four months. At the end of four months, both parties file motions for summary judgment.

Although the parties engaged in extensive discovery, they learn very little as a result. They do learn the accident took place at an intersection with a stop light. However, neither party has any evidence on one crucial point—whether Van's employee or the other driver ran a red light. There were no witnesses other than the two deceased drivers. The physical evidence provides no clues. Will the court grant either Art's or Van's motion for summary judgment? _____

117. Same facts as Problems 114 and 115. Assume the court postpones the hearing on the motion for summary judgment. Art and Van conduct extensive discovery. At the end of the discovery phase, both parties move for summary judgment.

Art hit the jackpot in discovery. As luck would have it, a photography class was being held near the intersection on the day of the accident. Five students happened to take photos at the very instant the two vehicles entered the intersection. Although Art has not seen the photos himself, he manages to obtain affidavits from all five photographers. All five state that their photos clearly reveal that the light facing Van's driver was red, while the light facing the other driver was green. All the students are neutral third parties.

Van objects to these affidavits. He correctly notes the affidavits are hearsay evidence and, as such, cannot be used as evidence at trial. And because neither party has any other evidence showing the color of the light, Van argues summary judgment for Art should be denied, and Van's motion for summary judgment should be granted. Is Van correct? _____

Answers

112. The court will not dismiss the action. A stipulation of dismissal bars a later action only if it specifies the dismissal is on the merits. Here the stipulation was silent. While Darrell should eventually prevail (using the defense of accord and satisfaction), he will need to introduce evidence of the settlement. The stipulation is not enough.

113. There will be a hearing. Because damages for personal injuries are not a sum certain, the court will need proof Paulette actually suffered the alleged harm. However, Darrell is not entitled to notice of the hearing. Under Fed. R. Civ. P. 55(b)(2), a party receives notice of the hearing only if he has "appeared." The facts specify that Darrell has done nothing, so he has not appeared in the case. Finally, Paulette cannot recover the additional damages at the hearing. A default judgment is limited to the specific prayer for relief in the complaint. Fed. R. Civ. P. 54(c). Of course, Paulette could still seek those damages. She could amend her complaint, but she would have to serve it on Darrell and give him another chance to respond.

114. Dismissal by notice is not available. Under Fed. R. Civ. P. 41(a), a party may dismiss by notice only before defendant answers or files a motion for summary judgment. Van has already moved for summary judgment.

115. Art will lose on timeliness, but is likely to prevail on his second claim concerning the hearing. A defendant may file a motion for summary judgment at any time until 30 days following the end of discovery. Fed. R. Civ. P. 56(b). It does not matter that Van has not yet filed an answer. However, the court should not hold the hearing right away. Instead, Rule 56(d) indicates the court should give Art time to collect evidence to bolster the assertions in his pleadings.

116. The court should grant Van's motion but deny Art's motion. This question involves the burden of production and inferences. Because Art is plaintiff, he has the burden of production on the question of whether Van's driver was negligent. If neither party has any evidence on that crucial point, Art loses.

Art is not completely bereft of evidence. We know the accident happened at an intersection with a light. Art wins if Van's driver ran a red light. Although there is no evidence on that point, if the court can infer from the known facts that Van's driver ran the light, the court should deny summary judgment. However, a court will *not* draw the inference that Art suggests. The court would infer that Van's driver ran the light only if that inference is the most likely under these circumstances. Here, the competing inference is at least as likely as the one Art needs to win. It is equally likely the other driver ran a red light, in which case Van is not liable. (Technically, there is a *third* possible inference here, which, if true, would also result in no liability. It is possible the light was malfunctioning, showing green both ways.)

Because the court will not draw an inference, there is no genuine issue of material fact here. *Neither* side has any evidence on the question of who ran the red light.

Here, both parties have filed a motion for summary judgment. Both are correct in saying there is no genuine issue of material fact. However, applying the second part of the summary judgment standard, only Van is entitled to judgment as a matter of law. Because Art has the burden of production on the issue of negligence, he loses if there is no evidence of negligence.

117. The court should grant Art's motion for a summary judgment. True, courts do not often grant summary judgment for a plaintiff. After all, if the jury does not believe all of plaintiff's evidence, defendant still wins.

Here, however, no one in her right mind would not be convinced by Art's evidence. The photographs were taken by people with no interest in the case and directly show the crucial fact. Nor does it matter that Art uses affidavits containing hearsay evidence to demonstrate this fact. Rule 56(e)(1) does not require that the affidavit *itself* be admissible as evidence, but only that the facts set out in the affidavit be admissible. The photographers all testify as to what the photos contained, a fact that would be admissible. The photographs thus switch the burden of production to Van. Van has no evidence at all to support his side of the case. Given that Art's evidence is overwhelming, the court should grant summary judgment for Art.

Exam Tips on
RESOLUTION WITHOUT TRIAL

If an exam question deals with resolving a case without trial or in the pretrial stages, it is important to consider all the different ways a dispute may be resolved. Different methods have their own advantages and disadvantages.

- ☞ **Settlement:** Settlement usually takes place without court oversight. While it is difficult to test on the *terms* of a settlement on a Procedure exam, it is possible to test on the means by which a settlement is effected (such as a stipulation of dismissal).

- ☞ Be sure to have a solid grasp on the differences—both legal and practical—between *mediation* and *arbitration*.

- ☞ As with settlement, it is difficult to test on pre-trial conferences under Fed. R. Civ. P. 16. However, if the exam indicates there was a Rule 26 order, it binds the parties for the remainder of the case.

- ☞ **Default:** Obtaining a default judgment involves several technical issues. Because default judgments for failure to defend are *highly disfavored* by courts, a party must carefully follow Fed. R. Civ. P. 55.

  - ☞ The default process has *two basic stages*: the *entry of default* and the *default judgment*.

  - ☞ The court may hold a *hearing* before entering a default judgment to require plaintiff to prove damages and possibly other issues. If defendant has *appeared* in any way, it is entitled to notice prior to this hearing.

  - ☞ It is relatively easy to reopen a default judgment, except for default judgments imposed as a sanction for failure to cooperate.

- ☞ **Involuntary dismissals:** Students sometimes do not recognize the *tremendously broad scope* of the involuntary dismissal rule. Most dismissals that result from a motion, spanning from subject matter jurisdiction to statute of limitations to failure to comply with discovery, are involuntary dismissals governed by Fed. R. Civ. P. 41(b).

☞ It may help to think of the involuntary dismissal for *failure to prosecute* as defendant's version of the default judgment. Like a default judgment, a defendant must make a strong showing before a court will dismiss for failure to prosecute.

☞ Fed. R. Civ. P. 41(b) also treats most dismissals as *adjudications on the merits,* which means they prevent the party from filing the same claim or claims again. However, the rule exempts certain types of dismissals and gives the dismissing judge the authority to exempt others.

☞ If a *federal* case based on state law is dismissed, and the plaintiff tries to refile in a different court, you should discuss the possible effects of the Supreme Court's *Semtek* decision.

☛ **Voluntary dismissals:** A plaintiff may dismiss her action in several different ways. Fed. R. Civ. P. 41(a) has provisions specifying whether plaintiff may file again. Study these provisions carefully because they can be tricky.

☛ **Summary judgment:** Conceptually, summary judgment is the most difficult of the various means to resolve a case before trial. This difficulty arises in large part because summary judgment *considers both the law and the facts.*

☞ Although the *timing* rules of Rule 56 allow a summary judgment motion to be filed very early in the case, judges typically grant a continuance if the opposing party needs more time to conduct discovery.

☞ **The standard for summary judgment:** The most difficult part of any summary judgment question is applying the "no genuine issue of material fact" standard.

☞ You may find it helpful to think of summary judgment as an earlier form of *judgment as a matter of law.* Although the standards for the two types of judgment are worded in different ways, they share certain basic similarities. In both forms of dismissal, you may face problems such as *burden of production* and *inference.*

☞ Although a judge is not supposed to gauge credibility, if one side's evidence is so overwhelming that the little bit of evidence offered by the other side cannot be believed, summary judgment may be appropriate.

☞ Understanding the *burden of production* is critical to understanding summary judgment. It is much easier for the party *without* the burden of production to prevail on a motion for summary judgment.

☞ One common type of test question involves a summary judgment motion by the party *without the burden*. In this case, first look to see if the party with the burden has introduced evidence on *each and every element of the claim*. If no evidence has been offered on even one element, the motion should be granted.

☞ Conversely, if the *party with the burden* is making the motion, summary judgment ordinarily is not granted. However, if the party with the burden has offered very strong evidence on every element, and the opposing party has offered little or no evidence to rebut it, summary judgment may be appropriate.

Chapter **10**

DETERMINING THE TRIER

ChapterScope

This chapter covers both jury trials and bench trials. It discusses when a party is entitled to a jury, as well as the process by which jurors are selected and challenged. Finally, it covers the process of challenging the judge assigned to a case.

- In some cases, the ***U.S. Constitution*** guarantees a right to a jury in federal court.

    - Determining whether there is a right to a jury requires a historic analysis. This focus makes applying the Constitution especially difficult in cases involving ***new rights that did not exist at common law*** or a ***mix of legal and equitable claims and defenses***.

- If a jury is impaneled, the jury decides ***questions of fact*** and the ***application of law to fact***. Pure questions of law are decided by the judge even when the case is tried before a jury.

- Selection of the actual jurors who sit in a case involves a two-step process.

    - First, the court draws a ***jury pool*** from the universe of available jurors.

    - Second, the parties select the actual panel through a process called ***voir dire***. During *voir dire*, potential jurors may be challenged ***for cause***, or a party may exclude a limited number of jurors without stating a reason by using a ***peremptory*** challenge.

    - A party may not use peremptory challenges as a back-door way to exclude jurors based on their race or gender.

- Parties may also challenge the judge assigned to sit in a case. In cases of bias or other difficulty, the judge should ***recuse*** himself from the matter.

I. RIGHT TO A JURY TRIAL IN FEDERAL COURT

The U.S. Constitution provides a right to a jury trial in certain civil cases.

A. **Seventh Amendment:** The Seventh Amendment to the U.S. Constitution provides in relevant part, "In Suits at common law, where the value in controversy shall exceed twenty dollars, the right of trial by jury shall be preserved. . . ."

   1. **Preserves, not creates, right:** The Seventh Amendment is unusual. It does not create a right, but instead *preserves* a right that existed before the Constitution was enacted. Therefore, to determine if a party has a right to a jury today, a court must determine if the underlying action would have been heard by a jury in *1791*, the year the Seventh Amendment came into effect.

   2. **Applies only to civil cases:** The Seventh Amendment applies only to civil cases. In criminal cases, the Sixth Amendment creates a right to a jury trial. The two amendments are interpreted differently.

3. **Applies to issues, not to entire case:** Although the Seventh Amendment on its face applies to "suits," it has been interpreted to apply only to those *issues* within a case that qualify for a jury. Thus, it is possible for a jury to decide some issues while the judge decides others.

4. **Not only source of right:** The Seventh Amendment is not the only source of a right to a jury trial. Some federal statutes give litigants a right to a jury.

5. **Amendment never *bars* jury:** The Seventh Amendment guarantees a right to a jury trial in certain cases. Neither the Seventh Amendment nor any other provision of the Constitution creates the converse right *not* to have a jury in situations falling outside the Seventh Amendment.

6. **Amendment does not apply to states:** Unlike most other provisions of the Bill of Rights, the Seventh Amendment has *not been extended to the states*. Therefore, state courts are not required by the amendment to impanel juries. However, many states do afford a right to a jury trial in their own constitutions or by statute.

B. **Features preserved by the amendment:** The Seventh Amendment does not require a jury exactly like those used in 1791. For example, in 1791 only men could serve on a jury.

1. **Size:** The jury at common law comprised 12 members. However, the federal rules allow a court to seat a jury of *"at least 6 and no more than 12."* **Fed. R. Civ. P. 48**. Rule 48 also provides that if the jury *falls below 6* members (due to illness, death, or disqualification), the jury may not return a verdict *unless the parties consent*. In practice, federal courts rarely seat a 6-person jury. Far more common are 9- or 12-member juries.

2. **Unanimity:** At common law, the jury verdict had to be unanimous. The federal rules *preserve the requirement of unanimity*. Fed. R. Civ. P. 48(b). However, the parties may stipulate to a non-unanimous verdict. By contrast, a majority of states do not require a unanimous verdict.

3. **Demand:** The right to a jury is a personal right that can be waived by the parties.

   a. Under *Fed. R. Civ. P. 38(b)*, a party must serve on the other parties a *written demand* for a jury within *14 days* after service of the *last pleading* dealing with the issue for which a jury is demanded. The demand may be (and usually is) included in a pleading.

   b. *Any party may file* the demand, even if that party does not raise any legal issues.

   c. Unless the demand specifies particular issues, a party will be deemed to have demanded a jury trial on *all issues triable by a jury*. Fed. R. Civ. P. 38(c). If a party limits the demand to certain issues, *any other party* may demand a jury trial on *any or all remaining issues* triable by a jury by serving its own demand within 14 days after service of the demand.

C. **Application of the Seventh Amendment—an overview:** The Seventh Amendment preserves a right that existed in 1791. As a general matter, in 1791 only actions tried in the *common law courts* were tried before a jury. Understanding this provision requires some understanding of how the English court system allocated jurisdiction among different courts.

1. **Different systems:** England historically maintained several different court systems, each of which could hear only certain categories of cases. The main systems were *Common Law*, *Equity*, and *Admiralty*. Although this somewhat byzantine system was not followed in most of the North American colonies, it nevertheless was incorporated into the Seventh Amendment.

2. **Jury at law:** Of these systems, only Common Law (sometimes called simply Law) would employ a jury to decide a case.

3. **Admiralty:** Admiralty included suits involving vessels in navigable waters. There is *no constitutional* right to a jury in these cases even today.

4. **Law vs. Equity:** When dealing with the right to a jury trial, the most problematic distinction is that between Common Law and Equity. The problem is that the authority of these courts overlapped to a significant extent. In many cases, a party could take a dispute either to Law or Equity, depending on how the case was structured.

   a. **Remedy:** In many cases, the remedy sought by the party dictated whether the case went to Law or Equity.

      i. **Remedies at Law:** The common law courts were limited to certain specific remedies. The most important remedy available in the common law courts was *damages*. However, a common law court could also grant certain forms of specific relief, such as *replevin* and *ejectment*.

      ii. **Remedies in Equity:** Equity was not confined to a fixed slate of remedies but could instead fashion a remedy to fit the facts. Nevertheless, certain remedies were often used in Equity, including *injunctions*, *specific performance*, *accounting*, *rescission* of a contract, *reformation* of a contract, and *restitution*.

   b. **Equitable claims and procedures:** Differences in remedy were not the only distinction between Law and Equity. Equity also recognized certain claims and allowed certain procedures that were not available in Law.

      i. **Claims:** Historically, only a court of Equity would hear certain claims for relief, including *breach of a fiduciary duty*, *subrogation*, *contribution*, and *indemnity*, and a debtor's claim to *redeem a mortgage* after foreclosure.

      ii. **Procedures:** Equity also demonstrated flexibility in procedure. Thus, a party who wanted to bring a case as a *class action* or who needed to use *discovery* could sue only in Equity, even if she sought damages.

      iii. **Remedy not controlling:** If a case involved one of the equitable claims or procedures, Equity could hear the claim notwithstanding that the remedy sought was available in Law. Thus, a party bringing a *class action for money damages* would historically sue in Equity.

   c. **Preference for Law:** Because of the significant overlap, the English system eventually worked out a compromise that established Law as the "preferred" court. After this compromise, a party could sue in Equity only if he could establish that *the relief available in Law was inadequate*. That same rule carries forward to this day, albeit to a more limited extent. Although few jurisdictions operate separate law and equity courts, in many systems a party may obtain an equitable remedy only by showing that the legal remedy, usually damages, is insufficient to redress the problem.

   Example: *P* wants to sue *D* to enforce a contract under which *D* agreed to sell *P* an old watch that used to belong to *P*'s great-grandfather. Although the market value of the watch is not that high, the watch has tremendous sentimental value. *D* refuses to deliver the watch. Because damages would not adequately compensate *P*, *P* would sue in equity for specific performance.

D. **Application of analysis to new claims:** Legislatures have created numerous new rights since 1791. Because these statutory claims did not exist in 1791, applying the history-based approach of the Seventh Amendment can prove difficult.

   1. **Three-part test:** In Tull v. United States, 481 U.S. 412 (1987), the Supreme Court established a two-part test to determine if a statutory claim must be tried by a jury. Later Court decisions added a third step, which is used only if the first two do not provide a definitive result.

      a. **Step one:** The first step is to identify the ***closest historic analogue*** to the action in eighteenth-century English practice and determine whether that historical analogue would be heard in Law or Equity.

      b. **Step two:** The second step is to analyze the ***nature of the remedy*** sought and determine if it is ***legal or equitable in nature***.

         i. **Second step predominates:** More recent decisions of the Court have made it clear this second step predominates over the first. Thus, even if the closest analogue is an action in equity, if the remedy being sought is essentially legal in nature, the parties are entitled to a jury.

            Example: An excellent example of how this two-part test applies is Chauffeurs, Teamsters & Helpers, Local No. 391 v. Terry, 494 U.S. 558 (1990). At issue in *Chauffeurs* was a claim against a union for breach of its duty to represent. Under the first step, the Court determined the closest analogue was the equitable claim for breach of fiduciary duty. However, that equitable claim was not entirely analogous. The Court then applied the second step and found the remedy (back pay) to be a form of damages, a legal remedy. Because the second step is more important in the analysis, the Court held there was a right to a jury.

            (a) **Continued relevance of first step:** A concurring opinion in *Chauffeurs* questions whether the first step has any continued relevance. However, if the statutory cause of action is a ***perfect analogue***—that is, if the legislature has simply codified an action that existed in 1791—codification should not affect whether the party gets a jury. In these cases, the first step may control.

            (b) **Applying the second step:** The second step of the analysis can be difficult to apply in some cases. A remedy is not legal merely because it involves money. Curtis v. Loether, 415 U.S. 189, 196 (1974). If a monetary remedy is essentially restitutionary in nature—that is, if it forces the party to disgorge money that ***defendant wrongfully gained***, as opposed to what plaintiff lost—it will be treated as equitable. Money that compensates for a harm caused to the claimant is damages and is legal in nature.

      c. **Possible third step:** In Markman v. Westview Instruments, 517 U.S. 370 (1996), the Court considered another factor, namely, whether the decision in question involved a function traditionally performed by juries. The decision in the case itself—construing the scope of claims in a patent for an invention—was a type juries did not historically perform, leading the Court to conclude the decision should be made by the judge. Later Court decisions, however, have made it clear this third step applies only if the first two do not produce a definite result.

E. **Application of analysis to new procedures:** Modern procedural innovations produce situations that did not exist in 1791 and thus cannot be resolved using a straightforward historical analysis.

1. **New remedies:** In addition to creating new substantive rights, legislatures occasionally create new remedies unheard of in 1791. One example is the declaratory judgment. See Chapter 6, Part I.C. In determining whether to grant a jury in a declaratory judgment case, courts look to the underlying dispute to determine *what action would eventually be brought* were the declaratory judgment option unavailable. If a party could demand a jury in that action, a jury is available in the declaratory judgment action. The analysis here parallels how courts analyze declaratory judgments for purposes of determining *federal question jurisdiction*. See Chapter 4, Part III.F.2.

2. **Effects of the merger of Law and Equity:** Because of Fed. R. Civ. P. 2, federal courts no longer hold separate proceedings for actions in Law and in Equity, but allow all claims, legal and equitable, to be brought in a single suit. This merger of Law and Equity affects the jury trial question.

   a. **Traditional equitable procedural devices:** As discussed above, certain procedural devices—such as the class action, interpleader, and discovery—were historically available only in Equity. Today, however, the federal rules make these devices available in all civil actions. Therefore, the mere fact that a case involves one of these procedural devices *does not affect whether the parties are entitled to a jury trial*. If the underlying claim is one that would otherwise be heard by a jury, the party's use of an equitable procedural device does not deny the parties their right to a jury.

      Example: *P*, as representative of a class comprising all first-year law students at City University Law School, sues the university in federal court for failing to provide adequate parking space. *P* seeks damages. Although a class action is an equitable procedural device, either party may demand a jury in the case.

   b. **Reclassification of equitable remedies:** In a few cases, the merger of Law and Equity results in traditional equitable remedies being "reclassified" as legal for purposes of jury trial. The best-known example of this phenomenon is Dairy Queen, Inc. v. Wood, 369 U.S. 469 (1962).

      i. The plaintiff in *Dairy Queen* sued for trademark infringement when defendant used plaintiff's trademark. One of the remedies it sought was an *accounting*, traditionally an equitable remedy. An accounting would require defendant to examine its records to ascertain how much profit it had made using plaintiff's mark.

      ii. The Court held the amount defendant would be required to calculate was essentially a measure of *damages*. The mere fact that the equitable remedy of accounting put the onus of calculating these damages on defendant rather than plaintiff did not change its essential character. Therefore, the Court held that the parties were entitled to a jury on the accounting claim, as it was essentially legal in nature.

   c. **Joinder of legal and equitable claims in single action:** After the merger of Law and Equity, legal and equitable claims can be combined in a single action, making it difficult to apply the historic test to the hybrid case. The Supreme Court set out the basic analysis for courts to use in this situation in Beacon Theatres, Inc. v. Westover, 359 U.S. 500 (1959). That decision held that a party is entitled to a jury on *all issues relevant to the legal claims*, even if some of those issues are also relevant to equitable claims.

      Example: *D* periodically visits an orchard and steals apples from the trees. *P* erects a barrier preventing *D* from entering the land. *P* then sues *D* for an order of *replevin*, requiring *D* to return the apples already taken, and an *injunction*, preventing *D* from trespassing again on *P*'s land. *D* defends by arguing that the city, not *P*, owns the land. *D* also files a counterclaim for *damages* for being excluded from the property. *P* demands a jury on all legal claims. A jury will hear *all issues related to the replevin* (recall that replevin is a legal remedy) *and damages claims*. This means the jury will also decide most issues relevant to the injunction claim, as that claim shares certain crucial issues—such as who owns the land—with the legal claims. The judge will decide only those few issues unique to the injunction claim, such as the balance of hardships and whether an injunction would be in the public interest.

3. **Agency adjudication:** Modern governments often use administrative agencies to deal with complex issues. Agencies may occasionally adjudicate the rights of individuals. However, administrative agencies historically *do not use juries*. To prevent Congress from sidestepping the jury trial requirement by assigning cases to agencies, the Supreme Court has created a *limited exception* as to when an agency may decide a case involving a *legal claim* without a jury. Atlas Roofing v. Occupational Safety & Health Administration, 430 U.S. 442 (1977). The exception has three elements.

   a. The underlying claim must be one *created by Congress* (that is, by statute).

   b. The claim must be litigated before an *agency tribunal*, not a federal court.

   c. The right being litigated must be a *public right*. Although there is no precise definition of public right, such rights are usually part of *a broad statutory scheme* designed to protect the *public interest*.

      i. The vast majority of public rights are *litigated by the government*. However, not all claims litigated by the government involve public rights.

         Example: Granfinanciera, S.A. v. Nordberg, 492 U.S. 33 (1989), involved a claim brought by the trustee in bankruptcy—a federal official—to recover a bankruptcy debtor's property for the bankruptcy estate. Although the claim was brought by the government, the Court found it involved a private, rather than a public, right. That finding led the Court to conclude a jury was required.

      ii. It may also be possible for an individual to sue to enforce a public right. For example, a claim by an environmental group under a comprehensive pollution statute may involve a public right. On the other hand, these sorts of claims are rarely litigated before agencies. If the matter is before a court, a jury is required even if the right is a public right.

Quiz Yourself on SEVENTH AMENDMENT RIGHT TO A JURY

118. Pamela sues David in federal district court for breach of contract and makes a timely demand for a jury. After some discussion, the parties stipulate to a nonunanimous verdict. The jury returns a 7-5 verdict for David. Pamela asks to have the jury verdict set aside. Although acknowledging she agreed to a nonunanimous verdict, Pamela argues both Fed. R. Civ. P. 48 and the Seventh Amendment to the U.S. Constitution require a unanimous verdict. What result? _____

ANSWERS
197

119. During the past 20 years, the United States has closed a number of military bases and related facilities. The government typically sells the land to private individuals, who may develop the land as they see fit. In some cases, however, the government had leased small portions of certain military bases to private parties while the base was in operation. When someone buys the base, these lessees often refuse to leave voluntarily. This "holdover" problem makes buying military land less attractive and therefore has reduced the government's proceeds.

Congress enacts a comprehensive new federal statutory regime to remedy the holdover problem. Under this statute, the new owner of a former military base may ask the court for a judgment ordering the holdover lessee to vacate the premises. The statute does not authorize damages or any other form of relief.

XYZ, Inc., recently purchased a former military base in Alabama. There are three holdovers on the property. XYZ brings an action in federal court against the three holdovers under the new federal statute. One of the defendants files a timely demand for a jury trial. XYZ and the other two defendants do not want a jury trial. They claim a jury should not be impaneled if a majority of the parties do not want one. They also claim that even if the demand was proper, there is no right to a jury. Will the court impanel a jury in the case? _____

120. Same facts as Problem 119, except the new federal statute creates another option. The statute creates a new federal agency to administer the sale of federal lands. In addition to (or in lieu of) suing in court for an order to vacate, the new owner may sue the holdover before the agency to recover any damages suffered by the owner due to the delay in taking possession. The statute specifically provides the agency will try the case without a jury.

XYZ brings a claim before the agency against the three defendants. Notwithstanding the language in the statute, one defendant demands a jury. Is a jury required for this case? _____

121. Pollock and Degas enter into a contract in which Pollock agrees to sell a painting to Degas. The parties negotiate the sale over the phone. Pollock describes the painting to Degas as a "Manet." However, Degas thinks Pollock said "Monet." When Degas discovers the painting is not what he thought, he refuses to close the sale.

Degas sues Pollock in federal court, asking to rescind the contract because of a mistake. Pollock denies there was a mistake. Pollock counterclaims for breach of contract, seeking $300,000 in damages. Degas files a timely demand for a jury, which Pollock contests. Will a jury be impaneled? If so, will it hear all issues in the case? _____

Answers

118. The nonunanimous verdict will stand. Although Fed. R. Civ. P. 48 generally requires a unanimous verdict, the parties may stipulate to a mere majority. Courts have upheld nonunanimous verdicts against Seventh Amendment challenges.

119. The case will be decided by a jury. First, Fed. R. Civ. P. 38(b) provides "any party" may demand a jury by filing a timely demand. A majority of the parties is not required. The facts also specify the demand here was timely.

Second, the Seventh Amendment right to a jury trial does apply to this claim. Because the claim was created by statute, it will be analyzed using the three-part test. Under the first part of the test, the closest analogue is an order of ejectment. Although ejectment is a form of specific relief, it was historically legal, not equitable. Second, the form of relief—an order requiring someone in possession to vacate—is also legal because it is exactly the form of relief provided in common law ejectment actions. Because the claim is legal, a jury is required. The third part of the test is not considered because application of the first two parts produces a definite result.

120. The case probably must be tried by a jury. Congress may allow an agency to adjudicate without a jury only if the case involves public rights. The right in question here—the right to force people to vacate privately owned land—is more likely to be a private, not a public, right. That the land was formerly used as a government base does not make the private owner's right a public right. Because the underlying claim (a suit for money damages) is indisputably legal, the case must be heard by a jury.

Note: This case also involves another issue: whether an agency can even hear this case. That issue is beyond the scope of most Civil Procedure courses and need not be addressed.

121. A jury will decide the case. Because the case involves a mix of legal (damages) and equitable (rescission) claims, the jury will decide all issues relevant to the legal claim, even if that same issue comes up in the equitable claim. In this case, the jury will decide all of the main issues, including whether there is a valid contract (which includes the question of whether the contract is voidable for mistake), whether the contract, if valid, is breached, and damages. There really are no remaining issues unique to the rescission claim, unless there are equitable defenses such as laches.

II. SELECTING JURORS

In every jury trial, the court must identify potential jurors, command them to come to court, and weed out those with unacceptable knowledge of or bias toward the given case. Although the notion of a "jury of one's peers" is often held out as the ideal, there is *no positive right* to a jury of people who are "like" a litigant. On the other hand, litigants and jurors alike may object if certain groups are *intentionally excluded* from serving on a jury.

   A. **Overview:** The process of selecting a jury comprises *two main stages*.

      1. **Selecting the pool:** The court identifies the universe of potential jurors. From that universe, the court selects, usually at random, a pool of jurors who are to be available for *jury duty* for a given period.

      2. **Selecting the panel:** The court, usually with the help of the attorneys for the parties, *questions* the jurors to uncover their views and any potential bias. Attorneys may exclude jurors by exercising *two different types of challenges*.

         a. **Challenge for cause:** An attorney may exercise a challenge for cause against a juror who holds a *bias* toward one of the parties or the subject matter, or who has too much *prior knowledge* of the facts of the underlying dispute. There is *no limit* to the number of challenges for cause.

         b. **Peremptory challenge:** An attorney may exercise a peremptory challenge against a juror the attorney wants to exclude for reasons that would not support a challenge for cause. Unlike challenges for cause, the number of peremptory challenges is *limited*.

   B. **Selecting the jury pool:** The process of selecting the pool of jurors varies among court systems. However, all systems strive to achieve the same basic end: to achieve a *broad cross-section* of those in the jurisdiction *qualified to serve as jurors*.

1. **State courts:** There are notable differences among the states in defining qualifications to serve as a juror. States also employ different means for identifying jurors.

   a. **Qualifications:** The most commonly used qualifications for jury duty in state courts are residency in the area, command of the English language, literacy, payment of taxes, lack of incapacity due to a prior felony conviction, and good health.

   b. **Identification of qualified jurors:** States use a number of different methods to identify those capable of sitting on a jury, including voting registration lists, driver's license information, telephone directories, and property tax records. Many states use multiple sources to ensure qualified jurors are not left out.

   c. **Exclusions:** States typically exempt certain people from jury duty.

      i. **Automatic exclusion:** Some people are automatically exempt from jury duty based on their health or the nature of their occupation. For example, military, police, and fire personnel are often excluded because of the demands of their work. In addition, some (but not all) states automatically exempt *judges* and *attorneys* from jury duty due to a concern they will unduly influence the other jurors.

      ii. **Exclusion by request:** Other jurors may seek exemption if jury duty poses an *individual undue hardship*. For example, an employee who is paid by the hour may be released from jury duty if the income lost during a long case would present a difficulty.

2. **Federal courts:** The jury selection system in the federal courts was completely revamped in 1968. *28 U.S.C. §§1861-1871* now dictate how the basic process operates.

   a. **Qualifications:** *28 U.S.C. §1865* provides a person is qualified to serve as a federal juror if she:

      i. is *a U.S. citizen*;

      ii. is *18 years old or older*;

      iii. has *resided* for *one year* or more within the judicial district in which she will serve as a juror;

      iv. can read, write, and understand the *English language* to a degree sufficient to complete the juror qualification form;

      v. can *speak* the English language;

      vi. suffers from *no mental or physical infirmity* that would preclude her from rendering satisfactory service;

      vii. has *no charge pending* against her for the commission of a crime punishable by imprisonment for more than one year; and

      viii. has *not been convicted* in state or federal court of a crime punishable by imprisonment for more than one year, unless her civil rights have been restored.

   b. **Identification of qualified jurors:** *28 U.S.C. §1863(b)* requires the universe of jurors to be gleaned from either *voter registration lists* or *lists of those actually voting* and, if necessary to ensure the underlying goal of a *fair cross-section of the community* (28 U.S.C. §1861), additional sources of names. The additional sources include many of the same lists as those used by state courts. Names of potential jurors are then placed on a *master jury wheel*.

c. **Exclusions:** *28 U.S.C. §1863(b)* also allows certain people to be excluded from the jury pool, according to definite standards.

   i. **Automatic exclusions:** *28 U.S.C. §1863(b)(6)* automatically excludes military personnel, members of police and fire departments, and government officials actively engaged in the performance of their official duties.

   ii. **Exclusion by request:** The statute allows other groups to be excluded by individual request.

     (a) *28 U.S.C. §1863(b)(5)(B)* allows members of volunteer firefighter groups, volunteer rescue squads, and volunteer ambulance crews to request exclusion *without the need to show hardship*.

     (b) *28 U.S.C. §1863(b)(5)(A)* allows each district to identify *other groups* and occupational classes, the members of which will be excluded provided they demonstrate *undue hardship or extreme inconvenience*.

     (c) *28 U.S.C. §1866(c)(1)* allows a court to excuse *individuals* who do not fall into the specified groups but nevertheless can demonstrate undue hardship or extreme inconvenience. However, exclusion under this provision is *temporary*, lasting only as long as justified.

3. **Constitutional restrictions in determining universe of jurors:** Several provisions of the U.S. Constitution restrict a court's ability to exclude people from jury duty.

   a. The *Equal Protection Clause* prevents government from discriminating in jury selection based on race, religion, national origin, and, to a more limited extent, age and gender.

   b. The *Seventh Amendment* not only guarantees litigants a jury in certain cases but also guarantees the jury will represent a *fair cross-section* of the community. Although this does not guarantee any party in an individual case a jury composed of particular categories of people, it does guarantee litigants that people will not be excluded from juries without good reason.

   Note: Because the Seventh Amendment does not apply to the states, a state may exclude classes of people from juries as long as the classification does not discriminate in a way forbidden by the Equal Protection Clause. For example, a state may create a jury of "experts" to decide a complex case. Exclusion of nonexperts would not violate the Equal Protection Clause.

4. **Selection of pool:** Periodically, the court will select a pool of jurors from the universe of potential jurors to serve in upcoming cases. In federal courts and in most states, the pool is selected at *random* although a court may then exclude those who have been selected in the recent past.

C. **Excluding jurors, formation of the panel:** The pool of jurors is narrowed to the panel that will hear a case through a process called *voir dire*. *Voir dire* involves questioning the jurors to determine their qualifications to sit in a particular case.

1. **Stages:** *Voir dire* typically happens in two stages. First, the entire pool is asked a series of general questions to determine if any members know the parties or have a personal bias toward or stake in the outcome of the case. Second, questions may be posed to individual jurors to determine other possible bases for challenge.

2. **Who conducts questioning:** The mechanics of *voir dire* vary from court to court. In some courts, the attorneys bear the primary responsibility for questioning the jurors. In others, the judge asks the questions.

3. **Challenges for cause:** Each party usually has an ***unlimited number*** of challenges for cause. Grounds justifying a challenge for cause include:

   a. a ***personal relationship*** with, or sometimes even knowledge of, the parties, their attorneys, the major witnesses, the subject matter, or the judge;

   b. that the potential juror is ***employed*** by one of the parties, or in some cases a person or organization closely affiliated with a party;

   c. a strong ***predisposition*** for or against one side based on reasons other than the law.

   Example: In Thompson v. Altheimer & Gray, 248 F.3d 621 (7th Cir. 2003), a small business owner in the jury pool stated her prior experience would affect her judgment and she believed some people filed spurious claims against employers. When asked whether she could judge the case fairly, she never gave an unequivocal answer. The court held that the juror could be challenged for cause.

4. **Peremptory challenges:** Each party has a ***limited*** number of peremptory challenges, which in most cases allow an attorney to exclude a juror ***without stating a reason***.

   a. **Number:** The number of peremptory challenges available to a party varies. In ***federal courts*** each party is limited to ***three*** peremptory challenges. However, the court may deem coplaintiffs or codefendants to be a single party or may allow additional challenges as it sees fit. 28 U.S.C. §1870.

   b. **Race- or gender-based challenges:** The Supreme Court has created a limited exception to the traditional rule that a party exercising a peremptory challenge does not need to justify the challenge. If the court detects a pattern of excluding jurors based on race, national origin, religion, or gender, the party may be required to justify the challenge by providing other, nonobjectionable reasons for the exclusion. Edmonson v. Leesville Concrete Co., 500 U.S. 614 (1991).

      i. Excluding a juror based on that juror's race, national origin, religion, age, or gender violates the juror's rights to ***equal protection*** under the Fourteenth Amendment.

      ii. If a party exhibits a ***pattern*** of excluding jurors who share one of these characteristics, that party will be asked to justify excluding each of the jurors for some reason other than the characteristic.

      (a) **Demonstrating a pattern:** A pattern of wrongful exclusion may be demonstrated if, for example, a party exercises two of its three peremptory challenges on people with the characteristic. What is necessary to establish a pattern also turns on other factors, such as the total number of people with that characteristic in the jury pool.

      (b) **Justifying exclusion:** The party who exhibited the pattern need not show he could have challenged the juror for cause. He merely needs to provide a ***rational basis*** for wanting to exclude the juror. Intelligence, attentiveness, and the like may well justify exclusion.

      iii. Challenging party need not share characteristic: The party challenging the exclusion of jurors need not share the characteristic in question. Thus, for example, an atheist could challenge the exclusion of Lutherans from the jury.

Quiz Yourself on JUROR SELECTION

122. The federal District of Carolina has recently amended its jury selection plan. Under the new plan, practicing attorneys are automatically excluded from the jury pool. The rationale is that an attorney would wield too much influence on the other members of a jury. A group of attorneys challenges this plan, arguing it does not comply with the federal statutes governing jury selection. Are the attorneys correct? _____

123. Kim, who is of Korean heritage, sues Jones in state court for defamation. Kim demands a jury trial.

Following its usual procedure, the state court compiles a pool of potential jurors by drawing names completely at random. The pool of 100 jurors includes 55 people of Korean heritage. Kim and Jones are both shocked to discover this because people of Korean heritage make up only 3 percent of the people both in the district's population and on the court's master list of potential jurors. Kim immediately files a motion asking the court to select a new jury pool. Jones opposes the motion. First, Jones claims that because Kim cannot show prejudice by the particular composition, he cannot challenge the jury. Second, Jones argues that even if Kim can challenge, the jury pool is constitutionally acceptable. Who should prevail? _____

124. Sneezy sues Doc in federal court for medical malpractice after Doc fails to cure Sneezy's cold. As the case nears trial, the parties conduct *voir dire.* The questioning reveals that one of the potential jurors, Marcus Welby, is a retired physician. In response to questions from Doc's attorney, Welby states he has been sued several times for malpractice, but always prevailed. Welby insists he can judge this case fairly. Sneezy challenges Welby for cause, arguing Welby is biased. Will Sneezy be able to exclude Welby? _____

Answers

122. The new plan does not comport with the federal statutes. 28 U.S.C. §1863(b)(6) automatically excludes certain government officials, but not attorneys. In addition, §§1863(b)(5)(A) and 1866 allow a district to exclude other individuals, but only on request and only on a showing of hardship. Because most attorneys otherwise meet the eligibility requirements, the district cannot exclude them as a class.

123. Jones is likely to prevail. Jones is wrong when she argues Kim cannot challenge the jury. Any party may challenge the composition of the jury pool, regardless of whether that party is a member of the group being excluded.

However, Kim will likely lose on the merits. The Constitution bars only systematic exclusion of jurors. Because the jurors were chosen at random from a list fairly reflecting the makeup of the district, most courts would find the exclusion of non-Koreans was not systematic. However, some courts would find otherwise.

Note that had this action been filed in *federal court*, the outcome would likely be different. Most courts have interpreted the jury selection statutes as preventing gross disparities of this sort, even if not attributable to systematic exclusion.

Note too that a juror's right to be free from systematic exclusion is based on the Equal Protection Clause, not the Seventh Amendment. Unlike the Seventh Amendment, the Equal Protection Clause binds the states.

124. It is unclear whether Sneezy can exclude Welby. Some courts would exclude, but most would not. The *potential* for bias is obvious since Welby may be sympathetic to another doctor. The problem is that other than the fact both Doc and Welby are doctors, there is no objective indication of bias. Even though he has been sued for malpractice, Welby has no reason to be sympathetic to Doc's cause. More important, as in Thompson v. Altheimer & Gray, Welby has insisted he can judge the case fairly. Nevertheless, a minority of courts would find the commonality of experience enough to sustain a challenge for cause.

III. DISQUALIFICATION OF JUDGES FOR BIAS AND OTHER GROUNDS

Like jurors, judges can be barred from hearing a case in situations where they might be biased. In addition to allowing the parties to challenge a judge, governing law often requires a judge to recuse herself without motion.

A. Constitutional concerns. If a judge is *likely to be biased* for or against one of the parties, the *Due Process Clause* of the U.S. Constitution requires a judge to recuse herself from a case. Unlike the statutes discussed below, the Due Process Clause applies both to federal and state court proceedings.

★ **Example:** In Caperton v. A.T. Massey Coal Co., Inc., 129 S. Ct. 2252 (2009), the chairman and president of one of the parties had donated almost $3,000,000 for the judge's election. The Supreme Court held it would deny due process to allow the judge to sit in the case.

B. Federal courts: In federal court, *28 U.S.C. §§144 and 455* determine when a judge will be disqualified from hearing a matter.

    1. No significant differences: On the surface, §§144 and 455 look very different. Section 144 speaks only in general terms, while §455 provides a detailed list of when a judge should not serve. Nevertheless, the courts have basically *interpreted the provisions in the same way.* Common features include the following.

        a. Same bases for disqualification: Courts have interpreted the general language in §144 as encompassing all detailed provisions in §455. Therefore, the grounds for recusal under each provision are the same.

        b. Procedure: Although §455, unlike §144, seems to require the judge to recuse himself, parties frequently make a motion under §455 to the judge asking for recusal.

    2. Grounds for disqualification: The standards justifying recusal are set out in §455, which, as noted just above, have been interpreted to apply equally to §144. Section 455 lists certain specific reasons for disqualification, as well as a general catchall provision.

a. **Specific grounds:** The specific grounds are set out in *§455(b)*. They include situations where:

i.   the judge has a *personal bias or personal knowledge of a party*;

ii. the judge has *personal knowledge of the underlying facts*;

iii. while in private practice, the judge, or a lawyer with whom the judge practiced, *worked on the matter*;

iv. the judge, or a lawyer with whom the judge practiced, has been a *material witness* concerning the matter;

v.   while working as a government employee, the judge participated as *counsel, adviser, or material witness* in the proceeding, or expressed an opinion concerning the merits of the controversy;

vi. the judge, his spouse, or a minor child living in the judge's household has a *financial interest* in the subject matter of the proceeding or one of the parties (for example, owning stock in one of the parties), or *any other interest* that might be affected; or

vii. the judge, her spouse, or someone closely related (as defined in the statute) is a *party, lawyer,* or *witness* in the proceeding, or has an *interest* that could be *substantially affected* by the proceeding.

b. **General grounds:** Section 455(a) provides a judge must recuse himself from any proceeding "in which his *impartiality might reasonably be questioned*." For example, if the judge wrote a law review article advocating the legal position taken by one of the parties, her impartiality is open to question.

c. **Waiver:** If the parties waive disqualification after full disclosure, a judge who would be disqualified only under the general grounds of *§455(a)* may continue to sit in the case. However, if any of the grounds of *§455(b)* apply, *waiver is not allowed* and the judge must recuse herself.

Quiz Yourself on DETERMINING THE TRIER

125. After a long and tempestuous relationship, Scarlett finally decides to break off her engagement with Rhett. Rhett sues Scarlett in a state court, asking for an order requiring Scarlett to return the engagement ring he gave her or, in the alternative, damages for the value of the ring. Rhett also demands a jury trial. The trial judge denies a jury. Rhett immediately files a special appeal of the trial judge's ruling to the court of appeals, arguing the Seventh Amendment requires a jury in this case. Will Rhett prevail? _____

126. Same basic facts as Problem 125, except Scarlett sues first. Scarlett files her claim in federal court. She seeks a declaratory judgment that the ring was a gift and that she is accordingly not liable if she sells it. Thirty days later, Rhett files an answer arguing Scarlett would be liable if she sold the ring. Three days after serving the answer, Rhett files and serves a written demand for a jury trial.

    Scarlett argues the case should be tried without a jury. First, she claims Rhett did not satisfy the procedural rules dealing with jury demands. Second, she claims that even if the demand was proper, there is no right to a jury. Who prevails? _____

127. The reputation of corporate America has been sullied in the last few years by a series of questionable, and often illegal, acts by corporate executives. As quickly as legislatures have responded, shady executives have dreamed up other devious schemes.

One recent scheme is the supplemental insurance plan. Corporate employees are given the option to purchase additional health insurance above and beyond the meager plans offered by the employer. Unbeknownst to the employees, however, this insurance does not cover the employees. It instead pays for corporate executives to take long "rest and recuperation" stays at posh resorts.

Congress reacts to this scheme by enacting a new federal statute. This statute gives employees the right to sue their employers for pushing a deceptive supplemental insurance plan. A prevailing employee may recover all money she paid into the plan.

Several employees of Megacorp, Inc., sue the company in federal court under the new statute, seeking return of the money they paid into an insurance plan. Some of the plaintiffs also appear on daytime talk shows, talking at great length about how they were "had" by the corporate executives.

One of the employees files a second claim against Megacorp. This employee claims he was demoted for arriving at work late one day. If true, that demotion would be illegal under federal labor laws. The employee asks the court to grant him the money he would have received had he not been demoted.

Megacorp files an answer denying liability. It argues its plan was not deceptive because it clearly spelled out the funds would be used for "executive health care." Megacorp also denies the demotion of the one employee was in any way wrongful. Finally, Megacorp files a counterclaim, asking the court to enjoin the employees from defaming the corporation on talk shows.

The employees demand a jury. Megacorp argues no jury should be impaneled in the case. Who will prevail? _____

128. Morris sues Jaatinen in federal court, claiming Jaatinen damaged a home he leases from Morris. Jaatinen, a Finnish citizen who is spending a year in the United States, denies liability, claiming the damage was caused in a storm. During *voir dire*, Morris exercises two of his three peremptory challenges against two jurors who emigrated to the United States from Finland. These two jurors, Nuutila and Korolainen, are the only two ex-Finns in the pool. Unlike Jaatinen, however, Nuutila and Korolainen are U.S. citizens. Jaatinen challenges the use of the peremptory challenges, demanding Morris justify the exclusion. Will Morris be required to provide a justification? _____

129. Same facts as Problem 128. Roberts is another potential juror in the pool. Roberts was walking along the street the day the damage to the home occurred. When asked whether she saw how the damage to the home occurred, Roberts said she had seen the entire event. However, neither Morris nor Jaatinen ask the juror to disclose *how* the damage had happened, for fear the information might sway the other jurors.

Jaatinen challenges Roberts for cause. Morris argues a challenge for cause is inappropriate because there is no showing of bias. How should the court rule? _____

130. Judge Judy has been assigned to hear a products liability class action suit against ACME, Inc. Several months into the case, plaintiff's attorney discovers that Judge Judy's husband owns a few shares of stock in ACME. It is clear, however, that Judge Judy does not know of her husband's stock. The plaintiff is considering asking Judge Judy to recuse herself from the case. However, plaintiff is not sure the husband's stock is grounds for recusal and does not want to take the chance of irritating Judge Judy. If plaintiff asks Judge Judy to recuse herself, is he likely to succeed? _____

Answers

125. Not only has Rhett lost Scarlett, but he will also lose his appeal. Rhett's case is in state court. The Seventh Amendment requires a jury only in federal court. Although the state constitution may also require a jury, Rhett relied only on the Seventh Amendment in his appeal.

126. Rhett will prevail. First, the Seventh Amendment provides a right to a jury in this case. Scarlett seeks the remedy of declaratory judgment, which by itself is neither legal nor equitable. To determine if there is a right to a jury for a declaratory judgment claim, one must ask what suit would eventually occur if the suit for declaratory judgment was never filed. Here, had Scarlett not sued for a declaratory judgment, Rhett would have sued her after she sold the ring. Once the ring is gone, Rhett could ask only for damages. A suit for damages for wrongfully disposing of property is clearly legal. Therefore, Scarlett's suit for a declaratory judgment will be treated as a legal claim, and the Seventh Amendment will afford a right to a jury.

Second, Rhett's demand for a jury is procedurally proper. It is in writing, as required by Fed. R. Civ. P. 38. Moreover, Rhett filed and served his demand within 14 days of the answer. Rule 38 requires that the demand be served within 14 days after service of the "last pleading directed to the issue" that will be tried by a jury. Rhett's answer, which denies the allegations of Scarlett's complaint, is the last pleading directed to the legal issue.

127. A jury will be impaneled, but only on the wrongful demotion issue. To begin, it is important to note that the right to a jury trial applies to issues and claims, not necessarily the entire case. This case involves three basic claims.

Megacorp's injunction is the easiest claim. This claim is purely equitable, and by itself does not create a right to a jury.

The federal statutory claim is also equitable. There is no clear historical analogue. The closest analogue would be fraud, which was usually heard in equity. Under part 2 of the test, the nature of the remedy is also equitable. In essence, the employees are seeking restitution of the money they paid into the plan. The employees had the money and turned it over to the employer for a particular purpose. Restitution is an equitable remedy. Therefore, the statutory claim, by itself, does not require a jury.

The wrongful demotion claim is legal. Again, there is no clear analogue. However, the employee is clearly seeking damages—the money he would have received had the employer not acted improperly. Therefore, the parties have a right to a jury trial on the wrongful demotion claim.

Because this case involves a mix of legal and equitable claims, the court must provide a jury for all issues involved in the legal claims. Therefore, a jury must hear all issues arising in the wrongful demotion claim. The jury will hear those issues even if they also arise in the equitable claims. Here, however, it is unlikely the wrongful demotion claim shares any common issues with the two equitable claims. Therefore, the judge will decide all issues relating to the equitable claims.

128. Morris should be required to provide a justification. Morris's exclusion of the only two immigrants from Finland makes a *prima facie* case of discrimination based on national origin. Jaatinen can challenge that exclusion even though he is not necessarily in the same "class" as Nuutila and Korolainen. Morris should be required to come up with a colorable, national-origin-neutral reason for excluding the jurors.

129. Roberts will be excluded for cause. Any potential juror with personal knowledge of the facts of the case can be challenged for cause. The challenging party need not show the juror is biased for or against him.

130. Judge Judy should recuse herself. The statutes make it clear that a financial interest of the judge or a spouse in the subject matter of the litigation is grounds for recusal. That Judge Judy does not know of the interest does not matter. The rule is designed to prevent not only actual bias but also the appearance of bias. Besides, once plaintiff makes the motion, Judge Judy will learn of the interest.

Exam Tips on DETERMINING THE TRIER

☞ If a question asks whether a case will be tried by a jury, you should always consider both the *procedural* and the *constitutional* aspects.

☞ Do not forget the Seventh Amendment applies only in federal court.

☞ Even if the Seventh Amendment guarantees a right to a jury in a particular case, a party must still make a timely demand for a jury trial. The time period for demanding a jury is fairly short: only 14 days following service of the last pleading directed to the issue.

☞ When analyzing a problem under the Seventh Amendment, it is crucial to have a solid understanding of the various types of remedies, as well as the various equitable claims and procedural devices.

    ☞ First, you must know which remedies, claims, and devices are legal and which are equitable. The only way to learn this is by rote. Be especially careful of ejectment and replevin, which look like equitable remedies but are legal.

    ☞ To apply the test for statutory remedies, you must also understand the general characteristics of each of the remedies.

☞ **Statutory rights:** Although the test for new statutory rights has three parts, the second, which looks to the nature of the remedy, is the most important.

☞ **Equitable procedures:** If a case involves a procedure that historically existed only in equity, your analysis should ignore the procedure. If the party brings a legal claim, but uses an equitable procedural device, there is a right to a jury trial.

☞ **Joinder of legal and equitable claims:** When legal and equitable claims are joined in one case, it is important to remember the Seventh Amendment requires a jury on *issues*, not the entire case. The basic rule is that the party receives a jury on all issues relevant to all the legal claims. Only any residual issues that relate solely to the equitable claim or claims will be decided by the judge.

☞ Congress can sometimes bypass the jury trial requirement by sending a case involving legal claims to an agency. However, before concluding that the case can be tried without a jury, make sure that all three parts of the "public rights" test are satisfied.

☞ When dealing with *selection of the jury*, recall there are two distinct phases.

    ☞ In the first phase, narrowing the universe to the pool, the primary considerations are to identify as many potential jurors as possible and to select the actual pool in a way that limits systematic exclusion of people based on their characteristics.

    ☞ In the second phase, selecting the actual panel, make sure you have a solid grasp of the reasons a juror may be excluded for cause.

☞ Because peremptory challenges usually do not require a reason, it is difficult to craft an
    exam question dealing with them. However, a peremptory challenge can be questioned if
    it appears motivated by improper reasons. Therefore, in a peremptory challenge question
    you should consider whether jurors were excluded based on race, national origin, religion,
    gender, or other objectionable characteristics.

☛ The rules governing disqualification of judges are fairly detailed. In addition to the specific grounds
    for objection, do not forget that 28 U.S.C. §455(a)—and possibly the Due Process Clause—allow a
    judge to be excluded in any case in which her impartiality might be called into question.

Chapter 11

THE TRIAL

ChapterScope

This chapter explores issues that may arise during a civil trial. The main focus is *jury trials*, which present special complications. The chapter discusses ways for the court to deal with improper influences on the jury and erroneous jury verdicts.

■ Courts have multiple tools at their disposal to prevent the jury from being influenced by *untrustworthy evidence* or *improper argument*. In addition to the *rules of evidence*, there are rules dealing with attorneys who make *prejudicial arguments* and jurors who attempt to conduct their own *investigation*.

■ Before sending the jury out to decide the case, the judge provides detailed *jury instructions* that inform the jury of the governing legal rules.

■ If the evidence presented at trial overwhelmingly favors one side, the court may decide the case by entering *judgment as a matter of law* rather than sending the case to the jury. In the alternative, the judge may let the jury decide the case, but render judgment as a matter of law *after the verdict* if the jury reaches an incorrect result.

■ If the trial goes awry, the judge may also grant a *new trial*. New trials are available in two basic situations:

■ where a verdict is against the *great weight of the evidence* (this gives the judge a less drastic option than rendering judgment as a matter of law); and

■ where a *procedural error* may have affected the outcome.

■ In some jurisdictions, it can be difficult for a party seeking a new trial to *use juror testimony* to attack a verdict.

I. PREVENTING IMPROPER INFLUENCE ON THE JURY

Although a jury in theory represents the "voice of the community," it decides cases in a very controlled environment. The jury may consider only evidence submitted to it at trial. Restrictions control what sort of evidence the jury may hear. After hearing the evidence, the jury is instructed in the legal principles to use to decide the case.

A. Rules of Evidence: The Rules of Evidence significantly limit the sorts of information that may be presented to a jury. As Evidence is a separate course, detailed discussion of the Rules of Evidence is beyond the scope of this outline. However, a few general principles may be useful.

1. Relevant evidence: A party may use only relevant evidence. Whether information is relevant depends on the form of the evidence and the purpose for which it is used. See Fed. R. Evid. 401 et seq.

2. **Hearsay evidence:** The Rules of Evidence limit use of hearsay evidence. Generally speaking, hearsay is an ***extrajudicial statement*** offered ***to prove the truth of the matter asserted***. Fed. R. Evid. 801(c). Although as a general rule hearsay evidence is not admissible, there are many situations in which it may be used. Fed. R. Evid. 803 and 804.

3. **Judicial notice:** A court may take judicial notice of certain matters that are either generally known or capable of being determined with relative ease. If a court takes judicial notice of a fact, no evidence need be introduced concerning that fact.

B. **Juror experimentation:** One of the jury's roles is to determine whether evidence is ***credible***. However, the jury cannot conduct its own tests to determine credibility. Juror investigation is grounds for a new trial. On the other hand, a juror is expected to use his or her own life experience in evaluating evidence. ***When the knowledge was acquired*** distinguishes permissible knowledge from impermissible knowledge.

1. **Before trial:** A juror may use knowledge acquired before trial in gauging credibility. To the extent the knowledge produces a bias in the juror, it is up to the parties to discover that bias during *voir dire*.

2. **During trial:** On the other hand, all information the jury acquires during trial must come from the parties. If one side introduces false or misleading evidence, it is up to the other side to counter it.

   Example: While sitting on his patio, *P* is injured by a flying rock. *P* concludes the rock was ejected by his neighbor's lawn mower. *P* sues *D*, the lawn mower manufacturer, for his injuries. *D* offers the testimony of an expert witness, who asserts the particular model of lawn mower could not possibly have propelled the rock that great a distance. Two jurors have knowledge that contradicts this testimony. Before being called for jury duty, Juror *X* read a blog claiming, without support, that several lawn mowers could propel rocks a distance at least as great as that in question. However, *X* cannot recall whether *D*'s lawn mower was one of those listed. During a break in the trial, *Y* goes home and performs his own test with his lawn mower, which is the same model as that which caused *P*'s injury. Only juror *Y*'s conduct is grounds for a new trial. Even though *Y*'s knowledge may be more reliable, it was acquired during trial.

C. **Attorney misconduct:** Although an attorney is supposed to represent her client, certain conduct goes too far and may result in a new trial. An attorney cannot supplement the testimony with her own facts or comment on the evidence. Nor may an attorney make an ***improper appeal to sympathy***, or ask the jurors to ***picture themselves in the party's situation***.

D. **Instructions:** Once the evidence is presented, the court instructs the jury as to the law to use in deciding the case. The instructions state both the legal standards governing the various claims and defenses and the logical sequence the jury should follow in deciding the case. For example, in a case where plaintiff alleges negligence and defendant contributory negligence, the judge will describe both the standard for determining negligence and the consequences of finding one or both parties negligent.

1. **Drafting the instructions:** Although the judge delivers the instructions to the jury, she usually solicits proposed instructions from the parties. Many jurisdictions have adopted ***form instructions*** for use in standard cases.

2. **Objections:** The parties may review the proposed instructions before they are submitted to the jury and may object to any items in the instructions, or failure to give a requested instruction. Fed. R. Civ. P. 51(c).

E. Judicial commentary: Some jurisdictions give the judge a limited authority to comment on the evidence. Federal courts, in particular, give the judge considerable leeway in this regard. However, the judge cannot indicate how she thinks the jury should decide the case.

II. JUDGMENT AS A MATTER OF LAW

A jury has a role to play only when the facts are in dispute. When it is clear from the evidence that one side should prevail, the judge may take the case from the jury by entering judgment as a matter of law (JML). ***Fed. R. Civ. P. 50.***

A. When available: A party may move for JML either before the case is submitted to the jury or after a verdict is returned.

    1. Terminology: Current Fed. R. Civ. P. 50 uses the term "judgment as a matter of law" to describe ***both the preverdict and postverdict judgments***. Prior to 1991, different terms were used for the two motions. Many states, and even some federal judges, still use the old terminology.

        a. The **preverdict** JML is sometimes referred to as a ***directed verdict***. Notwithstanding the term, the judge does not "direct" the jury how to decide the case, but simply enters judgment.

        b. The **postverdict** JML is sometimes referred to as a ***judgment notwithstanding the verdict*** or ***JNOV*** (from the Latin "judgment *non obstante veredicto*"). As the name suggests, the judge enters a judgment that ignores the jury verdict.

    2. Timing of preverdict JML motion: Although Fed. R. Civ. P. 50(a) allows a motion for preverdict JML to be made "at any time" before the case is submitted to the jury (Fed. R. Civ. P. 50(a)(2)), it also specifies that JML cannot be granted on a particular claim or defense unless the opposing party ***has been fully heard*** on that issue. Fed. R. Civ. P. 50(a)(1). Therefore, in practice such motions are filed at two stages.

        a. A ***defendant*** often files a motion for JML at the ***close of plaintiff's case***.

        b. ***Both parties*** may file a motion for JML at the ***close of all the evidence***.

    3. Timing of postverdict JML motion: A motion for JML after the verdict must be filed within ***28 days after entry of judgment***. Fed. R. Civ. P. 50(b).

        a. This 28-day period ***cannot be extended***. Fed. R. Civ. P. 6(b).

        b. If a party moves for a postverdict JML, the court may stay execution on the judgment. Fed. R. Civ. P. 62(b)(1).

        c. The reason the motion occurs "after entry of judgment" is Fed. R. Civ. P. 58, which requires the clerk to enter judgment "forthwith" following receipt of the verdict.

    4. Preverdict JML motion as prerequisite to postverdict JML: In the federal courts, and in most states with rules based on the Federal Rules of Civil Procedure, a party may not seek a postverdict JML unless she filed a motion for a preverdict JML. Fed. R. Civ. P. 50(b).

        a. "Renewed" motion: The rule creates a legal fiction: Even if the judge explicitly denies the preverdict motion, she is "considered" to have reserved decision on the motion. The party then "renews" the motion after the verdict and judgment.

        b. Rationale: This odd rule evolved because of the Seventh Amendment right to a jury trial. The common law courts allowed directed verdicts but did not permit a judge to overturn a verdict. Treating the judgment notwithstanding the verdict as a "delayed" ruling on the directed verdict motion avoids this constitutional problem.

   5. **New trial motion as alternative:** Fed. R. Civ. P. 50(b) allows a party moving for a postverdict JML to join a motion for new trial in the alternative. How the court deals with these alternate motions is discussed in Part III.

B. **Standard:** The standard for granting a JML is that *no rational jury* could find for the party opposing the motion.

   1. **Preverdict and postverdict compared:** Although the *standard is identical* for a preverdict and a postverdict JML motion, in practice it is more difficult to prevail on a postjudgment JML. After all, the judge in that case is faced with a jury verdict saying exactly what the movant claims "no reasonable jury" could decide.

   2. **Summary judgment compared:** Logically, the "no reasonable jury" standard used for JML motions is similar to the "no genuine issue of material fact" standard used for summary judgment (which is discussed in Chapter 9). However, there is one crucial practical difference. Because the judge considering a JML has *seen and heard live witnesses*, she is allowed a bit more leeway to *weigh the evidence* and *gauge credibility*. Even if there is evidence on both sides, it may be that no reasonable jury could decide for one of the parties if the evidence is overwhelmingly one-sided.

C. **Applying the standard:** Although a full appreciation for how courts apply the "no reasonable jury" standard can come only from a review of the case law, certain themes appear in the cases.

   1. **Basic principles:** Courts have established basic guidelines for applying this "no reasonable jury" standard.

      a. **Court's power limited:** Although the court may *weigh evidence*, its power is limited. If there is substantial evidence on both sides, the court must deny the motion for JML and let the jury weigh the evidence.

★   b. **Jury determines credibility:** Similarly, the judge should leave most *credibility determinations* to the jury. A judge may disbelieve a witness's testimony only if the testimony is completely unbelievable, either because it is internally inconsistent or because it was completely contradicted in cross-examination or by the testimony of other witnesses. See Pennsylvania Railroad v. Chamberlain, 288 U.S. 333 (1933) (although plaintiff's eyewitness's testimony was directly on point, it was impossible to believe given the distance and angle from which the witness viewed the event; therefore, as defendant had several witnesses who contradicted the testimony, JML for defendant was appropriate).

      c. **Issues within the province of the jury:** Some issues are considered particularly appropriate for jury determination. One example is *negligence*. A court is much less likely to grant JML on the issue of whether a party acted reasonably than it is on other issues in the case.

   2. **The problem of inferences:** As in summary judgment, one of the more difficult issues is when proffered evidence does not directly establish a crucial fact but instead asks the factfinder to draw an inference. The basic principles are the same in JML as in summary judgment. See Chapter 9, Part VII.D.1.d for a discussion of these principles.

   3. **The importance of burden of production:** Applying the "no reasonable jury" standard requires consideration of the burden of production. Again, the basic issues are the same in

JML as in summary judgment. See Chapter 9, Part V.D.2.b for a detailed discussion. However, application of these principles differs slightly in JML. Because a judge has more authority to weigh evidence and gauge credibility in JML, she has somewhat more authority to rule that a party has failed to meet his burden of production.

★ **Example:** Reid v. San Pedro, Los Angeles & Salt Lake R.R., 39 Utah 617 (1911), is a classic illustration of an inference problem. Plaintiff sued the railroad when her cow was killed on the railroad tracks. There were three possible ways the cow could have gone from the pasture to the tracks: through one of two open gates (in which case the owner would bear the loss) or through a stretch of broken fence (in which case the railroad would be liable). The cow was closer to the gates than the broken fence. The court held that because the inference the cow came through the gates was just as likely—if not more likely—than the inference she came through the broken fence, JML for defendant was appropriate. *P* had the burden of production and had failed to provide any evidence from which a jury could reasonably infer the cow came through the broken fence.

III. NEW TRIALS

In certain situations, a judge may order a case tried again before a new jury. A new trial is a less drastic alternative to a JML in cases where the evidence is one-sided. A new trial can also cure a judgment tainted by procedural defects or misconduct.

A. Basic principles: Most new trials are obtained pursuant to *Fed. R. Civ. P. 59*.

    1. Timing: A motion for a new trial under Rule 59 must be filed within *28 days after entry of the judgment*. Fed. R. Civ. P. 59(b).

        a. This 28-day period *cannot be extended*. Fed. R. Civ. P. 6(b).

        b. A party may move for JML and a new trial in the alternative. How a court deals with such a motion is discussed below.

    2. New trials under Rule 60(b): New trials may also be available under Rule 60(b). The time limit for obtaining relief under Fed. R. Civ. P. 60(b) is ordinarily at least a year. However, Rule 60 motions are rarely granted. Rule 60 relief is discussed in Chapter 13, Part V.A.

B. Two categories of new trial: Fed. R. Civ. P. 59 allows a court in a jury trial to grant a new trial "for any reason for which a new trial has heretofore been granted in an action at law in federal court." Fed. R. Civ. P. 59(a)(1)(A). Logically, there are two distinct categories of situations in which courts will grant a new trial:

    1. when the jury clearly *reached the wrong conclusion*; and

    2. when a *serious procedural error* occurred during the trial.

C. New trial to cure erroneous jury verdicts: If a judge is convinced the jury has reached the wrong result, he can order a new trial.

    1. Standard: A judge may grant a new trial when the jury verdict is *against the great weight of the evidence*.

    2. JML compared: This standard is *easier to satisfy* than the "no reasonable jury" standard that applies in JML cases. The new trial standard by its very nature allows the judge to weigh the evidence. By the same token, the judge may *evaluate credibility* to a certain extent. A court is therefore more likely to grant a new trial than a JML.

★   **Caveat:** Nevertheless, the standard is *great weight* of the evidence. If the evidence is close, or even somewhat in favor of the party who lost the jury verdict, the court should deny the new trial motion and let the verdict stand. See Lind v. Schenley Industries, 278 F.2d 79 (3d Cir. 1960), where the court of appeals reversed the trial judge's grant of a new trial, finding the judge had improperly substituted his interpretation for that of the jury.

  3. Combined JML/new trial motion: Because the new trial based on the weight of the evidence attempts to deal with the same basic problem as a JML, a party may want to bring both motions: hoping for a judgment in his favor, but willing to settle for a new trial as a second-best alternative. Fed. R. Civ. P. 50(b) accordingly allows a party to ask for both a JML and a new trial in a single motion. The new trial motion is a motion in the *alternative*.

    a. Court must decide both: Although granting a JML makes the new trial motion moot, *Fed. R. Civ. P. 50(c) requires the judge to rule on both*, even if the judge grants the JML. In such a case, the ruling on the new trial is treated as *conditional*.

       Note: The purpose of this requirement is to save time on appeal. If the appellate court reverses the JML, it is inefficient to remand, have the judge rule on the new trial motion, and possibly have another appeal. Requiring the conditional ruling on the new trial motion allows the court of appeals to deal with both.

    b. Application of standards: Because the "great weight of the evidence" standard that applies to new trials is easier to satisfy than the standard used for JML, a judge who grants a JML will also *ordinarily grant the conditional new trial*. However, this is *not always the case*. If the judge finds, for example, that plaintiff's only evidence on a certain point calls for an impermissible inference, she will grant a JML. However, if the court of appeals determines the inference *is* permissible, the evidence that was presented at trial would be enough to sustain the verdict, and a new trial would be unnecessary.

    c. New trial sought by winner: Fed. R. Civ. P. 50(e) allows a party who survives his opponent's JML motion to ask for a new trial if his opponent appeals. Thus, if the court of appeals decides the evidence overwhelmingly favored the opponent, it may nevertheless grant a new trial to the winner because of procedural problems that occurred at trial.

D. New trial to cure procedural defects: The second main reason for granting a new trial is because procedural errors occurred at trial.

  1. Prejudice required: No trial is ever perfect. Minor errors that occur during the trial process are not grounds for a new trial. Instead, the party must show the error *prejudiced* him by possibly changing the outcome of the case.

  2. Objection usually required: In addition, a party who fails to make a *timely objection* waives the error. However, in rare cases of "clear error," a party need not object. A clear error is an error committed by the court that is so blatant that it suggests the judge is biased.

  3. Common situations: New trials are often granted for:

    a. improper admission or exclusion of *evidence*;

    b. outside influences on the jury, including news stories that discuss the case in depth and juror experimentation;

    c. **prejudicial or improper arguments** by one or both attorneys;

    d. **improper commentary on the evidence** by the judge; and

    e. **improper deliberations**, including failure to reach a unanimous decision (when required) or a "quotient verdict" (where the jurors determine damages by stipulating beforehand the result will be the average of the amounts suggested by the jurors).

4. **Use of juror testimony to prove procedural error:** Many procedural errors occur in the courtroom and therefore are easily demonstrated. Showing outside influence or errors in the deliberation process, however, usually requires the use of juror testimony. To protect jurors from harassment after trial, many jurisdictions limit the use of juror testimony to challenge a verdict.

    a. Most courts allow the attorneys to *poll* the jury by questioning individual jurors. However, the attorneys may not harass or criticize the jurors.

    b. Obtaining information from the jurors is not the same as being able to use it. Courts differ significantly in the extent to which a party may ***use juror testimony to impeach a verdict***. There are three main approaches.

        i. **Common law rule:** Under the common law rule, a party cannot use a juror's testimony to impeach the verdict under any circumstances.

        ii. **Federal rule:** In the federal courts and some states, a party may only use juror testimony to impeach if it deals with ***extraneous prejudicial information*** or ***outside influence***. Fed. R. Evid. 606(b).

        Example: In Peterson v. Wilson, 141 F.3d 573 (5th Cir. 1998), the court applied the federal rule and held juror testimony could not be used to prove the jury had ignored the judge's instructions.

        iii. **Iowa rule:** Under the so-called Iowa rule, which is in force in a number of states, juror testimony can be used to prove ***overt acts*** but not matters that cannot be perceived through the senses.

        Example: During polling, the attorney for *D* discovers the damages award was the product of a quotient verdict. Under the common law and federal rules, the party cannot use the juror's testimony to impeach the verdict on that basis. Under the Iowa rule, by contrast, the party can use the juror's testimony because use of the quotient verdict is something that can be perceived through the senses. Under any of the approaches, the attorney could use other evidence (such as slips of paper in the wastebasket) to prove the quotient verdict.

E. **Partial and conditional new trials:** Courts may limit a new trial to one or more issues rather than the entire case. In addition, a court may grant a conditional new trial, in which case no new trial is held if the verdict winner agrees to a modification of the verdict.

1. **Partial new trials:** In many cases, the defect at trial does not affect all issues in the case. For example, improper evidence may affect one claim but not others. Or it may be that although the evidence supporting liability is overwhelming, the damages award is against the great weight of the evidence. In these cases, the court may limit the new trial to the affected issues.

2. **Conditional new trials:** A court may make its grant of new trial conditional. In some cases, if the verdict winner agrees to modify the judgment, the court denies a new trial and enters judgment for the modified amount.

   a. **When used:** Conditional new trials are most often used when the ***damages*** awarded by the jury are against the great weight of the evidence.

   b. **Remittitur and additur:** Courts often distinguish between cases of remittitur and additur.

      i. **Remittitur:** Remittitur occurs when the jury returns an ***excessive*** award. The jury grants defendant's motion for a new trial unless plaintiff agrees to reduce the damages award.

      ii. **Additur:** Additur is the logical converse of remittitur. It occurs when the verdict is ***too low***. If defendant agrees to an augmented damages figure, no new trial will occur.

         Note: ***Additur is unavailable in a federal court***. It has been found to violate the Seventh Amendment right to a jury trial. Remittitur, however, is available in federal court.

      iii. **The modified verdict:** Courts differ on how to calculate the proper damages figure in additur and remittitur. For example, in cases of remittitur, most courts hold the damages should be the ***highest figure*** that is not against the great weight of the evidence. Other judges determine for themselves what a reasonable award is.

   c. **Appeal:** A verdict winner who accepts the condition, and thereby avoids a new trial, normally may not appeal the modified judgment. The verdict loser may appeal, however, because her new trial motion was denied.

Quiz Yourself on
THE TRIAL

131. Chris Client sues Barry Sterr in federal court for attorney malpractice. Chris calls five experts who are experienced and well known in the field. The experts uniformly agree Barry acted unreasonably. Barry calls only one expert, who is not nearly as experienced. The witness contradicts himself several times on the stand and is unable to answer several simple questions.

   Before the judge sends the jury out to deliberate, she talks to the jury about Barry's expert. The judge points out the many inconsistencies in the expert's testimony. The judge closes by saying, "Personally, were I on the jury, I'd be much more inclined to believe plaintiff's witnesses than defendant's." Barry fumes but says nothing. The jury returns a verdict for Chris, and Barry files a timely motion for a new trial. Will the court grant Barry's motion for a new trial? _____

132. Same facts as Problem 131, except Barry objects to the judge's comment when it is made. The objection is denied. Will the court grant Barry's motion for a new trial? _____

133. You are the attorney for the plaintiff in a case in federal court. Your client's office building burned to the ground in a fire, and you brought suit on his behalf against the company that produced the sprinklers for the building. After a long trial, you are disappointed when the jury returns a verdict for defendant.

   Less than one-half hour after you leave the courtroom, you run into one of the jurors in the courthouse coffee shop. In casual conversation, you learn one of the other jurors was confused by the expert testimony in the case. Therefore, during a recess in trial, this other juror researched the matter further on the Internet. The juror shared what he learned with the other members, which turned many of them to defendant's side.

Armed with this information, you immediately ask the court for a new trial. Defendant opposes your motion. Defendant claims this casual conversation cannot be used as grounds for a new trial. In addition, defendant claims you acted unethically in talking to the juror without the judge's permission after the trial. Is your motion for a new trial likely to succeed? _____

134. Norton and Kramden are neighbors in a large apartment building. Norton sues Kramden for nuisance, claiming Kramden makes far too much noise. At trial, Norton introduces only one witness, a person who lives in an apartment building across the street. Although this person has never been in the building where Norton and Kramden live, she testifies that she has on many occasions heard loud voices emanating from their building.

When Norton is done presenting his case, he moves for judgment as a matter of law. The judge denies the motion. Did the judge make the correct decision? _____

135. Same facts as Problem 134. After the judge denies Norton's motion, Kramden introduces several witnesses who testify he is as quiet as a church mouse. Once he is done presenting evidence, Kramden moves for judgment as a matter of law, which is denied. Three days after judgment is entered for Norton on the verdict, Kramden files again for JML. How should the court rule? _____

136. Consider again the basic dispute in Problem 134. This time, however, Norton does not call any third-party witnesses. Instead, he himself takes the stand. Norton testifies that on certain specified dates he heard Kramden making loud noises in his apartment. Kramden calls five witnesses, all of whom testify that on the dates in question Kramden was either not at home or was as quiet as a church mouse.

Kramden moves for judgment as a matter of law at the close of all the evidence. The court denies the motion and sends the case to the jury. The jury returns a verdict for Norton and judgment is entered. Three days later, Kramden moves for judgment as a matter of law, or in the alternative a new trial. Norton argues the jury verdict should stand. Norton also argues the motion for a new trial is not procedurally proper. Although Norton admits the motion for judgment as a matter of law is timely, he argues Kramden may not move for a new trial because he did not make such a motion before the case was submitted to the jury.

How is the court likely to rule? _____

137. Rita is a meter reader with the city police force. Although her evaluations are stellar, Rita is fired from the force during a round of budget cuts. Rita sues Connie Stable, the chief of police, claiming state civil rights laws give her the right to a hearing prior to termination.

The state civil rights law provides a "good faith immunity" in cases like this. According to the statute, "an official can be held liable for a civil rights violation only if he or she knew that his or her actions were illegal." At trial, Rita proves beyond a doubt she did not receive a hearing. However, neither party offers any evidence concerning whether Connie knew firing Rita without notice and a hearing was illegal.

Rita and Connie both move for judgment as a matter of law at the close of all the evidence. Will the court grant either motion? _____

Answers

131. The court will deny Barry's motion because he did not object to the judge's statement when it was made. A party must make a contemporaneous objection to a procedural error.

132. Although Barry has now preserved his objection, he is not likely to win a new trial. A judge in a federal case has a limited power to comment on the evidence. Admittedly, the judge may have gone too far by telling the jury how she would decide. On the other hand, the comment was likely harmless error. Given Chris's strong evidence, the jury probably would have found for him notwithstanding the judge's comment.

133. The motion for a new trial is likely to succeed. First, there is nothing wrong with talking to a juror after trial, provided you do not harass the juror. This casual conversation certainly is not harassment. Second, the information the juror conveyed is grounds for a new trial. It is reversible error for a juror to conduct research on the matters being litigated. Third, although the only way you can prove the research is through juror testimony, you can use juror testimony in this situation. The case was litigated in federal court. Under Fed. R. Evid. 606(b), a party can use juror testimony to prove extraneous outside information. The Internet research is outside information.

134. The judge made the correct decision. A motion for judgment as a matter of law can be granted against a party only after that party has been fully heard. Kramden has not had a chance to present any evidence.

135. Now Kramden will prevail. He made a timely motion for JML during the case, preserving his right to move again after the verdict. He made the postverdict motion within 28 days following entry of judgment.

The court should also overturn the jury verdict. Norton has the burden of production. He does have evidence of loud noises. But that evidence requires an inference: namely, that it was Kramden making the noise. Given that the parties live in a "large apartment building," it is more likely that the loud noises came from someone else. Kramden also has evidence that contradicts the inference. Therefore, because the inference that Kramden made the noise cannot be allowed, Norton has no evidence on a crucial element of his claim. As Norton has the burden of production, he will lose.

136. The court will probably deny JML but grant the new trial. First, the new trial motion is timely. Although a party cannot move for a postverdict JML without a preverdict motion, Fed. R. Civ. P. 59 does not impose a similar requirement for new trial motions.

The court should deny JML. True, the evidence is fairly one-sided. There is also strong reason to doubt the veracity of Norton's self-serving testimony. Nevertheless, the evidence is inherently believable and calls for no inferences. The court has only a limited power to judge credibility when considering JML. A reasonable jury could believe Norton and disbelieve the five opposing witnesses.

However, the court should grant a new trial. The verdict, although within the realm of reason, is against the great weight of the evidence. Here, the judge has a greater authority to gauge credibility and should consider the self-serving nature of Norton's testimony.

137. Judgment as a matter of law is appropriate. However, it is not clear in whose favor judgment will be entered. The outcome depends on the burden of production. If Rita had the burden of coming forth with evidence to show Connie knew her acts were illegal, the court should grant Connie's motion because Rita has no evidence on a crucial element. However, if Connie has the burden of coming forth with evidence showing she did *not* know, JML for Rita is appropriate because the facts indicate she has conclusive evidence on the other elements of her claim. From the quoted language, it is not clear which party has the burden of production on this issue.

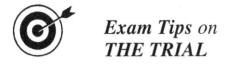

Exam Tips on
THE TRIAL

☛ If an exam question deals with ***procedural errors***, make sure the alleged error could have affected the outcome. A harmless error is not grounds for reversal.

☛ The issue of outside juror knowledge is one of the most vexing in new trials. Generally, only outside knowledge obtained during the proceeding is grounds for a new trial. Knowledge obtained before the proceeding may be grounds for a challenge for cause, but usually does not result in a new trial.

☛ When dealing with ***judgments as a matter of law***, you must determine who has the burden of production on the claim or defense. The analysis differs depending on whether the movant has the burden.

☛ A party must have made a preverdict motion for JML in order to move for JML after judgment.

☛ Problems involving inferences are common on law school examinations. Although there are rarely absolute right or wrong answers, make sure you are being reasonable when you determine whether an inference can be allowed.

☛ One issue students tend to find particularly difficult is the ***combined motion for judgment as a matter of law and new trial motion***. Many students try to memorize all the possible outcomes (for example, denying JML but granting NT). You will find the issue much easier if you simply work through each of the four possibilities and determine what the court of appeals would do.

☛ A judge who is considering a motion to grant a new trial because the verdict is against the great weight of the evidence has some ability to weigh the evidence presented in the case. However, she should not simply substitute her opinion for that of the jury.

☛ Recall that the 28-day limits for a postverdict motion for JML and new trial cannot be extended.

Chapter 12

APPEALS

ChapterScope

This chapter deals with appeals, the process by which court decisions are reviewed by a higher court. The discussion focuses almost exclusively on appeals in the *federal system*.

- Not every trial court ruling can be reviewed or reversed. There are limits on what issues can be appealed, when an appeal may take place, and how much deference the appellate court must give to the lower court's decision.

- A separate set of rules, the *Federal Rules of Appellate Procedure*, applies to appeals.

- Only someone who lost in the court below may appeal. However, the concept of "losing" a suit is quite flexible. Even a party who prevails may be able to appeal if the victory is not as complete as she would have liked.

- The most significant limitation on the timing of federal trial court appeals is the *final judgment rule*. Generally, a party may not appeal until the lower court has completely resolved the case.

  - However, the rule has several *exceptions*, some in the statutes and rules, others court-created.

- Once a case is properly appealed, the appellate court has only a limited *scope of review*. Its power to reverse a trial court's ruling depends on whether the issue being reviewed is one of *fact* or one of *law*.

I. DETERMINING WHAT ISSUES MAY BE APPEALED

The role of appeals courts is not to ensure a perfect result in every case. Instead, they correct only trial court mistakes that negatively affected a party. Therefore, a party may only appeal issues that resolved *adversely* to the party's interests and were likely to have affected the result. In addition, a party may need to give the trial court the chance to rectify the problem.

A. Adversity: Of course, a party who loses the case may appeal. But even a party who technically "wins" a judgment may appeal, provided the judgment affords that party less relief, or relief that is different in nature, than the party requested. In fact, it is fairly common for both plaintiff and defendant to appeal a judgment. Situations in which both parties appeal are called *cross-appeals*.

★ **Example:** *P* sues *D* to recover on an insurance contract covering a construction project. *P* sought relief on two theories: breach of contract and fraud, seeking the same sum under both theories. The trial court found for *P* under the contract, but not on the fraud claim. *P* nevertheless appealed, arguing that if *D* filed for bankruptcy, it could discharge (have the court negate) the contract debt, but not a debt for fraud. The court allowed the appeal, reasoning that *P* is entitled to a judgment not in the amount, but also "of the quality" it feels it is entitled.

B. Need to raise issue to trial court: A party who does not give the trial judge the chance to rule on an issue generally cannot appeal that issue.

1. **Legal theories:** An appealing party cannot raise a claim or defense for the first time on appeal. In addition, even if a party did present a legal theory at trial, he can *waive* that theory.

   a. **Exception:** One very important exception to this principle is *subject matter jurisdiction*. Either party (including plaintiff, who chose the court) may raise subject matter jurisdiction at any time, including on appeal.

   b. **Use of rejected theories by appellee:** The party who *won* at trial may use any legal theory that *appears in the record* to support the judgment, even if the trial court rejected that theory and the party did not pursue the theory any further at trial. Some courts even allow a prevailing party to raise new legal theories not appearing in the record on appeal.

2. **Objections to procedural mistakes:** With respect to matters other than legal theories, a party presents the matter to the trial court by objecting. Failure to object prevents a party from raising that issue on appeal.

   a. **Timeliness:** If an objection is not timely, the grounds for the objection are waived. A party must challenge evidence, for example, by objecting when the other side tries to introduce that evidence.

   b. **"Renewing" an objection:** If a mistake made at one stage of the trial has an impact at a later stage, the party may be required to object again at that later stage.

      Example: *P* sues *D* for negligent infliction of emotional distress after *D* destroys *P*'s family heirloom. *D* moves to dismiss for failure to state a claim, claiming the tort is not available for the destruction of property. The trial court denies the motion. Later, the trial court proposes jury instructions setting out the elements of negligent infliction. Even though *D* has already tried to convince the trial court the tort is not available, he should object to the instructions to preserve the issue for appeal.

   c. **Exception:** Some jurisdictions do not require an objection in the case of "*plain error.*" An error is plain when it is so blatantly incorrect that it calls into question the competence or partiality of the judge. Findings of plain error are very rare.

C. **Harmless error:** An error that does not "affect the substantial rights of the parties" cannot lead to reversal on appeal. *28 U.S.C. §2111.* Such errors—mistakes that did not affect the outcome— are called *harmless errors.* For example, if the lower court erroneously admitted evidence on a certain issue, but the party also had a considerable amount of admissible evidence showing the same thing, admission of the improper evidence might be harmless.

★   **Example:** Harnden v. Jayco, Inc., 496 F.3d 579 (6th Cir. 2007), represents a straightforward application of the harmless error rule. Plaintiff sought to overturn the trial court's summary judgment for defendant, arguing that an affidavit the trial court had considered was not in proper form. The appellate court found the error harmless, noting that if it reversed, defendant would simply refile the same affidavit, but in proper form.

II. TIMING OF THE APPEAL

In the federal courts, and in many states, a party may appeal only *final judgments* of the trial court. The following discussion focuses on the final judgment rule in the federal courts only. State practice may differ significantly.

A. Final decision rule: The final decision rule is set out in *28 U.S.C. §1291*, which allows appeals from all "*final decisions*" of the federal district courts.

1. Jurisdictional: Section 1291 is a jurisdictional statute. If the judgment is not final and fails to satisfy one of the exceptions, the appellate courts *lack subject matter jurisdiction*.

2. Appeals not covered by §1291: Not all appeals from the district courts fall within §1291. Certain cases go to the *Federal Circuit*. 28 U.S.C. §§1292(c), 1295. A handful of cases go directly from the district courts to the U.S. Supreme Court under 28 U.S.C. §1253.

3. *Final decision* defined: A final decision is "one which ends the litigation on the merits and leaves nothing to do but execute the judgment." Catlin v. United States, 324 U.S. 229, 233 (1945). In other words, the court hearing the case must have resolved all issues necessary to wrap up the dispute.

  a. Interlocutory rulings: Most of a trial judge's rulings during pretrial proceedings and trial do not completely resolve the case and therefore are not final. These decisions are called *interlocutory rulings*. Examples of interlocutory rulings include:

  i. most *discovery* rulings;

  ii. grant or denial of a *request for a jury*;

  iii. *denial* of a motion to *dismiss* or a motion for *summary judgment*;

  iv. *grant* of a motion to dismiss or summary judgment on *some, but not all, claims or defenses* (but see the discussion of Fed. R. Civ. P. 54 below); and

  v. orders granting a *new trial*.

★
  Example: Liberty Mutual Insurance Co. v. Wetzel, 424 U.S. 737 (1976), held a trial court's grant of summary judgment on liability, but not relief, was not a final decision for purposes of §1291.

4. Practical importance of finality: Section 1291 clearly prevents a party from filing an appeal too early. But it also determines whether a party has filed its appeal too late. Once a judgment becomes final, a party has only a limited period to file its appeal.

  a. In *federal courts*, a party usually has only *30 days* to file an appeal. An appeal filed too late cannot be heard by the appellate court. Fed. R. App. P. 4(a)(1)(A).

  b. The 30-day period may be extended if a party makes certain motions. See Fed. R. App. P. 4(a)(4)(A) and 4(a)(5).

B. Exceptions to the final decision rule: Federal statutes, the federal rules, and case law contain several exceptions to the final decision rule.

1. Final resolution of discrete portion of case under Rule 54(b): In a case involving multiple claims, the court may resolve some claims prior to others. If the trial court enters judgment on some but not all of the claims, Fed. R. Civ. P. 54(b) may allow the parties to appeal the ruling without waiting for a final decision on the entire case. Rule 54(b) has two basic requirements: that the judge enter judgment on a discrete "claim for relief" and that she expressly indicate there is no reason to delay entry of the judgment.

★
  a. "Claim for relief": The Fed. R. Civ. P. 54(b) term "claim for relief" is broader than it may appear. If a party sets forth a single basic wrong but seeks recovery for that wrong

under several different theories, the different theories are all part of the same "claim for relief." Therefore, if the court resolves only one theory, no immediate appeal of that ruling is possible under Fed. R. Civ. P. 54(b). Liberty Mutual Insurance Co. v. Wetzel, 424 U.S. 737 (1976).

    i. On the other hand, merely because two claims are related or share considerable facts does not mean they comprise the same claim for relief. Sears, Roebuck & Co. v. Mackey, 351 U.S. 427 (1956).

    Example 1: *P* and *D* are neighbors. *P* is upset because *D* has frequent cookouts at her house, and the smoke bothers *P*'s allergies. Moreover, at one of these parties, a guest threw a baseball through *P*'s window. *P* sues *D*. *P*'s complaint raises three claims: (a) nuisance, based on the frequent cookouts; (b) trespass, based on the smoke from the cookout entering *P*'s property; and (c) trespass, based on the baseball entering the property and causing the broken window. The trial court grants summary judgment for *D* on the smoke trespass claim, holding the movement of smoke particles cannot qualify as a trespass. The judge expressly certifies there is no reason to delay entry of the summary judgment. *P* cannot appeal the summary judgment at this time. The smoke trespass claim was merely one of two alternate claims for recovery arising out of the frequent cookouts.

    Example 2: Same facts as prior example, except the judge grants summary judgment for *P* on the baseball trespass claim. The judge certifies there is no reason to delay entry of the judgment. *D* can appeal the judgment immediately. (In fact, if *D* does not appeal within 30 days, she loses her right to appeal.) Although this claim, like one of the others, is for trespass, it involves a different core set of facts and is accordingly a discrete claim for relief.

    ii. A *counterclaim, cross-claim,* or *third-party claim* is *separate* from plaintiff's claim even if it arises from the same transaction or occurrence. Therefore, judgment on a counterclaim can usually be appealed under Fed. R. Civ. P. 54(b) even if the original claim remains pending.

    iii. Claims by or against *separate parties* are separate under Fed. R. Civ. P. 54(b). For example, if a court dismisses plaintiff's claim against one of two joint tortfeasors, the court has resolved a discrete "claim for relief."

  b. Express determination: In addition to the "single claim" requirement, Fed. R. Civ. P. 54(b) also requires that the trial judge expressly state there is *no reason to delay entry* of judgment.

    i. The purpose of this express determination requirement is to provide notice to the parties that the time for appeal has commenced.

    ii. However, a court of appeals is not bound by the trial judge's determination. Even if the trial judge certifies that immediate appeal is available, the court of appeals can determine for itself whether the single claim requirement was satisfied.

 2. Injunctions and other orders: *28 U.S.C. §1292(a)* provides that certain orders may be appealed immediately, notwithstanding the final judgment rule of §1291. The following three orders qualify:

   a. Injunctions: The most important of the §1292(a) exceptions deals with injunctions. Any order of the trial court that *grants, continues, modifies, refuses, or dissolves* an injunction may be appealed immediately. 28 U.S.C. §1292(a)(1). Although a *preliminary injunction* qualifies as an injunction under this rule, a *temporary restraining order* does not and therefore cannot be immediately appealed.

   b. Receivers: Any order appointing a receiver, refusing to wind up a receivership, or facilitating a receivership may be appealed immediately. 28 U.S.C. §1292(a)(2).

   c. Admiralty: Parties may also appeal any order in an admiralty case that finally determines the rights and liabilities of the parties. 28 U.S.C. §1292(a)(3).

3. Certification under §1292(b): 28 U.S.C. §1292(b) allows certain issues to be appealed if both the trial judge and the appellate court agree an immediate appeal is justified.

   a. Criteria: However, the statute places several conditions on such appeals.

     i. The order must involve a *controlling question of law* about which there is *substantial ground for difference of opinion*. Contested questions of fact cannot be appealed under the section no matter how important they are.

     ii. The trial judge must determine that allowing an immediate appeal might materially *advance the ultimate termination of the litigation*.

     iii. The trial judge must *certify in writing* that both (i) and (ii) are satisfied. The decision whether to certify is *within the discretion* of the trial judge.

     iv. The party who wants to appeal must apply to the appellate court within *10 days* of entry of the order.

     v. The appellate court must *agree to hear the issue on appeal*. Even if (i) to (iv) above are satisfied, the decision whether to hear the appeal is *within the discretion* of the appellate court.

   b. Rarely granted: Courts of appeal rarely certify appeals under §1292(b).

4. Certification of class actions: Fed. R. Civ. P. 23(f) allows for immediate review of the *grant or denial* of class certification. The court of appeals has *discretion* whether to hear the appeal.

5. Mandamus and prohibition: Writs of mandamus and prohibition are other ways to review an interlocutory order. These writs are not governed by §1291 and its final decision rule. However, writs of mandamus and prohibition differ from ordinary appeals in certain important ways.

   a. Definitions: Mandamus and prohibition are *original proceedings* brought against a public official. Because a judge is a public official, both writs are available as a way of challenging a judge's decision in a case. *Mandamus* orders the trial judge to *do something*. *Prohibition* orders the judge to *refrain* from doing something.

   b. Extraordinary relief: Mandamus and prohibition are both "extraordinary writs," available only in "exceptional circumstances amounting to a judicial 'usurpation of power.' . . . " Kerr v. United States District Court, 426 U.S. 394 (1976). Therefore, review under these writs is not frequently granted. However, *mandamus* is frequently granted in federal court when a trial judge improperly refuses to *impanel a jury*.

6. Practical finality: In addition to the exceptions listed above, the court-created *"collateral order" doctrine* allows appeal of some interlocutory orders.

a. Basic test: An order may be appealed under the collateral order doctrine if:

   i. the trial judge makes a ruling on an *important issue* that is *separate from the merits* of the case,

   ii. the issue is *conclusively settled*, and

   iii. the ruling would be *effectively unreviewable* if it cannot be appealed until after final judgment. Coopers & Lybrand v. Livesay, 437 U.S. 463 (1978).

b. Important issue separate from the merits: If the issue is tied up with the merits of the action, review under the collateral order doctrine is unavailable. This restriction saves the court of appeals from having to deal with the merits more than once.

   Example: A trial court denies a motion for summary judgment. The order is not appealable as a collateral order because it requires the court to consider the merits of the case.

   i. Fact or law: Unlike appeals under §1292(b), the "important issue" may be either an issue of fact or a combined issue of law and fact.

   ii. Important: The courts have given little guidance on what makes an issue important. Instead, they tend to focus on the "separate from the merits" language.

c. Conclusively determined: The trial court's decision must be one that is unlikely to be revised later in the suit.

d. Effectively unreviewable: The final element is that the decision be "effectively unreviewable" if the party is forced to wait to appeal until after final judgment. This is the *most difficult* part of the test to satisfy.

   i. The court must determine if the ruling will cause damage that cannot be repaired if the losing party must wait until an appeal following a final judgment.

   ii. In most cases, however, a *new trial* can cure the problem. Thus, collateral order appeals are limited to cases where a *new trial cannot repair the damage* done.

e. Application of test: Because this three-part test is very difficult to satisfy, most attempts to invoke the doctrine fail. Several cases help to illustrate when the doctrine applies.

   i. *Cohen*: Denial of bond in shareholder's derivative action: The Supreme Court opinion in Cohen v. Beneficial Industrial Loan Corp., 337 U.S. 541 (1949), allowed appeal of a trial court order refusing to require plaintiff in a shareholder's derivative action to file a bond as security for costs. The Court found the issue to be important (because it involved a question under the *Erie* doctrine) and completely separate from the merits (because the question turned solely on an interpretation of Fed. R. Civ. P. 23.1, not on the facts of the case). Moreover, although it would have been possible for the court to change its mind, that was not likely. Finally, the decision could not be effectively reviewed after final judgment. The purpose of the bond was to protect defendant from the *expenses of defending a frivolous case*. By denying the bond, the court took away that protection. Moreover, if defendant were forced to litigate the case to completion before appealing, it would suffer the very harm that the bond was designed to deal with, namely, the expenses of litigating a possibly frivolous case.

   ii. *Eisen*: Order to pay cost of notice: Similarly, in Eisen v. Carlisle & Jacquelin, 417 U.S. 156 (1974), the Court held an order requiring defendant to pay the costs of serving the members of the plaintiff class in a class action could be appealed under the collateral order doctrine. The decision turned on an interpretation of Fed. R. Civ. P. 23 and had nothing to do with the merits of the case. Nor was the decision effectively reviewable through normal avenues of appeal. Granting a new trial after final judgment in the case would not remedy the harm because defendant would already have paid the costs of service.

   iii. **Immunity:** The law provides immunities for certain categories of defendants. To the extent an immunity is a "right" not to be dragged into court at all, a ruling denying an immunity may fit within the collateral order exception doctrine.

     (a) However, the judge's ruling must deny the immunity as a matter of law, not based on whether certain facts alleged by plaintiff are in fact true. Thus, if the immunity is a *qualified immunity* that can be overcome by a showing defendant acted in bad faith, a decision denying immunity based on a finding defendant did act in bad faith cannot be appealed as a collateral order.

★   **(b)** An order refusing to enforce a forum selection clause in a contract is not a decision denying "immunity." A forum selection clause does not prevent litigation but merely defines where litigation must take place. Lauro Lines s.r.l. v. Chasser, 490 U.S. 495 (1989).

   iv. **Discovery orders:** The collateral order exception is almost never used for orders concerning discovery. A party subject to a discovery order can "appeal" the order by refusing to comply, being declared in contempt, and immediately appealing the contempt order.

   Example: Mohawk Industries, Inc. v. Carpenter, 130 S. Ct. 599 (2009), held that a ruling that certain information was not protected by the attorney-client privilege was not appealable under the collateral order doctrine. Even though the party might have to disclose certain secret information, the court could grant a new trial at which that information could not be used as evidence. The Court indicated the party could also refuse to divulge, be held in contempt, and appeal the contempt order.

Quiz Yourself on
APPEALABILITY, THE FINAL JUDGMENT RULE, AND EXCEPTIONS

138. Landowner sues Neighbor for trespass. At trial, Landowner calls a witness who testifies she saw Neighbor on Landowner's land on the date in question. Because Landowner did not disclose the name of the witness in either the initial or pretrial mandatory discovery disclosures, this witness proves a complete surprise to Neighbor's attorney. Nevertheless, the attorney, not wanting to look unprepared to the jury, does not object. The attorney regains his composure and conducts an effective cross-examination.

The trial continues for another day. Because Landowner has no other evidence showing that Neighbor trespassed, Neighbor moves for judgment as a matter of law. Neighbor correctly points out that the Federal Rules of Civil Procedure prevent Landowner from using the witness's testimony because Landowner failed to turn over the name in discovery. The judge denies the motion and submits the case to the jury. The jury rules for Landowner, and judgment is entered accordingly.

Neighbor appeals, arguing the judge erred in submitting the case to the jury. Assuming Neighbor would be entitled to judgment as a matter of law without the evidence of this one witness, will Neighbor prevail in this appeal? _____

139. Bunsen, a chemist, recently bought new laboratory equipment from ACME Co. The equipment explodes, causing serious injury to Bunsen. Bunsen sues ACME in federal court, alleging two separate claims. He first alleges ACME breached an express warranty set out in the purchase contract. Bunsen's second claim is for products liability, and asserts the equipment was negligently designed. The trial judge grants ACME's motion for partial summary judgment on the express warranty claim. Bunsen immediately files an appeal. May Bunsen appeal the summary judgment at this point? _____

140. Drake Yoola is a third-year law student who has a terrible aversion to the sun. He is accordingly quite upset that the Dean has arranged for the school's graduation ceremony to be held outdoors. Drake sues the Dean in federal court. Because graduation is in two weeks, Drake asks for a preliminary injunction requiring the Dean to hold the ceremony indoors. The court denies the request. May Drake appeal at this time, or must he wait until after trial? _____

Answers

138. Neighbor will not prevail because he did not object to the evidence in a timely fashion. An objection to the introduction of evidence usually must be made when the evidence is offered (a "contemporaneous objection").

139. Bunsen may not appeal at this time. The summary judgment is not a final decision because it resolved only one of the two claims in the case. Nor does this situation fit into the Fed. R. Civ. P. 54(b) exception. Even if the judge's order had specified there was no reason to delay entry of judgment, the judge did not resolve a complete "claim for relief." The warranty and products liability claims are both based on a single injury and therefore part of the same "claim for relief" under that rule.

140. Drake may appeal immediately. 28 U.S.C. §1292(a)(1) allows a party an immediate appeal from an order either granting or refusing an injunction. A preliminary injunction qualifies as an injunction under this statute.

III. SCOPE OF APPELLATE REVIEW

An appeal is not a new trial. An appellate court gives a certain amount of **deference** to the decisions of a trial court. How critically it reviews the lower court's decision **depends on the nature of the issues involved**.

A. **Issues of law:** Issues of law are reviewed **de novo**. Under *de novo* review, the court gives no deference whatsoever to the trial court's findings of law, but instead determines for itself what the law is.

   Note: In certain appeals from **agencies**, courts defer to the agency's interpretation of the law. This principle is unique to **administrative law** and does not apply to an appeal from a trial court.

B. Issues of fact: Issues of fact are reviewed under a *"clearly erroneous"* standard. The Supreme Court defined this standard: "A finding is 'clearly erroneous' when although there is evidence to support it, the reviewing court on the entire evidence is left with the definite and firm conviction that a mistake has been committed." United States v. U.S. Gypsum Co., 333 U.S. 364 (1948).

    1. Clearly erroneous standard applied: Clearly erroneous review is very deferential. The court of appeals may reverse only if it is convinced the trial court is incorrect.

        a. The court of appeals should not reevaluate the *credibility* of the witnesses.

        b. If there is *significant evidence on both sides* of the issue, the lower court's finding *cannot be clearly erroneous*.

        c. If the findings of fact are made by a *jury*, the standard is *even more difficult* to satisfy. Although often referred to as the clearly erroneous standard, in practice the court of appeals applies the *no reasonable jury standard* that applies in judgments as a matter of law under Fed. R. Civ. P. 50. See Chapter 11.

        Example: For an illustration of how these principles apply in actual practice, see Anderson v. Bessemer City, 470 U.S. 564 (1985), where the Court held a trial judge's finding of discriminatory intent was not clearly erroneous, even though it was based on minimal evidence and even though the judge had asked the parties to submit proposed findings of fact that the judge used in the opinion.

    2. Mixed fact and law: Many issues are mixed questions of law and fact. For example, whether a party breached a contract or acted negligently requires the factfinder to determine not only what happened but also how the law applies to the facts as determined.

        a. In the federal system, a mixed question of law and fact is *treated just like a question of fact* and is subject to the clearly erroneous standard.

        b. However, if the trial court's ruling on a mixed question was based on an error in law, the appellate court reviews the issue *de novo*.

    3. Documentary evidence: Sometimes, the only evidence on an issue at trial is contained in documents. For example, a court interpreting a written contract must read the contract itself. In such cases, much of the rationale for deferring to the trial court disappears, because the court of appeals is every bit as capable of reading and interpreting documentary evidence as the trial court.

        a. Federal view: Nevertheless, in the federal courts the *clearly erroneous standard applies* even when the evidence is comprised completely of documents and physical evidence. Anderson v. Bessemer City, 470 U.S. 564 (1985).

        b. Applying standard to instruments: As a practical matter, however, it is easier for a court of appeals to find a lower court's interpretation of a contract or other legal document clearly erroneous. Because interpretation of a legal document does not involve issues of credibility, the lower court's findings can be overturned if they are clearly at odds with the written words.

C. Issues within discretion of the trial judge: Certain issues, such as the decision whether to grant a new trial, are deemed particularly within the province of the trial judge. A court of appeals reviews these decisions under an *abuse of discretion standard*. As the name implies, a court of appeals will reverse only if it concludes that there is *no possible reasonable basis* for the decision. The standard is sometimes referred to as *arbitrary and capricious.*

Quiz Yourself on *APPEALS*

141. Lars, a citizen of Denmark, is on an extended driving trip in the United States. While in a very remote part of the country, Lars is stopped by Sheriff Smith. Hearing Lars's accent, Smith concludes Lars must be a spy and locks him in the local hoosegow. After Lars obtains his release, he sues Smith in federal district court, seeking recovery under state civil rights laws.

Smith moves to dismiss, citing a state statute that provides an absolute immunity to sheriffs. The trial court, however, rules the immunity does not apply to claims under the particular civil rights statute Lars is using. Smith files an immediate appeal to the court of appeals. Can the court of appeals hear Smith's appeal at this time? _____

142. Same facts as Problem 141, except the immunity statute contains an exception for acts done with "wanton disregard for someone's rights." Smith does not seek an immediate appeal of the trial judge's ruling. The case proceeds through discovery. After discovery is complete, Smith files a motion for summary judgment. Smith argues he can be held liable under the civil rights law only if he *knew* his actions were wrongful. Although Lars has evidence of negligence, he has no evidence Smith knew his actions were wrongful. The trial judge disagrees with Smith and denies the summary judgment motion, finding that an officer such as Smith can be held liable even if he was negligent.

However, the judge is unsure of her ruling on the standard of care. Therefore, she certifies the question of the applicable standard of care for review. In this certification, the judge states that because there is considerable doubt on the issue, allowing an appeal at this time might speed up the resolution of the case.

Does the appellate court have the authority to review the judge's findings concerning the standard of care at this time? _____

143. Same facts as Problem 141, except Smith does not seek immediate appeal of the trial judge's ruling. The case proceeds to trial, where Smith wins a judgment completely exonerating him from all liability. Lars appeals, based upon a number of alleged procedural errors made by the trial judge in the case. Smith is still sore about the trial judge's rejection of his immunity defense and is considering bringing that issue before the court of appeals. May Smith, as the party who won at trial, nevertheless challenge the trial judge's ruling on the immunity defense? _____

144. Until recently, Walter was a pastry chef at an upscale restaurant. Walter was fired by Paulette, the head chef, for incompetence. Walter sues Paulette in federal court, bringing two claims. The first is a wrongful termination claim, based on the firing. The second is a defamation claim, in which Walter claims Paulette spoke badly about Walter's social skills to his ex-workers, destroying several friendships.

After discovery, the trial judge grants summary judgment to Paulette on the defamation claim. The trial judge's written opinion states, "The evidence is clear plaintiff was (and is) a lousy pastry chef. Therefore, everything defendant said about plaintiff was completely true and cannot give rise to a claim for defamation. Because there is no reason to delay the entry of summary judgment on the defamation claim, I hereby grant summary judgment to defendant on that claim."

Four months later, the case goes to trial, where Paulette wins a judgment on the remaining wrongful termination claim. Walter immediately files an appeal. However, because the case was tried by a jury, Walter has little confidence he can prevail on the wrongful termination claim. Instead, he bases his appeal only on the defamation claim. Can Walter appeal on the defamation claim? _____

Answers

141. Smith's appeal is timely. Although none of the other exceptions apply, his case fits within the collateral order exception. That exception has been applied in cases involving an absolute immunity, for in those situations the very fact of exposing the protected person to trial is the sort of irremediable harm that the doctrine is designed to prevent. The key issue of whether the immunity is available to this type of defendant as a matter of law does not turn on the merits of the underlying dispute. The issue of immunity is also extremely important. Therefore, appeal is possible under the collateral order doctrine.

142. The final judgment rule is a rule that defines the jurisdiction of the courts of appeal. Therefore, unless the case fits one of the exceptions, the appellate court cannot hear this case merely because it wants to review it. Denial of summary judgment is not a final decision because the judge must still conduct a trial on the merits.

     The trial judge's certification of the question, however, may possibly allow review under §1292(b). The trial judge used proper language in the certification. In addition, the case meets the other requirements of §1292(b). The issue being appealed is one of law, as required by §1292(b). Although the judge evaluated the facts in making the ruling, the actual question of standard of care is one of law. In addition, allowing an immediate appeal might advance termination of the case. If the trial judge was incorrect and the standard of care is the "knowing" standard argued by Smith, the case is essentially over because Lars has no evidence of knowledge. Therefore, if the court of appeals elects to hear the case at this time, it has the authority to do so.

143. Smith is free to raise the immunity defense. A party who prevailed at trial may ask the appellate court to affirm the trial court's judgment on any grounds it chooses, including grounds presented to but rejected by the trial court.

144. Walter probably cannot appeal because he filed his appeal too late. The Federal Rules of Appellate Procedure give Walter 30 days following final judgment to appeal. He did file an appeal within 30 days of the trial judge's last ruling. However, he needed to file the appeal within 30 days of the grant of summary judgment. Under Fed. R. Civ. P. 54(b), the trial judge's ruling was probably a final judgment on the defamation claim. Moreover, the judge included the "magic language" about how there was no reason to delay entry of judgment. The ruling was accordingly a final judgment, starting the 30-day "clock" for appeal on that issue. Because trial did not commence until four months after the ruling, we know he did not meet this 30-day deadline. Walter did not move to extend the 30-day period for filing an appeal.

     The only debatable issue is whether the trial judge's ruling actually qualified as a final judgment under Fed. R. Civ. P. 54(b). In order for that rule to apply, the judge must entirely resolve a separate and distinct claim for relief. The firing and defamation are separate claims because they involve distinct injuries caused by separate acts. Paulette's statements were about Walter's social skills, not his skills as a chef.

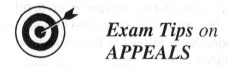

Exam Tips on APPEALS

☞ When dealing with a question concerning appeals, always consider three subissues: may *this party* appeal, may she appeal on *these grounds*, and is the appeal *timely*?

☞ **Who may appeal:** Recall that a party can "win" a suit and still be able to appeal.

☞ **Grounds for appeal:** Always make sure a party *has not waived* the grounds it is asserting for the appeal. In many cases, a party must ask the trial court to correct its own mistake when the mistake is made.

☞ **Time for appeal:** The final judgment rule is admittedly difficult. However, do not focus so much on that rule that you forget the other main limitation on appeal: the *30-day time limit*.

☞ When dealing with the final judgment rule, be sure you understand the various exceptions. Some of the exceptions, such as the provision allowing immediate appeal of either the grant or denial of an injunction, are relatively straightforward. Spotting one of these exceptions can save you valuable time, and if they apply you do not need to deal with the more difficult exceptions such as the collateral order doctrine.

 ☞ Before concluding appeal is possible under Fed. R. Civ. P. 54(b), make sure the trial judge's ruling contains language about "no just reason to delay" entry of the judgment.

 ☞ The most difficult issue in the *collateral order doctrine* is determining whether the issue is effectively reviewable. In the vast majority of situations, the erroneous ruling can be effectively cured by a new trial. It is only when the fact of the trial is *itself* the problem that the doctrine is likely to apply.

☞ **Scope of review:** The two main issues in scope of review are determining whether the issue in question is one of law or fact and how the various standards of review apply.

☞ Recall that a mixed question of law and fact—such as whether a party was negligent—is treated as a question of fact for purposes of review.

☞ Be very sure of yourself before you conclude a court of appeals should overturn a jury verdict. Jury verdicts are entitled to a very high degree of deference.

CHAPTER 13

RESPECT FOR JUDGMENTS

ChapterScope ━━━━━━━━━━━━━━━━━━━━━━━━━━━━━━━━━━━

This chapter deals with the effect a judgment in one case has on later litigation involving one or more of the parties. A judgment can affect later cases in three main ways. The first is as *precedent*, a topic not covered in this chapter. Second, a judgment can completely bar the litigation of certain *claims or defenses*, even those not raised in the first case. Finally, it can prevent relitigation of certain *issues* that were actually litigated and decided in the first action.

- The doctrine of *claim preclusion* (sometimes called *res judicata*) prevents parties from raising certain claims that were litigated or should have been litigated in the first action.

  - In certain cases, *defenses* will also be precluded. Both Fed. R. Civ. P. 13(a) and the common law compulsory counterclaim rule can bar defenses.

  - Claim preclusion applies only to later disputes between the *same parties* or those in *privity* with parties to the first action.

- The doctrine of *issue preclusion* (sometimes called *collateral estoppel*) prevents parties from relitigating certain issues that were actually litigated and decided in the first case.

  - Determining precisely what the first court decided is not always obvious from the judgment. Instead, it is necessary to dissect the judgment logically to determine what findings were actually made and necessary to the decision.

  - Unlike claim preclusion, courts increasingly allow people who were not parties to the first action to use issue preclusion. Whether such *nonmutual use* is allowed may depend on whether it is *offensive* or *defensive*.

- Claim and issue preclusion apply only to findings of either pure *fact* or *mixed questions* of law and fact. They do not apply to pure rulings of law.

- Courts have recognized certain *limits* on both claim and issue preclusion because of fairness and other policy concerns.

- Two other doctrines look similar to claim and issue preclusion.

  - The *law of the case* doctrine prevents a court from reopening a legal issue that was decided earlier in the case.

  - The notion of *judicial estoppel* may prevent a party who prevails on a position in one case from taking an inconsistent position in a later case.

I. CLAIM PRECLUSION

Claim preclusion forces plaintiffs to join all claims arising from a single basic event in one case.

A. **Overview**

1. **Policies:** Claim preclusion serves two main policy goals.

   a. **Efficiency:** First, by requiring parties to join all closely related claims in a single case, it helps ensure the most efficient use of judicial resources.

   b. **Consistency:** Claim preclusion also helps ensure consistency in litigation.

2. **Terminology:** Courts sometimes refer to claim preclusion as *res judicata*.

   a. Somewhat confusingly, at other times the phrase *res judicata* is used as a collective term to refer to the entire doctrine of preclusion, including both claim and issue preclusion.

   b. The terms *bar* and *merger* reflect two different aspects of claim preclusion.

      i. *Bar* means simply that someone who actually raises a particular claim in a case is barred from raising it again in later litigation.

      ii. *Merger*, by contrast, deals with claims (and sometimes defenses), that were ***not raised*** in the prior case. If such claims arise from the same basic set of events, the party may be precluded from raising them in the later case. A party who attempts to litigate the same basic claim in two actions is said to have ***split*** the action.

3. **Basic standard:** Generally, claim preclusion applies when:

   a. the first action resulted in a ***final judgment on the merits***, and

   b. the party raises a claim that was previously litigated or one arising from the same basic events as one that was previously litigated.

4. **Plaintiffs barred:** Generally, claim preclusion applies only to claims by parties who were ***plaintiffs in the first action***. If a party was not a plaintiff (or in certain narrow circumstances to be discussed below, a defendant), claim preclusion does not require the party to litigate its claim in the first action. One reason justifying the disparate treatment of plaintiffs and other parties is that plaintiff has the privilege of selecting the court.

B. **Barring claims:** A claim is barred if it ***was or should have been*** raised by a party who was a plaintiff in the prior action.

1. **Claims brought in action 1:** A party who litigates a claim in one suit can never again raise the ***same claim*** against the ***same defendant***.

   a. **Same claim:** Two cases involve the same claim if the party uses the ***same legal theory*** to recover against the ***same party*** based on the ***same underlying facts***.

      Example: *P*, a football quarterback, is injured when his blockers fail to prevent the defense from sacking him. *P* sues *Tackle* for his injuries, claiming *Tackle* was negligent in performing his blocking duties. *P* loses. *P* now sues *Guard* for negligence, seeking recovery for the same basic injury. Claim preclusion does not bar the claim. Even though the legal theory is the same and the same basic facts are involved, *P*'s claim against *Guard* is not the same claim as *P*'s claim against *Tackle*.

   b. A claim is barred only if it was ***resolved*** by the court in the first action. The final judgment requirement is discussed in Part I.D.2.

   c. Note it is ***irrelevant how the first case is resolved***. Plaintiff is barred from bringing a claim regardless of whether she won or lost the first case.

2. **Claims not brought in action 1:** Claim preclusion also bars a party who was a plaintiff in the first action from relitigating claims not brought in the first action but are *factually related* to claims presented in that action. *Courts differ significantly* on the test to determine whether a claim is sufficiently related to a claim raised in the first action to be barred by claim preclusion.

   a. **Majority view:** Most courts ask if the two claims arise from the *same transaction or occurrence*, or *series of transactions or occurrences*. This resembles the test used in the Federal Rules of Civil Procedure joinder rules. This is also the view favored by the *Restatement (Second) of Judgments*.

      i. Courts usually find the standard satisfied only if the claims share some of the *same relevant evidence*. Unlike the standard used in joinder, a mere logical relationship between the claims usually does not suffice.

      ii. As long as the claims share some of the same evidence, however, two claims can be sufficiently related notwithstanding that the legal theories are completely different.

         Example: *P* sells ground coffee under the trademark CONNOISSEUR. *D* starts to sell ground coffee under the trademark CONNISUER. *P* sues *D* for trademark infringement. Once that suit is complete, *P* sues *D* for false advertising, based on *D*'s claims—made in the same advertisements—that *D*'s coffee is "free trade." *P*'s second claim is barred. Both claims arise from the same occurrence, namely, *D*'s advertisements for its coffee.

   b. **Same cause of action approach:** A minority of courts use the "same cause of action" test. This test is much narrower; that is, it bars significantly fewer claims. It looks for *considerable overlap in the evidence* required to prove both claims. This test is satisfied only if the claims share many of the same basic elements, so that the evidence necessary to prevail on the second claim is by and large the same evidence that should have been presented in the first action.

      Example 1: Consider the example discussed just above. Under the same cause of action test, the false advertising claim is not part of the same cause of action as the trademark infringement claim. The trademark claim requires *P* to prove *D* used a similar mark in a way that caused customer confusion as to the source of the coffee. *P* need not offer evidence of the quality of the goods or other statements made in *D*'s advertising. The false advertising claim, by contrast, focuses on what *D* said about the coffee, whether those statements gave consumers an impression concerning the quality of the coffee, and whether the statements were true.

      ★ **Example 2:** For a case applying this approach, see Frier v. City of Vandalia, 770 F.2d 699 (7th Cir. 1985) (because the claims shared a significant overlap in evidence, the new claims were barred under Illinois law, which uses the same cause of action approach).

   c. **Same primary right test:** A few courts use the older "primary right" approach, which is an heir of common law pleading. Under this approach, the second claim is barred if it protects the same primary legally protected right of the plaintiff.

      Example: Again consider the trademark/false advertising example. Under the same primary right test, the false advertising claim is barred. Both claims, trademark infringement and false advertising, protect *P*'s same legal interest, namely, *its* right to sell its coffee to customers without unfair interference by competitors.

d. Installment contracts: Contracts performed in installments, such as a loan or lease, present special issues in claim preclusion. Generally, each installment is considered a *separate transaction*. Therefore, once one breach occurs, a party may bring an action for that breach without losing the right to sue for later breaches. However, this general principle is qualified by three important exceptions.

i. Acceleration clause: If the contract in question contains a clause under which breach of one installment *automatically* makes all installments due and owing immediately, the party must sue for breach of the entire contract. However, few acceleration clauses are automatic. Most give the nondefaulting party an option to accelerate.

ii. Material breach: If, as a matter of contract law, breach of a particular installment is so significant that it destroys the essential value of the contract, the party must sue for breach of the entire contract, not merely the installment.

iii. Rule of accumulated breaches: Although each installment is a separate transaction, the rule of accumulated breaches requires a party to join all breaches that have *already occurred* as of the moment he brings suit. However, the rule of accumulated breaches *does not apply to negotiable instruments*, such as a simple check.

C. Defenses in first action: In most cases, the common law doctrine of claim preclusion bars claims, not defenses. In certain narrow circumstances, however, the doctrine may also prevent a party from bringing a claim based on the same basic elements of a defense the party should have raised in the prior action. The Federal Rules of Civil Procedure significantly expand the scope of defense preclusion in federal courts.

1. Compulsory counterclaims: The starting point in any analysis of whether a party who was a defendant is barred from raising a claim is to determine whether there is a *compulsory counterclaim provision* in the governing Rules of Civil Procedure. If the jurisdiction in which the *first action* was litigated had such a rule, it is likely to control the issue. *Fed. R. Civ. P. 13(a)*, the compulsory counterclaim rule in the federal courts, is discussed in Chapter 14, Part I.B.

2. Common law rule: If the rules do not require a defendant to bring a particular counterclaim in suit 1, the party who was the defendant is free to raise the issue in suit 2—as either a defense or a claim—unless it falls within the narrow common law compulsory counterclaim rule. The common law rule asks whether the claim in the second case would *nullify the judgment* in the first case. If the claim would nullify the judgment by denying the other party certain rights found to exist in the first case, the claim is barred. Few counterclaims nullify the judgment.

Example: Smith hires Jones to install a new roof on Smith's house. Jones completes the project in satisfactory fashion. However, as Jones drives away from Smith's house, he negligently drives his truck through Smith's prize rose garden. When Smith refuses to pay, Jones sues Smith for breach of contract. Jones sues in a state that has no compulsory counterclaim provision in its Rules of Civil Procedure. Jones prevails in the suit.

Smith then sues Jones, seeking recovery on two separate claims. First, Smith alleges Jones committed fraud in his breach of contract action. Smith demands a refund of the damages Smith had to pay in that earlier case. Second, Smith sues Jones for negligence, for the damage to the rose garden.

The fraud claim is barred. If Smith were given a refund, it would deprive Jones of rights the first court found he had. However, Smith is free to bring the negligence claim. Jones's negligence does not nullify Jones's breach of contract claim, even though it may reduce Jones's ultimate recovery.

Do not forget that most jurisdictions have some sort of compulsory counterclaim rule. Thus, had the case in the prior example been subject to Fed. R. Civ. P. 13, Smith would also be barred from bringing the negligence claim because it arose from the same transaction or occurrence.

D. Other issues in claim preclusion: Other difficult issues may arise in claim preclusion.

   1. Same parties—the problem of privity: In most cases, claim preclusion applies only to claims between the same parties. Therefore, a plaintiff may sue two defendants for the same injury in different actions, even if those two defendants could have been joined in the same suit. Similarly, two people injured by a defendant's single act may sue separately. However, an important exception to the "same party" rule arises in cases of privity.

      a. Effect of privity: If *X* and *Y* are in privity, claim preclusion applies to both equally. Thus, if *X* is barred from bringing a claim against *D*, *Y* is also barred from bringing the claim against *D*. Similarly, in any situation where *X* could use claim preclusion to prevent *P* from bringing a claim, *Y* can also use claim preclusion against *P*.

      b. When privity exists: Privity exists when, because of the relationship between the parties, the two are litigating the *same legal right*.

         i. One situation where privity exists is when a party sues as the *legal representative* of another. Examples include a *guardian-ward* relationship and the class representative in a properly crafted *class action*.

         ii. Privity also exists where the two parties have a *mutual* or *successive interest* in the same property or contract.

            (a) This notion underlies the concept of "running with the land" in property law. Thus, if a person who regularly walks across land successfully sues the landowner and establishes an easement by adverse possession, anyone who buys the land from the landowner is bound by that judgment and takes the land subject to the easement. The landowner and buyer have successive interests.

            (b) An example of a mutual interest is a landlord and a tenant. If a tenant sues a nearby factory for nuisance, the outcome also benefits (if tenant wins) or binds (if tenant loses) the landlord.

         iii. Caveat: Privity is relatively rare. Before finding privity, ensure the two parties are indeed litigating the exact same legal right. For example, *joint tortfeasors* are not in privity. Similarly, parties with a *joint undivided interest in land* are not in privity.

★   **Example:** The case of Searle Brothers v. Searle, 588 P.2d 689 (Utah 1978), provides an excellent illustration of a situation that may look like one of privity but is not. In that case, a wife sued her husband for divorce. In dividing the marital assets, the court had to deal with a piece of property. The husband claimed he owned the property jointly with a partnership made up of the husband and two sons. The court rejected the claim and awarded the property to the wife.

The partnership then sued to protect its one-half interest in the same property. The wife claimed the husband was in privity with the partnership and that the partnership therefore was bound by the judgment. The court rejected the argument. Because the husband and the partnership owned the property jointly, they had neither mutual nor successive interests. Moreover, that the husband was managing partner of the partnership did not change the result.

c. **Privity-like relationships.** Courts sometimes try to apply claim preclusion when parties have a close relationship, even though that relationship does not technically qualify as privity. However, the Supreme Court has rejected some of these decisions.

★ **Example:** In Taylor v. Sturgell, 553 U.S. 880 (2008), the Court rejected the doctrine of "virtual representation," pursuant to which a party was barred if another person had fully and adequately presented the same arguments in a highly similar case. The Court emphasized privity is a narrow doctrine that applies only when there is a legal relationship between the person involved in the litigation and the person to be barred.

2. **Final judgment on the merits:** Not all court decisions have claim and issue preclusion effect. *Only final judgments on the merits qualify* for claim and issue preclusion.

a. **Final judgment:** A final judgment is one that completely wraps up the matter. In most jurisdictions, a judgment has claim preclusion effect even though it is currently on appeal.

b. **On the merits:** Claim preclusion bars all claims arising from the same core of facts. The doctrine applies only if the court actually *resolved one or more claims* involving those facts.

   i. **Rulings on the merits:** All jurisdictions agree that certain rulings are on the merits, including judgment after trial and summary judgment.

   ii. **Rulings not on the merits:** Other final determinations are clearly not on the merits, including a dismissal for lack of *jurisdiction*.

   iii. **Statute of limitations:** A judgment based on expiration of the statute of limitations is not considered a judgment on the merits by most courts. If a court grants judgment based on the statute of limitations, a party may still be able to sue in a different forum and gain advantage of that forum's longer limitations period.

   iv. **Issues where courts differ:** Other rulings are not as clear, including dismissal for failure to prosecute and dismissal for failure to state a claim upon which relief can be granted.

   v. **Effect of Rule 41(a) and (b):** Fed. R. Civ. P. 41(a) and (b), and similar rules in force in many states, deal with whether dismissals are on the merits. Dismissals are covered in Chapter 9. Several Supreme Court decisions have interpreted how these rules apply to federal dismissals.

      (a) A Rule 12(b)(6) dismissal for failure to state a claim has claim preclusion effect. Federated Department Stores v. Moitie, 452 U.S. 394, 399 n.3 (1981).

      (b) Because of the Supreme Court's *Semtek* opinion, Rule 41(b) may govern the preclusive effect of a federal dismissal only when the second case takes place in the same federal district. See Chapter 5, Part IV. In other courts, the preclusive effect of the dismissal will ordinarily be determined by the law of the state where the federal court that dismissed sits.

3. **Jurisdictional issues:** Claim preclusion tries to avoid inefficiency by encouraging a party to join all claims arising from the same basic facts. But joinder may not be possible in all cases. For example, federal courts have ***exclusive jurisdiction*** over certain claims arising under federal law. Claim preclusion may not apply when a party ***could not litigate*** a particular claim in the first action because of lack of jurisdiction.

   a. **Majority view:** Most state courts hold that a claim that could not be presented in the first case because of lack of jurisdiction is not barred by claim preclusion. This is also the view of the Restatement (Second) of Judgments. The rule is no different even if the party could have filed the first action in a different court that could have heard both claims.

★ b. **No special federal rule:** The Supreme Court has refused to create a uniform federal common law rule governing whether a state court judgment precludes a claim over which the federal courts have exclusive jurisdiction. Instead, whether the claim is precluded turns on the law of the state that heard the state court claim. Marrese v. American Academy of Orthopaedic Surgeons, 470 U.S. 373 (1985); Gargallo v. Merrill, Lynch, Pierce, Fenner & Smith, 918 F.2d 658 (6th Cir. 1990). As noted just above, most states do not bar litigation of the federal claim in a separate action.

Quiz Yourself on CLAIM PRECLUSION

145. Carol is the managing partner of a large law firm. The firm has two offices: a main office located in the city center and a small satellite office in the suburbs. Carol signs a contract with SpickandSpan, a janitorial service, under which SpickandSpan agrees to clean the firm's main office every night after normal business hours.

After a few months, Carol is so impressed with SpickandSpan's work that she signs another contract with SpickandSpan for the satellite office. The terms of this contract are virtually identical to the contract for the main office.

Three of the firm's largest clients have huge deals scheduled to close near the end of the year. Client *A* has scheduled its closing for December 30, at the main office. Client *B* has a closing scheduled for December 31, also at the main office. Client *C* is also scheduled to close on December 31, but at the satellite office.

SpickandSpan holds its annual New Year's Eve soiree on the afternoon of December 29. The liquor flows a bit too freely, and as a result, SpickandSpan's employees do not clean either of the offices on the 29th. Long-term hangovers cause the employees to do a very poor job of cleaning on the evening of the 30th. Clients *A*, *B*, and *C* are mortified at the condition of the firm's offices and immediately take their business elsewhere.

On January 22, Carol sues SpickandSpan to recover for the loss of client *A*. Carol wins a judgment of $10,000.

Buoyed by her success, Carol brings another action against SpickandSpan in which she seeks recovery for the loss of clients *B* and *C*. SpickandSpan brings a motion for summary judgment, alleging claim preclusion. How will the court rule? _____

146. Della, a law student, slips on the floor in the law school and falls, resulting in serious injury. Della learns that Jan Itor and Cass Todian, the law school's maintenance workers, had waxed the floors of the hallway a mere 30 minutes before Della's unfortunate accident. Della brings a negligence action against Jan. Although Della wins a judgment for $50,000, Jan has no assets to pay the judgment.

The next day, Della sues Cass. Della alleges in her complaint that because Jan and Cass were working together, they are jointly and severally liable for Della's injuries. In his answer, Cass argues Della's claim is barred by claim preclusion. Is Cass correct? _____

147. Radio Hut sells radios and other electronic devices at bargain-basement prices. For big purchases, Radio Hut has its own in-house financing system. Karl takes advantage of this financing system to buy a large stereo system from Radio Hut. Karl signs a note payable to Radio Hut and gives it a security interest in the stereo.

When Karl fails to make the October payment on the note, Radio Hut sues. The court enters judgment in favor of Karl, holding that Radio Hut failed to introduce evidence of a loan agreement. Several weeks later, Monolith, Inc., buys Radio Hut in a corporate takeover. Radio Hut is dissolved as a corporation, and all of its corporate assets are absorbed by Monolith, including all of the debts owed to Radio Hut under the in-house financing program.

When Monolith discovers that Karl missed the October payment, it sues Karl. Unlike Radio Hut, Monolith can prove that Karl owes the money. Karl moves for summary judgment based on claim preclusion. Monolith argues claim preclusion cannot apply to it because it had no chance to represent itself in the prior action. Does claim preclusion apply here? _____

Answers

145. The action dealing with client *B* is barred, but the action dealing with client *C* may proceed. With respect to client *B*, Carol is suing for breach of an installment contract. Each nightly cleaning is a separate installment. Although each installment is a separate obligation, when multiple breaches have occurred when the first action is filed, the rule of accumulated breaches requires the party to include all breaches that have already occurred. By omitting the December 30 breach when she sued in January, Carol has lost the right to recover on that claim.

The claim relating to client *C*, however, is not part of the same cause of action. Carol entered into two contracts on two different dates. Although the wording of each is very similar, they are still separate agreements. Therefore, Carol need not join breaches under the two contracts.

146. Della's claim is not barred. Even though Jan and Cass were acting in concert and accordingly may be jointly and severally liable for her injury, Della's claim against each of the maintenance workers is a separate and distinct claim.

147. Monolith's claim is barred by claim preclusion. It is suing for the exact same legal right as that involved in the prior case brought by Radio Hut. Monolith and Radio Hut are in privity with respect to this right because Monolith is a successor in interest to Radio Hut. Because the parties are in privity, Monolith is barred from bringing a second action to the same extent Radio Hut would be barred.

II. ISSUE PRECLUSION

Issue preclusion, or *collateral estoppel*, is a companion doctrine to claim preclusion. Even when claim preclusion does not bar a particular claim in the second action, issue preclusion may prevent the parties from relitigating certain issues relevant to that claim.

A. **Overview:** The analysis of issue preclusion differs significantly from the analysis of claim preclusion.

1. **Basic analysis:** Issue preclusion applies if:

    a. the *same issue* is involved in the two actions;

    b. that issue was *actually litigated*;

    c. that issue was *actually decided*; and

    d. the decision on the issue was *necessary to the outcome of the first action*.

2. **No merger:** Issue preclusion rarely applies if the issue was not actually litigated in the first case. Therefore, there is *no doctrine of merger* in issue preclusion. The *primary exception is jurisdiction*. A party who litigates a case to completion without challenging jurisdiction is ordinarily barred from claiming in a second action that the first court's judgment is invalid for lack of subject matter or personal jurisdiction.

B. **Same issue:** Issue preclusion applies only if the second action involves exactly the same issue as the first. Although this is often a relatively straightforward determination, certain situations are difficult.

1. **Differences in burden of persuasion:** Differences in the burden of persuasion on the issue in the two cases can lead a court to treat the same basic question as two separate issues for purposes of issue preclusion. A party who *fails* to meet a *higher burden* in the first case is *not precluded* from relitigating that same issue in a later case in which the *burden is lower*.

    Example 1: *D* destroys property belonging to State. Convinced that *D* acted intentionally, State prosecutes *D* for vandalism. In this state, any intentional destruction of property constitutes vandalism. The jury finds for *D*.

    State now brings a civil action against *D*, claiming conversion. Assume the action is not barred by claim preclusion. Like vandalism, a claim for conversion requires plaintiff to prove the intentional destruction of property. *D* argues issue preclusion, claiming the prior case found that *D* did not intentionally destroy the property. Issue preclusion does not apply. The issue in the criminal case was whether State proved intentional destruction *beyond a reasonable doubt*. In the civil case, however, State need only show by a *preponderance of the evidence* that *D* intentionally destroyed the property.

    Example 2: Same as the prior example, except reverse the order of the suits. State loses the civil suit for conversion. Now, State is precluded from prosecuting *D* for vandalism. If State could not prove intentional destruction under the lower standard, it logically should not be able to prove it under the more rigorous standard State must meet in a criminal prosecution.

2. **Series of related obligations or events:** It can be difficult to determine if two cases involve the same issue when a similar question of law arises in connection with separate but related obligations or events.

a. **When issue arises:** This problem often arises in an *installment contract*, when parties enter into a *series of contracts* using identical language, or when parties deal with each other repeatedly in the same way, giving rise to a tort or property claim.

b. **General rule:** In most cases, the issues are *not considered the same issue* for purposes of preclusion. Notwithstanding the facial similarity, each obligation or event is technically a separate legal situation, and each requires an independent legal determination.

Example: *L* leases an apartment to *T* for a term of two years pursuant to an oral lease. Rent is to be paid monthly. When *T* does not pay rent in January, *L* sues. *T* claims he need not pay rent because (a) the roof leaks, and (b) the oral lease is invalid under the statute of frauds. *L* prevails.

When *T* does not pay again in May, *L* brings a second action. (Claim preclusion does not apply because this is an installment contract.) *T* raises the same two defenses. Issue preclusion does not apply to the roof-leaking defense. Merely because the roof did not leak in January does not mean it does not leak now. However, issue preclusion does apply to the statute of frauds question. Although this is an installment contract, the issue of whether the lease is valid applies equally to all installments. See Cromwell v. County of Sac, 94 U.S. (4 Otto) 351 (1876).

C. **Actually litigated:** Unlike claim preclusion, issue preclusion applies only to issues that were actually presented to the court in the first action.

1. Because of this requirement, *default judgments* and *dismissals* do not have any issue preclusion effect (other than on the narrow issue of whether the defendant defaulted).

2. Again, there is no concept of merger in issue preclusion.

D. **Actually decided:** Perhaps the most difficult question in issue preclusion is determining what the first court actually decided. Plaintiffs often rely on *alternative theories* of recovery, and defendants may impose defenses to a claim. If the court simply declares who wins without clearly stating *why* that party won, it may be difficult to ascertain precisely what the court found.

1. **Analysis:** To determine what a court actually decided, it is necessary to dissect the decision logically. If a particular fact *must have been decided in a particular way* for the court to reach the result, issue preclusion will apply to that question. Conversely, if the court could reach the result in two or more different ways, and it is not clear which path the court followed, issue preclusion will not apply.

★ **Example 1:** Illinois Central Gulf R.R. v. Parks, 181 Ind. App. 141, 390 N.E.2d 1078 (1979), sets out a relatively straightforward application of this rule. *P* and his wife were injured by a train at a grade crossing. In suit 1, both sued the railroad, the wife for her own injuries and *P* for loss of consortium. The wife won, but *P* lost.

P then sued the railroad for his own injuries (under state law, *P*'s consortium claim and personal injury claim involved different legal "rights" and accordingly were not barred by claim preclusion). The railroad argued issue preclusion should prevent *P* from recovering.

The court disagreed and let the case proceed. The court reasoned *P* could have lost in the first case either because he was contributorily negligent or because he suffered no damages for loss of consortium. Although the contributory negligence issue was the same in both suits, damages would differ for the different claims.

Example 2: Same as Example 1, except *P* wins the first suit. Now, *P* claims issue preclusion prevents *D* railroad from arguing it was not negligent. Issue preclusion does apply, and the court will find *D* negligent. For the court to find for *P*, it was logically necessary for it to find *D* was negligent.

2. **Types of decisions:** The "actually decided" issue frequently arises in the context of a *jury trial* because of the predominance of the *general verdict*. In a bench trial, by contrast, the judge is required to discuss in detail all claims and defenses in her judgment. Similarly, in a jury trial involving a special verdict, the jury specifies what it finds on each question in the case.

E. **Necessary to the judgment:** The final requirement for issue preclusion is that resolution of the issue in question was necessary to the judgment. Obviously, mere dictum is not necessary. But the "necessary to the judgment" requirement may also prevent issue preclusion from applying to many findings that were actual issues in dispute at the first trial.

Note: Courts and commentators often treat "actually decided" and "necessary to the judgment" as a single question. However, logically each presents its own unique issues, and it is useful to think of the two separately.

1. **When problem arises:** The issue of whether a factual determination was necessary to the judgment arises whenever a judgment *explicitly* sets out *alternative bases for the holding*. Examples include:

   a. when a plaintiff seeks recovery for the same injury on *alternative claims*, and the court finds for *plaintiff* on two or more of those claims;

   b. when a defendant defends using *alternative defenses*, and the court finds for *defendant* on two or more of those defenses; and

   c. when a defendant asserts a *defense* to plaintiff's claim, and the court finds for *defendant* both on the defense and because plaintiff failed to prove its claim.

2. **Different from "actually decided":** Because the "necessary to the judgment" issue arises when the court explicitly states its finding on the issue, the problem is conceptually distinguishable from the question of how an issue was actually decided in a case involving a general verdict.

3. **No clear rule:** Courts are *split fairly evenly* as to whether any of the alternative holdings is entitled to issue preclusion effect. About half follow the view of the Restatement (First) of Judgments, under which *all* the alternative rulings have issue preclusion effect. The rest follow the view of the Restatement (Second) of Judgments, under which *none* of the alternative rulings have issue preclusion effect.

   Example: *P* sues *D* for specific performance of a contract. *D* defends in the alternative, first denying there was a contract, and second arguing that because *P* waited so long to seek enforcement, the defense of laches should apply. The court conducts a bench trial and eventually holds for *D*, explicitly finding both that there was no contract and that *P*'s claim is barred by laches. A month later, *D* takes action that *P* considers to be a new breach of the contract. *P* sues *D* again. *D* argues the prior judgment established there was no contract. Under the view of the Restatement (First), the court would apply issue preclusion. Under the view of the Restatement (Second), issue preclusion would not apply.

4. **Caveat:** The issue discussed above is a problem only when *fewer than all the issues* are relevant in the second case. If all the issues are relevant, all are precluded.

F. Parties benefited and burdened: Historically, both claim and issue preclusion applied only between those who were parties to the first suit or those in privity with the parties. Today, however, most jurisdictions have relaxed that requirement in issue preclusion.

1. **Traditional rule:** Courts historically required *"full mutuality"* before collateral estoppel applied. In other words, the rule was the same as in claim preclusion: Preclusion applied only when the parties in the second action were the same as those in the first action, or in privity with those parties.

2. **"Indemnity circle" exception:** Many jurisdictions recognize an exception to the requirement of full mutuality, which is commonly called the *indemnity circle*. If plaintiff sues someone who is ***primarily liable*** for an injury and ***loses*** that suit, that same plaintiff is precluded from arguing in a later action that another party is ***secondarily liable*** for that tort if that other party has a right to ***indemnity*** from the primarily liable party.

   Example: *P* is injured in a collision with a City bus. *P* sues the bus driver and loses. *P* then sues City, alleging it is vicariously liable for the driver's negligence. Under state law, an employer who is held vicariously liable has a right to indemnity from the employee. Issue preclusion prevents *P* from arguing that City is liable for the driver's negligence. However, *P* can still claim City was affirmatively negligent in other ways.

3. **Relaxation of mutuality requirement:** Most jurisdictions have abandoned the full mutuality requirement and allow ***nonmutual use of issue preclusion***. However, the extent to which nonmutual use is available may turn on whether the use is ***offensive*** or ***defensive***.

   a. **Offensive and defensive use defined:** Whether a particular use is offensive or defensive depends on the procedural posture of the party in the ***second action***.

      i. *Offensive use* is use by a party who is ***trying to recover on a claim*** in the second action. (Note this may be a plaintiff on a claim, or a defendant on a counterclaim.)

      ii. *Defensive use* is use by a party who is ***defending against a claim*** in the second suit.

   b. **When nonmutual defensive use allowed:** Most courts have completely abandoned the mutuality requirement in cases of defensive use. A person who was not a party to the prior action may freely use issue preclusion against someone who was a party to that first suit and is now bringing a claim against the person invoking preclusion.

      Example: *X* sues *Z* for patent infringement. *Z* argues a prior judgment has issue preclusion effect in this case and prevents *X* from prevailing on his patent claim. In this earlier action, *X* sued *Y* for infringing the same patent. The court entered judgment for *Y*, explicitly finding *X*'s patent had expired. *Z*'s alleged infringement occurred after *Y*'s (and patents cannot be renewed). Most courts would allow *Z* to use issue preclusion on the issue of the validity of *X*'s patent, even though *Z* was not a party to the prior action. *Z*'s use is *defensive*.

   c. **When nonmutual offensive use allowed:** Offensive nonmutual use has proven more problematic, and accordingly is subject to more limitations.

      i. **Problems with offensive nonmutual use:** Parklane Hosiery Co. v. Shore, 439 U.S. 322 (1979), discusses the problems with offensive use. The two main concerns are the *free rider* and *inconsistent judgment* problems.

         (a) **Free rider:** Because potential plaintiffs can only benefit from an earlier suit, they have an incentive to "sit and wait." If another party sues first, the potential plaintiff can sit out the action and, if offensive use is allowed, take advantage of any victory. If the other plaintiff loses, the potential plaintiff can still bring his action and not suffer any ill effects from the earlier loss. After all, preclusion may never be used against a person who was not a party to the first action, or in privity with a party.

(b) **Efficiency concerns:** Second, nonmutual offensive use creates a risk of *inconsistent judgments*. If plaintiffs sue separately, and none of the plaintiffs are affected by the prior results, different courts could reach different conclusions concerning the same basic issue.

ii. **Different rules:** Because of these concerns, jurisdictions differ as to the extent to which they allow nonmutual offensive use. Many jurisdictions allow nonmutual offensive use with certain limits designed to account for these policy concerns. The *federal approach*, which is set out in *Parklane* and has been adopted by many states, allows nonmutual offensive use *unless such use is unfair because*:

(a) there are *prior inconsistent judgments* (although one or two judgments in defendant's favor do not prevent issue preclusion if those are outweighed by many judgments against defendant);

(b) it would have been *easy* for the party seeking to use offensive nonmutual preclusion *to join in the prior action*; or

(c) there are *other reasons, such as procedural disadvantages in the first action,* making it unfair to use preclusion.

d. **Use against person who was not a party:** It is important to remember that the relaxation of the mutuality requirement applies only when preclusion is used against someone who was a *party in both actions*. It is a *violation of due process* to use claim or issue preclusion *against someone who was not a party* in the first action.

Example: *P* sues *D*, a large factory that emits noxious fumes, for nuisance. *D* attempts to use issue preclusion, relying on a judgment in *D*'s favor in a case filed by a different plaintiff. This other judgment held *D*'s factory did not constitute a nuisance. Even though this is a defensive nonmutual use, *D* cannot use issue preclusion against *P*. Because *P* was not a party to the prior action, the Due Process Clause entitles him to his day in court.

Note on privity: A person in privity with a party to the prior case not only may take advantage of preclusion, but also may have *both claim and issue preclusion used against her* without limitation. If privity exists, the person's rights were actually litigated in the prior case.

Quiz Yourself on
ISSUE PRECLUSION

148. Landlord hires Attorney to sue several tenants in Landlord's shopping mall. Attorney first sues tenant *A*. Attorney serves process in the case by taping the summons and complaint to the door of *A*'s store. Because this form of service is ineffective under state law, tenant *A* moves for and obtains dismissal of the case based on insufficient service. After the dismissal, Attorney sues tenant *B*. He serves the same way. Tenant *B* likewise obtains dismissal of the case.

Because Attorney's mistakes cost Landlord a great deal of money, Landlord brings a malpractice action against Attorney, based on the error made in the suit against tenant *A*. Following a bench trial, the trial judge grants judgment for Attorney. The sole basis for the judgment is the trial judge's explicit finding that Attorney was not negligent for failing to realize that service in this fashion was improper.

Landlord now brings a second malpractice action against Attorney, based on the error made in the suit against tenant *B*. This second action is not barred by claim preclusion. However, Attorney moves for summary judgment based on issue preclusion. Does issue preclusion apply in this case? _____

149. Jake is rudely awakened one morning when the engine from a jet airplane falls off the plane and crashes through his ceiling. The engine extensively damages the house and causes Jake serious bodily injury. Jake sues the airline for the injuries to his person. The airline's answer denies responsibility. After a short trial, the jury renders a general verdict for the airline, and judgment is entered accordingly.

Jake brings another suit against the airline, seeking damages for the harm to the house. Under the minority rule applied in this state, Jake is not barred by claim preclusion from seeking recovery for the property damage in a separate action. The airline nevertheless argues that issue preclusion prevents Jake from asserting the airline was negligent. Will the airline prevail on its issue preclusion argument? _____

150. Moe, Larry, and Curly are partners in a home repair service. While on a repair job at Shemp's house, all three are injured when Shemp's pet Pomeranian attacks them. Larry and Curly bring separate actions against Shemp for their injuries. Larry and Curly each allege Shemp was negligent in failing to restrain the dog. Larry's case reaches trial first, and Shemp prevails. The court enters judgment for Shemp. A few days later, the court in Curly's case enters a $3,000 judgment for Curly.

Moe now sues Shemp. Moe also claims Shemp was negligent for failing to restrain the dog. Moe further argues that issue preclusion prevents Shemp from arguing he was not negligent in failing to restrain the dog. Will issue preclusion apply? _____

151. McDougal's, Inc., operates a nationwide chain of fast-food restaurants. McDougal's has entered into franchise agreements across the nation. Each franchisee signs a detailed contract. One of the terms requires the franchisee to purchase "all ingredients used in preparing the food products" directly from McDougal's.

Fran operates a McDougal's franchise in New Mexico. To enhance her customers' dining experience, Fran includes a small tray of condiments on every table. Fran does not purchase these condiments from McDougal's. McDougal's sues Fran for breach of the franchise agreement. Fran answers, claiming condiments are not used in "preparing" food. The parties eventually reach a settlement under which Fran agrees to pay $2,000 to McDougal's. The parties agree on a consent judgment, which the court then enters.

One year later, McDougal's triples the price of its condiments. Fran therefore reverts to purchasing condiments from a third party. McDougal's again sues her for breach of the franchise agreement. Fran again argues that condiments are not used in "preparing" food. McDougal's argues issue preclusion prevents Fran from bringing up that issue in this suit. Is McDougal's correct? _____

Answers

148. Issue preclusion does not apply. In order for issue preclusion to apply, the two cases must involve the *same issue*. The basic legal question in both cases is the same, namely, whether Attorney's mistaken belief that he could serve by taping notice to the store door was negligent. However, although the legal question is the same, the issue of negligence requires the application of law to fact. Although it might not have been negligent to think that service by taping to the door was proper in the first case, the circumstances are different in the second case. Most important, the ruling in Landlord v. tenant *A* should have put Attorney on notice that this form of service was ineffective. Attorney served tenant *B* after this ruling, and should have learned from his mistake. Therefore, the cases do not involve the same issue, and issue preclusion does not apply.

149. Issue preclusion does not apply. Because the case was decided by a general verdict, we do not know why the jury held for the airline. It could have found that Jake failed to prove the airline was negligent. In the alternative, the jury could have found Jake suffered no personal injuries in the action. In the latter case, there would be nothing inconsistent about letting Jake prevail in the second case, where he seeks damages for harm to his property. Because we cannot be sure what was actually decided in the first case, issue preclusion does not apply.

150. Issue preclusion probably does not apply. Moe is trying to use offensive nonmutual collateral estoppel. Most courts apply a test like that in *Parklane Hosiery* for offensive nonmutual use. Under this test, the court allows offensive nonmutual use unless the current party could easily have joined in the prior action or unless allowing issue preclusion is unfair because of prior inconsistent judgments.

Here, Moe quite easily could have joined in the prior action. More important, it is unfair to Shemp to apply issue preclusion. Shemp has won one suit and lost another. It is unfair to let Moe take advantage of Curly v. Shemp while at the same time not be hindered by Shemp's victory in Larry v. Shemp.

151. McDougal's is not correct. Issue preclusion does not apply here because the issue was not fully litigated in the earlier case and the court did not actually decide the crucial issue. Consent judgments do have claim preclusion effect but not issue preclusion effect.

III. LIMITS ON PRECLUSION

The policies underlying claim and issue preclusion sometimes conflict with other concerns in the civil litigation process. As a result, courts have developed several exceptions to the preclusion doctrines.

A. Exceptions to claim preclusion: There are relatively few exceptions to claim preclusion. The most commonly recognized are the following four.

  1. A suit in another state to collect on a judgment: When a party obtains a judgment in one state, he may take that judgment to other states to seize assets owned by the judgment debtor in those states. Historically, it was necessary to bring a suit in each of the other states to enforce the judgment. Claim preclusion *does not bar* the judgment victor from suing on the judgment in one or more other states in order to collect the judgment.

  2. First court lacked subject matter jurisdiction over an omitted claim: This situation is discussed in Part I.D.3 of this chapter.

3. **By agreement:** Claim preclusion does not apply where the *parties agree* to allow claim-splitting or the court in the first action *expressly indicates* the party is free to bring one or more claims in a later action.

4. **Fairness requires:** In exceedingly rare situations, because of *overwhelming concerns for fairness*, certain claims may be brought in a later action.

B. **Exceptions to issue preclusion:** Restatement (Second) of Judgments §28 lists the more numerous exceptions to issue preclusion.

   Note: Although the Restatement lists these situations as "exceptions," many of them could also be dealt with under the "same issue" requirement.

   1. **No review available:** Issue preclusion does not apply if *no review of the judgment was available*. However, issue preclusion does apply if review is available but, for whatever reason, is not sought by the judgment loser.

   2. **Intervening change in law:** Issue preclusion does not apply if the issue involves the application of law to fact and there has been an *intervening change in the law or interpretation of the law*.

   3. **Procedural advantages:** Issue preclusion may not apply if there are *procedural advantages* available in the second suit that were not available in the first action. For example, if the first action did not allow for *discovery* or *cross-examination*, issue preclusion may not apply. Similarly, cases in *small claims* or similar tribunals usually are not entitled to issue preclusion because of the significant procedural limitations.

   4. **Burden of persuasion greater:** Issue preclusion does not apply if the *burden of persuasion* on the party who is to be burdened by issue preclusion was more rigorous in the first action than in the second. This issue is discussed at length in Part II.B.1 above.

★ 5. **Against public interest:** Issue preclusion does not apply if it offends the *public interest*. This rationale supports the general rule that *offensive* nonmutual issue preclusion is *not available against the federal government*. United States v. Mendoza, 464 U.S. 154 (1984).

   6. **No incentive:** Issue preclusion does not apply if the party to be bound did not have an *incentive to litigate* the first case fully and fairly, either because of the actions of others or because she could not appreciate the ramifications of the first action on later litigation.

IV. FULL FAITH AND CREDIT

To this point, the discussion has assumed the courts hearing the first and second actions are in the same jurisdiction. However, the U.S. Constitution and federal law also require courts to apply claim and issue preclusion to decisions rendered by other U.S. jurisdictions. This requirement is called *full faith and credit*. Although a full discussion of full faith and credit is beyond the scope of a first-year Procedure course, it is important to understand the basics.

A. **Governing law:** Both Article IV of the U.S. Constitution and federal statutes impose a full faith and credit requirement. The most important statute is *28 U.S.C. §1738*. There are also specialized statutes governing the full faith and credit effect of child custody determinations, *28 U.S.C. §1738A*, and child support orders, *28 U.S.C. §1738B*.

1. **State-federal issues:** The full faith and credit obligation applies between state and federal courts. State courts must give full faith and credit to federal judgments and vice versa.

2. **Foreign judgments:** Neither the Constitution nor the statutes apply to judgments of courts in foreign nations. Nevertheless, under the doctrine of *comity*, U.S. courts *may* give claim and issue preclusion effect to judgments of foreign tribunals, provided the foreign courts afford a fair process.

B. **What full faith and credit requires:** In essence, full faith and credit *extends claim and issue preclusion across state lines*. A court must afford preclusive effect to the decisions of other courts.

Example: *P* sues *D* in a state court in State *A*. The court enters judgment for *D*. *P* sues *D* again in a federal court in State *B*, raising a slightly different claim arising from the same facts. The federal court will grant *D*'s motion to dismiss based on claim preclusion.

1. **Governing law:** The rules governing claim and issue preclusion vary among different jurisdictions. When applying full faith and credit, the court in the second action must look to *the law of the jurisdiction that decided the first action* to determine whether the claim or issue is precluded.

Example: While riding her bicycle one lovely day, *P* gets into an accident with a City bus. *P* sues City for negligence in a state court in State *A*, seeking damages only for her personal injuries. City prevails. *P* now sues City in State *B*, seeking damages for the harm to her bicycle. City argues claim preclusion bars the second claim. The law of State *B* allows a party to sue separately for personal injuries and property damages stemming from the same accident. However, the court in *B* must look to the law of State *A*. If *P*'s claim would be barred under the law of *A* (which it likely would be), *B* is required by full faith and credit to apply claim preclusion. To refuse preclusive effect is to give "less than full" faith and credit.

2. **Giving *more* preclusive effect:** In some situations, a judge may want to give preclusive effect to a judgment even though the court that issued the judgment would not.

   a. **State courts:** A state court is *free to apply preclusion* even though the first court would not.

   Example: Same as prior example, except the laws of *A* and *B* are reversed—that is, *A* would not bar *P*'s claim, but *B* would. *B* is nevertheless free to apply the law of *B* and prevent *P* from suing a second time. Note, however, that although *B* *may* apply its own law in this situation, most states will not, out of a concern for fairness to *P*.

   b. **Federal courts:** A federal court *may not* give more preclusive effect to a state court judgment than the rendering state court would give. Migra v. Warren City School District Board of Education, 465 U.S. 75 (1984).

C. **Scope of full faith and credit:** The requirement of full faith and credit is *very strict*. A judgment is entitled to full faith and credit even though the court clearly made an error. A court must enforce the judgment of another state or federal court even though the underlying claim is illegal or violates the public policy of the enforcing jurisdiction. Fauntleroy v. Lum, 210 U.S. 230 (1908). However, there are exceptions.

1. **Orders affecting title to real property:** A court in one state cannot decree property rights in real property situated in another state. Fall v. Eastin, 215 U.S. 1 (1909). Therefore, such a decree is not entitled to full faith and credit.

2. **Lack of jurisdiction:** A judgment rendered without jurisdiction is void and not entitled to full faith and credit. In theory, then, a party may ***collaterally attack*** a judgment in the courts of another state by showing lack of jurisdiction. The limits on collateral attack are discussed in Chapters 2 and 4.

★   **Example:** The Supreme Court's decision in Durfee v. Duke, 375 U.S. 106 (1963), provides a classic example of the limits on collateral attack. The case involved ownership of land. The court's jurisdiction turned on whether the land was in Nebraska or Missouri, which was not clear. The parties had litigated the question of jurisdiction before the Nebraska courts in the first action, and the Nebraska court found the land was in that state. Duke, the loser in Nebraska, then tried to bring a second action in Missouri. The Court held Duke was precluded from arguing the land was in Missouri because he had appeared in the first case. However, the court's decision also makes it clear that other parties who had not appeared would be free to bring an action in Missouri and assert their rights to the same property. To prevail, however, those parties would need to prove the land was actually in Missouri.

3. **Divorce:** In order for a state to grant a divorce, one of the spouses to the marriage must be domiciled in that state. If a state grants a divorce when neither spouse lives there, the decree is not entitled to full faith and credit.

V. OTHER ISSUES IN PRECLUSION

Other procedural rules affect how claim and issue preclusion apply.

A. **Reopening judgments:** Most procedural systems place strict time limits on motions to amend the judgment or to file an appeal. The Federal Rules of Civil Procedure, for example, allow a party only 28 days to move to overturn or amend a judgment, and that time period cannot be extended. A party also has only 30 days to appeal in the federal system. However, the Federal Rules of Civil Procedure and some state rules provide a safety valve that allows judgments to be reopened. In the federal courts, the governing rule is ***Fed. R. Civ. P. 60(b)***, which allows a party to obtain ***relief from a judgment***—typically a new trial—in certain situations.

1. **Grounds for reopening judgment:** Fed. R. Civ. P. 60(b) allows a federal court to reopen a judgment in the following situations:

   a. When the judgment was the result of ***mistake, inadvertence, surprise, or excusable neglect***. Fed. R. Civ. P. 60(b)(1). Aside from default judgments where defendant did not receive service, courts require a very strong showing before providing relief under this provision. Ordinary oversights and mistakes do not suffice.

   b. When the party seeking relief discovered ***new evidence*** that a diligent search would not have uncovered in time to move for a new trial under Rule 59. Fed. R. Civ. P. 60(b)(2).

   c. When the judgment resulted from ***fraud, misrepresentation, or other misconduct*** of an adverse party. Fed. R. Civ. P. 60(b)(3). Here, the party must also show that the fraud or other misconduct was ***prejudicial*** to the party's chances to win the case.

   d. If the judgment is ***void***. Fed. R. Civ. P. 60(b)(4).

   e. If the judgment has been ***satisfied, released, or discharged***. Fed. R. Civ. P. 60(b)(5).

    f. If the judgment is ***based on an earlier judgment*** that was reversed or otherwise vacated. Fed. R. Civ. P. 60(b)(5). This language deals with the situation where a court applied claim or issue preclusion but the judgment given preclusive effect was reversed.

    g. If it is ***no longer equitable*** to apply the judgment prospectively. Fed. R. Civ. P. 60(b)(5).

    h. ***For any other reason justifying relief.*** Fed. R. Civ. P. 60(b)(6). Most courts interpret Rule 60(b)(6) so it does not overlap with (1) to (5). Therefore, if the situation fits within Rule 60(b)(1) to (5), the party cannot use Rule 60(b)(6) to bring the claim. This can be especially important because of the one-year bar on claims under (1) to (3), discussed below.

  2. Relief very rare: Other than default judgments, courts rarely grant relief under Fed. R. Civ. P. 60(b).

  3. Time limits: All motions under Rule 60(b) must be brought within a ***reasonable time***. Fed. R. Civ. P. 60(c). In addition, motions seeking relief under Fed. R. Civ. P. 60(b)(1), (2), or (3) must be made no later than ***one year*** after the judgment. This time ***cannot be extended***. Fed. R. Civ. P. 6(b)(2).

★   **4. Independent action for relief:** Rule 60 does not supersede the historic independent action for relief from a judgment, which is a ***new action*** brought to set aside a prior judgment. However, in United States v. Beggerly, 524 U.S. 38 (1998), the Supreme Court held that if the grounds for relief asserted in an independent action parallel the grounds listed in Rule 60(b)(1) to (3), the independent action is subject to the same one-year time limit.

B. Law of the case: Claim and issue preclusion apply between two or more separate judicial proceedings. The doctrine of "law of the case," by contrast, applies at ***different stages of the same action***.

  1. Basic rule: The basic rule of law of the case is that a court's interpretation of the law at one stage of the proceeding will bind that court, and all lower courts, at further stages in the proceeding.

    Example: *P* sues *D*. The trial court dismisses the action, finding *P* has no legal claim. *P* appeals, and the court of appeals reverses, finding *P* does have a viable claim. The court of appeals remands the case for trial. Obviously, the trial court must apply the court of appeals' ruling. At trial, *P* prevails, and *D* appeals. *D* attempts to argue that *P* has no legal claim. The court of appeals will apply the law of the case and rely on its prior determination.

  2. Limits: The law of the case applies only to ***rulings of law***, not findings of fact. Moreover, the earlier ruling ***only binds courts in the actual case***. A court may ignore its ruling (although not the ruling of a higher court) in a different proceeding, even if the legal issue is identical.

C. Judicial estoppel: Judicial estoppel is a somewhat amorphous doctrine that, like claim and issue preclusion, applies when a party is involved in two cases that overlap to some extent. Basically, the doctrine prevents a party who has taken a ***position*** in the first case from taking an inconsistent position in the second. Courts typically apply judicial estoppel when the party being estopped *prevailed* on the position it took in the first action. In issue preclusion, by contrast, the party usually either *lost* on the issue, or won less than what she now seeks.

Quiz Yourself on
RESPECT FOR JUDGMENTS

152. On Monday, Lucky Louie, a law student, is walking from the parking lot to the school when he is hit by a City bus. The mishap breaks Louie's arm. On Wednesday, while Lucky Louie is walking across the same street at the same time of day, he is again hit by a City bus. This accident leaves him physically intact but breaks the priceless heirloom watch he keeps in his pocket. The same driver was operating the bus on both dates.

Lucky Louie first sues the driver and the City for the Monday accident. Lucky Louie alleges that the driver ran a stop sign and that the City was negligent in training bus drivers. The court grants summary judgment *for* Lucky Louie against the driver but grants summary judgment *against* Louie on his claim against the City.

Lucky Louie now brings a second action against the same defendants, based on the Wednesday incident. Lucky Louie again alleges the driver was speeding and the City was negligent in training bus drivers.

Both defendants move for summary judgment, this time based on claim and issue preclusion. Will Lucky Louie's case be affected by claim and/or issue preclusion? _____

153. Pomum, Inc., and Fenster, Inc., both produce and sell tiny nanocomputers. Because their products are so small, the companies rely on a special computer chip produced by Chip's Chips, Ltd. Fenster enters into a contract with Chip under which Chip agrees to sell his entire output to Fenster. When Pomum learns of this, it sues Fenster in state court, alleging unfair competition. Fenster wins.

After judgment is entered, Pomum sues Fenster again in federal district court, alleging Fenster's exclusive contract also violates federal antitrust laws. Fenster files a motion for summary judgment based on claim preclusion. Pomum responds by correctly pointing out that federal courts have exclusive subject matter jurisdiction over antitrust claims, so Pomum could not have filed its antitrust claim in the first case. How is the court likely to rule on Fenster's motion? _____

154. Ann Ternett runs an Internet survey firm. She has a contract with USA Online, a major Internet service provider, for Internet access. Under this contract, Ann pays USA a monthly fee of $3,000, which provides all her employees unlimited access. USA sues Ann in March 2003 for $6,000, claiming she did not pay the fee for January and February of that year. Ann's answer denies liability. First, she argues she did pay the fee. Second, and in the alternative, she asserts she was not obligated to pay the monthly fee because USA made false representations to her when the parties negotiated the contract. The case is tried to a jury in September 2003. The jury returns a special verdict in which it explicitly finds (i) Ann had paid the $6,000 fee, and (ii) Ann was not obligated to pay anyway because of the false representations. Judgment is entered for Ann in conformance with this verdict.

After the case is complete, USA files another action against Ann in which it claims Ann did not pay the fee for May, June, and July 2003. Ann moves for summary judgment based on both claim and issue preclusion. How should the court rule? _____

155. One extremely hot day, a number of passengers board a Daisy Airways flight. Because of a technical glitch, the pilot keeps the passengers on the plane while the mechanics try to deal with the problem. The passengers remain in the plane for over five hours in stifling 100° F temperatures.

Pamela, a passenger, sues Deena, the pilot, in state court for damages. Pamela claims she suffered heatstroke on the flight. After a short bench trial, judgment is entered for Deena. The trial judge's ruling explicitly finds Pamela failed to prove Deena acted negligently in trying to deal with the problem on the tarmac.

Pamela now sues Deena a second time, this time in federal court. When Deena raises claim preclusion, Pamela responds by arguing the state court judgment was invalid for two reasons. First, a federal statute gives federal courts exclusive jurisdiction over claims arising out of injuries caused on airplanes. Second, a different federal statute makes a pilot strictly liable for all injuries suffered by passengers if he or she keeps the passengers on the tarmac for more than one hour in temperatures higher than 85° F. Although Pamela relied on that federal statute in her first case, the state court simply disregarded it, stating it was a "stupid law."

Deena acknowledges both of the federal statutes apply to Pamela's claim. She nevertheless argues Pamela's claim is still barred by claim preclusion. What result? _____

156. Husband and Wife are traveling in an automobile. Husband is driving. Distracted for a moment by something on the side of the road, Husband drives the car into a ditch, seriously injuring Wife. Wife sues Husband for her injuries. The trial court grants Husband's motion for summary judgment, holding that common law spousal immunity prevents Wife from suing Husband in tort. Wife appeals. The court of appeals reverses, holding that a new statute abrogates the common law immunity. The appellate court remands the case for a trial.

The trial results in a judgment for Wife. Husband appeals. Husband has done additional research and has discovered language in the statute that makes it clear it was *not* intended to override common law spousal immunity. Wife argues Husband is precluded from making that argument. How is the court of appeals likely to rule? _____

————————————————

Answers

152. This problem presents questions of both claim and issue preclusion. As a preliminary matter, that the first case was decided by summary judgment does not affect claim preclusion. Nor does it affect issue preclusion in this case, for Lucky Louie had a full chance to present his evidence.

Claim preclusion could be an issue for Lucky Louie's claim against the driver. If the two accidents arose from the same primary event, the claims would comprise a single cause of action under the majority approach. However, the two injuries did not result from the same event. Notwithstanding their similarity, the two accidents are two distinct events, caused by different acts of negligence. If the court applied the minority "same primary right" test, it would reach the same result. Louie would clearly have two separate injuries, which he could sue for separately.

With respect to the City, claim preclusion may apply. Unlike the driver, the same negligence of the City—the policy of defective training—was the cause of both injuries. Nevertheless, because Louie still suffered two distinct injuries, many courts would find claim preclusion does not apply.

However, although claim preclusion may not apply to the claim against the City, the City can use issue preclusion. We know Louie lost the first suit against the City. Ordinarily, we could not be sure whether he lost because he failed to prove negligence or because he failed to prove harm. In this case, however, we know Louie proved harm because he recovered against the driver. Therefore, the summary judgment for the City in the first case must have been based on a finding that Louie failed to prove a negligent training policy. Because that issue is the same issue as involved in this case, issue preclusion applies.

153. Fenster's motion is likely to fail, although there are not enough facts for a definite answer. First, there is an issue of full faith and credit. A federal court is required by 28 U.S.C. §1738 to afford full faith and credit to the judgments of a state court.

However, the federal court will bar the claim only if the claim would be barred under the law of the state that rendered the judgment. If the state will bar a claim that could not have been brought in the first court because of lack of jurisdiction, the federal antitrust claim here is barred. Although we do not know state law, most states will *not* bar a claim over which the court in the first action lacked jurisdiction.

154. Although Ann is not likely to prevail on claim preclusion, she may prevail on issue preclusion depending on the law in effect in this jurisdiction.

The contract is an installment contract. Therefore, as a general matter, USA is free to sue for each month's payment separately. Although the rule of accumulated breaches requires USA to join the claims for all installments already overdue, the majority rule is that the party need not include breaches that occur after suit is filed. Because USA filed its first suit in March, it did not need to include the May, June, and July breaches and is free to sue for them in this separate action.

However, issue preclusion may apply. Although each installment is a separate claim, they share issues. The problem is that the first case was decided on alternative bases. The first basis (nonpayment) is not the same issue as present in this case. That Ann paid for January and February does not mean she paid during May, June, and July. The second basis (misrepresentation) *may* be the same in the two cases. To the extent that USA has evidence that it now provides what it claimed it would provide, then the issue is different and issue preclusion does not apply. If the service has not changed, however, the issue is the same and issue preclusion may apply.

Assuming the issue is the same, whether issue preclusion applies depends on whether the state follows the view of the Restatement (First) of Judgments, under which the finding would have preclusive effect, or the Restatement (Second), under which the alternative ruling would have no effect. Courts are roughly evenly split, and there is no way to tell which rule this jurisdiction follows.

155. Pamela's claim is almost certainly barred by claim preclusion. 28 U.S.C. §1738 requires federal courts to give full faith and credit to state court judgments. The federal court must bar the claim to the same extent the courts of that state bar the claim.

As a general matter, a judgment rendered by a court without jurisdiction is void and accordingly not entitled to full faith and credit. However, to challenge a prior judgment on this basis, the party raising the challenge cannot have appeared in the prior case. Pamela not only appeared, but she selected the state court.

In addition, a court cannot refuse full faith and credit to a judgment merely because the first court erred or even because the second court strongly disagrees with the policy underlying the law used in the first case. Therefore, the federal court cannot refuse full faith and credit based on the fact the state court blatantly disregarded the federal liability statute.

156. Wife is likely to prevail. Neither claim nor issue preclusion applies because this is not a collateral attack on a final judgment. However, the doctrine of law of the case provides that once a court decides a legal issue, all courts at the same or lower level will not overturn that ruling in later proceedings in the case, even if the ruling is erroneous.

Exam Tips on RESPECT FOR JUDGMENTS

☞ You should consider claim and issue preclusion whenever you are presented with an exam question setting forth two separate actions.

☛ Do not forget that claim and issue preclusion are related concepts. Therefore, unless a problem makes it clear that you are to consider only one, analyze both.

☞ Consider *claim preclusion first*. If it applies, it has a much broader sweep, barring complete claims.

☞ If claim preclusion does not apply, consider whether individual issues involved in both actions might nevertheless be barred by issue preclusion.

☛ **Claim preclusion:** Do not forget that states apply different tests to determine if two claims are sufficiently related to qualify for claim preclusion.

☞ When dealing with counterclaims, recall that in most cases, Fed. R. Civ. P. 13, not the more complicated common law compulsory counterclaim rule, applies. As long as an answer was filed in the first case, Rule 13 trumps (unless, of course, Rule 13 does not apply for some reason).

☞ A plaintiff is generally free to sue two or more defendants in separate cases, even if defendants would be jointly and severally liable.

☞ Make sure you have a solid grasp of the sorts of rulings that qualify as a judgment on the merits for purposes of claim preclusion.

☛ *Privity* is a conceptually difficult doctrine. As a rule of thumb, however, privity does *not* exist between joint tortfeasors or between co-owners of property.

☛ When dealing with *issue preclusion*, first identify all the issues that should logically arise in each of the two cases. Second, identify which issues are common to *both* cases. In addition, make sure you know whether the first case was a bench trial or jury trial and, if a jury trial, the form of the verdict.

☞ In the case of a *general verdict*, analyze the first case very carefully in order to determine what must have been decided. If there are alternative theories under which the jury could have reached the same result and only one of those theories is relevant in the second case, issue preclusion does not apply.

☞ In a *bench trial* or *special verdict*, by contrast, you may well have to deal with the problem of specifically stated alternative holdings.

☞ In either of these situations, be on the lookout for a situation where *all* of the issues from the first case reappear in the second. In this case, it does not matter which theory the factfinder used in the first case.

☛ Lack of *mutuality* is permissible only in issue preclusion, not claim preclusion. In claim preclusion, the two cases must involve the same parties or people in privity.

☛ You should discuss *full faith and credit* in your answer whenever the two courts are in different jurisdictions. Although it may be obvious that the second court has to enforce the first judgment, you should at least mention the full faith and credit obligation in your answer.

☞ When dealing with full faith and credit, always recall that the preclusion law of the first court sets the floor.

☞ No matter how much the facts cry out for a different result, recall that a state cannot refuse to enforce another state's judgment because it disagrees with the underlying claim.

☛ Be very hesitant before concluding that a party may reopen any judgment (other than a default judgment) under Fed. R. Civ. P. 60(b).

CHAPTER 14

JOINDER OF CLAIMS AND PARTIES

ChapterScope

This chapter takes Procedure beyond the single plaintiff-defendant-claim case to cases involving multiple claims and/or parties. The chapter focuses almost exclusively on joinder under the Federal Rules of Civil Procedure. Discussion of class actions is deferred to the next chapter.

- Parties have tremendous freedom to add claims. Joining additional parties to the suit is, however, more limited.

- Plaintiff is not the only party who may join claims and parties to the case.

  - Defendants may file *counterclaims* against plaintiffs and *cross-claims* against each other.

  - Defendants (and in some cases plaintiffs) may *implead third parties* to the action for purposes of indemnity or contribution.

  - In some cases, third parties may *intervene* in cases to protect their interests.

- Many Federal Rules of Civil Procedure dealing with joinder use the *same transaction or occurrence* test.

- When a claim involving multiple claims and parties is litigated in *federal court*, it is crucial to consider whether the federal court has jurisdiction over the joined claims and/or parties.

  - Joinder and jurisdiction are separate issues. Although the analyses of the two often will dovetail, it is important to deal with each separately.

- Joinder of claims and parties is usually at the discretion of the parties. However, in certain cases joinder of parties is required by Fed. R. Civ. P. 19.

I. JOINDER OF CLAIMS AGAINST CURRENT PARTIES

Fed. R. Civ. P. 13 and *18* allow plaintiffs and defendants who are already in a lawsuit to file additional claims against the other. In most cases, these claims are optional; however, *certain counterclaims are compulsory*.

- **A. Adding additional claims:** *Fed. R. Civ. P. 18(a)* provides "A party asserting a claim, counterclaim, cross-claim, or third-party claim may join . . . as many claims . . . as it has against an opposing party." Note the rule applies to any "party," not merely plaintiffs.

  - **1. Not applicable to first claim:** Fed. R. Civ. P. 18 applies only when the party *already has asserted one claim* against the other party *under some other rule*. In essence, then, Rule 18 applies only to the second and subsequent claims.

  - **2. No relationship required:** Rule 18 *does not use the same transaction test*. A party may join additional claims regardless of whether the claims have anything to do with each other. By contrast, some of the other joinder rules, which dictate when a party may bring the *first* claim against the other party, do use the same transaction test.

3. **Jurisdictional limits:** In federal court, a party's ability to join unrelated claims is significantly restricted by the requirement that a federal court have *subject matter jurisdiction over all claims*. See Part V.B.

4. **Alternate claims allowable:** Rule 18 allows a party to join claims even if those claims are logically inconsistent.

B. **Counterclaims:** *Fed. R. Civ. P. 13* allows a defendant to bring any claims she may have against the opposing party. In some cases, however, a defendant *must* bring a counterclaim, or it will be lost.

1. **Permissive counterclaims:** *Fed. R. Civ. P. 13(b)* allows a defendant to bring any claim he has against plaintiff, regardless of whether it is related in any way to plaintiff's claim.

2. **Compulsory counterclaims:** If defendant has a claim that *arises from the same transaction or occurrence* as plaintiff's claim, defendant *must raise* the claim in his answer, unless one of the exceptions applies.

   a. **Same transaction or occurrence:** Rule 13(a) is one of several rules that turn on whether the claims arise from the same transaction or occurrence.

      i. **Rationale:** In interpreting this phrase, it is important to keep in mind the policy underlying joinder under the Federal Rules of Civil Procedure. The liberal rules of joinder serve two basic ends: *efficiency* and *consistency.* If two claims overlap to a significant extent, it is inefficient to have two courts decide the same issues in two separate cases. Similarly, different courts adjudicating the same key facts may reach *inconsistent results.*

      ii. **Tests:** Several tests are used to measure whether a claim and counterclaim meet the "same transaction or occurrence" standard.

         (a) **Logical relationship test:** This analysis asks whether the two claims are *logically related* in any significant way. The relationship need not be logical in the strict sense. In other words, the outcome of one claim need not turn on the outcome of the other. Instead, they must derive from the same underlying set of facts, even if the subset of facts relevant to each claim differs. In many cases, the analysis turns on whether it is *efficient* to try the claims together.

         (b) **Same evidence test:** This test asks if there is a significant overlap between the *disputed elements* of the two claims. The test is *narrower* than the logical relationship test. It is not enough that the claims arise from the same identifiable event; rather, the **core facts** giving rise to the claims must overlap to some degree.

            Note: Most courts apply both of these analyses. If either is met, the claims arise from the same transaction or occurrence.

         (c) **Other tests:** A few courts use other tests. For example, some ask whether the *issues of law and fact* raised by the two claims are largely the same. It is not entirely clear how this test differs from the same evidence test. Others ask whether claim preclusion (discussed in Chapter 13) would bar the claim if it was not brought with the other.

b. **Excepted claims:** Even if a counterclaim arises from the same transaction or occurrence, a defendant need not assert it if:

   i. defendant ***does not file an answer*** (Fed. R. Civ. P. 13(a) requires the counterclaim to be set forth in the answer);

   ii. the claim ***has not yet arisen*** when defendant files his answer;

   iii. adjudication of the claim requires the presence of ***third parties*** over whom the court cannot obtain personal jurisdiction;

   iv. at the time the answer is served the counterclaim is ***already being litigated*** in another state or federal action; or

   v. plaintiff's suit is based on ***in rem*** or ***quasi-in-rem*** jurisdiction.

c. **Failing to plead compulsory counterclaim:** Although the Federal Rules of Civil Procedure do not clearly specify this result, a defendant who fails to plead a compulsory counterclaim cannot assert it in later litigation. (Note, however, the liberal amendment provisions of Fed. R. Civ. P. 15 may allow defendant to amend the answer to add the omitted counterclaim.)

3. **Counterclaims by plaintiffs and others:** Fed. R. Civ. P. 13(a) and (b) permit counterclaims to be brought not only by defendants but also by any party against an "opposing party."

a. **By plaintiff:** Thus, if defendant files a counterclaim against plaintiff, plaintiff may include in her answer counterclaims against defendant. If plaintiff's additional claim arises from the *same transaction or occurrence* as defendant's counterclaim and does not fall into one of the Rule 13(a) exceptions, it is a compulsory counterclaim.

b. **By other parties:** Counterclaims may—and in some cases *must*—also be filed by third parties who have been added to the suit under Fed. R. Civ. P. 14 (impleader) or 13(h). These rules are discussed in Parts II.B and C below.

C. **Cross-claims:** Cross-claims are filed by one *co-party* against another—for example, by one defendant against another defendant. ***Fed. R. Civ. P. 13(g)*** governs cross-claims.

1. **Same transaction test:** A party may file any claim against a co-party arising from the same transaction or occurrence as ***either*** the ***original complaint*** or a ***counterclaim***, or relating to property that is the subject matter of the action. The "same transaction or occurrence" analysis is discussed in Part I.B. of this chapter.

   Example: *P1* and *P2* sue *D* in federal court. *D* files a counterclaim against both *P*s that does not arise from the same transaction or occurrence as the *P*s' original claim. *P1* wants to file a cross-claim against *P2*, seeking indemnity from *P2* should *D* prevail on the counterclaim. Because the cross-claim arises from the same transaction as the ***counterclaim***, *P1* may file the cross-claim in this action.

2. **Always voluntary:** Fed. R. Civ. P. 13(g) specifies a party "may" file a cross-claim. Cross-claims are always optional, never required.

3. **Cross-claims vs. counterclaims:** On the other hand, once a party is served with a cross-claim, many courts find that she and the claiming party become "opposing parties," and accordingly hold that Rule 13(a) requires her to file any factually related counterclaims she has against the claimant.

Example: In the prior example, suppose *P1* does file the cross-claim against *P2*. *P2* has a claim against *P1* that arises from the same occurrence as the cross-claim filed by *P1*. Under the majority interpretation, Rule 13(a) requires *P2* to file her claim against *P1* in this case.

II. JOINDER OF PARTIES

Many real-life disputes involve more than two people. The federal rules are fairly liberal in allowing multiple-party actions.

A. Multiple plaintiffs and defendants: *Fed. R. Civ. P. 20* allows multiple parties to join as plaintiffs in the action and allows plaintiff(s) to sue more than one defendant.

1. Parties joining as plaintiffs: Rule 20(a)(1) provides: "Persons may join in one action as plaintiffs if: (a) they assert any right to relief jointly, severally, or in the alternative with respect to or arising out of the same transaction, occurrence, or series of transactions or occurrences"; and (b) "any question of law or fact common to all plaintiffs will arise in the action."

a. Joint, several, or in the alternative: Plaintiffs sue *jointly* when they share a right, such as when they sue to collect for damage to a chattel in which they own an undivided interest. Plaintiffs sue *severally* when each has an individual right to recover, such as when a passenger and driver who were injured in an automobile accident sue for their respective individual injuries. When plaintiffs sue *in the alternative*, they allege that one of them, but not both, is entitled to recover. Taken together, these three situations cover all the ways in which plaintiffs might be entitled to recover.

Example: Testator leaves property in her will to "my favorite daughter." After Testator dies, her only two daughters, *P1* and *P2*, each claim to be Testator's favorite. *P1* and *P2* may sue the executor of Testator's estate in the alternative. Only one of the two will prevail.

b. Same transaction or occurrence: The second requirement is that the claims arise from the same transaction or occurrence or *series of transactions or occurrences*.

i. The "same transaction or occurrence" analysis is discussed in Part I.B of this chapter.

ii. Series of transactions or occurrences: Unlike Fed. R. Civ. P. 13, Rule 20 allows joinder either if the claims arise from the same transaction or occurrence or a *series of transactions or occurrences*. Although this language seems broader, courts have interpreted the language in Rule 20 no differently than they have in Rule 13.

★   **Example:** Mosley v. General Motors Corp., 497 F.2d 1330 (8th Cir. 1974), illustrates the reach of the same transaction or occurrence test under Fed. R. Civ. P. 20. In that case, ten plaintiffs sued their employer, alleging they had been the victims of race and sex discrimination. The court allowed joinder. Even though plaintiffs were subject to individualized acts of discrimination, the court emphasized plaintiffs had alleged a "general policy of discrimination" within the company. All their claims arose out of that general policy.

c. Common question: Finally, the claims must share a *common question of law or fact*.

i. Significance: The common question must bear a *significant relationship* to the action in order to qualify.

ii. **Not redundant:** Merely because two claims arise from the same transaction or occurrence does not guarantee they involve a common question of law or fact. Under the majority "logical relationship" test for same transaction or occurrence, it is possible for two claims to arise from the same basic facts but be based on entirely discrete subsets of that general fact pattern. In that case, there may be no question of law or fact common to the claims.

2. **Parties joined as defendants:** Fed. R. Civ. P. 20 also allows plaintiff to sue multiple defendants. The analysis is parallel to that used for multiple plaintiffs, using essentially the same three-part test.

   a. **Jointly, severally, or in the alternative:** Plaintiff must allege defendants are liable to him jointly, severally, or in the alternative. These three cover all possible bases of liability.

      i. **Joint and several:** In many states, two defendants are held jointly and severally liable for torts in which they both play a role. Joint and several liability meets the first requirement of Fed. R. Civ. P. 20.

      ii. **Alternative:** Defendants are liable in the alternative when plaintiff alleges one of the defendants is responsible, but is not sure which one.

   b. **Same transaction or occurrence:** The "same transaction or occurrence" analysis is discussed in Part I.B of this chapter.

B. **Adding parties to counterclaims and cross-claims:** If a party files a valid counterclaim or cross-claim, *Fed. R. Civ. P. 13(h)* allows her to add additional parties to the claim under the conditions specified in Rule 20. When dealing with the addition of parties under Rule 13(h), pretend the claim against the existing and additional parties is a separate suit and determine whether claimant could sue the parties as codefendants under Rule 20.

   Example: *P* sues *D*. *D* has a claim against both *P* and a party who acted in concert with *P*. *D* can counterclaim against *P*. Because Rule 20 would allow *D* to sue both *P* and the other party as codefendants in an original action, Rule 13(h) allows *D* to add the other party to the counterclaim.

C. **Third-party claims (impleader):** In many situations, multiple parties are legally responsible for an injury. In some situations, parties held liable have a right to seek *contribution* or *indemnity* from other responsible parties. If plaintiff does not (or cannot) sue all responsible parties, *Fed. R. Civ. P. 14* preserves defendant's right to seek contribution or indemnity by allowing defendant to bring the other responsible parties into the suit.

1. **Terminology:** Joinder of an additional party in this fashion typically goes by the name *impleader*. The person joined is called a *third-party defendant* (3PD). The party joining the third-party defendant is called a *third-party plaintiff* (3PP).

   Note on multiple names: Often, a court dealing with impleader refers to a party by its original role in the suit as well as its role in the impleader. Thus, a defendant who impleads another party may be called *defendant/third-party plaintiff.*

2. **When impleader available:** Fed. R. Civ. P. 14 allows a party to implead a 3PD "who is or may be liable to it for all or part of" *another party's existing claim against the 3PP*.

   a. **Who may use:** *Fed. R. Civ. P. 14(a)* speaks in terms of a defendant using impleader, and that is far and away the most common situation. However, *Fed. R. Civ. P. 14(b)* specifically allows a plaintiff to use impleader if a claim (such as a counterclaim or cross-claim) has been brought against that plaintiff.

b. **Permission of court:** A party need not obtain the court's permission to implead if she files the third-party complaint within *14 days* of serving her original answer to the claim. After that, court permission is required. Fed. R. Civ. P. 14(a).

c. **Common situations:** Impleader is available only when the third party is derivatively liable *to the 3PP* for all or part of what 3PP must pay plaintiff.

   i. **Joint and vicarious liability:** In cases where two parties are both liable, tort law often provides a right to seek *contribution* (in the case of joint liability) or *indemnity* (in the case of vicarious liability). If plaintiff sues only one of the parties, defendant may join the other(s) to assert the contribution or indemnity claim as part of the same suit, thereby providing for more efficient litigation.

   ii. **Contractual duty to indemnify:** The other main category of case in which a party uses impleader is when the 3PD has agreed by contract to indemnify the 3PP for sums the 3PP must pay the claimant. For example, a tenant in a lease may agree to indemnify landlord for any claims against landlord arising out of tenant's occupancy.

d. **Importance of substantive law:** *Rule 14 does not dictate whether a party has a right to indemnity or contribution*. Instead, the court must look to otherwise controlling law. A party can use impleader only if substantive law allows the 3PP to recover against the 3PD. Absent a tort or contractual right to contribution or indemnity, impleader is unavailable.

★   **Example:** In Price v. CTB, Inc., 168 F. Supp. 2d 1299 (M.D. Ala. 2001), the court reviewed Alabama law to determine whether it afforded defendant a cause of action against the third-party defendant. Finding that Alabama law allowed a claim for implied contractual indemnity, the court held impleader was proper.

   i. **Claim need not be matured:** However, the 3PP's right to contribution or indemnity need not yet be matured ("matured" means 3PP could currently sue 3PD on the claim). Fed. R. Civ. P. 14 allows impleader if the 3PD is *or may be* liable to the 3PP.

   Example: *P* sues *D* for a tort claim. *D* has an insurance policy with InsCo covering just the sort of situation set out in *P*'s complaint. However, the policy makes it clear InsCo's duty to pay does not arise until a claimant actually recovers a judgment against *D*. Notwithstanding this language, *D* may implead InsCo into the case. Of course, the court will determine whether *D* must pay *P* before entering judgment against InsCo. In essence, then, *impleader accelerates a lawsuit that ordinarily would not occur until later*.

   Note: Many jurisdictions do not allow evidence of insurance coverage to be introduced. Although the Federal Rules of Civil Procedure would allow impleader, a court in such a jurisdiction has discretion to deny impleader of the insurance company to keep the fact of insurance from the jury.

   ii. **"Him, not me":** Impleader is proper only if the *3PD is liable to the 3PP* for all or part of the *3PP's liability to plaintiff.* A defendant/3PP cannot use impleader by arguing it is not liable to plaintiff at all and that plaintiff has sued the wrong defendant. However, a defendant who joins a 3PD may allege **in the alternative** that she is not liable to plaintiff and that the 3PD is solely responsible.

e. **Unavailable against existing parties:** Fed. R. Civ. P. 14(a) makes it clear the 3PD must be someone who is a "*nonparty*." Thus, a party cannot use impleader to assert a contribution or indemnity claim against a codefendant or plaintiff. Such a claim would be asserted by a cross-claim or counterclaim, respectively.

3. **Additional impleader:** Additional levels of impleader are possible. A 3PD can bring its own third-party complaint if it alleges some other party is liable to it for all or part of its liability to defendant/3PP. Fed. R. Civ. P. 14(a)(5).

4. **Special service rules:** In order to hear a third-party claim, a court must have *personal jurisdiction* over the new 3PD. However, *Fed. R. Civ. P. 4(k)(1)(B)* contains a special provision designed to facilitate impleader. That rule provides that service is effective to create jurisdiction on *any party joined under Rule 14* who is served at any place within the United States that is *within 100 miles of the court that issued the summons*. Service under this provision can occur across state lines, and is effective regardless of whether the state long-arm statute would reach the party or whether there are any minimum contacts between 3PD and the state in which the action is pending.

5. **Venue:** Impleader does not affect venue under §1391.

6. **Procedure after successful impleader:** Impleader essentially creates a "suit within a suit." The 3PD must respond to the third-party complaint just as if it were an original complaint. Any counterclaims that arise from the *same transaction* as the third-party complaint must be brought or they are lost.

a. **Defenses to plaintiff's claim:** Since the liability of the 3PD turns on the validity of plaintiff's original claim, Rule 14 also allows the 3PD to assert any defenses the 3PP has to plaintiff's claim. Fed. R. Civ. P. 14(a)(2)(C).

b. **Plaintiff-3PD claims:** Rule 14 also allows the plaintiff and third-party defendant to file claims against each other.

i. **Same transaction:** However, plaintiff and 3PD may file against each other only claims arising from the transaction or occurrence that is the subject of an *original claim by plaintiff against the original defendant.* The factors that enter into the same transaction test are discussed in Part I.B of this chapter.

ii. **Compulsory counterclaims:** Nothing requires either plaintiff or 3PD to file related claims against each other. However, once plaintiff files a claim against the 3PD, the 3PD *must* file any claims she has against plaintiff that meet the requirements of Fed. R. Civ. P. 13(a) (the compulsory counterclaim rule). Fed. R. Civ. P. 14(a)(3). The rule is not clear if plaintiff must file any counterclaims it has in response when 3PD files a claim against plaintiff.

Quiz Yourself on BASIC JOINDER OF CLAIMS AND PARTIES

157. Saccharine Soft Drinks produces a variety of overly sweet beverages that it sells in glass bottles. Pamela and Peter are seriously injured when they each drink a Saccharine beverage containing small shards of glass. Pamela and Peter drink different types of beverages that they buy from different stores on different dates. Pamela notices the shards in the bottle but drinks the beverage anyway.

Can Pamela and Peter join as plaintiffs to sue Saccharine? _____

158. Same basic facts as Problem 157. Saccharine obtains its bottles from two different manufacturers, ACME and General. It is impossible to tell from an inspection of a given bottle which of the two produced the bottle. Under governing law, Saccharine and the manufacturer of the bottle are liable for any injuries caused to unsuspecting consumers because of glass shards in the bottle. However, they are not liable if the consumer knows the risk but drinks the beverage anyway.

Pamela tries to sue Saccharine, ACME, and General as codefendants in a single action. Both ACME and General object, pointing out it is logically impossible for *both* of them to have produced the bottle in question. Is joinder proper? _____

159. Same basic facts as Problems 157 and 158. The court rejects defendants' objection and allows Pamela's suit against Saccharine, ACME, and General to proceed.

Saccharine tests its products on live animals. When word of this animal testing becomes public, Pamela and other animal rights activists raid the laboratory and free the animals. This raid occurs well before Pamela is injured by the glass shards.

Saccharine tries to file a claim for the raid as a counterclaim in Pamela's action. Pamela objects, arguing the counterclaim does not arise from the same occurrence as her claim against Saccharine. Will Pamela prevail? _____

160. Same facts as Problems 157-159. Saccharine also files two claims against its codefendant ACME. First, Saccharine alleges ACME has revealed some of Saccharine's valuable trade secrets to one of Saccharine's competitors. If true, ACME violated a crucial term of its contract with Saccharine. Second, Saccharine alleges that if it is held liable for Pamela's injuries, ACME must indemnify Saccharine for any damages it must pay. Saccharine argues that if the bottle was defective, it was ACME's fault, not Saccharine's.

ACME files a timely objection to joinder of both claims. How will the court rule? _____

161. Same facts as Problems 157-159, except Pamela sues only Saccharine and ACME. Pamela's complaint specifically alleges ACME produced the bottle in question.

ACME denies liability. In the alternative, it decides to implead General, arguing the bottle in question came from General's plant instead of ACME's.

General objects to impleader. How should the court rule? _____

Answers

157. Pamela and Peter probably can join, but it depends on how they phrase their complaint. Fed. R. Civ. P. 20 sets out a three-part test. Under the first part, they are suing "severally," one of the three allowable forms (this part of the test is always met, but it is worth addressing anyway).

The second part of the test is the most difficult hurdle. The injuries are two separate occurrences. However, if Pamela and Peter allege the shards were caused by some defect in the bottling process, they should be able to join. That bottling process defect clearly meets the "logical relationship" test because both injuries are tied to the defect. The allegation should even meet the stricter same evidence test since Pamela and Peter would need to prove a defect to prevail.

If Pamela and Peter cannot allege in good faith that the shards were caused by a common manufacturing defect, they have a more difficult case. If the shards were created during, say, storage at the retailers' stores, the claims do not arise from the same occurrence or connected series of occurrences.

With respect to the third part, the cases share common questions of law (what standard of care applies to Saccharine?) and, if they phrase the complaint correctly, fact (what is wrong with Saccharine's bottling operations?). That Pamela has an additional unique fact (her knowledge of the shards) does not matter. The claims need only share some significant common issues.

158. Joinder of the defendants is clearly proper. True, only one of the two manufacturers can be responsible. But Fed. R. Civ. P. 20 allows a plaintiff to sue defendants in the *alternative*, which Pamela seeks to do here. With respect to Saccharine, it and the actual bottle manufacturer would probably be liable jointly.

The claims against defendants clearly arise from the same transaction—the injury to Pamela gave rise to all three claims.

Finally, the claims share a crucial common issue of fact: How did the shards end up in the bottle?

159. Pamela will lose. She is correct that the counterclaim does not arise out of the same transaction as the original claim. But Fed. R. Civ. P. 13(b) allows a party to file any claim, even those that are unrelated, as permissive counterclaims.

160. Both claims should be allowed. These are cross-claims governed by Fed. R. Civ. P. 13(g). Under that rule, a cross-claim must arise out of the same transaction as the original claim *or a counterclaim*. The trade secret claim does not arise out of the same transaction, even under the liberal "logical relationship" test. However, the indemnity claim clearly does arise from the same transaction as the original claim and is therefore a proper cross-claim.

Should the court dismiss the trade secret claim? No. Fed. R. Civ. P. 18 allows a party to join additional claims to a cross-claim, even though the additional claim is completely unrelated. Therefore, Saccharine can join its trade secret claim to the proper cross-claim under Rule 18. (On the other hand, the court could sever the trade secret claim for separate adjudication if it finds it unduly complicates things.)

161. The court should not allow impleader. Pamela is specifically alleging ACME made the bottle. By claiming General made the bottle, ACME is attempting to absolve itself from all liability, not to seek contribution or indemnity from General as required by Fed. R. Civ. P. 14.

D. Compulsory joinder: All the joinder methods discussed above allow, but do not ***require,*** joinder of new parties. But sometimes people ***must*** be joined to the action. Federal Rule of Civil Procedure 19 governs compulsory joinder in the federal courts.

1. Primarily a defense: Compulsory joinder is primarily a ***defense***, not a joinder method. Fed. R. Civ. P. 19 comes into play when a party ***moves to dismiss*** the action because one or more interested people is not a party.

a. How raised: Fed. R. Civ. P. 19 is usually invoked by defendant filing a ***Fed. R. Civ. P. 12(b)(7) motion*** or by raising the defense in the ***answer***.

b. Result of successful motion: If the court concludes the missing party should have been joined, it ***orders the nonmovant to join the person***. If the person cannot be joined (usually because of lack of personal jurisdiction or because it would destroy diversity), the court then considers whether the action should be dismissed.

2. **Development of doctrine:** The necessary party rule was originally a court-created doctrine. Several states still use the historic approach.

   a. The historic approach determines whether the absent person is "necessary" or "indispensable." An *indispensable party* is one who has an interest in the outcome of the pending litigation that would invariably be affected by the final decree in the litigation. A *necessary party* also has an interest in the case, but that interest is separable from those of the parties, allowing the court to issue a final judgment that would not unduly affect the party.

   b. If the party was *indispensable* and could not be joined, the court would *dismiss*. However, if the party was merely *necessary*, the court would *retain the case*.

3. **Rule 19:** The federal rule preserves the basic principles of the historical rule but significantly refines—and to some extent changes—the analysis.

   a. Different approach: Under Fed. R. Civ. P. 19, there are not separate categories of "necessary" and "indispensable" parties. Instead, there is only one category: *persons required to be joined if feasible*. If a court determines a party should be joined, but cannot be joined, the court then decides whether to dismiss. Therefore, there is no need to use the labels "necessary" and "indispensable" when applying Fed. R. Civ. P. 19.

   b. Three steps: Application of Rule 19 may involve up to three separate steps.

     i. Should the party be joined? *Fed. R. Civ. P. 19(a)* establishes the criteria for determining whether a person should be joined.

     ii. May the party be joined? If the court determines the person should be joined, it next determines whether the party can add the missing person. Although some rule will always allow for joinder of the missing person, *personal and subject matter jurisdiction* may prevent joinder.

     iii. Consequences of nonjoinder: If the person cannot be joined, the court must decide whether to dismiss the case, based on its evaluation of the factors listed in *Fed. R. Civ. P. 19(b)*.

   c. Persons to be joined if feasible: Fed. R. Civ. P. 19(a) lists *three situations* where a person should be joined if feasible.

     i. Absence precludes complete relief: Clause (a)(1)(A) specifies that a person should be joined if "in that person's absence, the court cannot accord complete relief among existing parties."

     Example: *P*, a law student, is upset because her law school has not offered Advanced Civil Procedure for 10 years. *P* sues Professor *D*, the professor who used to teach the course, and asks the court to order the professor to offer the course during the next academic term. At this law school, however, scheduling is the sole prerogative of the dean. The dean should be joined to this action if feasible, for even if *P* obtained an order against *D*, there is no guarantee the course would be offered.

     ii. Absence prejudices missing person: Clause (a)(1)(B) provides that a person should be joined if "that person claims an interest relating to the subject of the action and is so situated that disposing of the action in the person's absence may: (i) as a practical matter impair or impede the person's ability to protect that interest. . . ."

(a) It is not enough that the absent person is "interested" in the action. Instead, the absent person must have a "substantial legal interest."

Example 1: *P*, a competitor of *D*, sues *D* for false advertising, based on claims *D* made about its own product. *X* is another seller who makes claims similar to those made by *D*. *X* is not a necessary party. Although *X* is interested in the outcome of the case because of the *stare decisis* effect it might have on any false advertising claim brought against *X*, *X* has no *legal* interest in the outcome of this dispute because it involves *D*'s advertising, not *X*'s.

★

Example 2: *P* is a tenant in a shopping mall owned by *D*. In the lease, *D* agrees it will not lease any other space in the mall to a tenant who would compete with *P*. *D* nevertheless signs a lease with *X*, who sells the same goods as *P*. *P* sues to enjoin *D* from delivering possession of the store to *X*. *X* satisfies Rule 19(a)(2)(i). If *P* prevails, the outcome will directly affect *X*'s interest in the space. Helzberg's Diamond Shops v. Valley West Des Moines Shopping Center, 564 F.2d 816 (8th Cir. 1977).

Note: If *P* had sued for damages rather than an injunction, *X* would not be necessary because regardless of who won the suit, *X* would be able to take possession.

(b) Practical impairment: In addition to showing that the absent party has an interest, the movant must demonstrate that the pending lawsuit will "impair or impede" that interest.

1. **Likelihood enough:** The movant need not demonstrate impairment is certain or even likely. It need merely demonstrate that there is a distinct possibility the case could be resolved in a way that would impair or impede the absent person's interest.

2. **"As a practical matter":** Fed. R. Civ. P. 19(a)(1)(B)(i) requires only that the interest of the absent person be impaired *as a practical matter*. Therefore, it is not necessary to show the judgment would absolutely foreclose the interest. If the judgment would make it *significantly more difficult* for the absent person to protect her interest, she may need to be joined.

3. *Stare decisis* as "impairment": In many cases, the claimed impairment is due to the *stare decisis* effect of the first judgment. Most courts hold *stare decisis* is a sufficient impairment only when the "interest" claimed by the person is a property interest.

   Example: Consider the shopping mall situation discussed in the prior example. If *P* were to prevail in its suit, *X* would not be absolutely foreclosed from protecting its interest. *X* could bring a suit for specific performance against *D*. However, because there would already be an injunction against *D* preventing performance under the lease, *stare decisis* would make it extremely difficult for *X* to obtain an order directing *D* to deliver possession to *X*. And because *X* has a property interest due to the lease, this *stare decisis* effect is enough.

iii. Absence prejudices parties: Clause (a)(1)(B)(ii) provides that a person should be joined if that person "claims an interest relating to the subject of the action and is so situated that the disposition of the action in the person's absence may . . . (ii) leave an existing party subject to a substantial risk of incurring *double, multiple or otherwise inconsistent obligations* because of the interest."

(a) Interest: Analysis of whether the absent person has an "interest" is the same as it is under clause (a)(1)(B)(i), discussed above.

(b) Multiple or inconsistent obligations: There are two categories of cases where the "double, multiple, or inconsistent obligations" standard is likely to be satisfied. The first is where the existing party and the absent person both claim rights in the same property but only one of them by law is entitled to receive it. The second is when a party to the suit is insisting the law requires another party to act one way, while the absent party claims the other party is *required* by law to act in an inconsistent manner.

★   **Example 1:** A group of minority firefighters sues City, claiming City illegally discriminated based on their race when City made promotion decisions. Plaintiffs seek an order requiring City to give them preference in future promotions. Several nonminority firefighters, upon hearing of the suit, threaten a suit of their own, arguing the law forbids preferences based on race. Assuming the interest in being promoted is a substantial legal interest, the nonminority firefighters should be joined if feasible because failure to join them could leave City facing inconsistent legal obligations. Cf. Martin v. Wilks, 490 U.S. 755 (1989).

★   **Example 2:** In Temple v. Synthes Corp., 498 U.S. 5, reh'g denied, 498 U.S. 1092 (1990), the Supreme Court reaffirmed that nothing in Fed. R. Civ. P. 19 requires a plaintiff to join all joint tortfeasors. Although a judgment for the full amount might be entered against the named defendants, those defendants can seek contribution or indemnity from the missing defendants in a separate action. The availability of contribution or indemnity is a sufficient safeguard against multiple liability.

d. **Adding the missing person to the case:** If Fed. R. Civ. P. 19(a) requires someone to be joined, the person must be joined to the suit if possible.

   i. **Absent person properly a defendant:** If the absent person should be a defendant, plaintiff will join the person under *Fed. R. Civ. P. 20.* Someone who should be joined under Fed. R. Civ. P. 19(a) will always satisfy the requirements of Rule 20.

   ii. **Absent person properly a plaintiff:** Often a plaintiff is required to join an absent person as an additional plaintiff. Because Rule 20 does not authorize making a person a plaintiff against her will, Rule 19(a) explicitly allows the court to make the person a *defendant* or, in the proper case, an *involuntary plaintiff.* Note this is the only case where Rule 19 operates as a joinder rule.

   iii. **Potential problems with joinder:** Joinder of the missing person may be impossible because the court lacks *personal jurisdiction* over the party or because addition of the party would destroy *venue.* In addition, in a federal case, addition of the missing person may destroy *diversity jurisdiction.*

e. **Consequences of inability to join:** If a person who should be joined is not brought into the case, there is a chance the court will dismiss the case. *Fed. R. Civ. P. 19(b)* covers this situation.

   i. Plaintiff refuses to join: If plaintiff is ordered to join another person but refuses to, the court will ordinarily dismiss the case.

   ii. Plaintiff cannot join: If a plaintiff cannot join the missing person because of jurisdiction or venue limits, Fed. R. Civ. P. 19(b) requires the court to consider four factors in determining whether to dismiss:

      (a) the extent to which a judgment rendered in the person's absence would prejudice the absent person or the parties (this factor is similar to the analysis under Rule 19(a), but looks to the ***degree of prejudice***);

      (b) whether any prejudice could be reduced by protective provisions in the judgment, the shaping of relief, or other measures;

      (c) whether a judgment rendered in the person's absence will be adequate (this factor is redundant if the absent person is indispensable because of Rule 19(a)(1)(A)); and

      (d) whether plaintiff will have an adequate remedy if the case is dismissed.

   iii. Dismissal not favored: Courts usually go to great lengths to avoid dismissing a case under Fed. R. Civ. P. 19. They instead try to minimize prejudice by limiting or modifying the remedy in the case.

Quiz Yourself on
COMPULSORY JOINDER

162. Darla Decedent dies in 2016. Darla's last will and testament is dated August 9, 2010. The will leaves her entire estate to "my husband." From 1971 to 2012, Darla was married to Andrew. In 2012, however, she divorced Andrew and married Ben.

The executor of Darla's estate is convinced Darla meant to leave her estate to Andrew. The executor accordingly delivers all of the property in the estate to Andrew. When Ben learns of this, he sues the executor. Ben asks for damages, claiming he should have received the estate. The court agrees with Ben and awards $50,000 in damages. When Ben attempts to collect this judgment, the executor argues the judgment is void because Ben failed to join Andrew in the action. Is the judgment void?

163. Same facts as Problem 162, except the executor moves to dismiss Ben's suit for failure to join Andrew while the suit is still pending. Because of lack of personal jurisdiction, it is impossible to join Andrew to the action. Will the court dismiss Ben's suit? _____

164. Same facts as Problem 162, except Ben sues before the executor distributes the property. Ben seeks an order requiring the executor to distribute the property to him. The executor moves to dismiss Ben's suit for failure to join Andrew. Because of lack of personal jurisdiction, it is impossible to join Andrew to the case. Will the court dismiss Ben's suit? _____

Answers

162. The judgment is not void. The necessary party rule is simply a defense the executor could have asserted during Ben's case. Once that case is complete, the defense no longer has any effect. It does not affect the court's power to decide the case.

163. The court will not dismiss Ben's suit because Andrew is not a necessary party. The test is set out in Fed. R. Civ. P. 19(a), which lists three situations in which a person is deemed necessary. First, Andrew's presence is not necessary to afford complete relief. Ben is not asking for the estate itself but merely for damages. The executor does not need Andrew as a party to pay damages. Second, the suit in no way prejudices Andrew. Again, Ben seeks only damages, not the property that was given to Andrew. Third, there is no prejudice to existing parties. Although it looks as if the executor faces double liability, any liability would not result from inconsistent *judgments*, but from the executor's erroneous decision to give the property to Andrew rather than to Ben.

164. Now the court probably will dismiss. Andrew is a necessary party. Although Andrew's presence is not necessary to afford complete relief, failure to join Andrew not only results in prejudice to Andrew but also exposes the executor to double liability. Andrew is prejudiced, of course, because he would not receive the estate. The risk of double liability arises because Andrew could then turn around and sue the executor. Although the executor delivered the property to Ben in compliance with the court order, Andrew—who was not a party to Ben's suit—is not bound by that judgment and could still prevail in his suit against the executor.

Once it is determined Andrew is necessary, Ben must join him if feasible. The problem specifies, however, that the court lacks personal jurisdiction over Andrew.

If Andrew cannot be joined, the court needs to determine whether to dismiss or let the case proceed without Andrew. Here, it considers the factors in Rule 19(b). A judgment without Andrew would prove highly prejudicial to Andrew and possibly to the executor. Second, there *are* measures the court could take to reduce the prejudice. The court, for example, could order the executor to *interplead* Andrew and Ben. Or the court could refuse to order the executor actually to convey the assets but could simply require the trustee to hold the assets in trust until Andrew's claim is resolved.

Third, a judgment rendered without Andrew would not be completely adequate because it would leave the executor exposed to a later suit by Andrew. Finally, if the case is dismissed, Ben will have no adequate remedy. Although he could sue again in a forum with personal jurisdiction over Andrew, there is no guarantee that forum could exercise personal jurisdiction over the executor or the estate.

E. **Intervention:** Intervention allows a nonparty to join an ongoing action to protect her rights or interests. Intervention is governed by *Fed. R. Civ. P. 24*. In some cases, a party may intervene as of right; in others, court permission is required.

   1. **Permissive intervention:** *Fed. R. Civ. P. 24(b) governs intervention with court permission.*

      a. **Timely application:** Although no strict deadline is set forth, a request to intervene is more likely to be granted early in the lawsuit.

      b. **Grounds:** A party may seek permission to intervene *either* when a *federal statute* grants a conditional right to intervene or when the applicant's claim or defense shares a *common question of law or fact* with the existing suit.

      c. **Discretion:** The decision to allow or deny intervention is rarely reversed on appeal.

2. **Intervention by right:** *Fed. R. Civ. P. 24(a)* gives a party the right to intervene without court permission in certain situations.

   a. **Timely application:** The timely application requirement assumes a more important role in a case of intervention by right because it is the sole issue on which the court may exercise discretion. Whether the application is timely turns on whether delay in applying to intervene would ***prejudice*** the parties in preparing their suit.

   b. **Grounds:** A party has a right to intervene when *either* of the following conditions is met.

      i. A *federal statute* grants an unconditional right to intervene. Several federal statutes, for example, give the United States the right to intervene in actions challenging federal law.

      ii. The applicant (a) ***"claims an interest*** relating to the property or transaction that is the subject of the action" ***and*** (b) the applicant "is so situated that disposing of the action ***may as a practical matter impair or impede the movant's ability to protect its interest,"*** *unless* (c) the applicant's interest is ***adequately protected by existing parties.***

      (a) **Interest: Applicant must show a *significantly protectable interest.***

         1. **Need not be economic:** The interest in question need not be a property interest or other economic interest. However, some courts hold a mere economic interest outcome is insufficient.

         2. **Public concern:** The requirement of a significantly protectable interest is often relaxed when the suit involves a matter of public concern or when a public interest group seeks intervention.

         3. **Rule 19(a) compared:** The notion of an interest is the same under Fed. R. Civ. P. 24(a) as under Fed. R. Civ. P. 19(a). Glancy v. Taubman Centers, Inc., 373 F.3d 656 (6th Cir. 2004).

      (b) **Practical impairment:** The applicant must also demonstrate that its interest may be "impaired or impeded" by the ongoing litigation.

         1. **Practical, not legal:** The impairment need be only practical. Therefore, the applicant need not show that claim preclusion would bar any further action by applicant to protect its right.

         2. **May be impaired:** The applicant need not show impairment is certain, merely that it could occur if the lawsuit is resolved in a particular way.

         3. *Stare decisis* **as "impairment":** In many cases, the claimed impairment is due to the *stare decisis* effect of the first judgment. Most courts find *stare decisis* qualifies as sufficient impairment only when the "interest" claimed by the person is a property interest.

         4. Recent decisions tend to ***merge the interest and impairment elements*** of the analysis. The greater the impairment, the broader the scope of interests courts will protect.

      (c) **Unless adequate representation:** Even if the interest and impairment standards are satisfied, a party cannot intervene of right if the existing parties already protect the applicant's interest. However, it is fairly easy to show lack of adequate representation. An applicant need show only that the existing parties have a *possible incentive* not to represent the interests of applicant.

★   **Example:** NRDC v. U.S. Nuclear Regulatory Commission, 578 F.2d 1341 (10th Cir. 1978), discusses the adequate representation factor of Rule 24(a). An environmental group sued the U.S. Nuclear Regulatory Commission, challenging the Commission's decision not to conduct an environmental study before issuing a license to operate a uranium mill to Company *X*. Company *Y*, which also had filed an application for a license, sought to intervene in the action as of right. The court allowed Company *Y* to intervene. First, the court found Company *Y*'s interest in its own license was sufficient to allow intervention even though the suit did not directly involve *Y*'s application.

Second, the court found Company *Y*'s interest was impaired even though the lawsuit technically would not foreclose Company *Y* from making any arguments it wanted when its license application was considered. If the environmental group were to prevail in its suit dealing with Company *X*'s application, that ruling likely would affect how the agency handled all other applications, including that of Company *Y*. Finally, the court found Company *X* did not adequately represent the interests of Company *Y*. It hypothesized that Company *X* might have an incentive to argue for a ruling that would apply *prospectively only*, thereby leading the agency to undertake a full environmental study for Company *Y*'s application but not for Company *X*'s.

F.   **Interpleader:** Interpleader is a special type of joinder designed to deal with situations where a party faces **multiple, inconsistent claims**. Instead of waiting for the claimants to bring suit—which creates a risk of inconsistent judgments—interpleader allows the party who owes the obligation to join all claimants and let them fight it out amongst themselves.

1.   **Overview:** Interpleader is often used by a party who acknowledges it is liable to someone but is not completely sure to *whom*. For example, the executor of an estate may face conflicting claims to certain assets of that estate. Interpleader allows the executor to bring all claimants into a single action so that court can determine to whom the executor should deliver the assets. Because of the nature of the joinder device, the statutes and rules use a unique terminology to describe the parties and subject matter of an interpleader case.

   a.   The *stake* is the thing being claimed by two or more people. It can be property (as in the example of the executor posed just above) or an obligation (such as an insurance company's obligation to pay money).

   b.   The *stakeholder* is the person in possession of the stake.

   c.   The *claimants* are those who seek the property or performance of the obligation.

2.   **Two types of interpleader:** The federal system recognizes two separate forms of interpleader. The first, **rule interpleader**, is governed by **Fed. R. Civ. P. 22**. The second, **statutory interpleader**, is governed mainly by **28 U.S.C. §1335**. Statutory interpleader is far more useful because of special rules governing subject matter jurisdiction, personal jurisdiction, and venue.

3.   **Common features of rule and statutory interpleader:** Although there are important practical differences between rule and statutory interpleader, both share certain fundamental characteristics.

a. **How action initiated:** The stakeholder may initiate an interpleader action by naming the claimants as defendants in an *original action*. In the alternative, if the stakeholder has been sued, the stakeholder may initiate the interpleader action by *counterclaim* or *cross-claim*.

b. **When interpleader available:** Interpleader is not available merely because a party faces multiple claims. Instead, the claims must be inconsistent, leaving the stakeholder exposed to "*double or multiple liability*." Fed. R. Civ. P. 22(a)(1).

Example: A truck driver collides with a bus, seriously injuring 25 people. The driver has only $30,000 in assets to her name, plus a liability insurance policy with a maximum of $50,000 in coverage for a single incident such as this wreck. The injured passengers sue the driver and the insurance company in separate actions, asking for total damages in excess of $500,000. The *driver cannot interplead*. Even though the claims exceed her total assets, her liability is legally unlimited. Therefore, judgments against her do not present double or multiple liability. However, the *insurance company can interplead*. Its liability is limited by law to $50,000. Because the several plaintiffs seek more than that amount, there is a risk of separate judgments that exceed the policy limits.

4. **Rule interpleader:** *Fed. R. Civ. P. 22* allows a stakeholder to commence an interpleader action in a federal court. Notwithstanding the special terminology, a rule interpleader action is analyzed like any other federal action for purposes of determining jurisdiction and venue. This is the most significant difference between rule and statutory interpleader.

a. **Subject matter jurisdiction:** The court must have jurisdiction over *every claimant's claim against the stakeholder*. Few of these cases involve federal questions, so diversity is often the only option. The *complete diversity* rule can pose a special problem in these cases. Diversity jurisdiction exists under 28 U.S.C. §1332 only if the stakeholder is *diverse from all claimants* and the value of the stake exceeds $75,000.

b. **Personal jurisdiction:** For a court to hear the interpleader case, there must be personal jurisdiction over *all claimants*.

Note: Although an interpleader action essentially adjudicates who "owns" the stake, the Supreme Court held in New York Life Insurance Co. v. Dunlevy, 241 U.S. 518 (1916), that a court *cannot use quasi-in-rem jurisdiction* in interpleader. Personal jurisdiction over the claimants is required.

c. **Venue:** In a federal court, venue is proper either where all "defendants" reside or where a substantial portion of the events or omissions giving rise to the claim occurred, 28 U.S.C. §1391(b). If the stakeholder brings the interpleader as an original action, the claimants are the defendants. If the stakeholder brings the interpleader by counterclaim, it may be the sole defendant, and therefore venue would be proper in the district where the stakeholder resides.

5. **Statutory interpleader:** Although phrased as a jurisdictional statute, *28 U.S.C. §1335* has been interpreted to give federal courts authority to grant a remedy in interpleader cases. This "statutory interpleader" is *separate and distinct from rule interpleader*. Congress also enacted special rules governing subject matter jurisdiction, personal jurisdiction, and venue in cases brought under §1335.

a. **Subject matter jurisdiction:** As with rule interpleader, the federal court must have subject matter jurisdiction over every claim. However, 28 U.S.C. §1335 makes it much easier to obtain jurisdiction in diversity cases. It requires only *minimal diversity among the claimants* and an amount in controversy of only *$500*.

i.   **Minimal diversity among claimants:** Unlike the complete diversity requirement in rule interpleader, §1335 allows jurisdiction whenever at least one of the claimants is *diverse from any other claimant.* The citizenship of the stakeholder is usually not considered. However, some courts consider the stakeholder to be an additional claimant if it denies liability to all claimants and argues it should keep the stake.

ii. **Amount in controversy:** Unlike the $75,000 amount in controversy requirement in rule interpleader, diversity jurisdiction exists in statutory interpleader whenever the *stake is worth $500 or more.*

   Example: *P* files a statutory interpleader action against *D1*, *D2*, and *D3*. *P*, *D1*, and *D2* are all citizens of Ohio. *D3* is a citizen of South Dakota. The stake is worth $600. Diversity jurisdiction exists under §1335.

iii. **Federal question jurisdiction in statutory interpleader:** Because of the way 28 U.S.C. §1335 is worded, some courts hold that statutory interpleader is not available when the sole basis for subject matter jurisdiction is a federal question. Instead, the parties must satisfy the minimum diversity requirements of §1335 before they can use the special personal jurisdiction and venue provisions in statutory interpleader.

b. **Personal jurisdiction:** *28 U.S.C. §2361* complements §1335 by allowing the court to serve process *anywhere in the United States.* Therefore, as long as all claimants are domiciled, reside, or can be found anywhere in the country, the federal court can exercise personal jurisdiction over them.

c. **Venue:** *28 U.S.C. §1397* similarly sets out a special venue rule for statutory interpleader. Venue is proper in any judicial district where *one or more claimants reside.* Unlike rule interpleader cases, the statute does *not* look to where a substantial portion of the events or omissions occurred.

Quiz Yourself on
INTERVENTION AND INTERPLEADER

165. Jippy, Skiff, and Smackers are the nation's three largest producers of peanut butter. As most people know, not all peanut butter is the same. Jippy and Skiff add sugar and nonpeanut oils to their products, which makes them more appealing to children. Smackers, by contrast, takes the purist approach. Its peanut butter contains only ground peanuts and salt.

   Smackers sues Jippy under federal false advertising laws in federal district court. Smackers claims Jippy is misleading the public by calling its product "peanut butter," when in truth it contains many extra ingredients.

   Because Skiff uses many of the same extra ingredients, it is concerned about Smackers's suit against Jippy. Skiff fears that if Smackers prevails, the decision will effectively define what "peanut butter" is in the U.S. market. Skiff therefore wants to join the action. Federal false advertising laws, however, do not give Skiff a right to intervene. Will Skiff succeed in joining the lawsuit? _____

166. Horizon Communications operates a cellular telephone service. Recently, however, it has found itself in a bind. Two of Horizon's customers, Alice and Bob, both claim a Horizon representative promised them the valuable phone number 345-6789. However, when the representative set up the phones for Alice and Bob, she programmed a different number in each of the phones. Because Alice and Bob had business cards and stationery printed up with the 345-6789 number on them, they are threatening suit against Horizon. The number has not yet been assigned to anyone.

Horizon's troubles worsen when it receives a phone call from Callous Bank. Callous loaned money to Bob. In return, Callous claims, Bob gave it a security interest in all of his assets, including his cell phone account. When Bob failed to pay the loan, Callous foreclosed and now claims it owns the 345-6789 number.

Horizon is considering bringing an interpleader action to determine who really owns the number 345-6789. If it does bring such an action, it wants to be able to argue that *it* still retains the phone number. Is interpleader a proper way to deal with Horizon's dilemma? _____

Answers

165. Skiff may be able to intervene if the judge allows permissive intervention. However, it will not be able to intervene as of right.

The judge may well grant permissive intervention under Fed. R. Civ. P. 24(b). There are common questions of law or fact. The case may have some effect on Skiff, and allowing Skiff to join would not unduly complicate matters. On the other hand, permissive intervention is up to the discretion of the trial judge.

If the trial judge denies permissive intervention, Skiff will not be able to intervene as of right. First, it must file a timely application. That hurdle will not be difficult to clear. Second, because the false advertising laws do not give Skiff a right to intervene, Skiff must demonstrate it has an interest that will be impaired. Skiff is definitely "interested" in the suit. However, it has no significantly protectable interest in the dispute between Smackers and Jippy. On the other hand, a legally recognized interest is not always necessary—if the impairment is great enough, lesser interests may suffice.

The threat to Skiff is that a judgment in favor of Smackers would be *stare decisis* in a later suit by Smackers against Skiff. In some situations, courts will allow *stare decisis* alone to qualify for intervention of right. However, in those cases (see, for example, the *NRDC* case discussed in the text), the party had a *property* interest that was directly threatened. Skiff has no such interest. It has no property interest in the ingredients in its peanut butter. Skiff accordingly has no interest, and cannot intervene as of right.

166. Interpleader will deal only partially with Horizon's problems. Horizon can file an interpleader action against Callous and Bob. Those two parties have competing claims to the same basic right—the number that Horizon ostensibly assigned to Bob. It does not matter that Horizon claims it did not assign that number to either claimant. Under modern interpleader practice, the stakeholder (Horizon) can use interpleader even though it denies liability to anyone.

However, Horizon cannot use interpleader to join Alice to the suit. Alice's claim is not *logically* inconsistent with that of Bob/Callous. It is possible the representative did promise the number to two different people. Although Horizon obviously cannot give the same number to both, there is nothing inconsistent with holding it liable for making inconsistent promises.

III. SEVERANCE

In some cases, joinder of claims and parties results in an unwieldy case. Two Federal Rules of Civil Procedure, *21* and *42(b)*, give the court the power to *sever* the lawsuit into subsuits.

A. **No real difference:** Although the wording of the two rules differs slightly, there is no appreciable difference in how they apply.

B. **When severance granted:** Courts typically rely on two main arguments to justify severing claims. First, a court may sever when the case is *unmanageable or unduly complex*. The second main justification is when the presence of one claim may *prejudice* another claim. For example, if *P* sues two *D*s, alleging fraud against one and breach of contract against the other, the allegation of fraud may prejudice the breach of contract claim.

C. **Effect of severance:** Severance divides an existing case into two or more new cases. Plaintiff(s) need not serve defendant(s) a second time. Moreover, unless the court orders additional pleadings, the existing pleadings will be used in all the new cases.

IV. CONSOLIDATION OF ACTIONS

Fed. R. Civ. P. 42(a) allows a court to consolidate existing actions currently pending before it if they involve a "common question of law or fact." Although consolidation may occur at the initiative of the court, it usually is the result of a motion filed by a party in one of the actions.

V. JURISDICTION ISSUES IN JOINDER

Joinder of additional claims and parties raises issues of subject matter jurisdiction and personal jurisdiction. With the exception of interpleader, which has its own special rules that are discussed above, the basic principles of Chapters 2 and 4 apply in joinder. However, a brief review of those principles may be useful in this chapter.

A. **Personal jurisdiction:** A court must have personal jurisdiction over every party to the action, except voluntary plaintiffs, intervenors under Rule 24, and any other party who waives his right to contest jurisdiction. Thus, the court needs to be able to establish jurisdiction over *all defendants* and any other party *joined to the action against his will* (including involuntary plaintiffs under Fed. R. Civ. P. 19).

B. **Subject matter jurisdiction:** Subject matter jurisdiction may also bar an attempted joinder.

1. **Basic rule:** As discussed in Chapter 4, subject matter jurisdiction must exist over *every claim in the proceeding*.

2. **Federal question and diversity:** An individual claim can involve federal question or diversity jurisdiction if, standing on its own, it meets the requirement for jurisdiction.

3. **Supplemental jurisdiction:** If any claim does not qualify for either federal question or diversity jurisdiction in its own right, a federal court may be able to exercise supplemental jurisdiction over the claim. The basics of supplemental jurisdiction are discussed in Chapter 4. However, because the test for supplemental jurisdiction is similar to the test for certain forms of joinder, some types of joinder are likely to qualify for supplemental jurisdiction.

a. **Similarity in analysis:** The first step in the supplemental jurisdiction analysis is to determine whether the claim arises out of a *common nucleus of operative fact* as another claim over which the federal court has an independent basis for jurisdiction. 28 U.S.C. §1367(a). This test resembles closely the *same transaction or occurrence test* used in certain joinder rules.

   Note: Several recent decisions suggest the "common nucleus" test is actually *broader* than the same transaction test, which means supplemental jurisdiction may exist even for claims that do not derive from the same transaction or occurrence. These decisions do not affect the analysis below. Even under this view, as long as the same transaction test is satisfied, the claim will also satisfy §1367(a).

b. **Rules that will satisfy §1367(a):** Therefore, if a claim is joined to a suit on the grounds that it arises from the *same transaction or occurrence as a claim filed by a plaintiff*, and there is an independent basis for federal jurisdiction over the claim filed by plaintiff, the joined claim will usually meet the requirements of §1367(a). Examples of such claims include:

   i. **compulsory counterclaims** under Fed. R. Civ. P. 13(a);

   ii. **cross-claims** under Fed. R. Civ. P. 13(g) that arise out of the same transaction as the original claim by plaintiff (cross-claims are also proper if they arise out of the same transaction as a counterclaim; §1367(a) may not be satisfied in these cases);

   iii. **joinder of plaintiffs or defendants** under Fed. R. Civ. P. 20 (however, see Parts c and g.i for two very important limitations);

   iv. parties joined to counterclaims or cross-claims under Fed. R. Civ. P. 13(h);

   v. claims by a **third-party defendant against plaintiff** under Fed. R. Civ. P. 14(a)(2)(D); and

   vi. claims by a **plaintiff against a third-party defendant** under Fed. R. Civ. P. 14(a)(3) (however, see Part g.i for an important limitation).

   Note: As discussed below, joinder under these rules does not automatically qualify for supplemental jurisdiction. It merely satisfies the first element, the "common nucleus" test.

   Example: *P* sues *D1* and *D2* for negligence. The suit arises under state law. However, because both defendants are diverse from *P* and the case meets the amount in controversy requirement, *P* sues in a federal court. *D1* files a proper cross-claim against *D2*. *D2* files a compulsory counterclaim against *P* for an amount less than $75,000. Even though neither of the *D*s' claims has an independent basis for jurisdiction, both satisfy §1367(a), and therefore possibly qualify for supplemental jurisdiction, because they share a common nucleus of operative fact with *P*'s proper diversity claims.

c. **Exception for lack of complete diversity:** The *Exxon Mobil* case discussed in Chapter 4, Part V.C.2.iii.(b), sets out a very important exception to the rules discussed just above. If jurisdiction is based solely on diversity, and there is not complete diversity between plaintiffs and defendants, additional claims by plaintiff do not satisfy 28 U.S.C. §1367(a), regardless of whether all claims arise from a common nucleus of fact. *Exxon Mobil* holds the complete diversity requirement is part of the determination of whether the case is a "civil action of which the district courts have original jurisdiction" in §1367(a).

Example: *P1*, a citizen of Alpha, and *P2*, a citizen of Beta, sue *D*, a citizen of Beta. Plaintiffs' joinder satisfies Fed. R. Civ. P. 20 because the claims arise from the same transaction or occurrence. However, the case does not satisfy 28 U.S.C. §1367(a). The lack of complete diversity prevents this from being an original action of which the court has jurisdiction. (Note the court could hear *P1*'s claim.)

d. Impleader: Proper *impleader* claims *also satisfy §1367(a)*. Although Fed. R. Civ. P. 14(a) does not use the same transaction test, a proper impleader claim also *automatically meets the requirements* of §1367(a) since the liability of the third-party defendant ultimately traces back to the same underlying event as plaintiff's claim.

e. Permissive counterclaims: Because Fed. R. Civ. P. 13(b) permissive counterclaims *do not have to arise from the same transaction or occurrence*, permissive counterclaims ordinarily do not qualify for supplemental jurisdiction. However, some counterclaims do arise from the same transaction or occurrence but are not compulsory because they fall into one of Rule 13(a)'s listed exceptions. These "excepted" claims are permissive counterclaims. Such claims *satisfy §1367(a)* because they arise out of the same transaction or occurrence as the original claim.

f. Claims joined under Rule 18 may not qualify: Fed. R. Civ. P. 18 allows joinder of additional claims regardless of whether they are related to the original claim. Because Rule 18 does not use the same transaction test, the "automatic" rules discussed above do not apply to these claims.

Example: *P* sues *D1* and *D2* in federal court, based on a federal question. All the parties are citizens of Indiana. *D1* brings a state law cross-claim against *D2* that arises from the same transaction or occurrence as *P*'s claim. *D1* adds another state law cross-claim against *D2* that does not arise from the same transaction as the original claim by *P*. Although the original cross-claim satisfies §1367(a), the second cross-claim does not because it does not arise from a common nucleus of operative fact.

g. Remainder of §1367 must be satisfied: It is crucial to remember that meeting the same transaction or occurrence test *does not mean the claim automatically qualifies for supplemental jurisdiction*. Instead, it means only that the claim satisfies §1367(a), which is merely the first hurdle. The requirements of §1367(b) and (c) must also be satisfied. Section 1367(b) in particular bars supplemental jurisdiction over certain claims.

    i. Section 1367(b) and claims by plaintiffs: Section 1367(b) prevents a court from exercising supplemental jurisdiction over certain claims *by plaintiffs* when jurisdiction over the original claim is based on *diversity*. This provision defeats many joinder attempts by plaintiffs in diversity actions. See Chapter 4, Part IV, for a detailed analysis of this provision.

    Example 1: *P* sues *D1* and *D2* in a federal court, claiming that under state law the *D*s are jointly liable to *P* for $200,000. Jurisdiction is based on diversity. *P* and *D1* are diverse, but *P* and *D2* are citizens of the same state. Even if joinder of the two defendants satisfies the same transaction requirement of Fed. R. Civ. P. 20, *P cannot join D2* into this suit. There is no independent basis for subject matter jurisdiction. Because a plaintiff joins defendants under Rule 20, one of the rules listed in §1367(b), supplemental jurisdiction is not allowed.

Example 2: Same as the prior example, except that *P*'s claim against *D1* is based on federal law. *P*'s claim against *D2* is a state law claim. *P may use supplemental jurisdiction* (unless the court dismisses because of §1367(c)) because §1367(b) does not apply to situations where *P*'s federal claim is a federal question.

Example 3: *P*, a citizen of California, sues *D*, a citizen of Oregon, in a federal court based on diversity. *D* impleads *3PD*, a citizen of Nevada. *P* wants to add a claim against *3PD* for $50,000. *P cannot bring the claim* because there is no independent basis for jurisdiction (because the amount in controversy is not satisfied), and §1367(b) bars supplemental jurisdiction for a claim by *P* against *3PD*, a person joined under Fed. R. Civ. P. 14.

    ii. Section 1367(c): Even if a joined claim meets §1367(a) and (b), a court may still refuse to exercise supplemental jurisdiction over the claim based on the factors listed in §1367(c).

Quiz Yourself on JOINDER

167. Willard and Rosie, both citizens of Kentucky, are canoodling during a romantic horse-drawn carriage ride when a carriage wheel suddenly falls off. The frightened horse drags the carriage down the street with the couple inside, seriously injuring both. The horse and carriage are operated and owned by Ash Company, a citizen of both Delaware and Kentucky. Lea Company, a citizen of North Carolina, is the carriage manufacturer. Willard and Rosie join as plaintiffs in a federal court diversity action, seeking recovery against Ash Co. for negligent operation and against Lea Co. for products liability. Defendants object in timely fashion to both joinder and subject matter jurisdiction. How should the court rule? _____

168. The federal "lemon law" requires the seller of an automobile to disclose to a potential purchaser any defects of which seller is aware. If seller fails to disclose a defect, seller must repair the defect without cost to the injured purchaser. However, the statute also makes it clear that sale of a "lemon" is not grounds for canceling the sales contract.

Gail purchases a used car from Honest John. When she buys the car, Gail also takes advantage of Honest John's "on the lot credit" program where Honest John himself lends the purchaser the money to buy the car. A week later, Gail discovers a defect and immediately asks Honest John to fix the car, citing the lemon law. Honest John refuses, so Gail quits making payments under her loan. Two months later, after repeated efforts to get the car repaired, Gail sues Honest John in federal court for $200, the estimated cost of repair. Honest John denies liability, claiming the statute applies only to the sale of *new* automobiles. The court agrees with Honest John and enters judgment for him.

Now, Honest John has filed suit against Gail to recover on the loan. Gail has not made any payments. Does she nevertheless have a way to prevent Honest John from bringing all or part of his claim? Is this strategy likely to work? _____

169. Gary, Jeff, Heather, and Sarah just completed their first year of law school. During the past year, the four worked together in a study group. This group prepared joint outlines to use in reviewing the material in each course.

Gary and Sarah discover that Jeff, the entrepreneur, sold the group's Civil Procedure outline to Bar None Corp., a company that conducts bar reviews. Gary and Sarah, both citizens of Indiana, immediately sue Jeff, a citizen of Wisconsin, in federal court. Gary and Sarah allege that Jeff's actions infringe their copyright in the outlines.

Jeff immediately counterclaims against Gary, alleging that during the spring semester interview season, Gary and Heather told the interviewers that Jeff and Sarah conspired to cheat on examinations. Jeff claims these statements defamed him. Jeff's counterclaim not only names Gary but also attempts to join Heather, a citizen of Montana, into the action. Jeff seeks $300,000 in damages from Gary and Heather based on the tort theory of defamation.

Gary and Heather both object to Jeff's counterclaim, arguing that neither the joinder rules nor jurisdictional requirements are met. How should the court rule? _____

170. Same facts as Problem 169. Jeff files a timely third-party complaint against Bar None. This complaint contains two separate claims. First, Jeff correctly points out that federal copyright law does not prevent a party from reselling a legally obtained copy of a protected work. It would, however, prevent the party from selling a *copy* of that legally obtained copy. Jeff claims he merely sold his original outline to Bar None. Because only Bar None made a copy, Jeff's argument continues, only Bar None committed infringement. Therefore, Jeff concludes, only Bar None can be held liable to Gary and Sarah. Second, Jeff's third-party complaint also includes a federal antitrust claim against Bar None, which alleges Bar None has established an illegal monopoly in the bar preparation business.

Bar None objects to joinder, arguing that Jeff cannot join either of these claims in the copyright action. Is Bar None correct? _____

171. Caterpillar Tractor Company, an Illinois company with its principal place of business in Peoria, Illinois, manufactures bulldozers and other heavy-duty earthmoving equipment. Faced with declining demand due to a construction slump, Caterpillar decides to diversify its offerings. Caterpillar chooses to tap into the current craze for sports utility vehicles. Its engineers design the ultimate SUV: a bulldozer, with the blade removed, but equipped with a luxurious cabin replete with every creature comfort. Although the Catsplorer costs $335,000, uses three gallons of fuel for every mile traveled, and has a maximum speed of only 6 miles an hour, demand for the product exceeds Caterpillar's wildest expectations. In fact, two buyers—Tommy and Courtney—pay an extra $10,000 for the honor of owning the very *first* production Catsplorer.

When Tommy learns of Courtney's involvement, he sues Caterpillar. Tommy asks the court for an order of specific performance, requiring Caterpillar to deliver the first production Catsplorer to him.

Courtney reacts with lightning speed once she learns of Tommy's suit. She files a petition to intervene in the action. When the court denies her petition, Courtney claims the federal rules give her a right to intervene. The court has subject matter jurisdiction over Courtney's claim. Does Courtney have a right to intervene? _____

172. Reva, a citizen of Idaho, is an ardent "mall walker." While doing her laps early one morning, she stumbles over a diamond of approximately one carat in size. Reva takes the diamond to mall security. While she is there, three separate people—Mary, a citizen of Maryland, Ida, a citizen of Idaho, and George, a citizen of Georgia—come to the mall security booth. Each claims to have lost a similar diamond.

The diamond is worth at least $90,000. Reva is unsure what to do. Mary, less patient than Reva, sues Reva in a federal district court in Idaho. Although subject matter jurisdiction, personal jurisdiction, and venue requirements are clearly satisfied, Reva wants to have the action dismissed. What is her best strategy? _____

173. Same facts as Problem 172. Rather than dismiss the federal action, Reva wants to take this opportunity to interplead Ida, Mary, and George, and let the three claimants bicker over who owns the diamond. Can Reva use interpleader to avoid multiple liabilities? Assuming *arguendo* that interpleader is available, can Reva bring it in Mary's federal action? If Reva instead brings the interpleader as a separate suit, where can the case be heard? _____

Answers

167. Under Fed. R. Civ. P. 20, multiple plaintiffs can join, and multiple defendants can be joined, provided the claims and liability are joint, several, or in the alternative, the claims arise from the same transaction or occurrence, and there is a common question of law or fact. Here plaintiffs sue severally and are suing defendants jointly. The claims arise from a single occurrence: the accident. The common question of law or fact is who is responsible for causing the accident.

However, before the case may proceed, it must also be established that the court has subject matter jurisdiction. The action involves no federal question. Diversity is the only option. Because Willard and Rosie are citizens of Kentucky, they are diverse from Lea. However, Ash Co. is a citizen of Kentucky. Because Willard and Rosie are also citizens of Kentucky, complete diversity is absent.

The only other option is supplemental jurisdiction (28 U.S.C. §1367). The claims against Ash and Lea do arise out of a common nucleus of operative fact. However, supplemental jurisdiction does not apply in this case because of the lack of complete diversity. In cases where jurisdiction is based solely on diversity, the lack of complete diversity means that the case does not qualify as a case over which the district courts have original jurisdiction under 28 U.S.C. §1367(a). Although Willard and Rosie may sue Lea Co., Ash Co. must be dismissed from the action.

168. Gail's best strategy is to argue Honest John's claim was a *compulsory counterclaim* in the first action. Fed. R. Civ. P. 13(a) requires a defendant to allege in its answer all claims arising from the same transaction or occurrence as plaintiff's original claim. Failure to bring a compulsory counterclaim means the claim is lost.

Whether Gail will succeed in her attempt depends on which of the two tests the court uses to determine same transaction. Under the same evidence test, the counterclaim is not compulsory because there is no overlap in evidence. John's counterclaim is based on the loan, while Gail's claim is based on the sale. The disputed elements are different and would involve the presentation of different evidence. Note that the facts specify that a violation of the lemon law *does not affect the underlying sales contract*.

However, if the majority logical relationship test is used, John's counterclaim is probably compulsory. Both claims arise from the same general "transaction" —the sales/financing "deal" that was made on a single day.

Note that even under the logical relationship test, not all of Honest John's claims will be barred. Fed. R. Civ. P. 13(a) requires him only to bring claims he had when he filed his answer. Therefore, he would lose only installments due on or before the date he filed his answer. He is free to sue for later-accruing payments.

169. The court will allow the counterclaim against Gary and will allow Jeff to join Heather to that counterclaim.

Gary: This claim is a counterclaim. Fed. R. Civ. P. 13(b) allows a defendant to bring any claim he might have against plaintiff, regardless of whether it relates in any way to plaintiff's original claim. Joinder accordingly is not a problem here.

Jurisdiction is also easily satisfied for Jeff's claim. Because Jeff and Gary are of diverse citizenship and the claim exceeds $75,000, diversity jurisdiction is satisfied.

Heather: Fed. R. Civ. P. 13(h) allows a defendant to join additional parties to an action by way of a counterclaim if Fed. R. Civ. P. 20 would have allowed defendant to sue plaintiff and the additional party as codefendants in a single action. Jeff clearly could have sued both Gary and Heather in a single case, and so Rule 13(h) is satisfied.

Again, diversity is present between Jeff and Heather and the amount in controversy is satisfied, so jurisdiction is no problem.

170. Bar None is correct. The copyright claim is not a proper impleader claim. By arguing that only Bar None is liable for infringing the copyright, Jeff has made an improper "him, not me" argument. Impleader is proper only when defendant claims that the third-party defendant must reimburse *defendant* for all or part of defendant's liability to plaintiff.

Because the copyright claim fails, Jeff cannot use Fed. R. Civ. P. 18 to join the antitrust claim. Nor does that claim qualify for joinder under Rule 14, as it has nothing to do with the claims against Jeff. Both claims should be severed from the main case.

171. Courtney may intervene as of right. The governing rule is Fed. R. Civ. P. 24(a). First, Courtney has a significantly protectable interest in the first production Catsplorer based upon her contract. Moreover, that interest is very likely to be impaired by Tommy's suit. If Tommy prevails, he gets the vehicle. Courtney may still recover damages for breach of contract, but that is less desirable to her than getting the vehicle itself.

True, if Courtney does not join the suit, she is not barred from suing for the vehicle itself. But if Tommy wins his suit, the *stare decisis* effect of his victory qualifies as impairment of Courtney's interest. *Stare decisis* is a sufficient impairment when the suit is a dispute over property, such as this one.

172. Reva's best strategy is to move to dismiss for failure to join a necessary party.

First, it is clear both Ida and George are parties who should be joined under Fed. R. Civ. P. 19(a). Each claims an interest in the diamond. That interest could well be impaired as a result of Mary's suit. In addition, if the court orders Reva to deliver the diamond to Mary, Reva could still be sued in separate actions by Ida and George, raising the threat of multiple liability for Reva.

Given that Ida and George are necessary, they must be joined if feasible. Their claims are in the alternative with Mary's, so they should be joined as involuntary plaintiffs pursuant to the provisions of Rule 19.

Personal jurisdiction is clearly no problem with Ida since she resides in the forum state. It also seems George was present in the state, so there may also be personal jurisdiction over him if he is still there and can be served.

Subject matter jurisdiction, however, is clearly a problem. Although George is diverse from Reva, Ida is not. And since Ida can only logically "fit" in the case as a plaintiff, she cannot be joined to the action without destroying complete diversity.

The analysis then turns to Rule 19(b). A judgment rendered in Ida's absence will significantly prejudice her and, as noted above, pose a threat to Reva. Second, there are no clear protective measures that can be used here. Third, a judgment without Ida is not really adequate because additional litigation may well be necessary. Finally, if the case is dismissed for nonjoinder, Mary would have an adequate remedy because she could sue in state court. All in all, a court should order the case dismissed because of the inability to join Ida.

173. Interpleader is certainly proper here. Legally, only one of the claimants can truly be entitled to the diamond. If the three sue Reva in separate actions, however, the courts could reach inconsistent results, holding her liable to two or all three of the claimants.

Reva can file her interpleader action as a counterclaim in Mary's suit. In the alternative, she can file a new action in interpleader as a plaintiff.

If Reva chooses to bring the claim in a federal court (either in Mary's suit or in a new action), however, she will need to use statutory rather than rule interpleader. Under rule interpleader, there would have to be complete diversity between Reva on the one hand and all the claimants on the other. As noted in Problem 172, Reva and Ida are not diverse.

Statutory interpleader (28 U.S.C. §1335), by contrast, requires only that at least one of the claimants be diverse from any other claimant. Therefore, Reva may easily bring her action in the federal court against all the parties because the three claimants are diverse from each other and the amount in controversy is met (statutory interpleader also lowers the amount in controversy requirement to $500, but that is not an issue here).

Personal jurisdiction is not an issue. In statutory interpleader, nationwide service of process to all the claimants is available under 28 U.S.C. §2361.

Finally, venue is easy to satisfy. For statutory interpleader, 28 U.S.C. §1397 states that venue is proper in any judicial district where one or more claimants reside. Therefore, venue could be in Idaho, Maryland, and Georgia because one claimant resides in each state.

Exam Tips on JOINDER

☞ **Terminology matters:** Joinder has a confusing terminology. Separate standards apply to cross-claims and counterclaims. Worse still, you have to learn the differences between the similar-sounding devices *impleader*, *interpleader*, and *intervention*. Mastering the terminology can help you avoid misreading the question and discussing a joinder device not mentioned in the problem.

☞ **Joinder and jurisdiction:** Joinder is intimately tied to subject matter jurisdiction. Therefore, it is quite common for a joinder question to deal both with the joinder rules and jurisdiction. But this is not always so. Therefore, read the question carefully. Does it involve both joinder and jurisdiction, or only one?

   ☞ If a problem does raise issues of both jurisdiction and joinder, make sure your answer addresses each as a separate issue. Although the tests can be similar (especially when supplemental jurisdiction is an issue), you need to demonstrate you recognize the two are discrete parts of the total problem.

☞ **Same transaction or occurrence test:** Many of the joinder rules turn on whether the additional claim arises from the "same transaction or occurrence" (STO) as some other claim. Be adept at applying this test.

☞ Remember that courts differ on the standard for determining whether claims arise from the STO. Most find claims to arise from the STO if there is a *logical relationship* between the claims, or they involve the *same evidence*.

☞ Unless the problem tells you which approach is used in the particular forum (or unless your professor tells you otherwise), analyze every STO issue using the two-part majority test.

☛ **Quirks in individual joinder rules:** Many of the joinder rules have their own particular "red flag" issues.

☞ **Joinder of *P*s and *D*s under Rule 20:** When applying this rule, don't forget there are *three parts* to the test. In addition to your STO discussion, point out whether the claims involve a common issue of law or fact and whether the claims or liability are joint, several, or in the alternative.

☞ **Impleader:** The biggest issue in impleader is whether the claim by the third-party plaintiff is really one in the nature of impleader. The third-party plaintiff *must* seek damages from the third-party defendant to *reimburse the third-party plaintiff* for damages it must pay the original plaintiff.

☞ Be on the lookout for the *"him, not me"* situation, where the third-party plaintiff is trying to avoid liability altogether. Impleader is not proper in this situation.

☞ **Intervention:** First, *do not forget permissive intervention*. If the party is merely seeking to intervene, make sure to discuss why the judge might be inclined merely to allow the third party into the case.

☞ If the problem involves intervention by right, recall that Fed. R. Civ. P. 24(a) requires a "significantly protectable" interest.

☞ **Interpleader:** There are *two types* of interpleader, *statutory* and *rule*. The main differences between the two relate to jurisdiction and venue.

☞ Make sure the case is a proper one for the use of interpleader.

☛ **Compulsory joinder:** In most cases, joinder is *optional, not mandatory*. However, there are two important exceptions to this basic principle.

☞ **Compulsory counterclaims:** Counterclaims that arise from the STO as the original claim must be brought or they are lost.

☞ **Hint:** If a test question presents a situation where a party has *already filed a counterclaim*, it really does not matter whether the counterclaim is compulsory. All counterclaims are permissive under Fed. R. Civ. P. 13(b). The real effect of concluding that something is a compulsory counterclaim arises *after the pleadings* if the party should try to file the omitted claim later in the case or in a new action.

☞ **Necessary parties:** Fed. R. Civ. P. 19 also allows a party to object to another party's failure to join someone to the case. Because Rule 19 is primarily a defense, do not discuss it when dealing with parties who are attempting on their own to join someone to a case. You should discuss Rule 19 only when someone has *moved to dismiss* the case because someone is missing or if the problem somehow hints that a party is looking for a way to dismiss the case.

☛ **Joinder and subject matter jurisdiction:** As discussed above, joinder and subject matter jurisdiction are separate issues, and you should discuss them separately in your answer. Nevertheless, there is a clear logical connection between some forms of joinder and the doctrine of supplemental jurisdiction.

☞ However, do not make your life any more difficult than it needs to be. Instead of jumping right into supplemental jurisdiction, *first consider whether diversity or federal question jurisdiction exists*. Only if neither of these is available (or if there is some doubt as to their availability) do you need to engage in the more complex supplemental jurisdiction analysis.

☞ If you do need to consider supplemental jurisdiction, your analysis will often dovetail in some ways with your discussion of joinder. Basically, the *same Article III case test used in §1367(a) is functionally equivalent to the STO analysis* used in the Federal Rules of Civil Procedure.

☞ However, avoid bald statements like "supplemental jurisdiction is available because this is a compulsory counterclaim." Such statements are not always true because they fail to consider 28 U.S.C. §1367(b) and (c). In addition, even if they are correct in the case, such statements are so conclusory that you may lose points for failing to analyze the issue sufficiently.

☞ Instead, you might consider something like, "As discussed above, this claim is a proper cross-claim under Fed. R. Civ. P. 13(g) because it arises out of the STO as plaintiff's claim. Because the Article III "same case or controversy" of 28 U.S.C. §1367(a) is for all intents and purposes the same as the STO analysis, this claim forms part of the same Article III case as plaintiff's federal claim. Therefore, §1367(a) is satisfied."

☛ **Personal jurisdiction:** If a party is joined to a case, the court must be able to exercise personal jurisdiction over that party. In addition to the normal personal jurisdiction analysis discussed in Chapter 2, recall there are two special rules that apply to joinder: the *100-mile bulge* rule of Fed. R. Civ. P. 4(k)(1)(B), which applies to impleader under Fed. R. Civ. P. 14 and to involuntary plaintiffs joined under Fed. R. Civ. P. 19, and the *nationwide service* available in *statutory interpleader* actions.

CHAPTER 15

CLASS ACTIONS

ChapterScope ─────────────────────────────

This chapter deals with class actions: cases where a representative litigates both her rights and the rights of others. Although the chapter focuses on the federal class action rules, many of the principles also apply in state court.

■ A class action is a proceeding in which the rights or duties of every member of the class are litigated by a class representative.

■ Because the *Due Process Clause* of the U.S. Constitution prevents government from taking away certain rights without notice and an opportunity to be heard, class actions present constitutional concerns. Nevertheless, the Supreme Court has held that a class action does not violate the Due Process Clause if certain safeguards are present.

■ *Fed. R. Civ. P. 23* is designed to deal with these constitutional concerns. The rule places a number of strict controls on class actions.

  ■ The trial court must *certify* the case as appropriate for class action treatment.

  ■ The court must determine that the case fits one of *three categories* of class actions.

  ■ Rule 23 has strict rules about who can be a representative and, in some cases, requires notice and a chance to opt out to be provided to the class members.

■ Class actions also present unique *personal jurisdiction* concerns. Provided representation is adequate, however, a court in a typical class action can adjudicate the rights of the absent members even if there are no minimum contacts between those members and the forum.

■ *Settlement* is another difficult issue in class actions. There is a risk of a conflict of interest if defendant offers to settle the case in a way that benefits the representative personally but not the class. To avoid this, Rule 23 places strict limitations on settlement.

■ Class actions are not the only example of a case where a representative litigates the rights of others. Two other situations covered by the Federal Rules of Civil Procedure are *shareholder derivative actions* and suits involving members of an *unincorporated association*.

─────────────────────────────

I. OVERVIEW OF THE CLASS ACTION

In a class action, one or more *representatives* litigate not only their personal rights but also the rights of others similarly situated. The class action device offers the promise of judicial economy but also creates unique problems.

A. Governing rule: *Fed. R. Civ. P. 23* governs class actions in the federal courts.

B. Judicial control: One of the unique features of class actions is the extent to which the court plays a role in overseeing the case.

1. **Need for judicial certification:** A case cannot proceed as a class action without judicial approval. Whether the suit will proceed as a class action is typically a hotly contested issue. If the court agrees to certify, defendant may well settle the substantive dispute.

2. **Need judicial approval to settle:** Once certified, a class action cannot be settled without the approval of the court.

C. **Variations:** The typical class action involves a *single class* of people who would otherwise be *plaintiffs*, with one or more representatives representing the class. However, variations on this theme are possible.

    1. **Defendant class:** It is also possible for a plaintiff to sue a defendant class if the members of that class all acted in the same way toward plaintiff. One of the defendants represents the class.

    2. **Subclasses:** At times, the interests of people, although similar, are different enough to preclude them from being members of a single class. In these situations, it may be possible to divide the group into subclasses. Each subclass is treated as a separate class and must be separately certified.

    3. **Class action limited to particular issues:** It is also possible for the court to certify a case as a class action only with respect to certain issues. For example, in a products liability case, a court could certify the case as a class action on the question of liability only. If the court determines the manufacturer is liable, the damages for each victim are litigated in separate, individual actions.

II. CONSTITUTIONAL CONCERNS WITH REPRESENTATIONAL LITIGATION

The key feature of a class action—that one party litigates the rights of others—raises significant constitutional concerns.

A. **Due process:** Class actions pose concerns under the Due Process Clauses of the Fifth and Fourteenth Amendments to the U.S. Constitution. These clauses prevent government from depriving a person of *liberty or property* without *due process of law*.

    1. **Liberty or property:** A judgment requiring a defendant to pay money to another person constitutes a deprivation of property. An order requiring defendant to perform an action, or to stop doing something, is a deprivation of liberty. Conversely, although perhaps not as obvious, a plaintiff's right to a remedy against another person (even a non-monetary remedy like an injunction) qualifies as property for purposes of due process.

    2. **Providing due process:** The constitutional requirement of due process of law has several different components. With regard to class actions, however, there are two important, but separate, parts of the due process requirement.

        a. First, due process usually requires the person who possesses the property to receive *notice* and an *opportunity to be heard* by a tribunal.

        b. Second, due process is the constitutional basis for the requirement of *personal jurisdiction*.

★ B. **Notice and opportunity to be heard:** Even though members of a class can lose property without the chance to protect themselves at a hearing, a properly conducted class action satisfies the requirements of due process. The Supreme Court's watershed opinion in Hansberry v. Lee, 311

U.S. 32 (1940), both validated the basic concept of a class action and defined when a class action is constitutionally acceptable.

1. **Facts of *Hansberry*:** *Hansberry* involved a racially restrictive covenant on property, in the days before the Court declared such covenants unenforceable. The covenant had a provision stating it was not valid unless 95 percent of the landowners in the affected area signed it. In truth, only 54 percent of the landowners had signed.

   a. **Earlier action:** Before the *Hansberry* case arose, the validity of the covenant had been litigated in another action, which we can call A v. B. Both *A* and *B* had signed the covenant.

      i. When landowner *B* tried to sell his property to another in violation of the covenant, landowner *A* sued both *B* and the buyers. *A* designated her suit as a class action, with *A* representing a class comprising all property owners who had signed the covenant.

      ii. Even though only 54 percent of the homeowners had signed the covenant, *A* and *B* stipulated that 95 percent of owners had signed.

      iii. The court in A v. B found for *A*, upholding the validity of the covenant.

   b. ***Hansberry* case:** After this judgment, a different owner tried to sell to the Hansberrys, again in violation of the covenant. Yet another owner, Lee, sued the Hansberrys and their seller in state court to enjoin the sale.

      i. Defendants argued the covenant was invalid by its own terms because the 95 percent requirement had not been met.

      ii. However, the state court held that the party selling to the Hansberrys was a member of the class in A v. B and accordingly was bound by the judgment in that case upholding the validity of the covenant.

2. **Supreme Court holding:** The Supreme Court disagreed with the state court and held that defendants were not bound by the ruling in A v. B. The Court held that defendants' right to ***due process*** would be violated if they were to be bound by a suit in which their interests were not really represented.

   a. **Lack of adequate representation bars class action:** The Court noted that although the class representative in A v. B ostensibly represented the Hansberrys' seller, such representation was not constitutionally adequate.

      i. *A*'s interest—which was to enforce the covenant—was at odds with the interests of the Hansberrys' seller and the Hansberrys—which was not to enforce the covenant.

      ii. If the interests of the members were not adequately represented, then it ***violated due process*** for the court to issue a judgment adjudicating their rights or obligations.

   b. **When class action proper:** On the other hand, the Court also made it clear that a class action could constitutionally adjudicate the rights of absent members provided there was ***adequate representation***. One key to adequate representation is the lack of any ***divergent interests*** like those in *Hansberry*. In essence, a proper class action involves a situation where the interests of the representative and the class members are so closely aligned that the representative, by looking out for his own best interests, automatically also looks out for the interests of the class members.

      Note: This reasoning suggests the parties in the original A v. B suit in *Hansberry* structured the class action in the wrong way. Instead of a class of plaintiffs suing a single defendant, plaintiff should have named a ***defendant class action*** comprising all people who signed the covenant but did not want it enforced.

★ **C. Personal jurisdiction:** The Supreme Court has also dealt with the issue of personal jurisdiction in class actions. In Phillips Petroleum v. Shutts, 472 U.S. 797 (1985), the Court held that in the typical class action, a forum can adjudicate the claims of the absent members even absent minimum contacts between the members and the forum.

     1. Facts: *Phillips* was a plaintiff class action in a Kansas state court in which a representative sued an oil company on behalf of a class of 33,000 people who claimed they were owed royalties by Phillips under oil well leases. Phillips argued that because in many cases neither the owner nor the oil well was in Kansas, there were no minimum contacts sufficient to allow Kansas to adjudicate the claims.

     Note: Although a party usually may not challenge a court's lack of jurisdiction over *other* parties, the Court allowed Phillips to assert the defense. After all, if Phillips were to prevail in the case, it would want the judgment to bind all members of the class. However, the judgment could bind the absent members only if the court had personal jurisdiction.

     2. Supreme Court holding: The Supreme Court held the Kansas court ***could exercise jurisdiction*** over the absent members of the class. Although due process usually requires minimum contacts, the Court held that ***certain protections afforded by the class action*** device served as a ***substitute*** for minimum contacts. The Court noted the following features of class actions:

         a. the lack of any ***burden on the member*** to travel; instead, the burden of litigating the claim would be borne entirely by the representative;

         b. the guarantee of ***adequate representation*** of the members' interests;

         c. the provisions in Fed. R. Civ. P. 23 guaranteeing the members ***notice*** and the opportunity to ***opt out of*** the class;

         d. because courts would rarely allow a defendant to file a counterclaim against members of the class, the class action would result in ***no money judgment against*** the members.

     3. Limits of holding: Broadly read, *Phillips* could make personal jurisdiction a nonissue in class actions. However, the Court's opinion contains several significant limitations.

         a. Defendant class action: *Phillips* was a plaintiff class action. In theory, the rationale could apply to cases where a plaintiff sues a class of defendants. On the other hand, members of a defendant class would be subject to a money judgment. The Court specifically refused to deal with this question, stating in footnote 3 of the opinion that the opinion did not address defendant class actions.

         b. Nondamages class actions: Nor did the Court express an opinion concerning other types of class actions, such as those seeking specific relief. Again in footnote 3, the Court suggested that the result in those cases could be different. This limitation is especially important because, as discussed below, ***Fed. R. Civ. P. 23 does not guarantee*** members of a 23(b)(1) or (b)(2) class either ***notice or the right to opt out***, two features of class actions that were important to the rationale of *Phillips*.

Quiz Yourself on
CONSTITUTIONAL ISSUES IN CLASS ACTIONS

174. Major League Baseball has developed a bad reputation over the past two decades, in no small part because of the lack of player loyalty to their teams. Fans have grown increasingly frustrated by the annual parade of players leaving their favorite teams for higher salaries in other cities. To combat this, all the players in Major League Baseball sign a contract in which each promises not to take another position without the approval of at least 70 percent of the other players.

Soon after the contract is signed, Antoneres announces he is taking a position with another team. Ballou, one of his teammates, immediately brings an action in a federal court in California for damages. Ballou manages to have the case certified as a plaintiff class action, with the class comprising all players in Major League Baseball. All the players are served with notice and given the chance to opt out of the class. A few weeks later, however, the judge dismisses the case for failure to state a claim, holding that the 70 percent approval requirement in the contract violates federal antitrust laws and is unenforceable.

After final judgment is entered, Couture announces that he too is leaving his team for greener pastures. Dexter, one of Couture's teammates, sues Couture to enforce the contract. Couture defends by arguing that because Dexter did not exercise his right to opt out of the class, the class action judgment bars Dexter from suing. Dexter counters by arguing that he cannot be bound by the prior judgment because his interests were not represented. How should the court rule? _____

175. Same facts as Problem 174, except that rather than argue his interests were not represented, Dexter argues the California judgment does not bind him because of lack of personal jurisdiction. Dexter points out he has no contacts whatsoever with California. How should the court rule? _____

Answers

174. Couture should prevail. Dexter is bound by the class action judgment because, unlike in *Hansberry*, his interests were represented. Dexter is a member of the plaintiff class. The interest of that class was to enforce the contract. Here, too, Dexter seeks enforcement. The only way Dexter would not be bound is if he can show that Ballou compromised the case or otherwise did a poor job representing the interests of those who wanted to enforce the contract.

175. Couture again prevails. According to *Phillips*, absent members of a plaintiff class need not have contacts with a state to be bound by the judgment in a class action litigated in that state. The facts here specify that the class members received notice and were afforded a chance to opt out. Because the protections afforded by Fed. R. Civ. P. 23 provide all the process that is due, minimum contacts are unnecessary.

III. REQUIREMENTS OF RULE 23

The constitutional limits established by *Hansberry* underlie many of the requirements of Fed. R. Civ. P. 23. Most of the rule's requirements try to ensure the class representative adequately represents the interests of the class members.

A. **Overview of Rule 23:** Fed. R. Civ. P. 23 requires the court to **certify** the case as a class action using standards. The certification decision should be made **at an early practicable** time after the motion to certify. Fed. R. Civ. P. 23(c)(1). In practice, the decision to certify can take months, or even years in a complex case.

   1. **Result if no certification:** Without certification, any judgment in the action will bind only the **named parties**.

   2. **Two-step process:** FRCP 23 establishes a two-step process for certification.

      a. **Appropriateness:** First, the court must determine whether the case is appropriate for a class action, applying the factors of Fed. R. Civ. P. 23(a).

      b. **Which category:** Second, if the case is appropriate, the court must determine if the case falls into any of the Fed. R. Civ. P. 23(b) categories. This categorization is crucial because the rule sets out different procedural requirements for different types of actions.

   3. **Appeal:** *Fed. R. Civ. P. 23(f)* gives the appellate court the discretion to hear an immediate appeal of a decision granting or denying class certification, provided application is made to the court of appeals within 14 days of entry of the order.

B. **Is dispute appropriate for class action?** *Fed. R. Civ. P. 23(a)* contains the standards for determining whether a given dispute is appropriate for use of the class action device. The rule sets out four basic requirements: **numerosity, commonality, typicality,** and **adequacy.**

   1. **Numerosity:** *Fed. R. Civ. P. 23(a)(1)* requires that the class be "so numerous that joinder of all members is impracticable." Because of the complicated procedural requirements for class actions, the device makes sense only if the dispute involves enough class members to allow for economies of scale.

      a. There is **no fixed number** that will meet this requirement in every case. The minimum number turns on the particular features of the case. One key feature is the **amount of each claim**. If the claims are large, either individual suits or ordinary joinder is more likely to be workable because each party has an incentive to litigate her own rights. Another factor is how **widely dispersed** the members are.

      b. A few courts have allowed class actions with as few as 30 class members. However, in most cases, the threshold is significantly higher.

   2. **Commonality:** *Fed. R. Civ. P. 23(a)(2)* allows a class action to be certified only if "there are questions of law or fact common to the class." This notion of commonality defines the boundaries of the class.

      a. The commonality can concern **either law or fact**. Thus, unlike many other forms of joinder, the claims involved in a class action need not arise from the same transaction or occurrence.

      b. Commonality does not mean that all, or even most, questions of law and/or fact are common to the claims. However, if there are significant differences between the individual claims, a class action will not prove efficient because the court will have to spend too much time dealing with the individual issues.

      ★ **Example:** In Wal-Mart Stores, Inc. v. Dukes, 131 S. Ct. 2541 (2011), the Supreme Court overturned the lower court's certification of a massive class action brought by over a million female employees against the national retailer Wal-Mart. The class included women in all levels of employment. The Court held that the commonality requirement would be satisfied only if class members could demonstrate the same type of harm. Because there was no evidence the company had an overall policy of discrimination that applied to all women, only evidence of individual acts of discrimination, the commonality requirement was not satisfied.

3. **Typicality:** *Fed. R. Civ. P. 23(a)(3)* mandates that "the claims or defenses of the representative parties are typical of the claims or defenses of the class." Typicality turns on several factors, including the size of the claim, the legal source of the claim, and whether the representatives or members are subject to any defenses. Most courts find the requirement satisfied unless there is a major difference between the representatives' and members' claims.

4. **Adequacy:** *Fed. R. Civ. P. 23(a)(4)* requires that "the representative parties will fairly and adequately protect the interests of the class."

   a. **Policy:** This requirement attempts to deal with the constitutional problems identified in *Hansberry*. However, there is a significant overlap between the adequacy and typicality requirements.

   b. **Determining adequacy:** Courts consider several factors when determining adequacy of representation.

      i. **Parallel interests:** The interests of the representative must align closely with those of the class. If there is any sort of *conflict of interest*, actual or potential, representation may not be adequate.

      ii. **Counsel for the representative:** Another factor courts closely scrutinize is the competence of the attorneys for the representative. Although this is not always possible, courts prefer that counsel be both competent in the subject matter of the litigation and have experience dealing with class actions.

      iii. **Financial considerations:** Because a class action is a complicated case that can take years to complete, the court also considers the representative's ability to *fund the litigation*.

C. **Which category of class action?** If Fed. R. Civ. P. 23(a) is satisfied, the court applies *Fed. R. Civ. P. 23(b)* to determine whether the case fits into one of the *three acceptable categories* of class actions. If the case does not fit into any of the categories, the case cannot be certified as a class action.

   1. **Rule 23(b)(1)—numerous necessary parties:** The first category of class action covers situations where there are many absent parties, each of whom, generally speaking, meets the test for a "necessary party" under Fed. R. Civ. P. 19(a). The rule allows a class action when *individual actions* involving the class members pose a risk of either:

      a. *inconsistent or varying outcomes* with respect to the individual members that would expose the *party opposing the class to incompatible standards of conduct* (Fed. R. Civ. P. 23(b)(1)(A)), or

      b. results that as a practical matter would *dispose of the interests of the other members, or impair or impede their ability to protect* those interests (Fed. R. Civ. P. 23(b)(1)(B)).

      Example 1: *D* manufactures automobiles. A number of drivers are injured when the airbags in their automobiles deploy prematurely. One driver sues *D* for damages. *D* moves to certify the case as a class action, with the driver representing the class members. *D* argues that because it is unclear whether the airbag was defective, *D* faces inconsistent outcomes if the various injured parties are allowed to bring individual suits. The court will not certify the case under Fed. R. Civ. P. 23(b)(1). Although individual suits may result in inconsistent outcomes, those outcomes do not result in inconsistent standards of conduct. *D* can simply pay any plaintiffs who win and not pay those who lose. (*Note:* This case might be certified under Rule 23(b)(3), which is discussed below.)

Example 2: Same as the preceding example, except the driver sues *D*'s insurance carrier. The insurance policy has a limit of $1 million. Driver moves to have the case certified as a class action. Driver has proof that hundreds of people have been injured by the airbags in *D*'s cars and that those people have claims well in excess of $5 million. The class action meets the requirements of both Fed. R. Civ. P. 23(b)(1)(A) and (B). Under (b)(1)(A), plaintiffs might all prevail in their separate lawsuits, resulting in total judgments above the policy limit. Under (b)(1)(B), plaintiffs who obtain their judgments first might exhaust the policy, leaving later claimants with nothing from which to recover.

2. **Rule 23(b)(2)—injunctive or declaratory relief:** Fed. R. Civ. P. 23(b)(2) applies when "the party opposing the class has acted or refused to act on grounds that apply generally to the class, so that final injunctive relief or corresponding declaratory relief is appropriate respecting the class as a whole."

   Example: A city routinely captures unleashed dogs without providing notice and a hearing to the owners. A dog owner sues the city, claiming the practice violates due process. The owner sues for an injunction requiring the city to afford notice and a hearing before capturing a stray dog whose owner is known to the city. The case is proper for certification of a (b)(2) class comprising all dog owners in the city.

★ **Note:** Nothing in Fed. R. Civ. P. 23(b)(2) requires that the injunctive or declatory relief be the *only* remedy sought by the class. However, in Wal-Mart Stores, Inc. v. Dukes, 131 S. Ct. 2541 (2011), the Court held that certification under Rule 23(b)(2) is not available where the class members seek individualized monetary relief, even if they also seek an injunction. Rule 23(b)(2) certification may still be available in cases where nonindividualized, class-wide monetary relief is sought in addition to an injunction.

3. **Rule 23(b)(3)—the "damages" class action:** The (b)(1) and (2) class actions apply only in certain relatively narrow and clearly defined situations. The Rule 23(b)(3) class action, by contrast, is designed to deal with situations where class actions might still be appropriate but where the ***claims are not as intertwined*** as in the other two cases. Because the relationship between the various members is somewhat looser, Fed. R. Civ. P. 23 imposes additional restrictions on the Rule 23(b)(3) class action.

   a. **Basic standard:** A Rule 23(b)(3) class action is appropriate when:

      i. the ***common questions of law or fact predominate*** over questions affecting only individual members of the class, and

      ii. a ***class action is superior*** to either individual actions or a combined suit using other joinder devices for fairly and efficiently resolving the underlying controversy.

   b. **Determining superiority:** The rule also specifies the factors to be considered in determining whether a class action is the optimal method.

    i. The first factor is the extent to which the ***individual members*** have an ***interest*** in controlling the prosecution or defense of their own actions. Fed. R. Civ. P. 23(b)(3)(A). An individual member is more likely to litigate her own case if the amount at stake is large or if her claim or defense has advantages that are not present in the claims or defenses of other members of the class.

    ii. The second factor is whether ***litigation*** involving claims by or against members of the class is ***already pending***. Fed. R. Civ. P. 23(b)(3)(B).

    iii. The third factor is whether the chosen forum is a ***desirable place*** to concentrate litigation of the various claims. This factor focuses primarily on practical issues that may arise, such as the ease of discovery, availability of witnesses, and personal jurisdiction.

    iv. The fourth factor is other difficulties that may arise in ***managing the class action***.

  c. **Application of the standard:** The certification decision in every Rule 23(b)(3) class action depends on the idiosyncratic features of the particular case. However, there are a few themes that commonly arise in these cases.

    i. **Damages:** In ***personal injury*** and ***misrepresentation/fraud*** cases, the damages suffered by each member of the class may differ significantly. If there is a wide discrepancy, the individualized issues of damages may outweigh the common issues in the cases and thereby prevent certification.

    ii. **Defenses:** In many cases, defendant may have defenses to the claims of some class members. For example, some members may have signed waivers of liability or waited so long to bring their claims that they may be precluded by the statute of limitations. These individualized issues may prevent certification of the case as a Rule 23(b)(3) class action.

    iii. **Choice of law:** Class actions often involve members scattered across the country or in different nations. Depending on the circumstances, claims by or against these scattered parties may be governed by different substantive laws. Similarly, different states may recognize different defenses. Differences in governing law often preclude certification of a Rule 23(b)(3) class action because the individual issues of law are likely to predominate over the common issues.

    Example: A representative moves to certify a Rule 23(b)(3) class action comprising every person hurt by a drug produced by *D*. The victims purchased and used the product in dozens of different states. Certification is unlikely because different state laws are likely to apply in determining whether *D* is liable.

D. **Procedure after certification:** If the judge certifies the case as a class action, Fed. R. Civ. P. 23 imposes additional procedural requirements, which differ depending upon which Rule 23(b)(3) category of class action applies.

  1. **Notice and opt-out:** In *Fed. R. Civ. P. 23(b)(3)* class actions, the class representative(s) must give notice to all members of the class and afford those members the right to opt out of the class action.

    a. **Notice:** Rule 23(c) requires individual notice to ***all class members***. If a member cannot be found, the court ordinarily excludes the member from the class, and the judgment will not bind that person. In this regard, the notice requirements of Rule 23 go beyond the minimum requirements of due process.

        i. The notice must specify that:

           (a) the court will exclude from the class any member who requests exclusion by the date indicated in the notice;

           (b) if a member does not request exclusion, he will be bound by the judgment, regardless of whether the judgment is in his favor; and

           (c) a member who does not ask to be excluded may enter an individual appearance through counsel.

        ii. The requirement of individual notice to all members ***cannot be ignored or modified***. Notice by publication, for example, is not acceptable. Eisen v. Carlisle & Jacquelin, 417 U.S. 156 (1974).

        iii. Cost: The ***representative must bear the cost*** of notice. *Eisen.* In addition, the representative must bear the burden of ascertaining the identity of the class members. Oppenheimer Fund, Inc. v. Sanders, 437 U.S. 340 (1978).

    b. Opt-out: As indicated above, the notice must indicate that the member may request exclusion from the class. A member who so requests is said to opt out of the class action. In most cases, the class action notice includes a form the recipient can use to request exclusion from the class.

    c. Notice and opt-out in other categories: On its face, Rule 23(c)(2) requires notice and the right to opt out ***only in Rule 23(b)(3) class actions***. They are ***not required by Rule 23 in (b)(1) and (b)(2) actions***.

        i. Nevertheless, on occasion courts *do* require notice in (b)(1) and (b)(2) actions. Fed. R. Civ. P. 23(c)(2)(A) and 23(d)(1)(B) give a court the authority to require notice even in (b)(1) and (b)(2) actions.

        ii. However, courts ***rarely*** give members the right to opt out of Rule 23(b)(1) and (b)(2) actions. This tendency reflects the nature of those types of class actions.

           (a) In a Fed. R. Civ. P. 23(b)(1) class action, the members, for all practical purposes, are ***necessary parties***. If their presence in the action is needed to prevent prejudice to their interests or the interests of the litigants, it is counterintuitive to allow opt out.

           (b) A Fed. R. Civ. P. 23(b)(2) class action seeks injunctive or declaratory relief. If such relief is granted, as a practical matter it benefits the class members regardless of whether they are parties to the action. Therefore, it makes little sense to allow them to opt out of the action.

  2. Additional procedures: *Fed. R. Civ. P. 23(d)* allows the judge in a class action to issue any additional orders she deems necessary.

E. Settlement of class action: Settlement presents a special problem in class actions. If the party opposing the class can strike a favorable personal deal with the representative, the representative might settle the case even though settlement is not in the best interests of the class as a whole. Because of this risk, ***Fed. R. Civ. P. 23(e)*** places significant restrictions on settlement of a class action.

  1. Notice: Notice of any proposed settlement must be provided to all members of the class to allow them to challenge the proposed settlement. Unlike the notice required for class certification, notice of a proposed settlement must be provided ***in all categories of class actions***.

2. **Court approval:** No settlement is effective without court approval. This is a ***unique feature of class actions*** since courts do not approve settlements in other cases. In determining whether to approve a settlement, the court must ensure it is fair for all members of the class. The court also carefully scrutinizes the allocation of ***attorneys' fees*** in the settlement agreement.

3. **The "settlement class action":** At times, attorneys attempt to certify a class solely for the purposes of forcing settlement. Such cases often involve mass torts, and the class may comprise thousands of members. The attempt to certify may be made *after* an individual plaintiff or group of plaintiffs has negotiated a settlement with defendant. Defendant favors certification of a class as a way to resolve the dispute once and for all.

★   a. *Amchem*: The Supreme Court, however, significantly limited the use of settlement class actions in Amchem Products, Inc. v. Windsor, 521 U.S. 591 (1997). *Amchem* held that in a settlement class action where the class was defined as everyone who had ever been exposed to asbestos—regardless of whether any disease had yet manifested itself—it would be impossible to achieve adequate representation.

    b. *Amchem* does not completely prevent the use of settlement class actions. Indeed, the Court explicitly recognized that the fact that a settlement had been previously negotiated is a positive factor in the certification decision. As long as the claims are sufficiently similar that typicality and adequate representation are met, a settlement class action is still possible.

F. **Judgment in class action:** The judgment in a class action must identify the members of the class. Such identification is necessary to determine who is bound by the judgment. In a ***Fed. R. Civ. P. 23(b)(1) or (b)(2)*** case, the judgment should name every person who is a member of the class. In a ***Fed. R. Civ. P. 23(b)(3)*** case, the judgment should include only those members who ***received notice*** and ***did not opt out***.

Quiz Yourself on APPLICATION OF RULE 23

176. Peter Plaintiff is seriously injured by a food processor. Peter sues Kit's Kitchenwares, the manufacturer of the food processor, for damages. Peter argues Kit's was negligent in failing to put a warning label on the food processor. In addition to damages, Peter wants an order requiring Kit's to recall the food processors and add a warning label.

   Kit's and Peter seek to have the case certified as a class action, with the class comprising everyone who has been injured by this model of food processor. Peter will serve as representative. Kit's joins in the request for certification because it has already won four individual cases in which plaintiffs argued lack of a warning label was negligence. Therefore, Kit's wants to know whether such labels are required so it can decide how to act in the future. The 2,000 people who have been injured by the food processor live all across the country, and each purchased the product in his or her home state. Which Fed. R. Civ. P. 23(b) category of class action best fits this situation? _____

177. Same facts as Problem 176. The people who have been injured by the food processor work in a variety of occupations, from computer operators to law professors to concert pianists. However, all the victims bought the product from the same national retailer. All suffered injuries to their hands in operating the food processor, but the injuries vary significantly. Peter's injury is fairly typical. Peter provides voiceovers for radio commercials.

Is the proposed class likely to satisfy the Rule 23(a) requirements for a class action? _____

178. Same facts as Problems 176 and 177, except assume the court certifies a Rule 23(b)(3) class action. Notice is provided to all members, and 70 opt out of the case. Judgment is entered for Kit's in the class action. Shortly thereafter, one of the people who opted out brings her own individual suit against Kit's. Kit's argues that plaintiff is barred by the judgment in the class action from bringing an individual suit. How should the court rule? _____

Answers

176. This most likely is a Rule 23(b)(3) class action. Although Peter seeks a form of injunctive relief (the recall order), that relief is merely incidental to the individualized damages request. Rule 23(b)(2) is therefore inappropriate.

The situation also resembles the Rule 23(b)(1) situation in that Kit's is unsure how to act in the future. However, there is no risk of an inconsistent standard of behavior. Kit's may not know whether a label is required. On the other hand, nothing legally prevents Kit's from adding the label. Providing "too much" warning will not expose Kit's to liability.

Therefore, only Rule 23(b)(3) is an option. Note the case may not fit even this category. On the surface, the common questions of law and fact would seem to predominate—namely, the question of whether failure to have a warning label is a defect. However, because the victims live all over the country, their claims likely are governed by different laws. Although the issue of whether lack of a label is a defect arises in all the claims, the governing legal standard could be different.

Finally, if the other members of the class also suffered serious injury, a class action might not be the best way to resolve this dispute. Each of the members might have a sufficient incentive to sue on his or her own behalf.

177. The judge is unlikely to certify this case as a class action. Numerosity is met because there are 2,000 potential class members. Commonality, however, presents an issue. Because the victims are located all across the country and purchased their products in their home state, different laws may govern the various claims.

Another problem here is the disparity among plaintiffs, presenting problems with typicality and adequacy. First, the injuries suffered by the class members differ widely, even though all involve their hands. Second, the *consequences* of such injuries also differ. Damages for a hand injury are, other things equal, likely to be far greater for a computer operator or concert pianist than for a law professor. Moreover, because Peter, the class representative, does radio voiceovers, the injury to his hand might not be as devastating. As a result, his claim is not typical.

One option might be to certify the case as a Rule 23(b)(3) class for purposes of determining liability only, leaving it to individual cases to prove damages. This limited approach could solve the typicality and adequacy problems. On the other hand, with the difference in governing laws, commonality still remains a problem.

178. The suit is not barred. Although Rule 23 does not specifically say so, a party who opts out is not bound by the class action judgment.

IV. OTHER ISSUES IN CLASS ACTIONS

Class actions present a number of other unique problems.

A. Subject matter jurisdiction in federal court: Like other cases, a class action can be heard in federal court only if it involves a federal question, meets the requirements for diversity, or qualifies for supplemental jurisdiction.

  1. Federal question: Many class actions are brought under federal statutes such as securities or civil rights laws. Determining whether the claims involved "arise under" federal law involves the same considerations in class actions as in any other case.

  2. Diversity: Diversity jurisdiction has proven much more problematic. Supreme Court interpretations of 28 U.S.C. §1332 (the diversity statute) affect how one files a class action based on state law in federal court.

   a. Citizenship: In determining the citizenship of the class, courts consider *only the class representatives*. The citizenship of the absent members is ignored. Supreme Tribe of Ben-Hur v. Cauble, 255 U.S. 356 (1921).

   b. Amount in controversy: However, *every member of the class* must independently meet the amount in controversy to satisfy §1332. Zahn v. International Paper Co., 414 U.S. 291 (1973). Claims of the members cannot be aggregated to satisfy the requirement. Snyder v. Harris, 394 U.S. 332 (1969).

   c. "Mass" class actions. 28 U.S.C. §1332(d) is a special diversity provision applicable to class actions involving a total amount in controversy in excess of $5,000,000. The provision allows for jurisdiction regardless of the amount of any member's claim, and even if there is a lack of complete diversity. However, the provision contains numerous exceptions and limitations.

★   **i.** *Standard Fire*: In Standard Fire Insurance Co. v. Knowles, 133 S. Ct. 1345 (2012), the Court held a class representative could not prevent federal jurisdiction under §1332(d) by stipulating that the class would not seek total recovery in excess of $5,000,000.

  3. Supplemental jurisdiction: *28 U.S.C. §1367* also may prove useful in a federal class action relying on diversity jurisdiction.

   a. When supplemental jurisdiction might apply: In theory, the doctrine of supplemental jurisdiction proves useful when some of the members' claims independently qualify for federal subject matter jurisdiction, while others do not. If the claims arise from a *common nucleus of operative fact*, the basic requirements of §1367(a) are satisfied. See Chapter 4.

   b. Supplemental jurisdiction may apply in diversity cases when some of the claims meet the amount in controversy and others do not.

★   **i.** *Exxon Mobil*: Exxon Mobil Corp. v. Allapattah Servs., Inc., 545 U.S. 546 (2005), upheld the use of supplemental jurisdiction in a class action where not all the members' claims met the amount in controversy requirement.

     ii. Inapplicability of §1367(b): As discussed in Chapter 4, Part V, §1367(b) bars most claims by plaintiffs in cases where jurisdiction is based solely on diversity. However, it does not bar all claims. Instead, it bars only claims by plaintiffs against parties joined *under certain listed rules*. Rule 23 is not one of the rules listed in §1367(b).

    c. Caveat: Section 1367(a) makes it clear that supplemental jurisdiction is not available if the claims do not arise from a ***common nucleus of operative fact***. Not all class action claims will satisfy this requirement. The commonality requirement in Rule 23(a) merely requires that the claims share ***common questions of law or fact***. If claims share an issue of law but do not arise from the same event or series of events, they do not qualify for supplemental jurisdiction.

B. Attorneys' fees: Attorneys' fees are an important consideration in class actions. Because of the procedural complexity and sheer size of a class action, the attorneys' fees are likely to be quite large.

    1. Paid from fund: If the class action results in a cash settlement or money judgment for the class, the attorneys' fees are paid out of the fund. It is not uncommon for the fees to exhaust the lion's share of the amount recovered, leaving little for the members of the class.

    2. Court approval: The requirement of court approval for class action settlements gives the court considerable control over the fee. If the court determines the attorneys charged more than a reasonable amount, it will not approve the settlement.

V. OTHER EXAMPLES OF REPRESENTATIONAL LITIGATION

Class actions are not the only form of representational litigation. ***Fed. R. Civ. P. 23.1 and 23.2*** authorize federal courts to hear shareholder derivative actions and actions involving unincorporated associations.

A. Shareholder derivative actions: A shareholders' derivative action is usually brought against the ***officers and/or directors of a corporation***. It seeks compensation for harm caused to the corporation by the officers and directors.

    1. Corporation as plaintiff: In theory, because the harm is suffered by the corporation, the action should be brought by the corporation itself.

    2. Not through officers or directors: However, a corporation acts through its officers and directors—who are unlikely to sue themselves.

    3. Stockholder sues instead: To resolve this dilemma, the shareholders' derivative action allows a person who ***owns stock*** in the corporation to sue the officers and/or directors on behalf of the corporation. Rule 23.1 allows federal courts to hear these cases, provided the requirements for jurisdiction are satisfied.

    4. Action by member of unincorporated association: Rule 23.1 also allows an action *by* a member of an unincorporated association against the association's officers or directors, which is conceptually similar to a shareholders' derivative action.

    5. Requirements of Rule 23.1: Rule 23.1 places several restrictions on shareholders' derivative actions and actions by members of unincorporated associations. The ***complaint*** in the action must be ***verified*** and must make certain specific allegations. In addition, plaintiff must ***fairly and adequately represent*** the interests of similarly situated shareholders or members. Finally, the rule requires ***court approval*** for dismissal or settlement.

B. **Unincorporated associations:** In most cases, suits by or against unincorporated associations (clubs and other groups) must be filed by or against all members of that association. However, *Fed. R. Civ. P. 23.2* allows suits involving these organizations to take a form similar to class actions.

> **Note:** Suits involving unincorporated associations under Fed. R. Civ. P. 23.2 differ from those under Rule 23.1. In the case of Rule 23.1, the suit is *against the association's officers or directors*. In Rule 23.2, by contrast, the *association is suing or being sued by* a third party.

1. **One or more representative parties:** The rule allows a suit by an unincorporated association to be brought by one or more representative parties. Similarly, a party suing the association may sue one or more representatives.

2. **Fairly and adequately protect interests:** However, Rule 23.2 allows the representative suit only if the court finds the representatives will fairly and adequately protect the interests of both the association and its members.

3. **Other protections:** Rule 23.2 also adopts protections from class action procedure. For example, *settlement* must meet the standards of Fed. R. Civ. P. 23(e), including the requirement of *court approval*.

Quiz Yourself on CLASS ACTIONS

179. Poppy sues Drugco, a major pharmaceutical company, in federal district court. Poppy seeks to recover damages for a serious allergic reaction she suffered when taking one of Drugco's products. Poppy wants to have the case certified as a class action, with a class comprising all people who suffered the same allergic reaction. Poppy, who would be the class representative, is a citizen of a different state than Drugco, and her claim is well in excess of $75,000. However, a number of members of the class cannot bring individual diversity actions against Drugco, either because they are from the same state or because their injuries involve damages of less than $75,000. Assuming the case can be certified as a class action, does the federal court have subject matter jurisdiction over the entire action? _____

180. Same facts as Problem 179, except assume the court certifies the case as a Fed. R. Civ. P. 23(b)(3) class action. Notice and a chance to opt out are given to all the class members. A few months later, Poppy receives what she feels is an excellent settlement offer from Drugco. The trial judge agrees and is willing to approve the settlement. Is Poppy free to go ahead and settle the case? _____

181. John "Jack" Russell absolutely loves the breed of small terrier that shares his name. A rich and somewhat eccentric man, Jack decides not to leave any of his vast estate to his relatives. Instead, his will specifies his money is to be divided equally among "everyone who owns a purebred Jack Russell terrier on the date of my death."

   After Jack dies, Ed Executor, the executor of Jack's estate, finds himself in an intractable situation. Thousands of people have written to Ed claiming a share of the estate. However, it is difficult for Ed to determine whether the claims are valid and whether there are others out there who have not asked for a share of the money. To solve this problem, Ed brings a class action in a North Carolina state court. He names four of the claimants as the representatives of a defendant class. The judge certifies the class under the appropriate Rule 23(b) category, concluding that to allow each of the owners to sue Ed separately would present a risk of multiple liability to Ed, as well as imperil the interests of the other owners. After a long and difficult trial, in which the parties diligently seek to find all of the people entitled to funds, the court enters a judgment and the estate is distributed.

After the case is complete, Russell Jackson sues Ed. Russell claims he is entitled to a share of the estate. Although the court did consider Russell's claim in the class action proceeding, it eventually determined Russell did not buy his dog until after Jack had died. Therefore, Russell received nothing. Russell nevertheless claims he is not bound by the class action judgment. First, he points out he received no notice of the case. Second, he correctly notes that he has no contacts whatsoever with North Carolina. Because of these issues, Russell claims, it violates his due process rights if the judgment binds him.

Is Russell free to seek additional funds? _____

182. The Wolf Network (TWN) is a major player on the national broadcasting scene. TWN takes an unapologetically arch-conservative viewpoint. Much of its so-called news is spent bashing politicians whose views do not comport with those of TWN's staff. In addition, TWN refuses to air campaign advertisements from politicians who do not have TWN's arch-conservative views. Many politicians complain to the Federal Communications Commission, to no avail.

One of the politicians takes a different course. He sues TWN in state court, seeking an injunction requiring TWN to accept and air the campaign ads of all politicians willing to pay TWN's fees. The politician seeks to have the case certified as a class action, with a class comprising all politicians who will be running for office in the future and would like to advertise on TWN, but are likely to have their ads rejected because of their views. As described, this class includes thousands of members who will be running for national, state, and local offices on different dates. The case nevertheless satisfies the requirements of Rule 23(a). Will the court certify it as a class action? _____

Answers

179. The federal court probably does have jurisdiction. The citizenship issue is not a problem. When applying 28 U.S.C. §1332 to class action cases, the court considers only the citizenship of the named representative. Because Poppy is diverse, this requirement is met.

The amount in controversy presents a more serious problem. Under 28 U.S.C. §1332, *all* class members must have claims in excess of $75,000. However, because of *Exxon Mobil*, supplemental jurisdiction may be available. Provided all the claims arise from a common nucleus—which is probably the case, as all the claims involve the composition of the drug—§1367(a) is satisfied. And §1367(b) does not bar the claims because Fed. R. Civ. P. 23 is not among the rules listed in that provision.

180. Before settling the case, Poppy needs to give notice to all the class members. Fed. R. Civ. P. 23(e). Notice is provided in the manner dictated by the court. If Poppy does not give notice, a member might not be bound by the settlement.

181. Russell's suit probably is barred, but the precedent is not entirely clear. His claim of lack of notice probably will fail. The case as described was certified as a Rule 23(b)(1) class action. The reasons given by the trial judge describe the Rule 23(b)(1) necessary party class. Class members in a Rule 23(b)(1) case are not entitled to notice. Although *Phillips* casts some doubt as to whether this is constitutional, lower courts typically have followed the rule and not ordered notice.

The lack of contacts argument stands a stronger chance of succeeding. *Phillips* is again the most important case. That case held the protections afforded by the class action device satisfied due process, and, as a result, minimum contacts between the absent class members and the forum were not required. However, *Phillips* was a Rule 23(b)(3) plaintiff class action, and the Court explicitly limited its holding to plaintiff class actions. In most respects, there is no appreciable difference between a plaintiff and defendant class action. Nevertheless, because the *Phillips* Court did not decide the issue, the rule of that case may not apply, and minimum contacts could be necessary.

182. The court should certify this as a Rule 23(b)(2) class action. TWN has acted the same way toward everyone in the class. An injunction would remedy the claims of everyone in the class. The disparity in the claims is not a factor under Rule 23(b)(2).

Note that unless federal law governs the claims, the case might not satisfy the commonality requirement of Rule 23(a). However, the facts state that Rule 23(a) is satisfied.

Exam Tips on
CLASS ACTIONS

☛ Do not overlook the serious constitutional concerns surrounding the class action device. Understanding these core concerns helps you understand the many technical provisions in Fed. R. Civ. P. 23.

☛ With respect to personal jurisdiction, do not forget that the holding in the *Phillips* case is explicitly limited to plaintiff class actions under Fed. R. Civ. P. 23(b)(3) in which the class seeks damages. Although the rationale might seem to apply to other class actions, the precedent is not clear.

☛ When dealing with the question of certification, be sure to treat the Fed. R. Civ. P. 23(a) and 23(b) analyses as two separate steps.

☛ When dealing with Rule 23(a), the following hints may prove helpful.

    ☞ Commonality may be destroyed when the claims arise under state law and the parties are from different states. In these situations, different laws may govern the different claims.

    ☞ Typicality and adequacy are interrelated to some extent. A case will present a typicality or adequacy problem when the representative's claim is different in kind from those of the members or significantly different in degree.

☛ When dealing with Rule 23(b), remember that some situations do not fit any of the three categories and accordingly may not be brought as a class action.

    ☞ Although Fed. R. Civ. P. 23(b)(3) is a catchall category, it applies only when the common questions *predominate*.

☛ As a general matter, be very sure of yourself before concluding that a class action is proper in the following cases:

    ☞ mass tort cases involving serious injuries (because the parties have the incentive to bring individual cases), and

    ☞ cases where parties scattered across the nation would be bringing state law claims (because of choice-of-law problems).

☛ Recall that notice and opt-out are required only in Rule 23(b)(3) cases.

    ☞ On the other hand, Rule 23(e) requires an additional notice should there be a proposed settlement. This additional notice must be provided in all cases.

☛ Recall that subject matter jurisdiction presents special concerns in the class action context. One of the special considerations is that as long as some of the members' claims meet the amount in controversy requirements for diversity, supplemental jurisdiction may be available for the other claims.

Essay Exam Questions

QUESTION 1 (Suggested time: 75 minutes): In 2014, Axel Griess, a citizen of Germany, left his homeland and moved to Eau Claire, Wisconsin. A mechanic by trade, Axel set up a small automobile repair shop in Eau Claire. This operation has developed into a thriving business. Although he has not yet acquired U.S. citizenship, Axel enjoys Wisconsin and fully intends to remain there for many years.

While driving through Eau Claire one day, Carol, a citizen of the state of South Dakota, discovers that her automobile is having brake problems. Carol stops in Axel's shop for repairs. Axel notices her South Dakota license plates and strikes up a lively conversation with Carol about South Dakota as he fixes the brakes.

Carol thinks her brake problems are solved, and she pays Axel in cash. However, when she returns to South Dakota, her brakes fail, and she is seriously injured. Carol sues Axel in a federal court in South Dakota, seeking $300,000 in damages. Carol asks Axel to waive service, and he agrees. But Axel then moves like greased lightning, filing a pre-answer motion to dismiss for *forum non conveniens* the day after he receives the request for waiver of service. After considering the matter for three full weeks, the judge denies that motion.

Two days after the judge's decision on his motion, Axel files and serves an answer. In addition to denying liability on the merits, Axel's answer argues that the chosen court lacks both subject matter and personal jurisdiction. Carol counters with several arguments. First, she argues that Axel filed his answer well after the deadline. Second, she argues that even if the answer was timely filed, Axel waived his subject matter and personal jurisdiction defenses by failing to include them in his pre-answer motion. Third, Carol argues that even if the defenses were not waived, the court has both subject matter and personal jurisdiction.

You are a clerk for the federal district judge assigned to hear this case. Your judge wants you to write her a short memorandum addressing the following issues:

1. Did the judge err in denying Axel's pre-answer motion?

2. Was Axel's answer filed too late?

3. Did Axel waive the personal and subject matter jurisdiction defenses by failing to include them in his pre-answer motion?

4. Assuming (without affecting your answer to issue 3) that the jurisdictional defenses were raised in timely fashion, how should the judge rule on the merits?

Discuss each issue separately.

QUESTION 2 (Suggested time: 30 minutes): Same basic facts as Question 1. Assume (without affecting your answer to that question) the court finds it has subject matter jurisdiction over the case and personal jurisdiction over Axel. Axel files a timely third-party complaint impleading Bosch GmbH, a German corporation with its principal place of business in Germany. In this third-party complaint, Axel alleges that Carol's accident was caused entirely by a design defect in the brakes. Axel further alleges that he did not know the brakes were faulty, and that he did not act negligently in installing the brakes. Although Axel acknowledges that he can be held liable to Carol even if he was entirely without fault, he argues that Bosch should reimburse him for any judgment he might have to pay Carol.

Bosch responds by filing a timely motion that raises two arguments. Bosch first argues that Axel is raising a "him not me" argument, and that impleader is accordingly improper under the governing rule. Second, Bosch argues that even if the impleader is procedurally proper, the court does not have subject matter jurisdiction over the third-party claim. Bosch correctly notes that when ruling on Axel's earlier motion to dismiss, the court found that Axel was not a permanent resident alien. Bosch therefore concludes that because the third-party claim involves one alien suing another, the federal court cannot exercise subject matter jurisdiction.

How should the judge rule on Bosch's arguments?

QUESTION 3 (Suggested time: 75 minutes): Smith and Jones are co-employees at ACME, Inc. Although both started with the company at roughly the same time, Jones has a much larger and nicer office than Smith. During the three-odd years the two have worked at the company, this fact has made Smith increasingly jealous.

Unable to take it any more, Smith sues Jones and Olson (ACME's office manager, who assigns offices to all new employees). Smith brings his case in a federal court that has subject matter jurisdiction, personal jurisdiction, and venue over the action. Smith claims he is legally entitled to the office currently occupied by Jones. ACME company policy provides that when two or more employees join ACME during the same time period, the person who "first began to work for the company" gets first choice among the vacant offices. Smith's first day on the job was July 10, 2012. However, Smith was not given a choice of offices but was merely assigned to his current small office by Olson. Smith asserts that Jones's first day on the job was not until August 1, 2012. In his complaint, Smith asks the court to grant an injunction requiring Olson to reassign Jones's office to him. With respect to Jones, Smith asks for a writ of ejectment requiring her to vacate her current office.

Olson files and serves his answer 3 days after receiving the complaint. Jones, a procrastinator, does not file her answer until December 1, 2015—a full 45 days after the answer was due. Both defendants deny that Smith is entitled to relief. Although they agree that the company policy is enforceable in court, they argue that Jones actually "began to work for the company" before Smith within the meaning of the company policy. The defendants assert that Jones *accepted* her offer of employment before Smith, even though her first day of work was later. Jones also argues in the alternative that even if "beginning to work" is measured by one's first day on the job, she had worked at ACME one day in June 2012 before taking an extended vacation.

You are the attorney representing Smith in this action. It is now early on the morning of December 12, 2015. Smith has left you a message indicating that he wants to meet with you later in the day to discuss the next steps in the lawsuit. In this message, Smith first asks you whether it is possible to have the action tried before a jury.

Second, Smith has several questions about discovery. He has in his possession two tangible items that he fears must be disclosed to the defendants in the initial mandatory disclosures. One is a letter he received from Pearson, who was ACME's director of personnel at the time Smith and Jones were hired. Because this letter makes it clear that Smith received his offer before Jones, Smith would rather not reveal it now, but instead save it to surprise Jones and Olson at trial. The other item is a transcript of a telephone call. When Smith called Pearson to accept the offer of employment, he recorded the call, and then typed up a verbatim transcript of the tape. The tape has since been accidentally destroyed, but Smith still has the transcript. Although the transcript shows that Smith accepted his offer before Jones, Smith does not want to disclose it at this point, again because he would rather use it to surprise Jones and Olson. Smith's next discovery question involves a different matter. Smith is sure Jones is lying when she claims that she actually worked one day in June. Based on that statement, Smith suspects Jones is a pathological liar. Smith therefore wants to know whether it is possible to force Jones to submit to a mental examination to determine if she is, in fact, a pathological liar.

Finally, Smith wants to talk to Pearson, who he feels will support his argument that he, not Jones, actually began to work for ACME first. However, as Pearson has now retired and moved to Hawaii, Smith would rather not bother taking Pearson's deposition. Instead, Smith wonders if you can simply send Pearson a set of interrogatories to obtain the information.

How will you respond to Smith's questions concerning the jury trial, letter, transcript, mental examination, and interrogatories? Discuss.

QUESTION 4 (Suggested time: 45 minutes): One day, Jay Walker decides to cross a busy street. In a hurry, he crosses in the middle of the block rather than at the crosswalk. Shortly after reaching the other side, Walker is accosted by Lou Tennant, a police officer who works for York City in the state of York. Tennant throws Walker to the ground, beats him severely, and then arrests him—all for the minor offense of jaywalking.

Infuriated, Walker sues Tennant in a federal district court in the state of York. His complaint contains two counts. The first is under 42 U.S.C. §1983, a federal civil rights statute. To state a claim under §1983, a party must allege (a) that the person who engaged in the objectionable behavior was acting under "color of state law," and (b) that the objectionable behavior deprived plaintiff of a right guaranteed by the U.S. Constitution or federal law. Count I of Walker's complaint attempts to meet these requirements by using the following language:

Count I
2. Defendant works for, and at the time of the incident described in paragraphs 3 and 4 below was acting on behalf of, the City of York, State of York.
3. On October 4, 2016, Defendant seized Plaintiff after Plaintiff jaywalked across Elm Street in the City of York.
4. Although Plaintiff did not resist arrest, Defendant severely beat Plaintiff, causing serious injuries.
5. These actions denied Plaintiff his right to due process of law as guaranteed by the Fourteenth Amendment to the U.S. Constitution.

Walker's second count is based on title 12, §123 of the York statutes. This section creates a cause of action against police officers who abuse their authority. The portion of Walker's complaint that deals with this count states:

Count II
6. Plaintiff repeats the allegations of paragraphs 2 through 4.
7. Said acts also violated title 12, §123 of the York statutes.

The complaint also contains a jurisdictional statement and a prayer for damages.

Defendant Tennant concedes that the York federal court has jurisdiction and venue. However, he files a timely motion to dismiss the complaint for failure to state a claim. His motion cites two provisions of the York Pleading Rules. The first is the basic provision setting forth York's system of Code pleading, which requires a pleader to set forth "a statement of the facts constituting the cause of action, in ordinary and concise language." The second provision is a specific pleading statute that applies only to actions under title 12, §123. This provision reads as follows:

> In any civil action brought under title 12, §123, the plaintiff must certify that he or she has met with the defendant(s) prior to filing suit in an attempt to reach an amicable, nonlitigated settlement, and that such meeting failed to produce such a settlement.

Walker's complaint contains no such statement. In fact, Walker never tried to meet with Tennant because he feared Tennant would again cause him physical harm.

How should the court rule on Tennant's motion to dismiss? Discuss.

QUESTION 5 (Suggested time: 35 minutes): Clampett recently sued his banker, Drysdale, in the federal district court for the Southern District of California. Clampett alleges that Drysdale negligently invested Clampett's funds in pork bellies. Drysdale immediately files a timely motion to dismiss Clampett's case. Drysdale bases his motion on the deposit agreement that Clampett signed when he turned his funds over to the bank. Not only does that agreement explicitly authorize Drysdale to invest the funds in pork bellies, but it also requires that all disputes concerning the bank's management of the money be settled by binding arbitration. Drysdale argues in his motion that the arbitration clause divests the federal court of its power to hear the case and that accordingly the court should dismiss the action.

The trial judge disagrees with Drysdale and denies the motion. Although recognizing that as a general rule agreements to arbitrate are enforceable in federal court, the judge finds that the clause in the Clampett-Drysdale agreement is unenforceable because Drysdale had lied to Clampett about the contents of the agreement before it was signed. Hoping to forestall Drysdale's inevitable request to reconsider, the trial judge includes the following language in her opinion denying Drysdale's motion:

> This ruling is the absolute final judgment of this court on the issue of whether this dispute will be arbitrated. If defendant Drysdale disagrees with this court's ruling, he is encouraged to appeal. In fact, this court sees no reason why such an appeal cannot occur immediately.

Drysdale takes the hint and immediately files an appeal in the proper court of appeals. May the court of appeals hear the case at the present time? Discuss.

Essay Exam Answers

SAMPLE ANSWER TO QUESTION 1

1. Ruling on *forum non conveniens*: The judge correctly denied the motion. A court may dismiss an action based on *forum non conveniens* when there is another forum in which it would be significantly more convenient to hear the case. A court will consider both private and public factors when deciding whether to dismiss. The facts here do not provide much information as to whether some other state (probably Wisconsin) is significantly more convenient. But even if some other state is more convenient, the court made the correct decision. Carol filed her case in *federal* court. When the more convenient forum is in another state, the court will not dismiss the action, but instead transfer it to a federal court in that state under 28 U.S.C. §1404.

2. Timeliness of answer: Axel's answer was not filed too late. The "default" rule is that a party has 21 days after being served to answer. Fed. R. Civ. P. 12(a)(1)(A)(i). However, the facts specify Axel waived service. In cases where the defendant waives service, the time for answering is extended to 60 days following the day the request was sent. Fed. R. Civ. P. 12(a)(1)(A)(ii). Although the facts are not entirely clear, it seems highly likely that Axel met this 60-day deadline. We know he served his motion the day after he *received* the request for waiver of service. We also know that the judge took "3 full weeks" to rule on that motion, and that Axel then filed his answer "2 days" after the judge's ruling. Therefore, Axel's answer was filed about 24 days (1 day plus 21 days [3 weeks] plus 2 days) following his receipt of the request. However, the 60-day period of Fed. R. Civ. P. 12(a)(1)(A)(ii) is measured from the date the request was *sent*, not the date it is received. Given that a request for waiver must be sent by "first class mail or other reliable means," Fed. R. Civ. P. 4(d)(1)(G), it is very likely that it reached Axel in far fewer than 26 days. If so, Axel answered within the allowed time. In the highly unlikely event that it took more than 26 days for the request to be delivered, Axel's answer was too late.

Note that Axel probably cannot avail himself of the extension of time provided by Fed. R. Civ. P. 12(a)(4)(A). That rule applies only when a party serves a motion *under this rule*, that is, Rule 12. As discussed just below, a motion to dismiss for *forum non conveniens* is not a Rule 12 motion.

3. Waiver of defenses: Axel filed a pre-answer motion to dismiss and then raised the subject matter and personal jurisdiction defenses in his answer. Under Fed. R. Civ. P. 12(g), a party may waive certain Rule 12(b) defenses by omitting them from a pre-answer motion. Therefore, we must first address whether Axel waived the jurisdictional defenses by failing to include them in the *forum non conveniens* motion.

Subject matter jurisdiction is not one of the defenses that are waived by failure to include it in a pre-answer motion. Pursuant to Fed. R. Civ. P. 12(h)(3), a party may raise lack of subject matter jurisdiction at any time and in any manner. Axel's challenge to subject matter jurisdiction is therefore timely.

The personal jurisdiction defense is a closer case. Personal jurisdiction *is* a defense that can be waived by failure to include it in a pre-answer motion. However, Axel's motion to dismiss did not result in a waiver. Under Rule 12(g), the only pre-answer motions that result in waiver are motions raising a defense that "this rule" (that is, Rule 12) permits to be raised by motion. *Forum non conveniens* is not a defense listed in Rule 12 (it is instead a court-created argument) and therefore does not trigger the waiver rule of Fed. R. Civ. P. 12(g). However, one could make a policy argument that *forum non conveniens* should be treated like the defenses listed in Rule 12. Like the Rule 12(b) issues, a successful *forum non conveniens* does result in dismissal of the case from the chosen court. Although that argument might convince a sympathetic judge, it nevertheless is inconsistent with the express terms of Fed. R. Civ. P. 12.

4. Jurisdiction: The merits

a. Subject matter jurisdiction: Axel's motion to dismiss for lack of subject matter jurisdiction will be denied because the court has diversity jurisdiction. Carol is a citizen of South Dakota. Axel is a citizen of Germany because the facts say that he has not yet acquired U.S. citizenship. Although the problem does not make it clear whether he has acquired permanent resident alien status, that fact will not make a difference. If he has not, he is a citizen of Germany for purposes of §1332, and alienage jurisdiction will exist. If he has acquired permanent resident alien status, §1332 would deny jurisdiction only if he resides in the same state as Carol. Because the facts state that Axel currently resides in Wisconsin and intends to remain there "for many years," his domicile is Wisconsin. Therefore, regardless of whether Axel has acquired permanent resident alien status, diversity exists. The amount in controversy for the claim is $300,000, which clearly exceeds the $75,000 floor under §1332.

b. Personal jurisdiction: As noted above, Axel's challenge is timely. And he should prevail on the merits. *Service* is not an issue, because Axel waived service. However, waiver of service is not waiver of personal jurisdiction. Fed. R. Civ. P. 4(d)(5).

The South Dakota federal court may not exercise personal jurisdiction over Axel. Because of Fed. R. Civ. P. 4(k)(1), filing a waiver of service in a federal action establishes jurisdiction only if a state court could exercise jurisdiction over that same defendant. We do not have enough facts to know whether South Dakota's service rules would allow a state court to serve Axel in this case. However, regardless of the state service rules, it would violate due process for a South Dakota state court to exercise jurisdiction over Axel. Axel has no contacts with South Dakota sufficient to establish jurisdiction. Although he did intentionally deal with a citizen of that state, that transaction is not sufficient to establish jurisdiction. A connection with a state constitutes a contact only if it constitutes purposeful availment of the benefits and protections of a state's law. By repairing an automobile in Wisconsin, Axel did nothing to gain the benefits and protections of South Dakota law. In particular, Carol paid Axel in cash in Wisconsin, so Axel would not need to use South Dakota courts to recover on a debt.

Therefore, because he does not have sufficient minimum contacts with South Dakota, the Due Process Clause would prevent a South Dakota state court from exercising jurisdiction. Because the state court could not exercise jurisdiction over Axel, Fed. R. Civ. P. 4(k) likewise prevents a federal court from exercising jurisdiction.

If Axel had had purposeful contacts with South Dakota, the "fairness" side of the test would not preclude the exercise of jurisdiction. The burden on Axel in traveling to South Dakota is not that great. In addition, the plaintiff and that state itself clearly have an interest in the outcome of the case. Carol is a South Dakota citizen, which gives South Dakota an interest. Again, however, because minimum contacts are lacking, the fact that it might be fair to exercise jurisdiction is not enough to meet the constitutional requirements.

SAMPLE ANSWER TO QUESTION 2

1. Propriety of impleader: Bosch will lose the motion. The governing rule is Fed. R. Civ. P. 14 because Axel added Bosch as a third-party defendant (3PD). Although that rule places a time limit on joining 3PDs, the facts specify that the impleader was timely.

Rule 14 allows a defendant to join as a 3PD anyone who is or may be liable to the defendant for all or part of the defendant's liability to the plaintiff. Axel's claim meets this test. More particularly, it is *not* a "him not me" type of claim. Admittedly, Axel claims he was entirely without fault. However, his claim recognizes that even without culpability, he can be held liable to Carol for installing the brakes. By asking Bosch to reimburse him for any liability, his claim meets the requirements of Fed. R. Civ. P. 14.

2. Subject matter jurisdiction: Bosch will also lose its subject matter jurisdiction argument. Diversity (or more technically, alienage) jurisdiction does not exist. Because of the trial judge's earlier finding that Axel was not a permanent resident alien, his claim involves a citizen of Germany suing another citizen of Germany. Bosch, a German corporation with its principal place of business in Germany, is also a German citizen because of 28 U.S.C. §1332(c).

However, the court will have supplemental jurisdiction over the impleader claim. The first step is to determine if the claim arises from a common nucleus of operative fact as Carol's original claim against Axel. This requirement is satisfied. Carol's accident gave rise to both Carol's claim against Axel and Axel's claim against Bosch. Bosch's act of designing the brakes that ended up in her car form the common nucleus of operative facts.

Nor do §§1367(b) and (c) preclude the exercise of supplemental jurisdiction. Although this is a case in which diversity is the sole basis for jurisdiction, §1367(b) does not bar Axel's claim because it is not a claim by a plaintiff. Axel is a third-party plaintiff, not a plaintiff. Similarly, none of the §1367(c) discretionary elements are significant factors in this case, at least from the facts presented. The state claim does not dominate over Carol's federal claim, the claim does not seem to be new or original, and the federal court has not dismissed Carol's original claim. Therefore, the court should be able to exercise supplemental jurisdiction over the impleader claim.

SAMPLE ANSWER TO QUESTION 3

1. Jury trial: The Seventh Amendment preserves a right to a jury trial (a) in cases in federal courts, and (b) for any claims and issues that would have been heard by a jury at common law. Smith's action is in federal court, so the first criterion is satisfied. However, his case presents a mix of legal and equitable claims. Smith's claim against Olson seeks only an injunction. Because an injunction is purely an equitable remedy, the Seventh Amendment would not require a jury on that claim.

Smith's claim against Jones seeking ejectment presents a claim at common law. Although ejectment is specific relief, historically it was a common law remedy for which a jury would be impaneled.

In cases presenting a mix of legal and equitable claims, a party is entitled to a jury on all *issues* relating to the legal claims, even if those same issues are also relevant to the equitable claims. Thus, Smith is entitled to a jury on all issues relevant to the ejectment. Because his claims against Jones and Olson are so intertwined, this also means that a jury could decide all of the common issues arising in the claim against Olson (which will constitute virtually all of the issues in that claim, too).

Even when a party has a constitutional right to a jury trial, she must demand a jury in timely fashion. Fed. R. Civ. P. 38(b)(1) requires Smith to file his demand within 14 days from service of "the last pleading directed to the issue. . . ." In this case, the last pleading directed to the legal claim was Jones's answer. The fact that the answer was served late does not matter. Assuming the demand can be filed immediately, you can make a timely demand for a jury, as the 14-day period has not expired.

2. Disclosing the letter: The letter need not be disclosed. Under Fed. R. Civ. P. 26(a)(1)(A)(ii), Smith must disclose the letter only if he may use it to support his claim. This letter is not relevant to Smith's claim. Although he and Jones disagree on what it means to "begin to work for ACME," no one is claiming that the term means the date of the *offer*, which is what the letter covers. (Of course, Smith really will not be able to use the letter to "surprise" Jones unless she happens to testify about the date of the offer, a trivial point.)

3. Disclosing the transcript: The transcript should be disclosed since Smith will almost certainly use it to support his case in one way or another. Even if it contains hearsay evidence, Jones can use the statements to find other supporting information she can use at trial.

That Smith wants to use the information to "surprise" the defendants at trial is not a sufficient excuse. The purpose of the mandatory disclosure rules is to prevent just this sort of surprise. The only exception is when a party has information that it will use solely for impeachment. Here, Smith almost certainly will present this information as part of his case, not merely in response to testimony by Jones or Olson.

Nor does the transcript qualify for the word product qualified privilege. Although it is a document, it was not prepared in anticipation of litigation. Smith had no reason to anticipate that he would go to court over a claim concerning his office.

4. Mental examination: Smith cannot obtain a mental examination of Jones. The issue of Jones's mental condition has not been placed into controversy. Although a party can place her own condition into controversy in her pleadings, nothing in Jones's pleadings raises a question as to her psychological condition. For an opposing party to place a party's condition into controversy, *Schlagenhauf* requires more than the "suspicion" that Smith has. Smith would need to file affidavits or other real evidence providing facts that tend to show Jones has a problem with the truth.

5. Interrogatories: Only a party to a suit is required to answer interrogatories. Because Pearson is not a party, he is under no obligation to respond to interrogatories in this case. On the other hand, if Pearson willingly answers the interrogatories, nothing prevents Smith from using the information to the extent permitted by the Rules of Evidence.

SAMPLE ANSWER TO QUESTION 4

This question actually involves two separate *Erie* issues.

1. Code pleading: First, there is a question as to whether the federal court must follow the York Code pleading rules. Note that *Erie* is an issue even when, as here, the federal court is exercising federal question jurisdiction.

The York rule probably does conflict with federal law. Fed. R. Civ. P. 8(a) requires only a short, plain statement of the cause of action. Walker's complaint meets this standard because it sets out the legal theory coupled with enough basic facts to make its claim plausible. However, the complaint does not contain sufficient facts to satisfy York's Code pleading standard. If state law applies, the suit could be dismissed for failure to state a claim.

Because the federal law is a Federal Rule of Civil Procedure, the *Erie* analysis turns on whether Fed. R. Civ. P. 8(a) is "procedural" within the meaning of the Rules Enabling Act (28 U.S.C. §2072). The rule meets this test. It is not meant to make it easier or more difficult for a party to recover but merely controls how the plaintiff apprises the court and other parties of the claims it is asserting. Nor does Rule 8(a) abridge, enlarge, or modify the rights or defenses in any way. It only affects what a party must say to get into court, not what it must do to prevail on its claim.

2. Certification: On the surface, there is a conflict between the York rule and the Federal Rules of Civil Procedure because the rules do not require a party to certify that he met with the defendant. However, that conflict actually proves to be fairly narrow. The Federal Rules of Civil Procedure do not deal with the issue of *whether* the plaintiff must actually meet. (Indeed, the defendant's right to negotiate might be deemed a substantive right that could not be impaired by the Federal Rules of Civil Procedure.) The rules deal only with whether the complaint must *specify* that a meeting occurred. A rule, such as Rule 8, that does not require a statement does not infringe the defendant's right to have such a meeting. Therefore, Rule 8 is procedural, and Walker need not specify that a meeting occurred. However, because the Federal Rules of Civil Procedure do not affect the state law requirement of meeting, Tennant will still be able to dismiss the case on other grounds because no meeting occurred.

SAMPLE ANSWER TO QUESTION 5

As a general rule, a federal appellate court may hear appeals only of "final" judgments. 28 U.S.C. §1291. The decision here is not final within the meaning of §1291 because it does not wrap up Clampett's claim. The suit for misuse of funds remains to be resolved.

There are, however, several exceptions to §1291. Many of these are obviously inapplicable. The order did not grant or deny an injunction or receivership and therefore does not qualify under §1292(a). Nor is discretionary review under §1292(b) available because the trial judge did not properly certify the decision as indicated in that section. Moreover, Drysdale's appeal is not a mandamus or prohibition.

Two other exceptions remain a possibility. The first is appeal of a "discrete part" of a case under Fed. R. Civ. P. 54(b). Although the trial judge's language looks like a proper certification under Rule 54(b), the case cannot be appealed under that section. Rule 54(b) applies only when the trial court enters a final judgment on one or more discrete *claims*. As indicated above, the decision here did not wrap up any claims, merely the arbitration issue.

The only other possible exception is the collateral order doctrine. This exception applies when the court (i) conclusively determines, (ii) an important issue, (iii) that is completely separate from the merits, and (iv) the decision would be effectively unreviewable if the loser must wait for an ordinary appeal. The first two requirements are met. The judge is certainly done with this issue. Moreover, the issue of arbitration is important, especially because federal statutes may require the court to honor this arbitration agreement.

It is unclear whether the issue is separate from the merits. The basis for the judge's decision— unconscionability—might also be an issue in the underlying dispute. Clampett must deal with the term in the deposit agreement explicitly authorizing investments in pork bellies. One way to accomplish that goal is to argue that the contract was entered into by fraud.

Finally, even if the other requirements are met, appeal under the collateral order doctrine should not be allowed because the decision would be effectively reviewable if Drysdale appeals after final judgment. The court of appeals could simply vacate any judgment in favor of Clampett and order the parties to arbitrate the dispute. Note, however, that a court could conclude that the right to arbitrate is a right not to be sued at all in a court (like the immunity issue discussed in *Lauro Lines*). This result is unlikely because binding arbitration, unlike immunity, does allow a third party to adjudicate the defendant's rights. However, if the court of appeals treats arbitration like an immunity, the decision denying arbitration *would not* be effectively reviewable via an ordinary appeal. Requiring a full trial prior to appeal would violate Drysdale's "right" not to have to go to court. Again, however, this result is unlikely.

315

Table of Cases

Table of Statutes and Rules

Federal Rules of Evidence

Subject Matter Index

Purposeful availment, 17, 19-20
Quasi in rem, 12
Service. *See* Notice under this heading
Specific jurisdiction, 15
State of incorporation, 21
Stream of commerce, 19-20

PHYSICAL EXAMINATION. *See* DISCOVERY

PLEADING
See also AMENDMENTS; ANSWER; COMPLAINT;
        MOTIONS
Certification, 133-134
Claim for relief, 114-116
"Code" pleading, 112
Common law pleading, 112
Discovery, interplay of pleading with, 115
Exhibits, 113
Federal Rules of Civil Procedure, 114-127
Federal Forms, abolition, 114
Form of pleadings, 113
Historical development, 112
Plausibility standard, 114-115
Reply, 113
Rule 11, 132-135. *See also* Sanctions under this heading
Certifications made, 133
Discovery, 132
Documents governed, 132
Failure to sign, 133
Who must sign, 133
Sanctions, 134-135
    Allowed, 135
    Court's initiative, 134-135
    Discretion in determining appropriate, 135
    Motion, 134
    Order, 135
    Persons subject to, 135
    Process, 134-135
    Safe harbor, 134
Signing requirement, 132-133
Types allowed, 112-113

PRETRIAL CONFERENCES, 173

PRIVILEGES. *See* DISCOVERY

QUASI IN REM JURISDICTION. *See* PERSONAL
        JURISDICTION

REMEDIES
Generally, 99-105
Attorneys' fees, 106-107
American rule, 106
Compensatory damages, 100
Complaint, prayer for relief, 116

Declaratory judgment, 102
Ejectment, 193
Enforcement, 99-100, 101
Equitable, 101-102
Garnishment, 100
Liquidated damages, 100
Multiple damages, 100
Prayer for relief, 116
Provisional remedies, 102-105
    Attachment, 104-105
    Due process requirements, 104-105
    Preliminary injunction, 102-103
    Temporary restraining order, 103-104
Punitive damages, 101-102
Replevin, 193
Statutory damages, 100

REMITTITUR. *See* NEW TRIAL

REMOVAL
Generally, 70-73
Defendants, 70, 72
Devices to defeat, 71, 73
Diversity, 71
Federal question, 70-71, 72
Multiple claims, 72
Nonremovable cases, 70
Objections, 73
Procedure, 72-73
Remand, 73
Separate and independent claims, 72
Supplemental jurisdiction, 72
Timing, 72-73
Venue, 38, 72

REPLY. *See* PLEADING

SERVICE OF PROCESS. *See* PERSONAL
        JURISDICTION: NOTICE

SETTLEMENTS, 169-170
Class actions, 169, 296-297
Confidentiality, 170
Consent decree, 169, 170
Judicial approval, 169
Postjudgment, 170
Settlement agreement, 170

SUBJECT MATTER JURISDICTION
See also AMOUNT IN CONTROVERSY
        REQUIREMENT; REMOVAL;
        SUPPLEMENTAL JURISDICTION
Generally, 49-50
Challenges to, 50
Class actions, 299-300